# USING QUARKXPRESS 3.0

# USING QUARKXPRESS 3.0

TIM MEEHAN

M&T BOOKS

**M&T Books**
A Division of M&T Publishing, Inc.
501 Galveston Drive
Redwood City, CA 94063

© 1990 by Tim Meehan

Printed in the United States of America

All rights reserved. No part of this book may be reproduced or transmitted in any form or by any means, electronic or mechanical, including photocopying, recording, or by any information storage and retrieval system, without prior written permission from the Publisher. Contact the Publisher for information on foreign rights.

**Limits of Liability and Disclaimer of Warranty**
The Author and Publisher of this book have used their best efforts in preparing the book and the programs contained in it. These efforts include the development, research, and testing of the theories and programs to determine their effectiveness.

The Author and Publisher make no warranty of any kind, expressed or implied, with regard to these programs or the documentation contained in this book. The Author and Publisher shall not be liable in any event for incidental or consequential damages in connection with, or arising out of, the furnishing, performance, or use of these programs.

Library of Congress Cataloging-in-Publication Data

Meehan, Tim
  Using QuarkXPress
    p.   cm.
  Includes index.
  ISBN 1-55851-128-8
    1. QuarkXPress (Computer program) 2. Desktop publishing.
I. Title.
Z286.D47M43    1990b
686.2'2544536—dc20                                  90-13383
                                                                         CIP

93 92 91        4 3 2

Apple is a trademark of Apple Computer, Inc.
Linotronic is a trademark of Linotype Corp.
Macintosh is a trademark of McIntosh Laboratories, Inc.
PANTONE is a registered trademark of Pantone, Inc.
QuarkXPress is a trademark of Quark, Inc.
All products, names, and services are trademarks or registered trademarks of their respective companies.

---

                  **Editor**: Phillip Robinson    **Cover Design**: Lauren Smith Designs
                                 **Cover Photograph**: C & I Photography

*For Ray. You're a fine pup.*

# Contents

**Why This Book is for You** .................................................................1
**Introduction** ...........................................................................................3
   The Old Way ........................................................................................3
   The Desktop Publishing Way ..............................................................6
   Why the Macintosh? ............................................................................7
   Why QuarkXPress? ..............................................................................8
   How to Use This Book .........................................................................8
      Play Around With Your Mac ........................................................8
      Try As You Fly ..............................................................................9
   Where to Look .....................................................................................9
   Who Should Read This Book .............................................................10
   What You Need to Use QuarkXPress ................................................10
      RAM ..............................................................................................10
      Disk ...............................................................................................10
      Display .........................................................................................11

**Chapter 1. Where to Begin** ..............................................................13
   Introduction .......................................................................................13
   The Mac Interface ..............................................................................13
   Icons ....................................................................................................13
   Control: Keyboard and Mouse ..........................................................14
   Select an Object, Then an Operation ................................................14
   Menus, Submenus, and Dialog Boxes ..............................................16
   The Apple Menu ................................................................................17
   Tool Palettes .......................................................................................18
   "Ease of Use" — A Standardized Approach ...................................18
   The QuarkXPress Interface ...............................................................19
   Menus .................................................................................................20
   Palettes ...............................................................................................22
      Tools Palette ................................................................................22
      The Two Most Important Tools: Item and Content ................22

| | |
|---|---|
| Rotation and Zoom Tools | 23 |
| Boxing Tools | 23 |
| Line Tools | 23 |
| Linking Tools | 24 |
| Customizing the Tools: Preferences | 24 |
| Tool Practice | 24 |
| Measurements Palette | 25 |
| Getting Help | 26 |

## Chapter 2. QuarkXPress Basics .................................................. 29

| | |
|---|---|
| Opening Documents and New Documents | 29 |
| Working with an Existing Document | 30 |
| Working with a Template | 31 |
| Creating a New Document | 32 |
| Document Setup | 32 |
| Preferences | 34 |
| General Preferences | 35 |
| Typographic Preferences | 37 |
| Tool Preferences | 39 |
| Viewing Your Document and Tools | 40 |
| Master Page Formats | 43 |
| Creating New Master Pages | 44 |
| Changing Existing Master Pages | 46 |
| Naming Master Pages | 47 |
| Deleting Master Pages | 47 |
| Document Page Layout | 47 |
| Automatic Page Insertion | 49 |
| Moving Between Pages | 50 |
| Page Numbering | 50 |
| "Smart" Page Numbering — "Continued On" References | 51 |
| Sections | 53 |
| Items: Text Boxes, Picture Boxes, Lines | 54 |
| Grouping Items | 57 |
| Library | 60 |
| Frame Editor | 62 |
| Saving | 66 |

Printing ........................................................................................... 67
    Page Setup ................................................................................. 67
    Print ........................................................................................... 68

## Chapter 3. Word Processing with QuarkXPress ........................ 71
First Create or Select a Text Box .................................................... 71
Importing Text ............................................................................. 73
Entering Text ............................................................................... 75
Selecting Text .............................................................................. 76
    Text Selection with the Mouse ................................................. 76
    Text Selection Using the Keyboard ........................................... 77
Editing Text ................................................................................. 79
    Deleting Text ........................................................................... 79
    Moving Text ............................................................................. 79
    Copying Text ........................................................................... 80
    Replacing Text ......................................................................... 80
Undoing Edit Changes .................................................................. 80
Styling Text .................................................................................. 81
Formatting Text ............................................................................ 83
Style Sheets .................................................................................. 86
Stylesheet Adventure .................................................................... 91
Finding or Replacing Text ............................................................. 94
Find/Change with Attributes ......................................................... 97
Spell Checking ............................................................................. 98
    Spell Checking a Word ............................................................. 98
    Spell Checking a Story or Document ........................................ 99
    Auxiliary Dictionaries for Spell Checking ................................ 101
Save Text ................................................................................... 103

## Chapter 4. Typography ........................................................... 105
Terminology of Type ................................................................... 106
Macintosh Screen Fonts .............................................................. 108
Macintosh Printer Fonts .............................................................. 109
Font Usage ................................................................................. 110
Kerning and Tracking ................................................................. 111
    Kerning .................................................................................. 112

    Changing Kerning Tables ................................................................ 113
    Exporting and Importing Kerning Values ....................................... 116
    Tracking ............................................................................................ 116
    Custom Tracking Tables ................................................................. 121
Horizontal Alignment .............................................................................. 124
Leading .................................................................................................... 125
    Specifying Leading in QuarkXPress ............................................... 128
    Size Subheads Carefully and Reduce the Leading ......................... 130
Baseline Shift .......................................................................................... 131
Text Inset ................................................................................................ 132
Vertical Alignment .................................................................................. 133
    Top Vertical Alignment ................................................................... 134
    Center Vertical Alignment .............................................................. 135
    Bottom Vertical Alignment ............................................................. 136
    Justified Vertical Alignment ........................................................... 136
Hyphenation and Justification ................................................................ 137
    Suggested Hyphenation and Hyphenation Exceptions ................... 140
Widows and Orphans .............................................................................. 142
Special Effects with Type ....................................................................... 144
    Horizontal Scaling .......................................................................... 144
    Reversed Text ................................................................................. 145
    Text Box Rotation ........................................................................... 145
Drop Caps ............................................................................................... 147
    Hanging Drop Caps ........................................................................ 149
    Drop Caps with Drop Shadows ...................................................... 150
Special Characters .................................................................................. 153
Tips for Type .......................................................................................... 154
    Type Reversed Out of Type ............................................................ 154
    Upside-Down Type ......................................................................... 155

## Chapter 5. Graphics .............................................................................. 157
    Lines ................................................................................................ 157
    Line Types ....................................................................................... 157
    Creating a Line ............................................................................... 158
    Changing Lines — Moving, Stretching, Shrinking ........................ 158
    Line Styles ...................................................................................... 160

Anchoring Lines to Text ................................................................. 163
Pictures ........................................................................................ 166
Creating Picture Boxes ................................................................. 166
Drawing a Polygon Picture Box ................................................... 167
Reshaping Picture Boxes .............................................................. 168
Moving and Positioning Picture Boxes ........................................ 170
Framing a Picture Box ................................................................. 172
Picture Box Runaround ................................................................ 173
Runaround Pitfalls ....................................................................... 179
Importing Images ......................................................................... 179
Import File Types ......................................................................... 182
    TIFF and RIFF Images ............................................................ 183
    PICT Images ............................................................................ 183
    EPS (PostScript) Images .......................................................... 183
Moving Pictures Inside a Box ...................................................... 183
Styling and Formatting Pictures ................................................... 185
Editing Picture Boxes and Pictures .............................................. 188
Anchoring Graphics to Text ......................................................... 189
Save Page as EPS ......................................................................... 191
The Library .................................................................................. 192
Picture Usage ............................................................................... 193
Halftone Advice ........................................................................... 194
    The Split Fountain Effect ........................................................ 195
Using What You've Learned ........................................................ 195
    The Starburst Outline .............................................................. 195
    The Variable Drop Shadow for Any Object ........................... 196

## Chapter 6. Color ................................................................................. 199
Why Color is Important in Design ............................................... 199
Planning Color ............................................................................. 200
How to Use Color in QuarkXPress ............................................... 200
Applying Colors ........................................................................... 200
Coloring Selected Text Elements ................................................. 201
Coloring Body Text ..................................................................... 201
Coloring Lines .............................................................................. 202
Coloring Frames ........................................................................... 205

Coloring Graphic Images ................................................................. 205
Creating a Color Palette .................................................................. 206
Viewing the Palette ......................................................................... 216
Adding or Changing (Editing) Colors ............................................. 218
Duplicating a Color ......................................................................... 219
Color Models and the Color Picker ................................................ 219
Seeing Color: HSB .......................................................................... 219
Showing Color: RGB ...................................................................... 220
Printing Color: CMYK ................................................................... 221
Making Color: PMS ........................................................................ 222
Hardware's Effects on Color Models and Matching ..................... 223
Back to Creating a Color Palette .................................................... 224
    Appending Colors ..................................................................... 224
    Specifying Traps, Spreads, and Chokes ................................... 224
Setting Trap Values ......................................................................... 225
    Automatic Trapping Specifications ......................................... 226
    Custom Trapping Values .......................................................... 226
Tips on Printing Color .................................................................... 227
Some Special Tricks with Color ..................................................... 229
    Graduated Lines ........................................................................ 229
    Alphabet Blocks ........................................................................ 231

## Chapter 7. Sample Assignment #1:
## Creating a Newsletter Format ................................................... 233
Creating the Layout ........................................................................ 234
The Masthead .................................................................................. 241
Flowing the Text ............................................................................. 245
The Bold Subhead ........................................................................... 245
Smart Page Numbering ................................................................... 247
Adding the Pictures ........................................................................ 248
The Table of Contents .................................................................... 250
The Innards ...................................................................................... 252
The Advertising ............................................................................... 256
Saving Your Work ........................................................................... 261
Enhancements ................................................................................. 261
    Justify the Text ......................................................................... 261

Set the Text Outset...................................................................262
Enhancing the Image Output ...................................262
Color ...........................................................................262

## Chapter 8. Sample Assignment #2: Creating a Two-Color Magazine Ad..............................................................265
Getting Ready .............................................................265
The Headline...............................................................274
The Flag......................................................................274
The Logo.....................................................................276
Printing the Ad............................................................278
Enhancements .............................................................280

## Chapter 9. Sample Assignment #3: Color Corporate Brochure......281
First Step: On Paper....................................................281
Building the Pieces .....................................................286
Other Graphic Elements ..............................................290
Page Numbering ..........................................................294
The Third Layout Spread.............................................299
Putting It Together ......................................................302
Setting Up Style Sheets ...............................................303
Now for the Text.........................................................310

## Glossary ............................................................................317

## Appendix A. Keyboard Shortcuts .....................................325

## Index..................................................................................335

# List of Illustrations

| | | |
|---|---|---|
| 1-1 | A variety of icons | 14 |
| 1-2 | Examples of pull-down menus from different programs | 15 |
| 1-3 | Example menus with pop-up and grayed-out selections | 16 |
| 1-4 | Example of a dialog box | 17 |
| 1-5 | The Apple menu (pulled down) | 18 |
| 1-6 | The QuarkXPress interface | 20 |
| 1-7 | Item tool | 22 |
| 1-8 | Content tool | 22 |
| 1-9 | Rotation tool | 23 |
| 1-10 | Zoom tool | 23 |
| 1-11 | Text box tool | 23 |
| 1-12 | Picture box tools | 23 |
| 1-13 | Line tools | 23 |
| 1-14 | Linking tools | 23 |
| 1-15 | Tool Preferences dialog box | 25 |
| 1-16 | The Measurements palette | 26 |
| 1-17 | The About QuarkXPress... box | 26 |
| 1-18 | A page from the Help file | 27 |
| 2-1 | Initial QuarkXPress display | 30 |
| 2-2 | Open dialog box for opening existing documents | 31 |
| 2-3 | New dialog box | 33 |
| 2-4 | Document setup dialog box | 33 |
| 2-5 | Preferences pop-up menu from the Edit menu | 35 |
| 2-6 | General Preferences dialog box | 36 |
| 2-7 | Typographic Preferences dialog box | 38 |
| 2-8 | Tool Preferences dialog box | 39 |
| 2-9 | The View menu with keyboard shortcuts | 41 |
| 2-10 | Example display with several horizontal and vertical ruler guides | 42 |
| 2-11 | The View percent field | 43 |
| 2-12 | The Document Layout palette for master page work | 44 |
| 2-13 | Page menu with display pop-up menu | 45 |
| 2-14 | The Master Page format L-Master A display | 46 |

| | | |
|---|---|---|
| 2-15 | Adding another Master Page icon in the Document Layout palette | 46 |
| 2-16 | Naming field for master pages | 47 |
| 2-17 | Document Layout palette | 48 |
| 2-18 | The Insert Pages dialog box | 49 |
| 2-19 | The Move Pages dialog box | 49 |
| 2-20 | Section dialog box | 53 |
| 2-21 | The Item menu | 55 |
| 2-22 | Step and Repeat dialog box | 56 |
| 2-23 | Space/Align dialog box | 56 |
| 2-24 | Grouped items enclosed by the group's dotted boundary line | 57 |
| 2-25 | Using the Group Specifications dialog box | 58 |
| 2-26 | Library dialog box, for opening or creating a library | 61 |
| 2-27 | Library window, for selecting items from or adding items to a library | 62 |
| 2-28 | Frame Editor selection of frame elements | 63 |
| 2-29 | Drawing in the Frame Editor | 63 |
| 2-30 | The Style Selection box of the Frame Editor | 64 |
| 2-31 | Save As dialog box, with the Template button marked | 66 |
| 2-32 | Page Setup dialog box | 67 |
| 2-33 | Sample Print dialog box | 68 |
| 3-1 | The Get Text dialog box | 75 |
| 3-2 | The Style menu's pop-up submenus for formatting text | 82 |
| 3-3 | The Character attributes dialog box for formatting text | 82 |
| 3-4 | Formatting text with the Measurements palette | 83 |
| 3-5 | The Paragraph Formats dialog box | 83 |
| 3-6 | The Tabs dialog box | 85 |
| 3-7 | Style Sheet pop-up menu within the Style menu | 86 |
| 3-8 | Style Sheet dialog box | 87 |
| 3-9 | Edit Style Sheets dialog box | 88 |
| 3-10 | Character Attributes dialog box | 89 |
| 3-11 | Paragraph Formats dialog box | 89 |
| 3-12 | Paragraph Rules dialog box | 90 |
| 3-13 | Paragraph Tabs dialog box | 90 |
| 3-14 | The style sheet as of Step 6 | 92 |
| 3-15 | The style sheets that you've created through Step 10 | 93 |
| 3-16 | Find/Change dialog box | 95 |
| 3-17 | The expanded Find/Change dialog box — using Attributes | 96 |

| | | |
|---|---|---|
| 3-18 | The Check Word dialog box for spell checking | 99 |
| 3-19 | The Check Document dialog box for spell checking | 101 |
| 3-20 | The Edit Auxiliary Dictionary dialog box | 103 |
| 4-1 | Typographical units of measure together for comparison | 107 |
| 4-2 | The Font Usage dialog box | 110 |
| 4-3 | The Kern... dialog box | 113 |
| 4-4 | Kerning Table Edit dialog box | 114 |
| 4-5 | Kerning Values for dialog box (with -20 em kerning) | 117 |
| 4-6 | Kerning Values for dialog box (with 10 em kerning) | 117 |
| 4-7 | The upper headline could benefit from some kerning finesse | 118 |
| 4-8 | Copy fitted to text box before and after tracking | 119 |
| 4-9 | Track... dialog box | 120 |
| 4-10 | Example of a horrendously overtracked paragraph | 121 |
| 4-11 | Tracking Edit dialog box | 122 |
| 4-12 | Tracking Values for dialog box | 123 |
| 4-13 | Tracking Values for dialog box with a changed values curve | 124 |
| 4-14 | Alignment menu in QuarkXPress | 125 |
| 4-15 | Example of unevenly spaced text in columns | 125 |
| 4-16 | Examples of different leading values | 127 |
| 4-17 | The Typographic... preferences dialog box | 129 |
| 4-18 | Specifying leading incrementally | 129 |
| 4-19 | Example of sizing subhead text | 131 |
| 4-20 | Reduced leading for a subhead | 131 |
| 4-21 | Baseline shift example | 132 |
| 4-22 | Text Box Specifications dialog box with callout to text inset value | 132 |
| 4-23 | Vertically aligned text — all four examples | 133 |
| 4-24 | Vertical Alignment pop-up menu | 134 |
| 4-25 | First baseline specifications for vertical alignment | 135 |
| 4-26 | Example of columns of text evenly justified | 136 |
| 4-27 | H&J dialog box | 138 |
| 4-28 | Edit Hyphenation & Justification dialog box | 140 |
| 4-29 | Suggested Hyphenation example | 141 |
| 4-30 | Hyphenation Exceptions dialog box | 141 |
| 4-31 | Widow and orphan control with the Paragraph Formats dialog box | 143 |
| 4-32 | Horizontal scaling | 144 |
| 4-33 | Reversing text in its own text box | 145 |

| | | |
|---|---|---|
| 4-34 | Examples of rotated text boxes | 146 |
| 4-35 | Paragraph Formats dialog box with Drop Caps option checked | 148 |
| 4-36 | Drop Cap limits | 149 |
| 4-37 | Hanging drop caps | 150 |
| 4-38 | Large drop cap with drop shadow | 152 |
| 4-39 | An example of white type reversed over black type | 155 |
| 4-40 | Upside-down type created by rotating and grouping text | 155 |
| 5-1 | The Orthogonal Line tool | 158 |
| 5-2 | The conventional Line tool | 158 |
| 5-3 | The Mode pop-up menu in the Modify dialog box | 159 |
| 5-4 | Using the Measurements palette to adjust a line | 160 |
| 5-5 | Line styles through the Style menu (using style as example) | 161 |
| 5-6 | Line styles through the Modify dialog box (using color as example) | 162 |
| 5-7 | Line styles through Measurements palette (using ends as example) | 162 |
| 5-8 | Paragraph Rules dialog box | 163 |
| 5-9 | Expanded Paragraph Rules dialog box | 164 |
| 5-10 | The four picture box shapes | 166 |
| 5-11 | Picture box creation tools | 167 |
| 5-12 | Picture Box shape menu | 168 |
| 5-13 | Making a cartoon balloon | 170 |
| 5-14 | The Picture Specifications dialog box settings | 171 |
| 5-15 | The Measurements palette settings | 171 |
| 5-16 | Frame Specifications dialog box | 173 |
| 5-17 | Example of simple Runaround... for a picture box | 174 |
| 5-18 | Runaround... dialog box | 174 |
| 5-19 | Examples of the four runaround modes | 175 |
| 5-20 | Customizing runaround by moving a control point in Manual mode | 177 |
| 5-21 | Using different Text Outset values to customize runaround | 177 |
| 5-22 | Text only flows down one side of a picture box within a text box | 178 |
| 5-23 | Inverted runaround | 179 |
| 5-24 | The Get Picture dialog box | 180 |
| 5-25 | Auto Picture Import preference setting | 181 |
| 5-26 | Picture Box Specifications dialog box and Measurements palette | 184 |
| 5-27 | Style choices for Picture boxes | 185 |
| 5-28 | Positive and negative images | 187 |
| 5-29 | Normal contrast and high contrast | 187 |

| | | |
|---|---|---|
| 5-30 | The effects of posterization | 187 |
| 5-31 | Example of anchored picture within text box | 190 |
| 5-29 | Anchored Picture Box Specifications dialog box | 190 |
| 5-30 | Save Page as EPS dialog box | 192 |
| 5-31 | The Library window | 193 |
| 5-32 | Starburst outlines with text added | 197 |
| 5-33 | Starburst with a drop shadow | 198 |
| 6-1 | The Style menu approach to coloring text | 202 |
| 6-2 | The Character dialog box approach to coloring text | 202 |
| 6-3 | An effective use of color in a text object | 203 |
| 6-4 | Some ways color can enhance the impact of large initial caps | 204 |
| 6-5 | Color as a background for reversed text or shape | 204 |
| 6-6 | Using the Style menu to color a line | 205 |
| 6-7 | Using the Modify dialog box to color a line | 206 |
| 6-8 | The Frame Specifications dialog box for coloring a box border | 207 |
| 6-9 | Grayscale RIFF image colored red | 207 |
| 6-10 | This image won't separate into its component color plates | 208 |
| 6-11 | Contrast | 209 |
| 6-12 | Colors dialog box | 209 |
| 6-13 | The Edit Color dialog box | 210 |
| 6-14 | The Color Picker, using the HSB model | 210 |
| 6-15 | The Color Picker with the RGB model selected | 211 |
| 6-16 | The Color Picker with the CMYK model selected | 211 |
| 6-17 | The Color Picker with the Pantone model selected | 212 |
| 6-18 | The Append Colors dialog box | 212 |
| 6-19 | Trap Specifications dialog box | 213 |
| 6-20 | The widened line of Step 2 | 213 |
| 6-21 | The graduated line as of Step 12 | 214 |
| 6-22 | Capital A centered and evenly spaced in text box — Step 2 | 214 |
| 6-23 | Frame Specifications dialog box (Step 3) | 215 |
| 6-24 | Colored Text character, box, and frame from Step 4 | 215 |
| 7-1 | New Document dialog box with attributes for Chapter 7 exercise | 234 |
| 7-2 | Drawing lines on both pages — Step 5 | 236 |
| 7-3 | Line weight field highlighted on the Measurements palette | 236 |
| 7-4 | Step and Repeat dialog box with values for Step 7 | 237 |
| 7-5 | Layout with lines after Step 7 | 237 |

| | | |
|---|---|---|
| 7-6 | Small text box for smart page numbering — Step 8 | 238 |
| 7-7 | Automatic page numbering text highlighted — Step 7 | 239 |
| 7-8 | Repositioned and formatted page-number text after Step 11 | 239 |
| 7-9 | Master Page icon selected and new name typed in — from Step 14 | 240 |
| 7-10 | Results in Document Layout palette | 241 |
| 7-11 | Large Masthead text box | 241 |
| 7-12 | Actual size view of text in Masthead box | 242 |
| 7-13 | Masthead box rotated and moved to right page margin | 244 |
| 7-14 | Subhead text box drawn across two columns of text | 246 |
| 7-15 | Formatted subhead text with overflow icon in text box | 246 |
| 7-16 | Text box with reference to page for text continuation | 247 |
| 7-17 | Text linking arrow from Step 31 | 248 |
| 7-18 | New picture box displacing text, as in Step 33 | 249 |
| 7-19 | Text reflowing around a rotated picture box, from Step 35 | 249 |
| 7-20 | Text box for table of contents | 250 |
| 7-21 | Character attributes for table of contents text box | 250 |
| 7-22 | Formats for table of contents | 251 |
| 7-23 | Stray text between new table of contents box and TIFF image | 251 |
| 7-24 | Experimenting with the Runaround... specifications | 252 |
| 7-25 | Character attributes for subhead of Step 44 | 253 |
| 7-26 | Paragraph formats for text — from Step 45 | 254 |
| 7-27 | Offset and weight values for rules of Step 46 | 254 |
| 7-28 | Replacing initial paragraph letters with numbers — Step 47 | 255 |
| 7-29 | Square picture box after step-and-repeat operation — Step 50 | 256 |
| 7-30 | The new text box of Step 51 | 257 |
| 7-31 | Large, bold, attention-grabbing subhead from Step 54 | 258 |
| 7-32 | Spacing and alignment settings for Step 55 | 258 |
| 7-33 | New picture box with imported Bicycle image — Step 58 | 259 |
| 7-34 | Decimal Tab to locate the model name and price — Step 63 | 260 |
| 7-35 | Finished layout | 261 |
| 8-1 | Settings and preferences for the document | 266 |
| 8-2 | More settings and preferences for the document | 266 |
| 8-3 | The Runaround Specifications box with the Mode pop-up menu | 267 |
| 8-4 | Setting the colors — Step 4 | 268 |
| 8-5 | Importing the picture — Step 5 | 268 |
| 8-6 | Headline text box and body copy text box in place — Steps 7 and 8 | 270 |

| | | |
|---|---|---|
| 8-7 | Setting the number of columns and the gutter space for body text | 271 |
| 8-8 | Selecting Drop Caps in the Paragraph Formats dialog box | 273 |
| 8-9 | Flag box and initial cap with inverted coloring, from Step 19 | 275 |
| 8-10 | New picture box | 276 |
| 8-11 | Logo and slogan styled and tracked, picture skewed | 278 |
| 8-12 | The finished ad | 279 |
| 8-13 | Page Setup | 280 |
| 9-1 | New Document dialog box with Page Specifications for Step 1 | 282 |
| 9-2 | Edit Color dialog box — Step 2 | 283 |
| 9-3 | Document Layout palette — Steps 4 and 5 | 284 |
| 9-4 | Narrow text box dimensions for Step 7 | 286 |
| 9-5 | Polygon picture box overlaying the text box — Step 9 | 287 |
| 9-6 | Grouped boxes, the result of Step 12 | 288 |
| 9-7 | The moved and rotated group of Step 13 | 289 |
| 9-8 | Rectangle picture box from Step 15 | 291 |
| 9-9 | Choosing polygon picture box from the Item menu — Step 16 | 292 |
| 9-10 | Reshaped, slanted picture box from Step 17 | 293 |
| 9-11 | Grouped picture boxes | 293 |
| 9-12 | Results of Step 20 | 294 |
| 9-13 | Automatic page numbering box | 295 |
| 9-14 | Repositioned stripes — Step 35 | 298 |
| 9-15 | Results of Step 38 | 300 |
| 9-16 | Error message when trying to save a document | 300 |
| 9-17 | Last master page, as in Step 40 | 301 |
| 9-18 | Pages in the thumbnail view and the document layout | 302 |
| 9-19 | Text imported and wrapping around illustration | 304 |
| 9-20 | Paragraph formats for Step 48 | 305 |
| 9-21 | Character Attribute settings for Step 50 | 306 |
| 9-22 | Imported pictures of Step 53 | 308 |
| 9-23 | Results of picture importing in Step 54 | 309 |
| 9-24 | Rotating the bike images using the Measurements palette | 310 |
| 9-25 | Pages 10 and 11 with pictures imported during Step 56 | 311 |
| 9-26 | Stray text illustration for Step 62 | 312 |
| 9-27 | Text fitting clean-up of Step 65 | 313 |
| 9-28 | Paragraph Rules dialog box (Step 66) | 315 |
| 9-29 | The finished project | 316 |

# Acknowledgements

Starting at the top. No acknowledgement written for any Apple- or Macintosh-related product is complete without paying homage to the legendary "Two Steves" for making Apple and the Macintosh happen "...for the rest of us." (Where would any of us be?)

I would also like to acknowledge:

**Everyone at Apple** who shared my vision of the potential for this wonderful system and helped make it what it is today. Their support and encouragement have been invaluable to me from day one (January 24, 1984).

**Tim Gill**, the amazing programming wizard, and his dedicated crew at Quark, Inc., including all the current and past employees of Quark. They are among the thousands of software professionals who really make the Macintosh dance and sing.

**Alice Price**, my agent extraordinaire, without whom none of this would have come to pass. Alice's expert guidance, confident enthusiasm, encouragement, and faith helped drive this project from concept to printed page.

**The dedicated and all-too-blunt editing staff at M&T Books**, who helped make readable the eccentric rantings of a first-time author.

**My family**, who have always provided moral and emotional support and encouragement and helped me grow — and love me anyway.

And finally **you, the reader**. You have the vision and intelligence to see the potential this system and software have to offer anyone composing anything for the printed page. You have the wisdom and foresight to use the Macintosh and, more importantly, the common sense to enhance that investment by buying this book. Thank you.

# Foreword

We at Quark are fortunate to have a wide variety of professionals using QuarkXPress. Among them are many graphic artists who are telling their friends about our product and showing them how to use it. We find this very exciting and want to encourage more graphic artists to join the growing community of QuarkXPress users.

We are grateful to Tim Meehan — a very talented artist and enthusiastic QuarkXPress user — for sharing his experience and perspective with others in his professional field. As an authorized Quark trainer, he has introduced many new users to QuarkXPress and provided them with guidance and support. As a graphic artist, he has put his considerable talents to work in creating imaginative page designs that show off the power of the electronic medium — and QuarkXPress.

Given Tim's background and skills, we feel confident that he has produced a significant book for designers and other professionals who want to explore QuarkXPress. We wish his readers a pleasant and fruitful experience with *Using QuarkXPress 3.0*.

Tim Gill
Vice President of Research and Development
Quark, Inc.

# Why This Book is for You

Whether you're new to the Macintosh and QuarkXPress or already familiar with them, this book can help you create more effective, memorable graphic designs. You'll become familiar with the terminology and concepts of desktop publishing and find out how QuarkXPress differs from other graphic design software for the Macintosh.

This book is of particular interest to:

- *QuarkXPress novices.* If you're new to QuarkXPress, you'll learn the basics of graphic design and page layout through step-by-step explanations and tutorials.
- *Everyday users.* You'll find tips on making anything you print look more interesting and professional as well as shortcuts to make the Macintosh and QuarkXPress work for you.
- *Corporate desktop publishing users.* If you're creating brochures, presentations, ads, or reports of any kind, *Using QuarkXPress* will show you how they can be produced more easily and in less time than you would have expected.
- *Graphic designers and production artists.* QuarkXPress 3.0 and the Macintosh can produce professional results and substantial cost savings by automating repetitive, labor-intensive functions normally performed by your printer. This book will show you how to optimize the advantages of using a computer to design and produce camera-ready art.

# Introduction

Desktop publishing is the new computer technology that makes it faster, easier, and cheaper than ever before to create and produce newsletters, brochures, letterheads, advertisements, menus, flyers, package designs, and annual reports. When you use a personal computer as a design and layout tool to combine and position text and graphics, you can spend more time being creative and less time on the boring, repetitive tasks of graphic production. With the right software, the computer can offer you quick, precise control of the text and graphics that make up a page.

**The Old Way**

To fully appreciate the advantages of desktop publishing and QuarkXPress, you need to know what graphic design and publishing were like in the old days. (Which, incidentally, wasn't all that long ago. . . .)

Graphic-design projects began with the copywriters spinning out copy ideas while the designers created the roughs and thumbnail sketches to go with them. Then the copy writers revised their copy and the designers produced comprehensive roughs to go with it. Everybody revised everything once more for good measure. Publishing projects began with writers creating text, artists sketching illustrations, and photographers snapping pictures. Editors edited and checked the text, illustrations, and photographs, and these elements were revised as necessary. These first steps are still part of the desktop process for both graphic design and publishing.

At this point in a graphic design project, the copywriter provided you (the designer) with a type-written, semi-final, approved bundle of copy, labelled and marked for headlines and body text. You then painstakingly counted every character in the entire piece. With the aid of a calculator and font tables, which gave you an approximate idea of how many characters per pica each typeface would occupy, you determined the probable type size to use so that the copy would fit into the allotted space on the layout. Then you sent your type order off to the typesetter. Publishing work followed a similar path, though you wouldn't have to make such exact calculations for the large body text. These were only required for the pull-quotes, headlines, sub-heads, and other special parts.

The typesetter (who has worked in the same way for the past 30 years or so) received pages of your typewritten text marked up with character counts and editing marks, along with a copy of the rough layout. The typesetting machine had a big keyboard and a screen that showed a hodgepodge of tiny letters and codes in steady little lines. The typesetter retyped all of your copywriter or writer's work (later some typesetting machines could accept text files on disk) and inserted code characters that told the machine what typeface, size, line spacing, type, and column widths might possibly fit your layout. The machine was then instructed to run your galleys on photosensitive paper, which the operator would develop and dry. The typesetter then compared the galleys to your comp or rough, measuring the galleys against all the line lengths and text columns you had spent all afternoon drawing in with your markers. The text was revised and galleys were rerun until the type fit your rough sketch.

Meanwhile, you sent all of your photography and artwork to your in-house camera room or outside stat shop to have position stats made, and you placed them on the camera-ready mechanicals to indicate the exact location of the photos and artwork.

The next day (if you had agreed to pay rush charges) or the day after (if you hadn't), you received your finished type galleys back from the typesetter. You often discovered then that your characters-per-pica calculations weren't quite right. No matter how well you had calculated and counted, the galleys rarely came back looking as you expected. After you ran the type and stats through a

# INTRODUCTION

machine that coated the back side of the paper with wax so it would stick to the mechanical boards, you started the actual paste-up process by cutting the copy and art apart with an Exacto knife and metal ruler. As you began to lay the individual pieces together on hotpress illustration boards (which you also had to prepare in advance with keyline guides for registration and production), you started to get an idea of how close you came with your type spec calculations.

If your calculations (or your typesetter's interpretation of them) were a little off, you might have decided to have the type rerun and/or the camera work re-shot to different sizes. If there wasn't enough time for this, you had to cut up each individual word or line of text and rearrange them to fit your original layout. You pasted down the position stats in position and cut amberlith windows for the images where needed. Finally, you positioned overlays and flaps to indicate where the color breaks occurred.

After you finished all of this labor-intensive production work, you learned that the president of the client's company or the editor managing the publishing project had somehow suffered a brainstorm the night before. The runoff from that storm meant the project had to be completely revised to accommodate a new angle and graphic image!

Since there wasn't enough time left to make all the revisions on all the elements, you left in the original graphics and photography and just had the copy rerun.

After working until 2 a.m. on Sunday night to complete all of the design and layout by the Monday morning deadline (the typesetter wouldn't work on weekends, so you had to individually cut, paste, and rearrange every single word in the final paragraph to make it fit), the deadline was extended.

Final revisions were approved, the typesetter re-ran the copy to fit the new layout, and your project was finally off to the print shop. The printer immediately tore off all of the amberlith windows you worked on so hard and replaced them with his own stripping work.

The bluelines and color keys came back and were approved. After the printer finished making all of the negatives and plates, the job was finally ready for printing (only weeks past the original deadline). The press check went smoothly and the art director approved the job. Returning to the office later that evening, the art director found a message from the receptionist stating that the client's name was misspelled in the headline, or that the times and prices mentioned in an article were all wrong.

Well, you know the rest of the story. The art director went into the darkroom and spent the evening crying quietly. The writers started looking for real jobs in a bank somewhere. In the morning, the account rep and the production artist were fired and your design agency reprinted the job at its own expense. In the publishing scenario, a retraction was printed on the back page of the next issue, the project editor was promoted to a position where he could do less harm, and everyone argued over who was to blame while they struggled with the next missed deadline.

## The Desktop Publishing Way

With desktop publishing, all of the steps from initial typesetting to final revision (before sending the materials to the print shop) can be handled on a personal computer. In fact, the early steps — the original work by the writers and artists — can also be handled by PCs.

Writers process their words and submit files on disk (or through a telephone modem) to the page designer. Artists draw with programs and submit disk files or use a scanner to capture sketches and photos they've created without a computer. The graphic designer or page-layout pro then uses a desktop publishing program to combine the two elements.

# INTRODUCTION

Imagine a system where you can produce multiple versions of any comprehensive layout in the same time that it used to take to create just one. Imagine being able to quickly and easily produce design comps that accurately show the particular fonts and typestyles proposed for a project and the exact photographs and illustrations being used in any design. Imagine being able to completely sidestep most of the mechanical-production and stripping steps prior to printing a piece. Now imagine having all of that flexibility, accuracy, speed, and productivity at a fraction of the usual cost. Best of all, imagine making last-minute changes in the blink of an eye, without headaches or ulcers. That's why desktop publishing is such a success.

## Why the Macintosh?

The Apple Macintosh was the first personal computer to do desktop publishing, and it's well-suited to the work. Most of the programs that run on the Macintosh, even those dedicated to such tasks as engineering and financial calculations, offer a variety of text fonts and styles and can intermix text and graphics. These programs can also print those mixes, because of Apple's dedication to the high-resolution LaserWriter laser printers as the natural and primary printers for the Mac. Because the LaserWriter uses the sophisticated PostScript printing language, it can accurately reproduce what you design on the Macintosh screen. Coincidentally, these same characteristics that are fundamental to the Mac are also the basis of desktop publishing. That isn't true of some competing personal computers, such as the systems compatible with IBM's PC and PS/2.

The Mac's interface — the images it presents on the computer screen — is based on the intimate combination of text and graphics. It's a graphic display of icons for documents, menus for commands, and a mouse for selecting screen positions that's ideal for many design tasks (see Chapter 1 for more details on the interface). That too makes the Mac a natural for desktop publishing. Because the interface puts similar commands in the same places for all programs, it also eases the job of learning the many desktop-publishing-related programs, such as

7

drawing and painting applications, word processing applications, and other utilities.

A final answer to "Why the Macintosh" is "QuarkXPress 3.0 runs on the Mac." And QuarkXPress is one of the premier desktop-publishing programs for the Macintosh.

## Why QuarkXPress?

The QuarkXPress program is famous for its power in design and publishing; it's the software of choice for both professionals and amateurs. When sized up against other Macintosh desktop-publishing programs in comparison reviews, QuarkXPress often takes the honors for its long list of features and its many options. With the Macintosh and QuarkXPress 3.0, you can produce final composition and more accurate proofs in much less time than with conventional methods. This translates directly and immediately into increased productivity and profitability.

You don't have to have an expert's knowledge of graphic design and the Macintosh to use QuarkXPress. Just learning the QuarkXPress basics can make you productive almost immediately. As your skills and familiarity with the program increase, you can move up into QuarkXPress's advanced capabilities.

## How to Use This Book

Here are a few simple guidelines to help you get more from reading this book.

**Play Around with Your Mac.** This is probably the most important tip in this chapter. Set aside about 30 minutes every day to play with your Mac. Play some games if you have them, play with QuarkXPress, play around with some other applications. Make sure you are playing — not working.

During this time, make sure you're not doing anything productive; this can lead to frustration if you aren't successful. This lets you concentrate on just using the Macintosh. You'll get better at handling the Mac's mouse and interface and will acquire an instinctual feel for finding commands in menus and moving items on the screen.

If you dedicate some time each day to these nonproductive pursuits, you'll find it easier to learn new material when you start working with QuarkXPress and the Mac. The intimidation factor is 98 percent of what keeps you from learning any new software (or hardware) effectively.

**Try as You Fly.** Don't just read about QuarkXPress commands — try them. Run QuarkXPress in front of you as you read the book and step through the tutorials, experiment with the commands, and analyze the results. The examples and tutorials in this book don't require any special fonts or software tools other than those found in your basic Macintosh system.

## Where to Look

To begin learning QuarkXPress, start with Chapter 1, which explains the Mac's interface and QuarkXPress tools, menus, and palettes.

Chapter 2 shows you how to open and size a document, set up master pages for it, and dictate your preferences for its units and behavior.

Chapter 3 introduces the process of entering, importing, and manipulating text.

Chapter 4 discusses sophisticated typography and text control.

Chapters 5 teaches you how to incorporate lines, boxes, and images into your documents.

Chapter 6 is devoted to color — how it works and when to use it.

Chapters 7, 8, and 9 are sample assignments for you to work through.

## Who Should Read This Book

You don't have to be a computer expert to use QuarkXPress or to read this book. All you need is either some familiarity with the Mac or the willingness to learn to mouse your way around its menus and icons. QuarkXPress can be used for everything from creating a company newsletter to designing a professional advertisement or brochure to laying out a commercial magazine or book. If that's the work you do, then QuarkXPress and this book are for you. After reading this book, you'll be able to produce most, if not all, of your desktop-publishing and graphic projects on the Macintosh using QuarkXPress.

## What You Need to Use QuarkXPress

You'll need a certain amount of basic Mac hardware to run QuarkXPress and more to run it efficiently. Here are the details.

**RAM.** QuarkXPress 3.0 will run on any Macintosh with 2 megabytes or more of RAM. If you are currently using a Macintosh with less memory, an upgrade to 2 megabytes is not as expensive as it used to be. Besides, Apple's new System 7.0, expected in January 1991, will require 2 megabytes of memory, so you should definitely have an upgrade on your shopping list. Keep in mind that you can never have too much RAM. Some Macintosh configurations allow you to install up to 32 megabytes of RAM — an expensive proposition. QuarkXPress 3.0 will run very smoothly with 4 megabytes of RAM, so you shouldn't have to go to those lengths to make your software run efficiently.

**Disk.** You'll need a hard-disk drive with about 3 megabytes of free space to store QuarkXPress 3.0 and all the filters, extensions, drivers, and other files that it needs for operation. It's a good idea to have another 2 megabytes of free space for a working file as you create new documents.

The amount of hard disk space you need depends to a great extent on what types of documents and images you're working with. Placing and manipulating images in QuarkXPress 3.0 will be a lot smoother and faster if the picture files are stored on a hard-disk drive instead of on a floppy disk or other external storage device.

You can save and store QuarkXPress 3.0 documents on standard floppy disks or on other high-volume storage devices — such as a removable-cartridge hard drive — for easy transportation or archiving. Fortunately, QuarkXPress does not embed the programming code for each image in the document file. This lets you use as many images as you need in your documents without their growing to huge proportions.

If you use grayscale or high-density 24- or 32-bit color images, file-compression software will be a good investment. It can reduce the file sizes and, if necessary, segment files to spread a single huge file across several floppy disks.

Check with your service bureau to see if it has a preference for a particular type of high-volume system for transporting files. Modem transfers of large files can be inconvenient (even at 9600 baud), so it's always a good idea to do some research before investing in another piece of expensive hardware.

**Display.** QuarkXPress 3.0 is adept at handling color production and separation on the Macintosh, even without a color monitor. On a Macintosh with a monochrome or grayscale monitor, you won't be able to see the actual colors you're working with, but you'll still be able to manipulate and separate colors with QuarkXPress. This feature will be discussed and demonstrated in more detail in Chapter 6.

## CHAPTER 1

# Where To Begin

### Introduction

The first step in learning QuarkXPress is to become comfortable with the Macintosh controls — the interface of icons, pull-down menus, and mouse and keyboard commands that are native to any Mac program. Then you're ready to learn the interface of the QuarkXPress program itself: to notice its approach to design and layout, to browse through its menus, to recognize its major tools, and to find help when you need it. In this chapter you'll do just that.

### The Mac Interface

The Macintosh is famous for its interface, the way it shows the operator what it's doing and the way the operator tells it what to do. This interface is widely credited with popularizing desktop publishing. You need to be comfortable with it to master QuarkXPress.

### Icons

The Macintosh display mimics traditional office and design tools to simplify the work of moving from the old manual way (as described in the Introduction) to the computer way. For example, the Mac uses icons, or small graphic images, to represent files (individual computer documents), folders (to hold files), and even a trash can (for throwing files away). As you can see in Figure 1-1, documents created with different applications — such as a word-processing program, spreadsheet program, or database-management program — have different icons that easily distinguish them from each other.

USING QUARKXPRESS

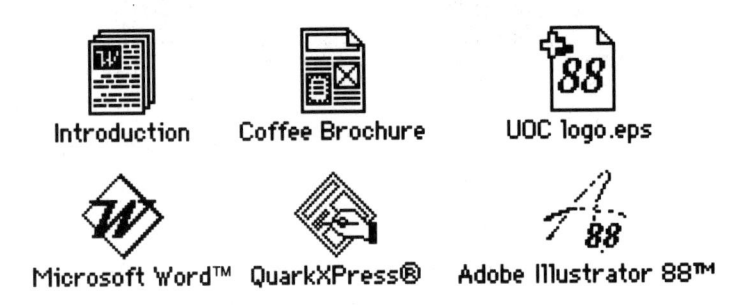

Introduction   Coffee Brochure   UOC logo.eps

Microsoft Word™   QuarkXPress®   Adobe Illustrator 88™

Figure 1-1, a variety of icons, including several document icons from different applications.

## Control: Keyboard and Mouse

You control the Macintosh by selecting commands with the keyboard or the mouse. Use the keyboard by pressing a combination of the **Shift**, **Command** (or ⌘, the key with the Apple and square-cloverleaf patterns on it), **Control**, and **Option** keys while simultaneously pressing a letter or number key (such as **C** for a copy operation). Use the mouse by moving its cursor to a menu, where commands are organized, then holding down the mouse button. This pulls down a menu and shows its command selections, as shown in Figure 1-2. Move the mouse cursor again, stop on any item within the pulled-down menu, and release the mouse button to invoke that command or option. The keyboard shortcuts for these commands are noted with the corresponding menu selections, as shown in Figures 1-2 and 1-3.

## Select an Object, then an Operation

Most Macintosh operations begin when you select something to work on. Then you choose the "operation" (or command) to perform on the selected object. You select icons on the Mac display or text and graphics within a program display by pointing the mouse cursor at the item and pressing and

| File | | File | | File | |
|---|---|---|---|---|---|
| New | ⌘N | New... | ⌘N | New... | ⌘N |
| Open... | ⌘O | Open... | ⌘O | Open... | ⌘O |
| Close | ⌘W | | | Place... | |
| Save | ⌘S | Close | | | |
| Save As... | | Save | ⌘S | Close | |
| Delete... | | Save as... | | Save | ⌘S |
| | | Revert to Saved | | Save As... | |
| Print Preview... | ⌘I | | | | |
| Print Merge... | | Get Text... | ⌘E | Page Setup... | |
| Page Setup... | | Save Text... | | Print... | ⌘P |
| Print... | ⌘P | Save Page as EPS... | | | |
| | | | | Quit | ⌘Q |
| Open Mail... | | Document Setup... | | | |
| Send Mail... | | Page Setup... | | | |
| | | Print... | ⌘P | | |
| Quit | ⌘Q | | | | |
| | | Quit | ⌘Q | | |

**Figure 1-2. Examples of pull-down menus from different programs.**

releasing (clicking) the mouse button. The selected item changes color, or is highlighted. You can select several items at once by "shift-clicking," pressing the **Shift** key while clicking on each item in turn. You can select an area of text within a document by placing the text-editing cursor at one end of the area, pressing the mouse button, then dragging the cursor across the area while holding down the mouse button. The selected area can then be cut away entirely or merely copied (in either case a copy of the selected area is kept on a clipboard in the computer's memory), and if desired, pasted (retrieved from the clipboard) in some other place on the document. The dragging operation can also be used to move icons or graphic images from one position to another.

You can open, or launch, a program simply by selecting its icon or one of its document icons on the Macintosh desktop and choosing the **Open** command from the **File** menu, or by using the simple shortcut of double-clicking on the icon.

## Menus, Submenus, and Dialog Boxes

Many commands and menu entries have layers of more-detailed options and choices. The Macintosh presents these in several ways. Sometimes a menu item leads to a sub-menu, or pull-out menu, of more choices, as you can see in Figure 1-3. You find these by clicking the mouse on a main menu, then settling the mouse cursor on any selection with an arrow pointing to the right. The pull-out menu appears to the right, and you select from it by continuing to hold the mouse button down while you move the mouse cursor to the entry you want.

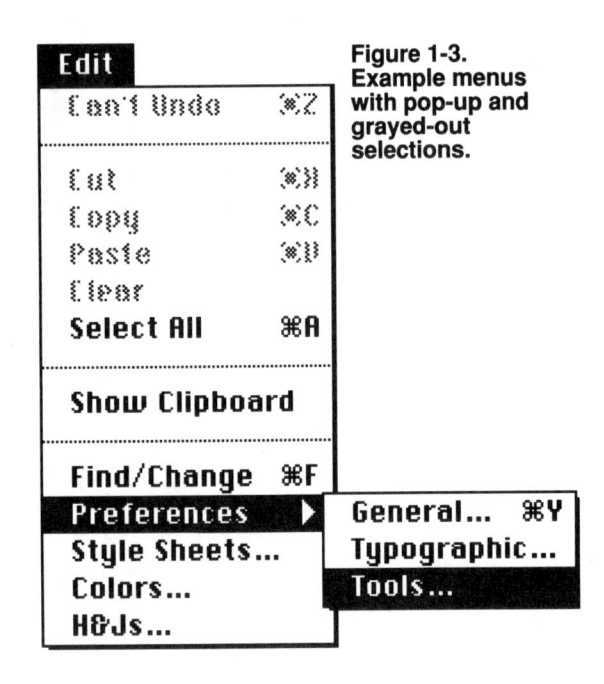

**Figure 1-3. Example menus with pop-up and grayed-out selections.**

Menu options displayed in a light gray instead of the solid black (see Figure 1-3) indicate that the option isn't available. This keeps you from choosing something that shouldn't or can't be used in a particular situation.

Mac commands followed by three dots indicate that they're accompanied by dialog boxes, which present you with buttons you can click on to select options, and fields you can fill in by that the Mac is easier to use and remember than other computers are. And after learning your first program, the second one can be a breeze.

You can access most commands in other Mac applications in much the same way, by using the mouse or keyboard shortcuts. And commands common to all applications are in the same places, within the same menus. For example, commands used to open, close, save, print, copy, and cut are in the same menus in much the same places in every application, from simple paint programs to complex spreadsheets, to advanced desktop-publishing and page-layout software. If you learn one Mac program — such as a word processor, paint/draw program, or database manager — you've already learned the basics of any other application.

### The QuarkXPress Interface

You can see the QuarkXPress interface in Figure 1-6, which displays a QuarkXPress document already open. These are the menu commands and palette tools you'll use to create, edit, and print QuarkXPress documents.

The **Tool** palette is usually on the left of the screen, though it is a "floating" palette — you can move it to any other position on the screen by clicking on its top bar with the mouse and dragging it to another position. You can also close, or hide, this palette by clicking in the tiny box in the corner of the top bar, as you do with other Macintosh windows.

At the bottom of the display, you'll often see the **Measurements** palette. This precisely reports the attributes (position, rotation, text style, scaling, and so on) of any selected item in the document.

The main working area, or pasteboard (representing the real boards where pages are manually pasted up), takes up most of the screen, displaying the graphics and text that you're positioning and editing. This window too can be moved. You can also change its size by dragging the double-box icon in its

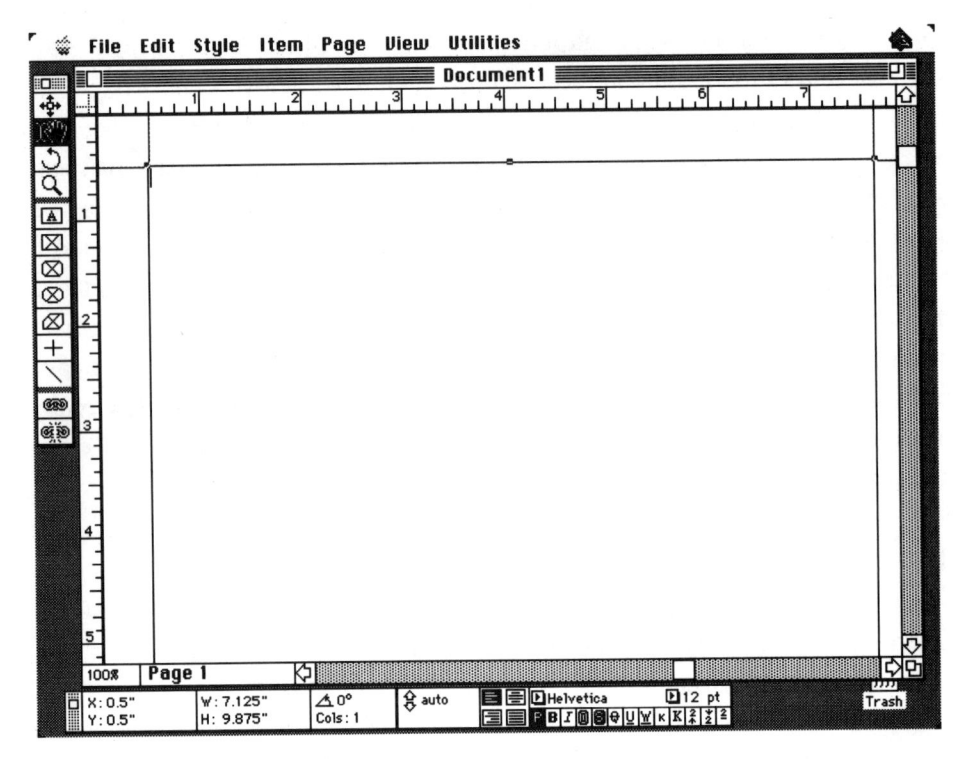

**Figure 1-6. The QuarkXPress interface.**

bottom right corner (another standard Macintosh action). You may want to change the window's size if you want to open and view more than one QuarkXPress document at a time or use MultiFinder to activate another program alongside QuarkXPress (see your Macintosh manual for more information on MultiFinder).

## Menus

QuarkXPress's pull-down menus — **File**, **Edit**, **Style**, **Item**, **Page**, **View**, and **Utilities** — run across the top of the screen. You can browse through them by clicking on each of the menu titles. **Edit** and **File** are common Mac menus and usually appear the same in each Mac program. The **File** menu is dedicated to opening, closing, saving, importing information, and printing. The **Edit** menu lets you perform basic text- and graphic-editing commands such as **Cut, Copy,** and **Paste** (as mentioned earlier). QuarkXPress adds its own selections to the **Edit** menu for dictating settings that apply to the full document, such as hyphenation and justification; color choices; style sheets; and typographic, page-layout, and tool defaults. The **Style** menu holds the text control commands, where you can set the size, shape, color, and other typographic attributes. It also controls graphic image specifications when a picture box is selected, and line attributes when a line is selected. The **Item** menu is loaded with commands to edit or move items, the boxes that hold text or graphics. The **Page** menu enables you to number and navigate through the pages of a document. The **View** menu lets you dictate what the screen displays — which tools appear and what size, or magnification, you see the document in. And the **Utilities** menu is a collection of utilities and controls, including commands for text formatting, editing, and graphics storage.

There is more than one way to control any graphic element in QuarkXPress. For example, while the **Item** and **Content** tools in the palette allow direct (but imprecise) manipulation of elements, and the **Style** menu offers options that give you control over some aspects of each object, the **Modify...** command under the **Item** menu offers ultimate precision and control over all aspects of any selected element.

The brief descriptions above should give you the gist of what the seven menus offer. Remember that the menus change depending on the different conditions of your document and that some selections may be grayed out if you try to do something that the selection is unable to perform.

The rest of this book explains all of the key menu selections in the context of creating a document, adding text to it, formatting that text, adding graphics, editing the graphics, and saving the results.

USING QUARKXPRESS

## Palettes

**Tools Palette.** Almost everything you do in QuarkXPress involves the tools in your floating **Tools** palette. Here's a brief description of what they do and how to make them do it.

**The Two Most Important Tools: Item and Content.** The **Item** tool (Figure 1-7) is first on the palette. This tool lets you select, move, cut, copy, paste, or delete items (boxes) in a document. It also allows you to manipulate and edit some kinds of items.

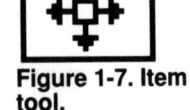

**Figure 1-7. Item tool.**

Next is the **Content** tool (Figure 1-8), which lets you select, edit, move, cut, copy, paste, or clear the *contents* of the items in your documents.

**Figure 1-8. Content tool.**

Here's a good rule of thumb: If you need to change something *inside* a box, select that box with the **Content** tool. Whenever you need to change the attributes of the *box itself,* use the **Item** tool.

There are some areas where the tools' capabilities overlap. For example, when you want to delete an item or group of items on the page, select them with the **Item** tool and press the **Delete** key. Selecting the item with the **Content** tool and pressing the **Delete** key deletes the contents of the item, but not the item itself. However, you can delete an item you've selected with the **Content** tool by pressing the keyboard equivalent of the **Delete** command, ⌘+K, or by choosing **Delete** from the **Item** menu.

You can change many other attributes or qualities of the selected object in the **Measurements** palette (another floating palette — you reach it by choosing **Modify** frcm the **View** menu). See the **Measurements** palette section below for more information.

22

# WHERE TO BEGIN

**Figure 1-9. Rotation tool.**

**Rotation and Zoom Tools.** The next two tools down the palette are **Rotation** and **Zoom**. The **Rotation** tool (Figure 1-9) lets you rotate any selected object around any origin point you create by clicking. The rotation angle can be refined with the **Measurements** palette.

**Figure 1-10. Zoom tool.**

The **Zoom** tool (Figure 1-10) lets you magnify any portion of the page on your screen. It works two ways: click on the **Zoom** tool and then on the item you want to enlarge, or select the area on the page with the **Zoom** tool by dragging the mouse diagonally across the area. You can enlarge any portion of the page up to 400% of its original size.

**Figure 1-11. Text box tool.**

**Box Tools.** The next set of tools on the palette creates new boxes in a document. The first creates new text boxes and is shown as a boxed **A** (Figure 1-11). The next four create picture boxes (Figure 1-12). Three tools make picture boxes in preset shapes (rectangle, rounded rectangle, and ellipse) and one creates picture boxes in shapes you design yourself. The **Text box** tool is described in Chapters 2 and 3. The **Picture box** tools are explained in Chapter 5.

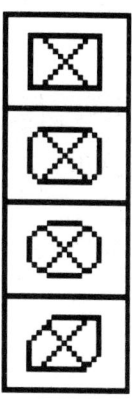

**Figure 1-12. Picture box tools.**

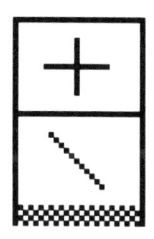

**Figure 1-13. Line tools.**

**Line Tools.** The line tools (Figure 1-13) are next. The first creates new "constrained" horizontal or vertical lines (no matter how you drag the tool, it only draws horizontal or vertical lines). The other tool draws lines at any angle. You can edit lines drawn with either tool with the **Measurement** palette, **Style** menu, or the **Modify** command under the **Item** menu. That means that even if you have drawn a constrained horizontal line, you have several ways to change its angle, weight, color, shade, or location. These tools are explained in Chapter 5.

23

# USING QUARKXPRESS

**Linking Tools.** The last two tools control the flow of text from one text box to another (Figure 1-14). The **Text Chain Linking** tool lets you set up the flow of text from box to box on the same page or across several pages. Its counterpart, the **Text Chain Unlinking** tool, lets you interrupt and rearrange the flow of text in a document or story.

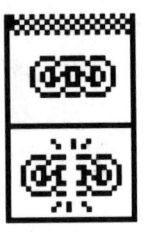

**Figure 1-14. Linking tools.**

**Customizing the Tools: Preferences.** You can define the ways you want these tools to perform by choosing **Preferences** and then **Tools** from the **Edit** menu. Each tool has its own controllable setting. For instance, you can define the **Zoom** tool's enlargement increments with each click of the mouse button, or you can define the default line thickness that either line tool draws for new lines.

You can modify the box tools to change the appearance of each new box you draw. For text boxes, you can designate border style, border thickness, text runaround, and text inset attributes. For picture boxes, you can assign border style, border thickness, text runaround style, and picture scale.

### Tool Practice

1. Double-click on one of the line tools.

2. Select the constrained line tool when the **Tool Preferences** dialog box appears (Figure 1-15).

3. Click on the **Modify** button to change any of the attributes of the line that the tool draws next. Click on **OK** or **Cancel** when you're finished making modifications.

4. Notice that the **Frame** button in the **Tool Preferences** dialog box is grayed and unavailable because lines don't have frames (borders).

24

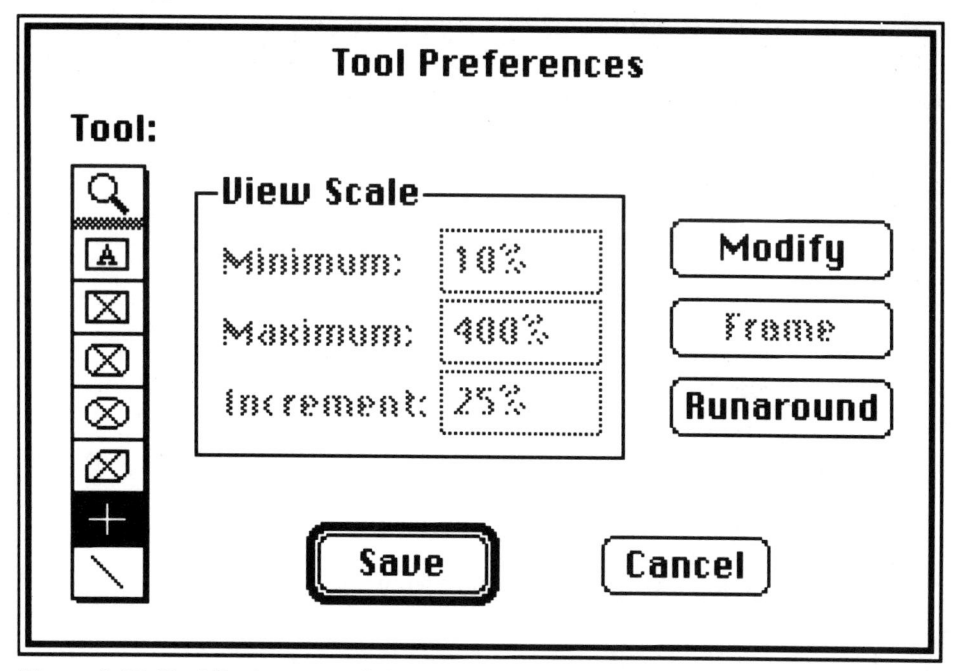

Figure 1-15. Tool Preferences dialog box.

5. You can also designate whether a line you've drawn is automatically opaque or transparent using the **Runaround** mode button. (See Chapter 6 for more details about setting an item runaround attribute.)

**Measurements Palette.** The **Measurements** palette (see Figure 1-16) is new to QuarkXPress 3.0. It "floats" as the **Tool** palette does: You can move it or hide it. It gives you precise reports on the location, size, rotation, styles (for type), picture skew and angle, and other attributes of an item you select in the working display area. You can also use it to enter precise new values for those attributes. To do so, click on the desired attribute, type a new value, then press **Return** or click somewhere else on the palette or display. It should be more convenient for experienced QuarkXPress designers to use this palette than to navigate through several layers of menus, submenus, and dialog boxes.

## USING QUARKXPRESS

**Figure 1-16. The Measurements palette.**

### Getting Help

If you need answers to a question about using QuarkXPress, you can:

1. Use this book.

2. Check the **Help** window that comes with the program by choosing **About QuarkXPress...** on the **Apple** menu (see Figure 1-17). Select a topic from the list, and click on **Help**. After you read the information, you can jump forward to the next topic, back to the previous, return to the index in **Topics**, or quit **Help** altogether and return to QuarkXPress. Figure 1-18 shows an example page from the **Help** file.

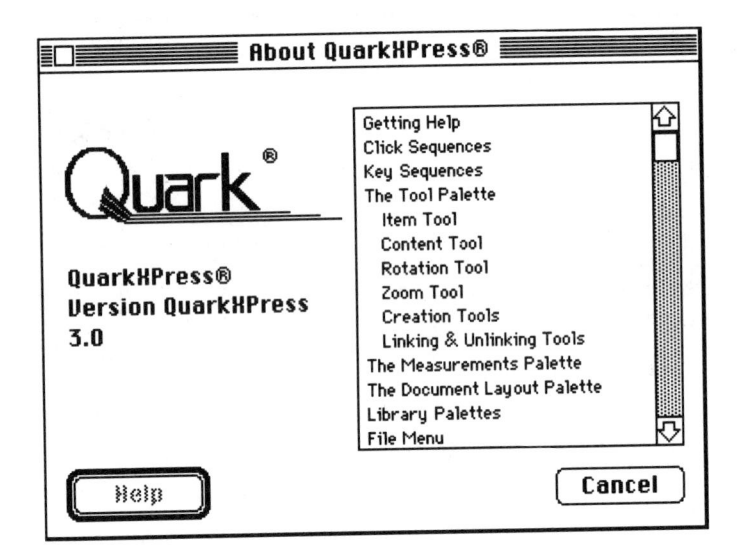

**Figure 1-17. The About QuarkXPress... box.**

3. Check the QuarkXPress manuals. These have more detailed explanations than does the **Help** file.

4. Call QuarkXPress technical support. Before you do this, make sure you record the details of your problem or question in a notebook, such as what you wanted to do and what happened, and what hardware you were using. This will help to diagnose your problem and determine a solution.

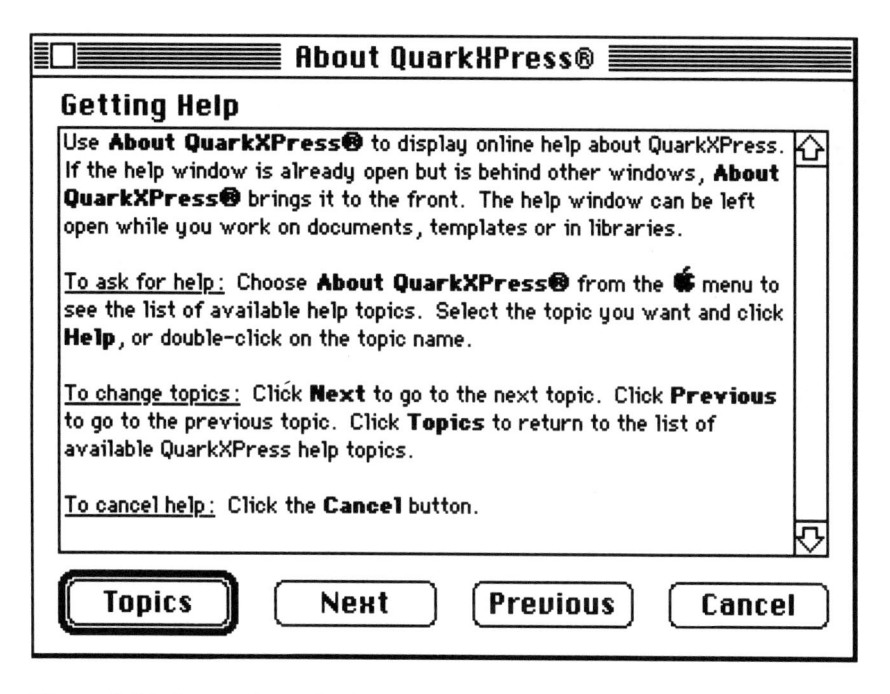

**Figure 1-18.** A page from the Help file.

### CHAPTER 2

# QuarkXPress Basics

Before you begin entering and manipulating text and graphics, you need to know how to get QuarkXPress up and running.

First, you should know your way around a Macintosh — at least the fundamentals of running and commanding your Mac. The Macintosh manuals and disks, your own experience, and Chapter 1 tackle that topic.

Second, you need to install and start QuarkXPress. See the QuarkXPress manual for installation information.

Third, you need to open or create a new document, set your preferences for QuarkXPress commands, set up the palettes and windows you're going to use, and be able to find your way around the document. That's what this chapter covers.

## Opening Documents and New Documents

When you start QuarkXPress you'll see a display such as that in Figure 2-1. Your first choice is whether to work on an existing document (opening a file), a template (a new document based on an old one), or a new document (creating a file).

Work on an existing document if you need to make changes to it. Work on a new document based on a template if you've saved some previous design or layout as a template to use its setup and layout in new compositions. (Templates can save you a lot of time, and help create consistency between various projects.) Any changes you make to the opened template document won't affect the actual

USING QUARKXPRESS

template file on disk – they'll only be saved as a new file on disk, leaving the template for future projects. Work on a new document without the aid of a template if the current project doesn't bear a close resemblance to any of your previous work.

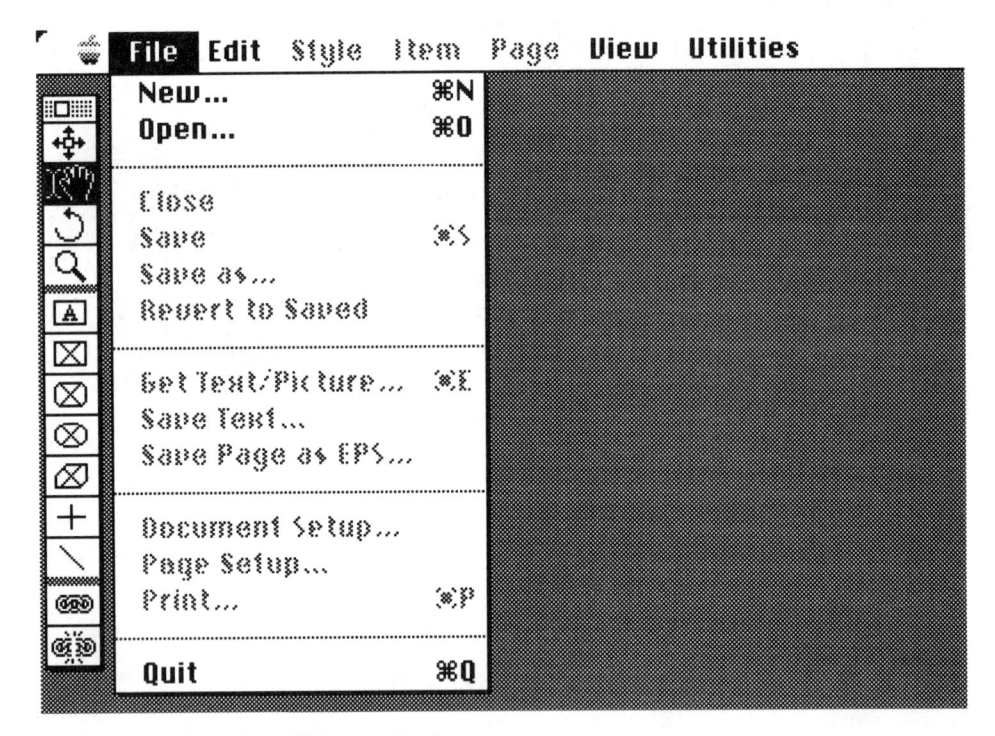

**Figure 2-1. Initial QuarkXPress display.**

## Working with an Existing Document

To work on a document that already exists, you simply:

1. Choose **Open** from the **File** menu.

2. From the **Open** dialog box (as in Figure 2-2) select the drive and folder where the document sits on disk.

3. Click on the name of the file you want to select.

4. Click on **Open** in the dialog box. The document will appear on the display.

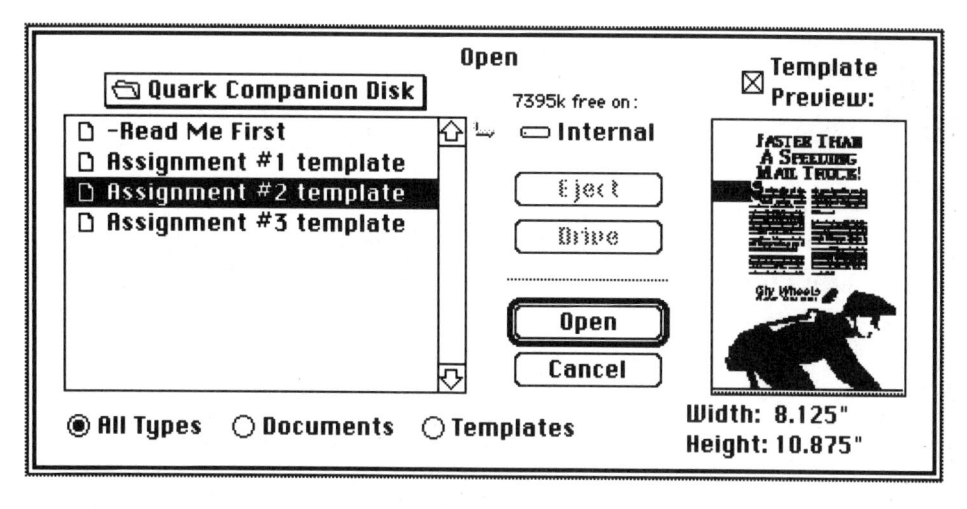

Figure 2-2. Open dialog box for opening existing documents.

## Working with a Template

To work on a document that is based on a template:

1. Choose **Open** from the **File** menu.

2. From the **Open** dialog box (as in Figure 2-2) select the drive and folder where the template sits on disk.

3. Click on the name of the template you want to select. If there are many files, you may want to click beside **Templates** at the bottom of the dialog box. This option will display only templates in the list.

4. Click beside **Template Preview** to see a thumbnail image of the template. This can help you see if it's the template you wanted.

5. Click on **Open** in the dialog box. The template will appear on the display.

## Creating a New Document

To work on a new document:

1. Choose **New** from the **File** menu. The **New** dialog box will appear – as shown in Figure 2-3. This is where you'll set the layout for the document's first page and the original Master Page A.

2. Set the page size for your new document.

3. Set the margin guides for the document. (If you click in the Facing Pages box you can create a document with different left and right page formats.)

4. Decide on the number of columns and the gutter width between columns.

5. Decide if you want a text box to automatically occupy the first page.

6. Click **OK**. The first page will appear, with your layout in place, surrounded by a "pasteboard" area of display for working edits. Blue (dotted on non-color displays) "page guide" lines will show the page margins. These lines won't print.

## Document Setup

If you're unsure of the page size of a new (or any) document, just select **Document Setup** from the **File** menu. The dialog box that appears (see Figure 2-4) will fill you in.

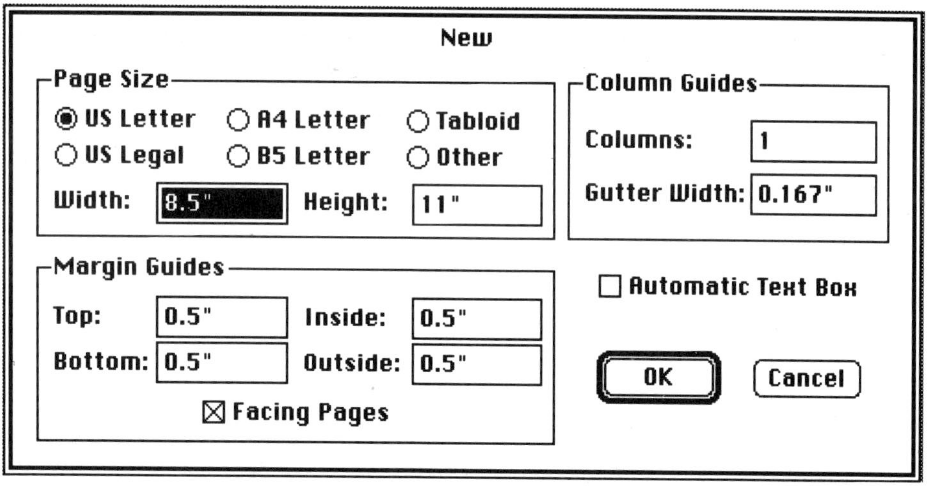

*QUARKXPRESS BASICS*

Figure 2-3. New dialog box.

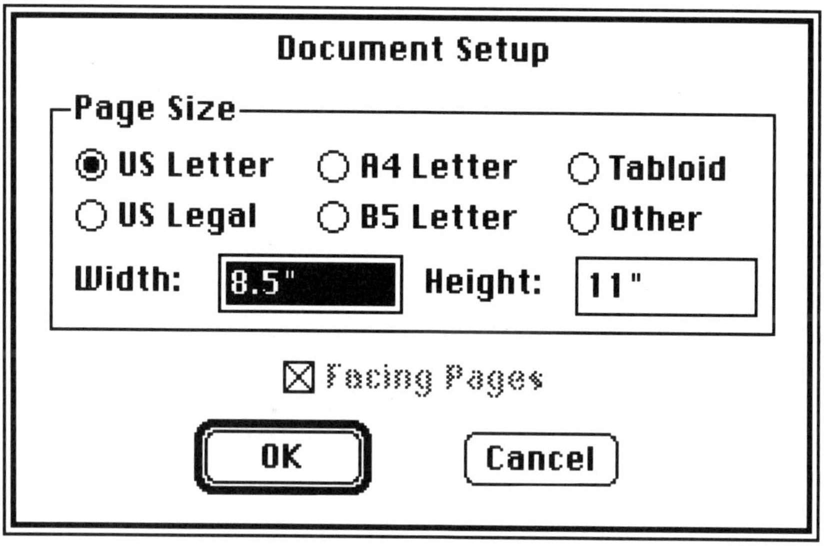

Figure 2-4. Document Setup dialog box.

## Preferences

After starting a new document or opening a template, you should check and change, if necessary, the document's preferences. These are all of the details of approach that QuarkXPress lets you choose, such as:

- units of measure (do you want to work in inches, points, or millimeters?)

- item coordinates (should they be by the page or by the entire spread?)

- superscript position (should the default be 33% above the line, or less, or more?)

- zoom amount (should it zoom in 25% each time, or 50%, or how much?)

- picture box color (should the default be black, no color, or some other color?).

If you're a beginner, you may not want to change any of these now. Even experts sometimes set only the units of measure. But for full control of QuarkXPress and for efficiency you'll find yourself coming back to **Preferences** as you work. For example, by setting the preference for the rectangular picture box tool frame to 12 points wide and black, that's what will automatically appear every time you use the tool. You won't have to dig around in the style menu each and every time to change the frame's width and color.

**Preferences** are divided into three sets: **General**, **Typographic**, and **Tools**. You reach them all through the **Edit** menu, as shown in Figure 2-5.

Figure 2-5. Preferences pop-up menu from the Edit menu.

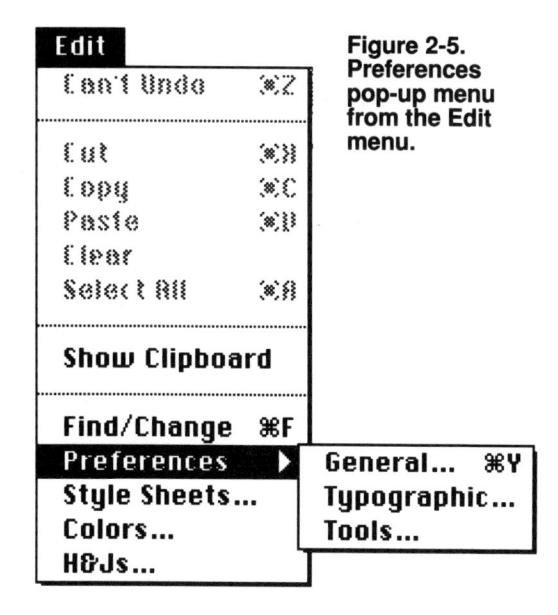

## General Preferences

The **General Preferences** dialog box (reach it through the **Edit** menu) is shown in Figure 2-6. Set the preferences you want here, by choosing from a pop-up menu (click on the menu and move the cursor to the selection you want), by clicking in a box, or by typing a value in a blank. Then click **OK**.

**Horizontal Measure:** specifies the measurement marks on the horizontal ruler.

**Vertical Measure:** specifies the measurement marks on the vertical ruler.

**Auto Page Insertion:** if you import more text to a text box than can fit, QuarkXPress automatically inserts a new page in your document with a text box to hold the overflow. This menu decides where that new page is added within the document.

**Framing:** specifies if frames should be inside or outside the perimeter of boxes.

**Guides:** determines if ruler and page guides should be in front of all items or behind them.

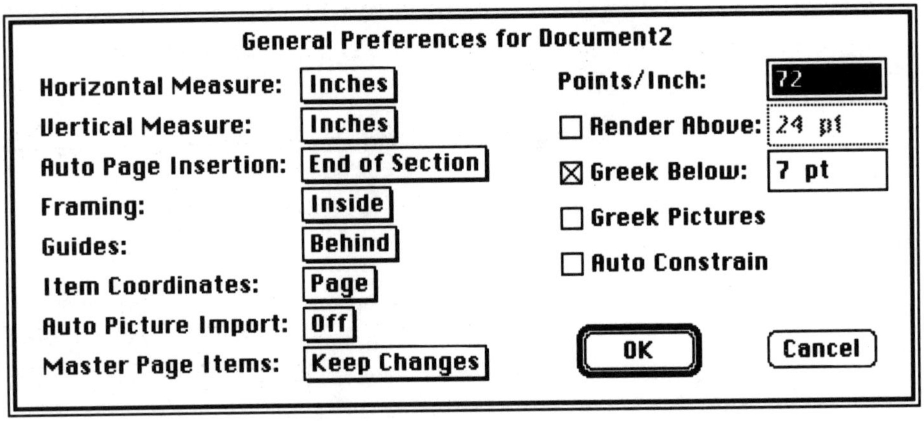

```
                General Preferences for Document2
Horizontal Measure:  [Inches]         Points/Inch:      [72]
Vertical Measure:    [Inches]         ☐ Render Above:  [24 pt]
Auto Page Insertion: [End of Section] ☒ Greek Below:   [7 pt]
Framing:             [Inside]         ☐ Greek Pictures
Guides:              [Behind]         ☐ Auto Constrain
Item Coordinates:    [Page]
Auto Picture Import: [Off]                [ OK ]      [Cancel]
Master Page Items:   [Keep Changes]
```

Figure 2-6. General Preferences dialog box.

**Item Coordinates:** sets either a separate horizontal ruler for each page, or one ruler across multiple pages.

**Auto Picture Import:** allows pictures that have been modified since a document was last opened to be automatically updated from their disk files.

**Master Page Items:** allows items on a page that came originally from applying a master page, but have been modified, to be removed when a new master page is applied.

**Points/Inch:** sets how many points should there be per inch (from 72 to 73).

**Render Above:** specifies which size text should be rendered smoothly on screen (rendering takes more time, but looks better — all fonts are rendered when printing).

**Greek Below:** sets which size text is small enough to "greek," to show only as grey bars. (This saves time in changing the display. Use it for text that is too small to read anyway or when reading the text is less important than seeing its general placement. No text is greeked when you print.)

**Greek Pictures:** allows pictures within a document on screen be shown only as gray (this saves time when changing the display, such as when zooming or changing pages). No pictures greek when you print.

**Auto Constrain:** determines if items such as boxes should automatically "constrain" newer items created within them. For instance, a smaller box within a larger box could not be moved or sized beyond the borders of the larger box if it is constrained.

## Typographic Preferences

The **Typographic Preferences** dialog box (reach it through the **Edit** menu) is shown in Figure 2-7. Set the preferences for type operations such as the positions of superscripts and subscripts here, by typing values in blanks or by choosing from a pop-up menu (click on the menu and move the cursor to the selection you want). Then click **OK**. (Chapter 4 has more details on typographics.)

**Superscript Offset, VScale, HScale:** measured in percent of the normal font size; the offset from the baseline and the size of superscript characters.

**Small Caps:** measured in percent of the normal font size; the size of small caps characters.

**Superior:** measured in percent of the normal font size; the size of superior characters.

```
┌─────────────────────────────────────────────────────────┐
│         Typographic Preferences for Document2           │
│ ┌─Superscript──┐ ┌─Subscript───┐ ┌─Baseline Grid──────┐ │
│ │ Offset: 33%  │ │ Offset: 33% │ │ Start:     0.5"    │ │
│ │ VScale: 100% │ │ VScale: 100%│ │ Increment: 18 pt   │ │
│ │ HScale: 100% │ │ HScale: 100%│ └────────────────────┘ │
│ └──────────────┘ └─────────────┘                        │
│                                   Auto Leading:  20%    │
│ ┌─Small Caps───┐ ┌─Superior────┐  ☒ Auto Kern Above: 10 pt│
│ │ VScale: 75%  │ │ VScale: 50% │                        │
│ │ HScale: 75%  │ │ HScale: 50% │  Char. Widths: Fractional│
│ └──────────────┘ └─────────────┘  Leading Mode: Typesetting│
│                                                         │
│              ( OK )      ( Cancel )                     │
└─────────────────────────────────────────────────────────┘
```

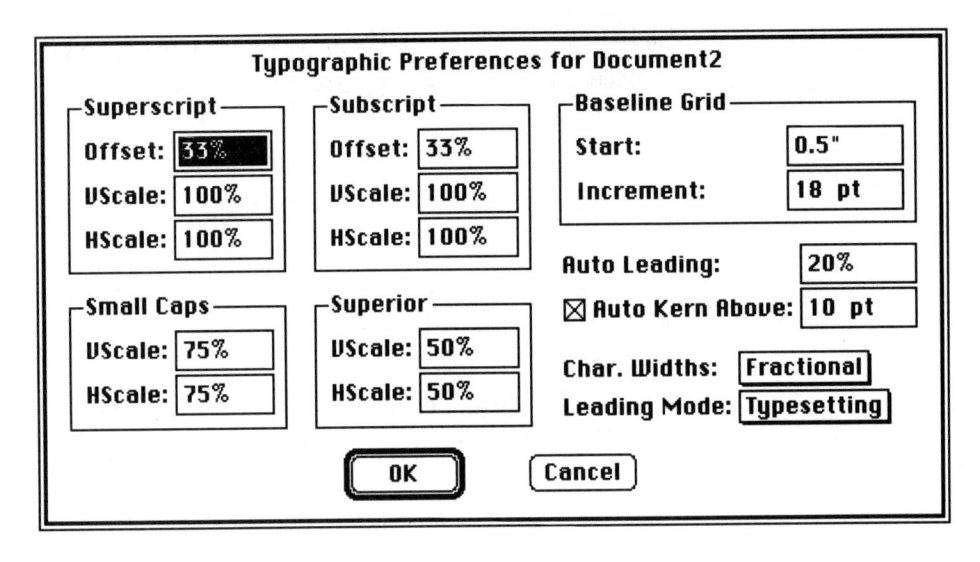

Figure 2-7. Typographic Preferences dialog box.

**Baseline Grid:** the place to start and the interval between lines of the invisible grid to which you can lock baselines of text in paragraphs (to align baselines across multiple columns).

**Auto Leading:** the amount of leading in paragraphs that are set to automatic leading (see Chapter 4).

**Auto Kern Above:** sets the size font above which to automatically kern and track text from the built-in kerning and tracking tables.

**Character Widths:** the way to display and print characters. Use fractional for laser and PostScript printers and integral for dot-matrix printers.

**Leading Mode:** typesetting mode to measure upward from the baseline of text to the next baseline, word processing to measure downward from the top of ascent on one line to the top of ascent on next.

## Tool Preferences

The **Tool Preferences** dialog box (reach it through the **Edit** menu) is shown in Figure 2-8. Set the action of the **Tool** palette icons here, by clicking on the relevant tool, then selecting from the options in the dialog box (these depend on the selected tool). Then click **OK**.

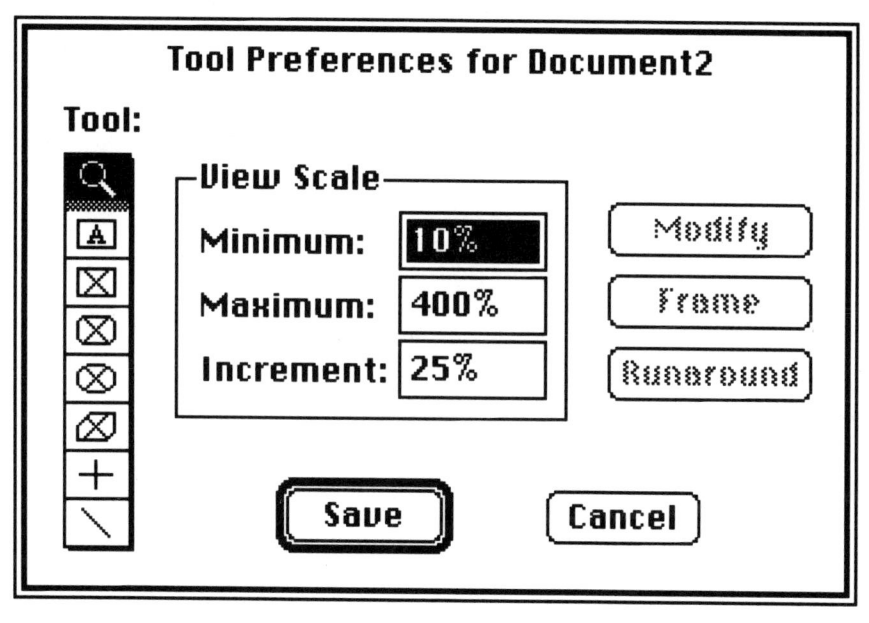

**Figure 2-8. Tool Preferences dialog box.**

**Zoom:** sets the minimum and maximum zooms, and the increment (magnification factor) for each time you use the tool.

**Text box:** sets the modify (vertical alignment, background color and shade, text inset, number of columns), frame (color, width, style), and runaround modes (for wrapping around overlapping items) for all new text boxes.

**Picture box** (any shape): sets the modify (scale, offset, picture angle and skew, background color and shade), frame (color, width, style), and runaround modes (for wrapping around overlapping items) for all picture boxes.

**Lines** (either type): sets the modify (style, endcaps, width, color, shade) and runaround modes (for wrapping around overlapping items) for all lines.

## Viewing Your Document and Tools

You can choose your viewpoint on many of QuarkXPress' tools and on the displayed document with the **View** menu (see Figure 2-9).

You can show or hide the:

- **Measurements** palette

- **Tool** palette

- Rulers

- Guides (page guides, ruler guides, and box outlines)

- **Document Layout** window (where you handle master page settings, as explained below)

- Invisibles (these non-printing characters are listed in the reference manual and include the new paragraph marker ¶ and the word space).

You can view your document at:

- 50% of actual size

- 75% of actual size

# QUARKXPRESS BASICS

> **Extra!**
>
> *Ruler Guides*
>
> *You can create non-printing "ruler guide" lines on your document pages to help you align items. Just click within a ruler and drag onto the page. You can click again on the guides and drag them to move them, even to delete them by moving them off of the page entirely. To delete all horizontal or vertical guides, hold the Option key and then click on the horizontal or vertical ruler. See Figure 2-10 for a display with several rulers of each type.*

- Actual size

- 200% of actual size

- Thumbnail versions of the pages (each page only an inch or so square)

- Fit in Window size (where all of the document fits into the Mac's displayed window)

- Zoomed size (click on the Zoom tool in the palette and then click on the document or drag across a rectangular area of the document to zoom in on or out from a particular spot or area of the document. Set the zooming amount and the limits in the **Preferences** box).

```
View  Utilities
─────────────────────────
  Fit in Window      ⌘0
  50%
  75%
✓ Actual Size        ⌘1
  200%
  Thumbnails
─────────────────────────
  Hide Guides
✓ Snap to Guides
  Show Rulers        ⌘R
  Hide Invisibles    ⌘I
─────────────────────────
  Hide Tools
  Hide Measurements
  Show Document Layout
```

**Figure 2-9.** The View menu with keyboard shortcuts (when available) listed to the right of the selections.

41

USING QUARKXPRESS

### Shortcut

**Zooming**

You can zoom in on your document to see more detail, or away from it to see more of the document at once. You can do this with:

- **View** menu commands
- **Zoom** tool
- **View** percent field

The **View** percent field is tucked into the bottom left corner of the display window. See Figure 2-11 for an example. Click in this tiny field and type the zoom value you want to use. Then press **Return** to see the results.

Figure 2-10. Example display with several horizontal and vertical ruler guides.

42

Use the **Fit in Window** size to get a feel for the page layout. Use **Thumbnail** to move pages around within the document or between documents. (You can drag the thumbnails about with the mouse). Use the **200%** view when you want to view text or graphics up close.

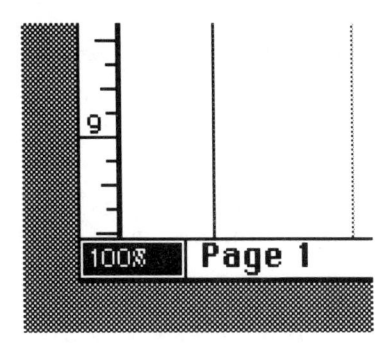

**Figure 2-11. The View percent field.**

## Master Page Formats

**Master Page Formats** let you create a series of page templates with common design elements appearing on each page. Design elements can consist of any graphic element or combination of elements that can be created or imported to QuarkXPress 3.0, such as:

- page headers

- format lines

- borders

- chapter titles

- page numbers

- imported graphics.

Create master page formats to identify and separate sections of larger documents, as in chapters and section heads. You can create a common page format that appears throughout a document, with different identifying headers or section markers. QuarkXPress lets you create up to 127 different master page formats in any document. You can choose to work on master pages individually or globally in the **General Preferences** dialog box. The changes you make will be applied to all of the master pages sharing that format.

When you're working on a new document, you should start by creating master page formats. Even on existing documents or when working from templates you should take a look at the master page formats; they set the ground rules for the entire project's design.

The **Document Layout** palette, shown in Figure 2-12, controls the master pages, with help from the commands in the **Page** menu (Figure 2-13). It lets you create click and drag icons that represent your different master page formats and place them into any order, without using the menus. This is an independent window that you can size and move to the most convenient position.

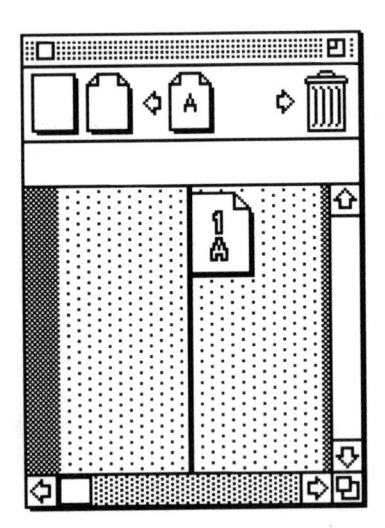

**Figure 2-12. The Document Layout palette for master page work.**

### Creating New Master Pages

It's easy to create new master page formats. QuarkXPress always begins each new document with a default standard page that is shown in the **Document Layout** palette. To create a master page format for this page:

1. Choose **A-Master A** from the **Page** menu's **Display** pop-up (see Figure 2-13). (You can also just double-click on the master page icon in the **Document Layout** palette.) The master page layout for this document is shown by the default text chain icon in the upper left corner, and the name of the master page (if you

**Figure 2-13.**
**Page menu with display pop-up menu.**

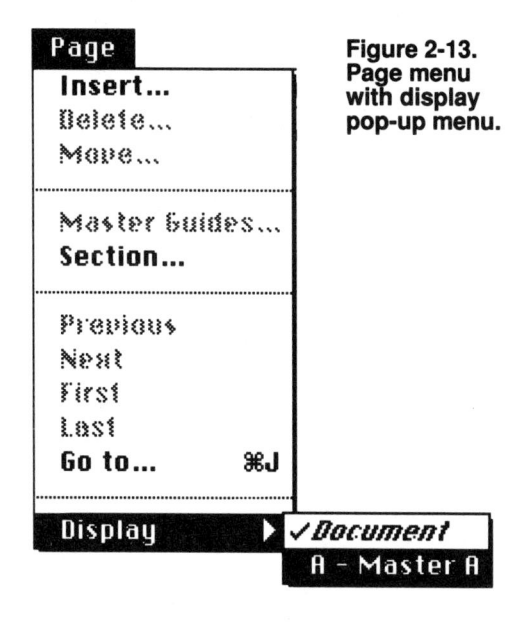

have given it one) appearing in the lower left corner of the document window. See Figure 2-14.

2. Now start adding the graphic and text items that you want to appear on every page sharing this master page format. Everything on this page will appear on every page you create from this moment on. If you've already created a series of pages, every page sharing this master page format will have the elements you place on this page.

3. To create another master page, drag one of the page icons from the left side of the **Document Layout** palette into the space between the tiny arrows on the **Page Layout** palette. (If you selected the **Facing Pages** option when you created this document you'll be able to place opposing pages with spreads in the **Document Layout** palette. The page icon in the **Document Layout** palette with the corners turned down is for insertion of spreads.) You'll see a new **Master Page** icon appear, as in Figure 2-15 where a master page B has been added. (The tiny arrows are for scrolling through long lists of **Master Page** icons.)

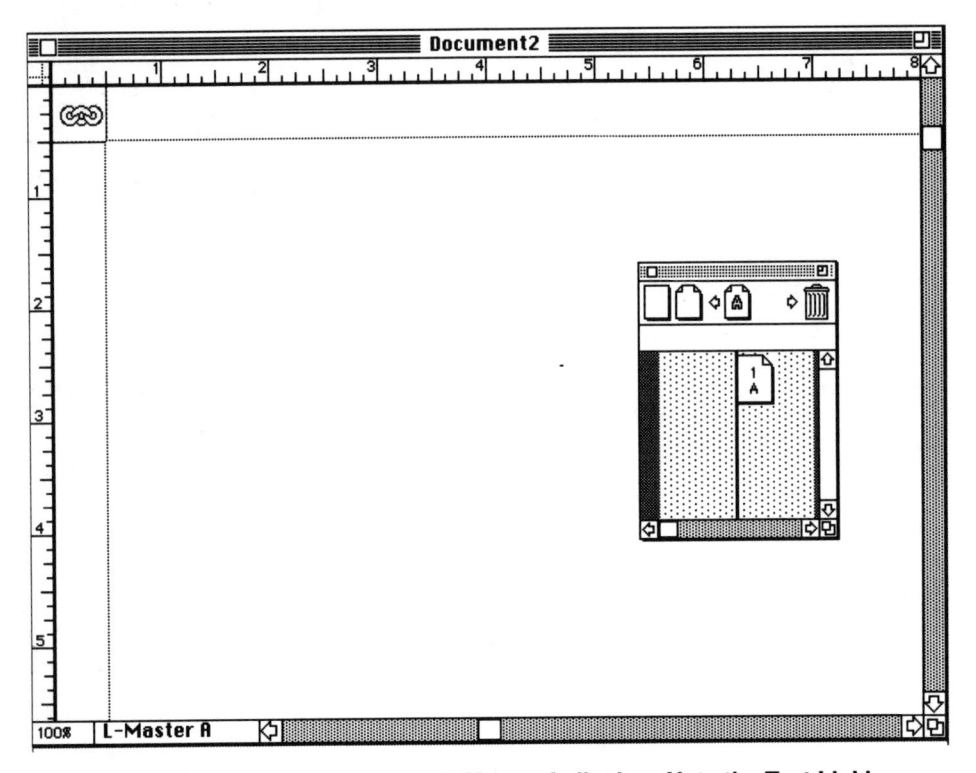

Figure 2-14. The Master Page format L-Master A display. Note the Text Linking icon (upper left) and the master page name (lower left).

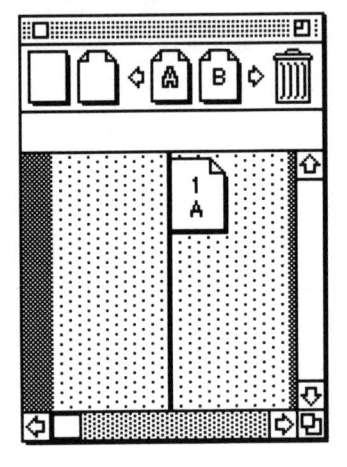

Figure 2-15. Adding another Master Page icon in the Document Layout palette.

## Changing Existing Master Pages

Choose the master page you wish to edit from the pop-up menu that appears when in the **Display** choice of the **Page** menu (or double-click on the **Master Page** icon you want to edit in the **Document Layout** palette).

46

The master page will be displayed in the document window. Any changes you make to this master page will automatically affect any document pages based on this master.

You may also choose **Master Guides** from the **Page** menu to change the margin and column settings for the master page format.

### Naming Master Pages

You can assign any name you like to a master page. Just click on its icon in the **Document Layout** palette, and type a new name for it in the naming field, shown highlighted in Figure 2-16.

### Deleting Master Pages

To throw away a master page, drag its icon in the **Document Layout** palette to the palette's trash can.

### Document Page Layout

After you've created any master page formats for your document, you can create the actual document pages. For this you use the **Document Layout** palette, as shown in Figure 2-17. The **Master Page** icons occupy the top line of the palette. The next field displays the name of any selected master page or document page. The area below is devoted to the document pages. These are numbered and labeled with any applied master page format. (In Figure 2-17 there are pages that follow **Master Page A**, **Master Page B**, and one document page with no applied master page format.)

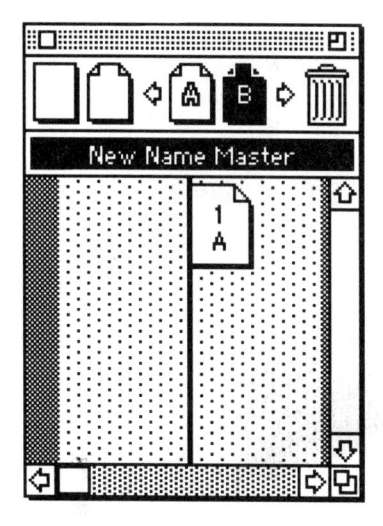

**Figure 2-16. Naming field for master pages.**

47

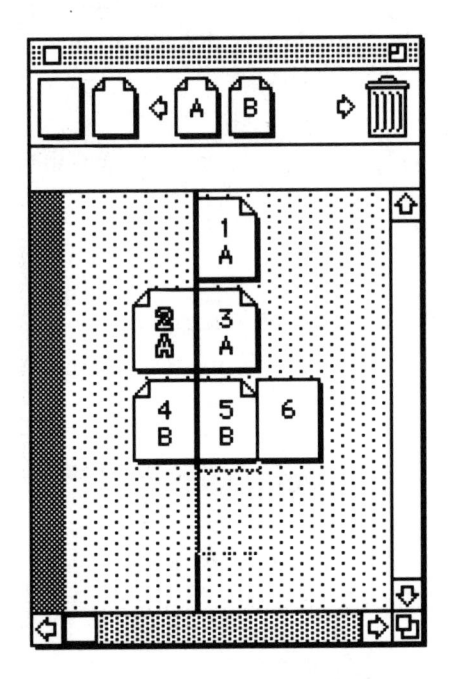

**Figure 2-17. Document Layout palette showing multiple document pages and the addition of a new document page.**

To add pages to the document:

Drag either a standard icon (the one in the top left corner of the palette) or one of the master page icons down onto the **Document Page** area, or select **Insert** from the **Page** menu, and then from the dialog box that appears (see Figure 2-18) choose a master page format and a position for the page.

To delete pages from the document:

Drag their icons from the **Document Page** area to the palette's trash can, or select **Delete** from the **Page** menu and then specify the pages to be deleted (by page number).

To move pages within the document:

Drag their icons from one position in the **Document Page** area to another position. Their page numbers will automatically change; or select **Move** from the **Page** menu and then specify which pages to move, and where to move them (as shown in Figure 2-19).

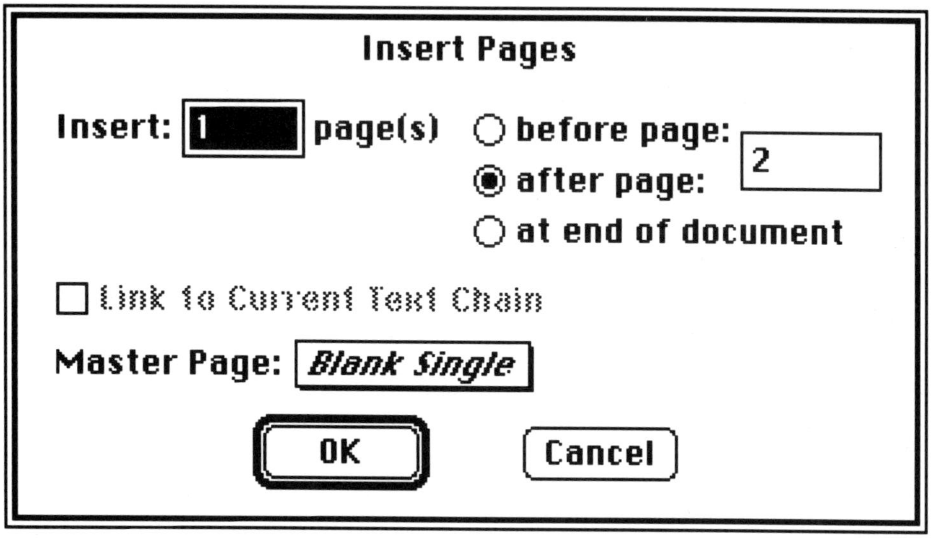

Figure 2-18. The Insert Pages dialog box.

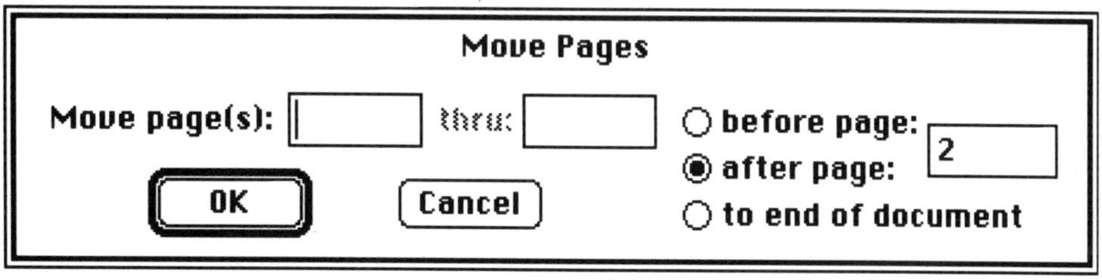

Figure 2-19. The Move Pages dialog box.

## Automatic Page Insertion

QuarkXPress 3.0 automatically inserts new pages when there is more text than will fit on the first page of a new document. When you have more text than will fit in a box in a new document, or two or more boxes linked together, QuarkXPress automatically creates new pages with the default text box. (This feature can be controlled or disabled by using the **General Preferences** dialog box under the **Edit** menu.)

## Moving Between Pages

You can move from one page of a document to another in several ways:

1. Scroll the Macintosh display using the scroll bars and elevator boxes on the edges of the document windows.

2. Double-click on the page's icon in the **Document Layout** palette.

3. Use the **Previous, Last, Next, First,** or **Go to** commands in the **Page** menu. The number and name of the page you're on will be outlined in the **Document Layout** palette.

## Page Numbering

When you're creating the pages for your document, you don't need to manually number them. Not only are they numbered automatically in the **Document Layout** palette, but you can have these numbers appear and print on the pages themselves. To do this:

1. Open any document or start a new one.

2. Under the **Page** menu, choose **Display** and any of the master pages. (You can double-click on the **Master Page** icon for that page in the **Document Layout** palette.)

3. Create a small new text box and position it where you want the page number to appear.

4. With your cursor in the box, hold down the ⌘ key and type 3. Then select the <#> character that appears there and format it to your preference.

5. From now on, every page that shares that master format, and any new pages you create with that master will have the current page number in

the new small text box, with the style and format you specified in Step 4. The page number will replace the <#> symbol in the document.

## "Smart" Page Numbering – "Continued On" References

QuarkXPress 3.0 can also make "smart" page numbers. If you have a text chain that continues to another page, you can create a box containing a reference to the next or previous page to or from where the text continues.

This is a great feature for documents such as newsletters or magazines, where text carries (or jumps) from one page to the next. The characters are smart because they automatically update the reference if the page order changes. For example, if you are continuing a text chain from page 1 to page 10, and sometime before the final output you insert four more pages between pages 1 and 10, the reference on page 1 that previously read "Continued on page 10" will automatically change to read "Continued on page 14," since what was page 10 has now become page 14. (Remember you've inserted four new pages between pages 1 and 10.) The reverse is true for text continuing from a text box on another page. The auto page numbering feature and the smart page numbering features are handy to use and quick to establish.

Here's an example of smart page numbers:

1. Create a new document using the standard defaults.

2. Create a text box on page 1.

3. Insert four pages after page 1.

4. Go to page 5. (The keyboard shortcut is ⌘+J.)

5. Create another new text box on page 5.

## USING QUARKXPRESS

6. Choose **Fit in Window** from the **View** menu. (The keyboard shortcut is ⌘+O.)

7. Now select your **Text Linking** tool from the **Tool** palette.

8. Click once on the new text box you created on page 1.

9. Scroll down to page 5 and click on the new text box you created. Now these two text boxes are dynamically linked. Any text that overflows beyond the text box on page 1 will automatically flow directly to the linked text box on page 5. Select the new text box on page 1 using the **Content** tool. Choose **Get Text...** from the **File** menu, and select any text file to flow into the text box.

10. Place a new small text box inside each of the new text boxes you created on pages 1 and 5.

11. On the new text box on page 1, type "Continued on page" followed by a character space (space bar). Then hold down the ⌘ key and type 4. This is telling QuarkXPress to list the page number that this text chain continues on. It should read "Continued on Page 5."

12. Go to Page 5. Select the new text box you created there with the **Content** tool and type "Continued from Page," a character space, then hold down the ⌘ key and press 2. This tells QuarkXPress to list the page number that the selected text chain is continued from. It should read "Continued from Page 1."

13. Choose **Insert...** from the **Page** menu. Insert two pages after page 2. Click **OK.**

14. Select **Insert...** from the **Page** menu. Insert three pages before page 1.

52

Click **OK**.

15. Choose **Go to...** from the **Page** menu, type 4. This will take you to page 4. The text box in which you typed "Continued on" should now read "Continued on Page 11." Now check the text box on page 11. It should read "Continued from Page 3." Though the order of the pages has been rearranged, the smart page numbering automatically updates the page number references.

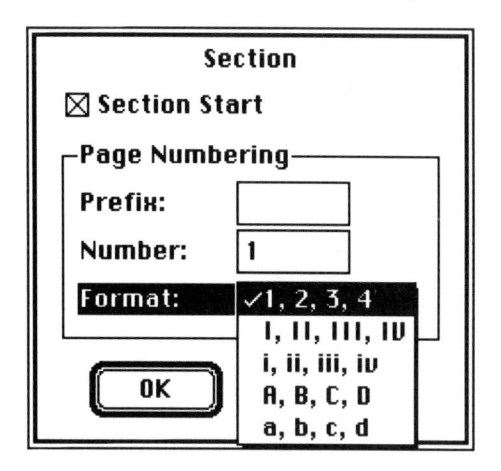

**Figure 2-20. Section dialog box.**

## Sections

One of the most sophisticated features of QuarkXPress 3.0 is its ability to divide a long document into "sections." Each section can have its own numbered pages. A document can have any number of sections. The page numbering within a section can start on any value and can be displayed in any of five different formats (shown in Figure 2-20). Automatic page numbering affects only the pages within a section, not those in other sections of the same document.

To specify pages as a section:

1. Move to the first page of the section-to-be.

2. Select **Section...** from the **Page** menu.

3. Click in the **Section Start** box, and choose a section numbering format and starting number.

53

Now all of the pages that follow this page, until the next section start page, are in a section of their own.

## Items: Text Boxes, Picture Boxes, Lines

Once you have:

- created a document

- set up the document

- chosen preferences

- arranged the view

- created master page formats

- created document pages to work on

- numbered the document pages

you're ready to place "items" on those document pages. QuarkXPress works with three kinds of items: text boxes, picture boxes, and lines.

All text, including numbers, letters, special symbols, page numbers, and punctuation is kept in text boxes. Chapters 3 and 4 cover the details.

All imported graphic images are kept in picture boxes. Chapter 5 covers the details.

Straight lines can be drawn in QuarkXPress, and don't need to be in boxes. Chapter 5 covers these too.

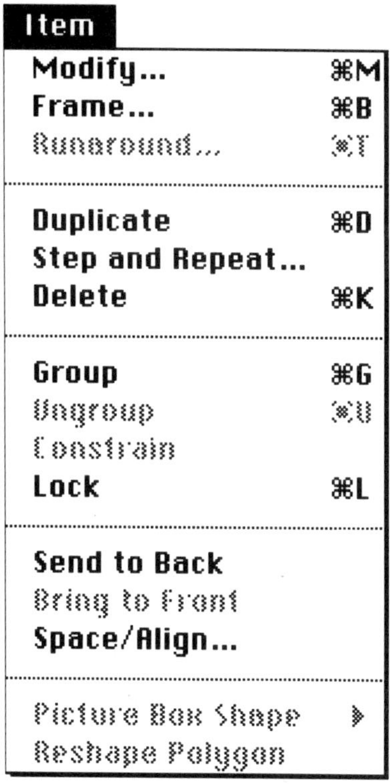

## QUARKXPRESS BASICS

```
Item
─────────────────────────
Modify...            ⌘M
Frame...             ⌘B
Runaround...         ⌘T
─────────────────────────
Duplicate            ⌘D
Step and Repeat...
Delete               ⌘K
─────────────────────────
Group                ⌘G
Ungroup              ⌘U
Constrain
Lock                 ⌘L
─────────────────────────
Send to Back
Bring to Front
Space/Align...
─────────────────────────
Picture Box Shape    ▶
Reshape Polygon
```

**Figure 2-21. The Item menu.**

Each item type has its own tools in the palette, its own **Style** menu (though there are similarities between the style menus), and its own behavior.

But all three items are subject to a core set of commands in the **Edit** and **Item** menus. (The **Item** menu is shown in Figure 2-21.) These differ slightly in application, but apply to all items. They are:

**Cut, Copy, Clear,** and **Paste** (in the **Edit** menu): select any item with the **Item** tool (or select them all with ⌘+A) to use these commands (as well as **Undo**). (To edit the text in a text box, or the picture within a picture box, you need to select them with the **Content** tool.)

**Duplicate:** to make an immediate copy of the item (instead of using **Copy** then **Paste** from the **Edit** menu).

**Delete:** to delete a selected item or group of items.

**Step and Repeat:** to make multiple copies, offset horizontally and vertically, in one operation. The dialog box to control the operation is shown in Figure 2-22. (The **Repeat Count** field is the number of copies.)

**Group** and **Ungroup:** to convert a collection of several selected items into a single item that can itself be handled by these **Item** commands. (See the detailed explanation below.)

55

USING QUARKXPRESS

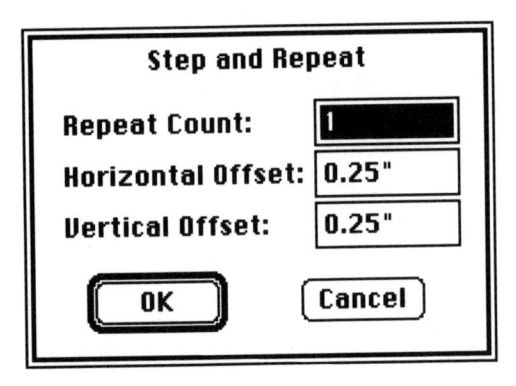

Figure 2-22. Step and Repeat dialog box.

**Lock** and **Unlock**: to prevent an item location from being changed.

**Constrain** and **Unconstrain**: to limit the resizing and movement of items in a surrounding box to stay within the box.

**Send to Back, Bring to Front**: to dictate the order of items that overlap, to determine which is completely displayed and which obscured.

**Space/Align**: to position several selected items with respect to one another. You can space them a certain distance apart or distribute them evenly along a line. (See Figure 2-23 for these controls.)

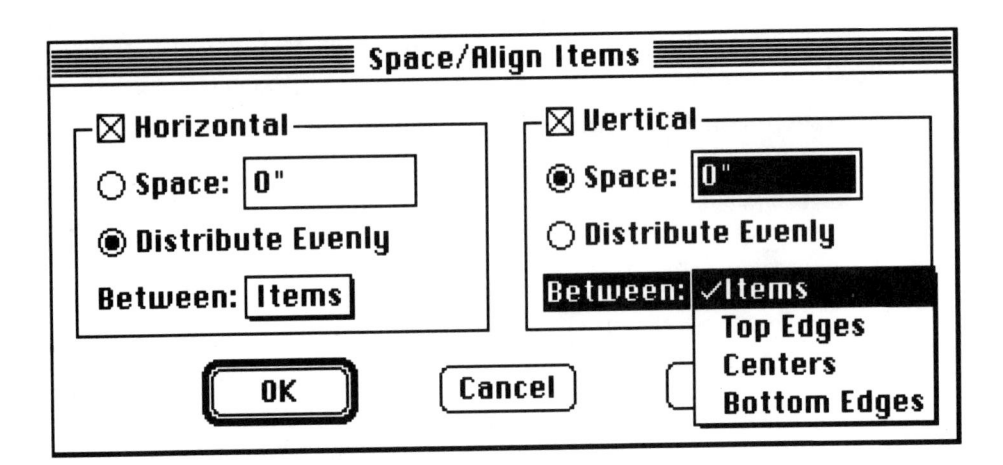

Figure 2-23. Space/Align dialog box.

56

**Movement:** move items by selecting them with the **Item** tool and then dragging them with the mouse, or by then entering new position coordinates for them in the **Measurements** palette or **Modify** dialog box.

**Modify:** brings up a dialog box where you can specify just about every attribute of an item. You can also set the **Modify** dialog box by double-clicking on an item with the **Item** tool. (The **Modify** options are explained in each chapter.)

**Runaround:** brings up a dialog box where you dictate how text will wrap, or not wrap, around overlapping items. (**Runaround** is explained in depth in Chapter 5.)

**Frame:** brings up a dialog box where you specify the style, width, and color of the border for the item (this does not apply to lines). The **Frame** options are explained in each chapter. (A separate Frame Editor program comes with QuarkXPress 3.0. You use the Frame Editor to create your own frame styles, as explained below.)

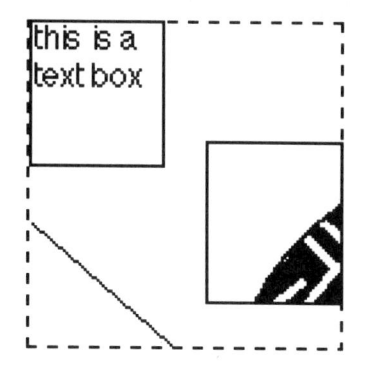

**Figure 2-24. Grouped items enclosed by the group's dotted boundary line.**

**Library** (in the **Utilities** menu): you can store items in a library for use later. (See the detailed explanations below.)

## Grouping Items

QuarkXPress 3.0 lets you group items together to make it easier to move and manipulate more than one item at a time. This is handy if you have spent time precisely positioning items and then have to move them somewhere. By grouping them together they will retain their spatial relationship to each other and act as a group.

## USING QUARKXPRESS

```
                    Group Specifications
                                    ┌─Background─────────
    Origin Across:  0.38"
                                    │  Color:  ■ Black
    Origin Down:    7.181"          │
                                    │  Shade:  ▶
    Angle:          0°              └─────────────────────

    ☐ Suppress Printout              [   OK   ]   [ Cancel ]
```

**Figure 2-25.** You use the Group Specifications dialog box to modify the attributes of a group of unlike items.

Grouped items will have a dotted line boundary, as in Figure 2-24. You can modify a group of items by choosing **Modify** from the **Item** menu, though only attributes that are common to all the items in the group will be fair game. For example, if a group consists of different types of items (a text box and a line, or a picture box with a text box), choosing **Modify** from the **Item** menu will display the **Group Specifications** dialog box, as in Figure 2-25. This dialog allows you to manipulate the group's location, angle background color, and shade. If the group is made up of the same types of items (two or more picture boxes, two or more lines, etc.), the **Modify** dialog box allows for the manipulation of common attributes. (You can group together groups of items, but the **Modify** command will not be available. However, the **Measurements** palette is available for changes to location and rotation angle attributes.)

Groups of items may be moved together with the **Item** tool. Using the **Content** tool on individual members of a group lets you adjust their individual attributes including location and contents, even as they remain members of the group.

1. Create two picture boxes.

2. Choose the **Item** tool and group the items together by holding down the **Shift** key while you select one item and then the other.

3. Then choose **Group** from the **Item** menu.

4. Choose **Modify** from the **Item** menu. The **Modify** dialog box will have all but the size field available for editing (unless the two boxes are identical in size).

5. Change an attribute such as **Background Shade**. The attribute you've chosen will be reflected on both items when you click **OK**.

6. Now choose the **Content** tool.

7. Select either of the two boxes and choose **Get Picture** from the **File** menu. Paste in any picture.

8. You can change the location of the selected box by holding down the ⌘ key while you click and drag the box around on the page. Remember, holding down the ⌘ key while you are using the **Content** tool changes the cursor to the **Item** tool, allowing you to click and drag, moving the selected item around.

9. Change the background color, size, and location of the box while you still have the **Content** tool selected.

10. Now choose the **Item** tool again and select the grouped items.

11. Choose **Modify** from the **Item** menu. Notice that some attributes have no values in their fields, indicating which attributes are no longer common to both items. Since you're using the **Item** tool again, you can click and drag anywhere on the grouped items and move them around as if they were a single item.

## Library

A new QuarkXPress 3.0 feature is the library. The library lets you store groups of items together for easy selection and use later, in the same document or in another document. The library will hold any item or combination of items.

You can have up to 2,000 items in each library and up to 127 different libraries. However, you can have only seven different libraries open at any one time. (In fact, you can only have a combined total of seven documents, templates, and libraries open at a time.) This is especially helpful if you have created a complex conglomeration of items that you can group into a single item. Items moved into the library retain all of their formatting, size, color, style, and runaround information when they are moved back into any QuarkXPress 3.0 document. This means that if you've formatted a column of text in a text box and moved it into the library, all of the style and format information remains when it is moved into any other document.

**To use a Library:**

1. Choose **Library** from the **Utilities** menu.

2. From the **Library** dialog box that appears (as in Figure 2-26), click on **New** to start a new library or select a library by name from the disk directory list and open it. (If you start a new library, you'll have to give it a name.)

3. The **Library** window will appear, as shown in Figure 2-27.

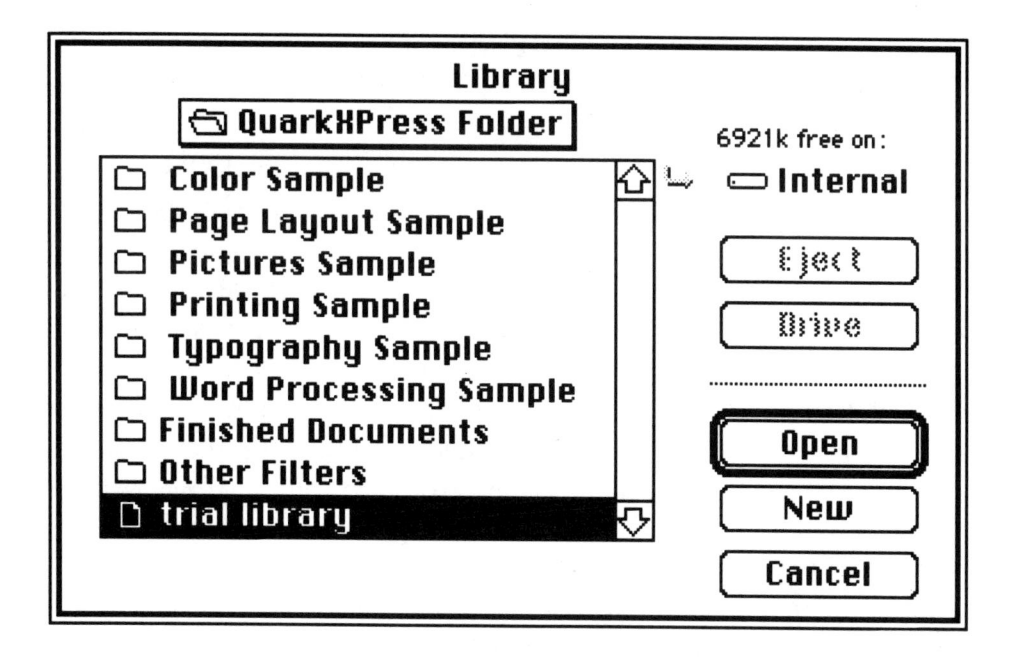

Figure 2-26. Library dialog box, for opening or creating a library.

4. You can drag items from the document into the library, or you can paste them in (after cutting or copying them in the document).

5. You can drag items from the library to the document, or you can paste them into the document (after cutting or copying them in the library).

6. You can find items in the library by scrolling through the library's display list or you can use the library's pull-down menu to locate an item by its label (its name).

7. You can label items by double-clicking on them, then typing a name in the dialog box that appears.

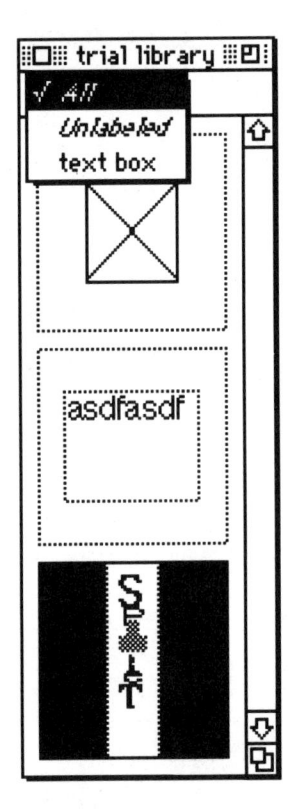

**Figure 2-27.** Library window, for selecting items from or adding items to a library.

## Frame Editor

QuarkXPress 3.0 also has a powerful frame-editing feature that lets you edit and create your own custom borders. The QuarkXPress Frame Editor is a separate application that runs outside of QuarkXPress. To use it you must exit from QuarkXPress, return to the Finder, and start up Frame Editor 2.1 from the desktop. Both applications will not run at the same time, even if you are using Multifinder. The frames you create in the Frame Editor will become part of the XPress Data file, and so will be pulled into and available in QuarkXPress when you're done.

### To Create a New Frame Style:

1. Start the Frame Editor.

2. If you are creating a new frame style from scratch, choose **New Style...** from the **File** menu.

3. The Frame Editor will ask you what size you want your new border to be. Type in a size. The frame sizes are measured in pixels, about 1/72 of an inch (just about the same size as a point). If you are making an ornately detailed frame, it will look better if you construct it at a very large size and use it at a smaller size in your documents.

4. Select a frame element to start your design from the assortment shown (as in Figure 2-28). QuarkXPress will confirm the size of the element you want to create. Click **OK** if it is correct.

## QUARKXPRESS BASICS

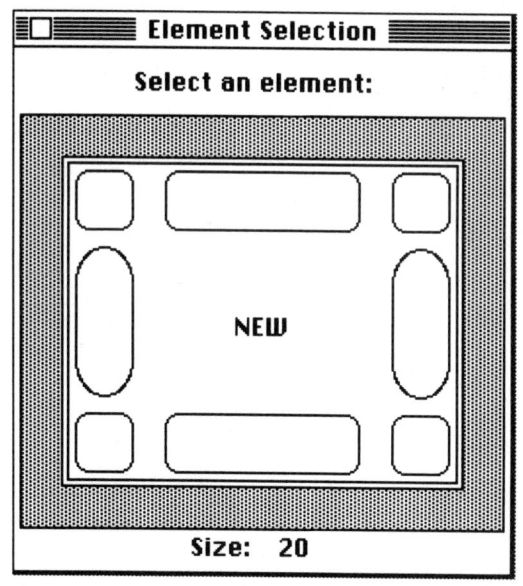

**Figure 2-28.** Frame Editor selection of frame elements.

5. Start drawing your frame design using the crosshair cursor as a pencil tool, as demonstrated in Figure 2-29. If the size you've specified is larger than the standard drawing window that QuarkXPress uses, scroll bars will appear to help you navigate through your art.

6. If you have some bit-mapped art you would like to use as your pattern, you can paste it

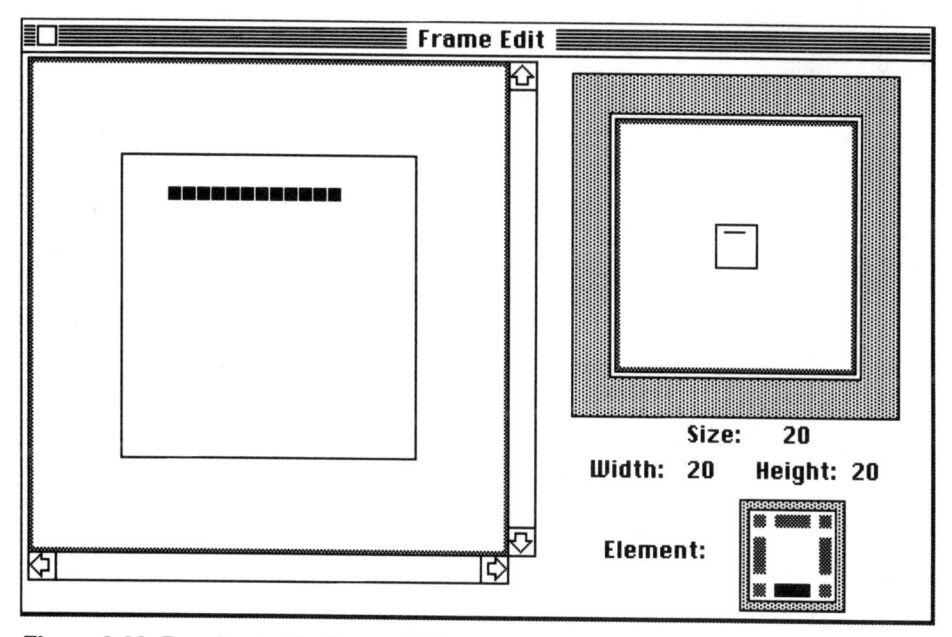

**Figure 2-29.** Drawing in the Frame Editor.

63

in from the clipboard or from the scrapbook. Unfortunately, there are no provisions for filling areas with patterns outside of this, and any edits you make must be done one pixel at a time. (It's tedious, but rewarding.)

7. When you have finished creating the artwork for that element click the **Close** box in the upper left-hand corner of the window. QuarkXPress will show the **Element Selection** window again. You'll see that QuarkXPress has duplicated your element design into the other elements as a convenience to save you the trouble of recreating that design into these elements if they are all symmetrical. If you want to change one of the other elements, just click on it and you'll be led through the process again.

8. Finally, when you are satisfied with your new frame design, click the **Close** box in the **Element Selection** window. QuarkXPress will confirm that you are finished by asking if you want to save the changes you've just made. If you are finished, choose **Quit** from the **File** menu.

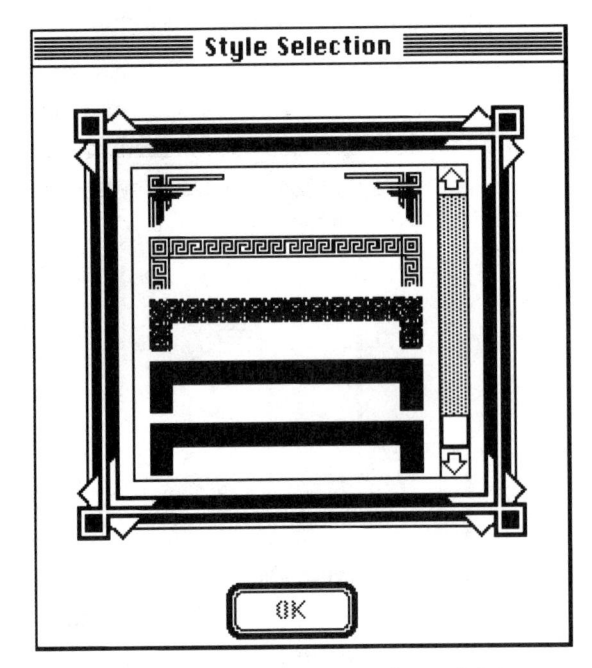

**Figure 2-30. The Style Selection box of the Frame Editor.**

If you want to create your new frame using an existing frame as a template:

1. Select one of the frame styles in the **Style**

**Selection** window that appears when you start Frame Editor (see Figure 2-30). Click **OK** or press the **Return** or **Enter** keys. (Or just double click the selection.)

2. Choose **Duplicate** from the **File** menu to create a duplicate of the frame style.

3. Follow steps 3 through 8 of the preceding instructions.

There are occasions when a frame may not be built onto a box. If you've defined a box as a constraining box (meaning that anything placed or created within that box cannot be moved outside of that box without cutting or pasting with the **Moving** tool), it can affect whether a frame can be built around that box. If a constraining box has within it a box that is resting against its side, and you've specified that frames are to be built on the outside of boxes, there will not be space to build a frame around the inside box. Similarly, if you've specified frames to be built on the inside of boxes, and you want to frame the outer (parent) box in the same situation, it will not have space to build a frame inside either, as the inside box is resting against the place where the frame would be

> **Warning: Frame printing**
> *Remember to Include Your XPress Data File*
> *This is probably the most important thing to remember when printing a document that has a custom border on it. If you are printing your document on another printer or at your service bureau, remember to include your XPress Data file with your document file. All of the information defining your new frame style is contained there. If you do not include your XPress Data file, the border will neither appear in the document nor will it print.*

built. QuarkXPress 3.0 will display a dialog message saying "Frame too large for this box."

## Saving

While you're working on a document, and certainly when you're done with it, you should save it. You have several choices:

1. **Save Text** (in the **File** menu). The text box must be selected with the **Content** tool. You may save selected text or all of the text in a chain as a text file on disk, in any of several different formats. (This is explained in Chapter 3.)

2. Save the page as EPS (in the **File** menu). You may save a single page as a PostScript file (EPS means Encapsulated PostScript) for use in another program. You choose the page number, the scale, and whether to save as color or black and white.

3. Save the file as a **Document** (in the **File** menu). This is how you should save most work.

4. Save the file as a **Template** (in the **File** menu). In the **Save As...** dialog box, as shown in Figure 2-31, click on the **Template** option button. Then give the file a name and click on **Save**. You can then open this

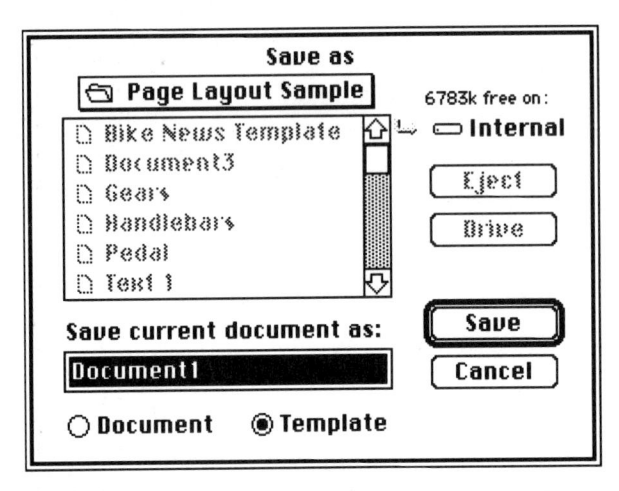

**Figure 2-31. Save As dialog box, with the Template button marked.**

66

file any number of times later as the setup and layout foundation for other new documents, without ever changing the original template file.

## Printing

Naturally, printing is vital to design and publishing projects. You may want to print drafts to see how you're doing, and you will certainly need to print final copies, even if the absolute final will roll off a high-resolution typesetting machine somewhere else.

To print you need to specify the page setup, then use the print command.

## Page Setup

Each printing device comes with its own page setup routines. You use the **Chooser** desk accessory to select a printing device (see your Macintosh manual for information on this), then you select **Page Setup** from the **File** menu. You'll see a dialog box such as that in Figure 2-32. Here you'll set paper size, printer effects, orientation, and more.

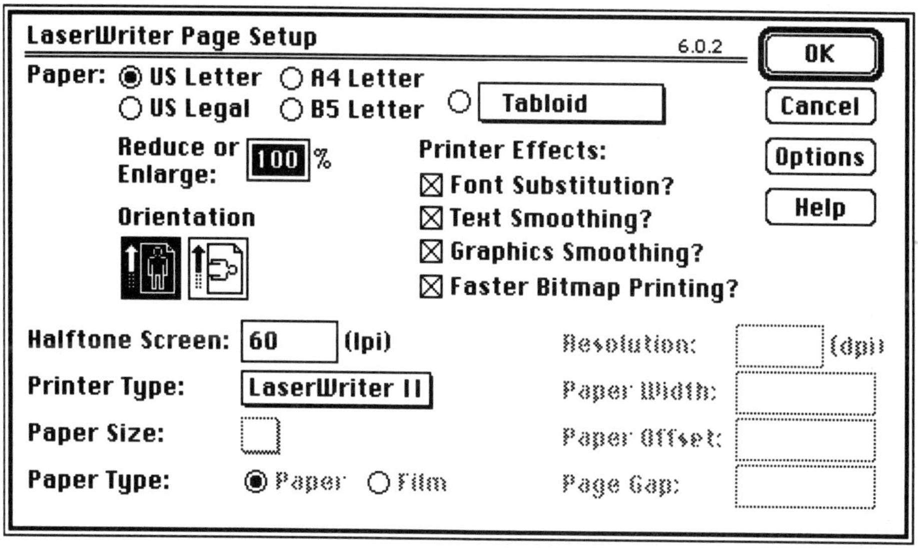

Figure 2-32. Page Setup dialog box.

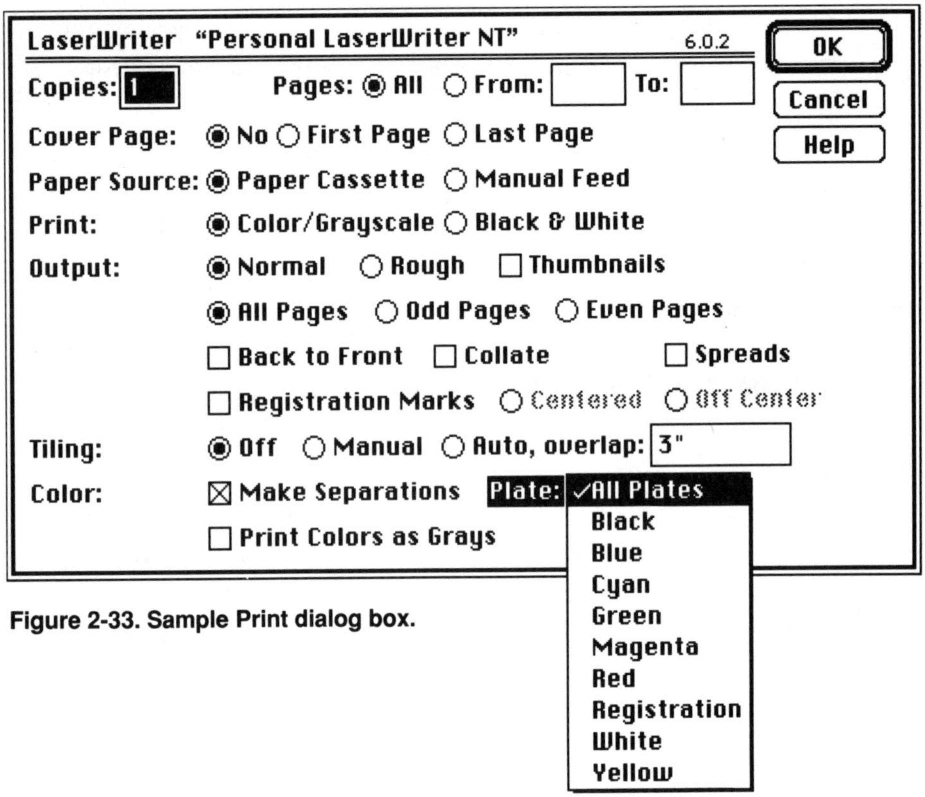

USING QUARKXPRESS

```
LaserWriter  "Personal LaserWriter NT"              6.0.2    [  OK  ]
Copies: [1]      Pages: ● All  ○ From: [  ] To: [  ]        [Cancel]
Cover Page:   ● No ○ First Page ○ Last Page                 [ Help ]
Paper Source: ● Paper Cassette ○ Manual Feed
Print:        ● Color/Grayscale ○ Black & White
Output:       ● Normal    ○ Rough    ☐ Thumbnails
              ● All Pages  ○ Odd Pages  ○ Even Pages
              ☐ Back to Front  ☐ Collate      ☐ Spreads
              ☐ Registration Marks  ○ Centered  ○ Off Center
Tiling:       ● Off  ○ Manual  ○ Auto, overlap: [3"]
Color:        ☒ Make Separations  Plate: ✓All Plates
                                         Black
              ☐ Print Colors as Grays     Blue
                                         Cyan
                                         Green
                                         Magenta
                                         Red
                                         Registration
                                         White
                                         Yellow
```

Figure 2-33. Sample Print dialog box.

## Print

After you specify the page setup, all that's left to do is print. Select that command from the **File** menu and you'll see a dialog box for the printing device you're using. Figure 2-33 shows an example. Most of the choices are easy to understand, and there is often help information tucked away behind one of the buttons. You'll dictate:

- which pages to print
- whether to print a cover page
- how to feed the paper
- whether to print black-and-white or color
- whether to print a rough draft or final

- the order in which to print the pages
- whether to print registration marks in the corners of pages (for precise positioning)
- whether to tile the pages (how to print images that cross over page boundaries)
- whether to print colors as gray shades
- whether to print color separations, and which separations to print.

Now you're ready to learn about each type of item QuarkXPress handles, and to practice putting them into designs and documents.

CHAPTER 3

# Word Processing with QuarkXPress

Most desktop publishing programs combine text from a word processing program with art from various graphics programs. This means you really need at least three separate programs to create a finished design. It can also lead to shuttling text or graphics back and forth between the desktop publishing program and the word processor or graphics program, as you modify or edit the material.

QuarkXPress doesn't bog you down with these cumbersome procedures — its features include a word processing application. Though it doesn't have all of the features you find in a program dedicated to word processing, it has far more editing ability than do most desktop publishing programs. You can create your own text in QuarkXPress without resorting to another word processor, or you can import text from other word processors and use that in your documents and designs. Either way, you can handle more of the text-editing work in QuarkXPress than you can in other desktop publishing programs.

## First Create or Select a Text Box

Before you import text or enter new text from within QuarkXPress, you need a text box to work in. Either select a text box that's already in your document or create a new text box to hold the text. Chapter 2 explains how to do both, but here's a quick review.

To select a text box in the document:

1. Click on the **Content** tool on the **Tool** palette.

2. Click on the box you want to select (its frame highlights and sprouts handles).

3. Move the cursor (which now appears as an editing I-beam) to the point of existing text where you want to edit or import more text.

To create a new text box:

1. Open a document.

2. Set up whatever rulers and guidelines you need to position the box.

3. Click on the text box creation tool (the capital letter **A**).

4. Move the cursor to one corner of the place where you want to create a new box.

5. Press the mouse button and drag the cursor diagonally to the opposite corner of the new box position (you'll see the box stretch to fit the area). When you've created the box, release the mouse button and you'll see the box frame is highlighted and has handles, which shows that this box is selected.

You can change the size of any selected box, new or old, by clicking on one of its handles and dragging that handle to a new position or by entering new numeric values in the **Measurements** palette. (See Chapter 2.)

You can also move any box by selecting it with the **Item** tool, clicking within the box, and dragging the box to a new position. Again, you can also enter new values for the box position in the **Measurements** palette.

## Importing Text

You can import word processing documents from several other word processors, then edit and rearrange them to fit your layout. QuarkXPress understands more than just the bare letters and numerals in these imported files. It automatically and completely translates the style tags in the documents — the codes that define such attributes as paragraph formats, bold-face type, and tabs. QuarkXPress works with these file types:

- ASCII text
- Claris MacWrite 5.0
- Claris MacWrite II
- Microsoft Word 3.0
- Microsoft Word 4.0
- Microsoft Write
- Microsoft Works 1.1
- Microsoft Works 2.0
- WordPerfect 1.0
- WordPerfect 1.02
- WriteNow 2.0

QuarkXPress also saves text in almost any word processing format, in case you do need to move text back to the original program to distribute or edit outside of QuarkXPress.

If you're not sure if QuarkXPress will read a document's format, it's best to change the document to the ASCII format. ASCII text is the most basic form of text information, containing no formatting codes that could confuse the importing operation. ASCII files strip out all special typestyle, spacing, and other attributes, leaving only the bare characters. Almost all word processing applications have an option to save their documents as ASCII text.

To import text in any format:

1. Select or create a text box, as explained in the previous section (and in Chapter 2).

2. Place the cursor within the box. Click on the **Content** tool and move the cursor to the spot where you want the text to go (the new text also replaces any highlighted text).

3. Choose **Get Text...** from the **File** menu. You'll see the dialog box shown in Figure 3-1.

4. Find the text file you want and click on it. The dialog box shows the file's size and format.

5. In the **Get Text...** dialog box, you can choose to bring in the file's style sheets with the text and to convert any quotation marks in the file into their typographical equivalents (changing simple vertical quotes and apostrophes, ' and ", into smart quotes and apostrophes, ", ", ', and '). Click on the relevant boxes to select these options. (When they are selected, the boxes will be marked with an X.)

6. Click on **Open.**

The text fills the box. If there's too much to fit in the selected box, a small icon with an X in it appears in the bottom right corner of the text box.

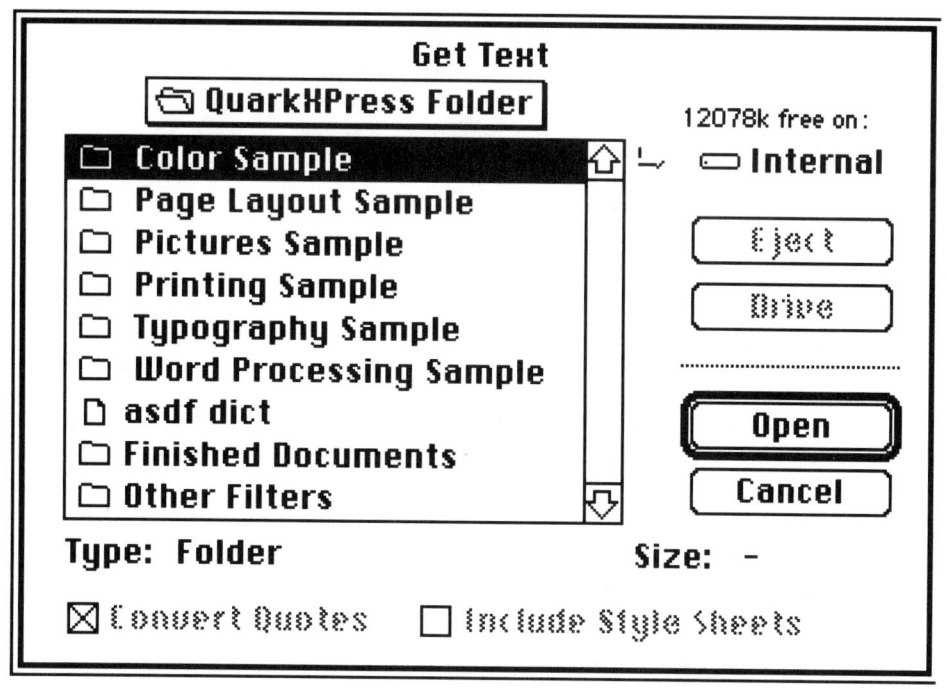

**Figure 3-1.** The Get Text dialog box.

## Entering Text

QuarkXPress lets you create and edit text documents just as you would with a conventional word processor. QuarkXPress even has an 80,000-word spelling dictionary, and it offers you the option of creating your own auxiliary dictionaries to use with individual documents.

Entering text is simple:

1. Select or create a text box in a document (as explained in the first section of this chapter and in Chapter 2).

2. Click on the **Content** tool (also known as the **Editing** tool) and click

inside the text box at the point where you want to enter text (in an empty box, the cursor automatically goes to the upper left corner). The text insertion cursor starts flashing in the upper left hand corner, ready for you to start typing.

3. Type in your new text. Any new text starts at the cursor position and replaces any highlighted text in the box.

## Selecting Text

In QuarkXPress and most other Macintosh word processing applications, you can easily use the mouse or keyboard to select the text you want to edit.

**Text Selection with the Mouse.** To select text with the mouse, just click and drag the cursor across the text, which highlights as you drag across it.

When you're selecting large pieces of text, you can use a special variant of the mouse technique:

1. Click where you want the selection to begin.

2. Scroll the screen down (with the elevator box or the scrolling arrow at the edge of the window) to where you want the selection to end.

3. Hold down the **Shift** key and click the cursor at the end of your selection.

All of the text between those two points is selected and ready to edit. This technique is especially useful if you must select several pages of text at one time.

There are also some mouse shortcuts to selecting text:

- Double-click on a word to select the entire word.
- Triple-click to select the entire line.

- Quadruple-click to select the entire paragraph.
- Quintuple-click (five clicks, whew!) to select the all of the text in the text chain.

**Text Selection Using the Keyboard.** There are also keyboard shortcuts, listed below, that come in handy if you're tired of using the mouse. (Note that some of these shortcuts deal not only with text in your selected box but also to any other boxes that are linked to it — to all of the boxes in a linked chain, as explained in Chapter 2 and later on in this chapter.)

| | |
|---|---|
| ⌘+Shift+Left Arrow | Selects the next word. |
| ⌘+Shift+Right Arrow | Selects the previous word. |
| ⌘+Shift+Down Arrow | Selects the next paragraph. |
| ⌘+Shift+Up Arrow | Selects the previous paragraph. |
| ⌘+Shift+Down Arrow | Selects the next paragraph. |
| ⌘+A | Selects all text within the current text chain. |
| Option+⌘+Shift+Up Arrow | Selects all text up from the cursor to the beginning of the document or continuous text chain. |
| Option+⌘+Shift+Down Arrow | Selects all text from the cursor down to the end of the document or continuous text chain. |

77

**Option+⌘+Shift+Left Arrow**     Selects all text from the cursor up to the beginning of the current line.

**Option+⌘+Shift+Right Arrow**     Selects all text from the cursor down to the end of the current line.

> **Extra!**
>
> ***Moving About...***
> *Using these keyboard shortcuts without the **Shift** key moves the cursor in the same manner without selecting text.*

You need to move the cursor to the point where you want to use a keyboard shortcut. Do it with the mouse, or, if you are using a Macintosh with Apple's extended keyboard, use the keys located on the right side of the keyboard, including the **Arrow** keys and the **Page Up**, **Page Down**, **Home**, and **End** keys.

The **Home** key brings you immediately to the top right-hand corner of the document's first page.

The **End** key brings you to the end of the document.

The **Page Up** and **Page Down** keys move the cursor forward and backward one screen length at a time.

The **Arrow** keys move you one line up or down, or one character to the left or right.

## Editing Text

After you've selected text (as described above), you can delete it, move it, copy it, replace it, and style it.

Deleting, moving, copying, and replacing are explained in the following sections. Styling is more complex, and is described later in this chapter.

**Deleting Text.** To delete text, use the **Edit** menu commands **Cut** or **Clear.** (Cut removes selected text from the box and makes a copy of it on the **Clipboard.** You can then paste the text somewhere else.) You can also delete text using these keyboard shortcuts:

| | |
|---|---|
| **Delete** | Delete selected text. |
| **Delete** | Delete previous character. |
| **Shift+Delete** | Delete next character. |
| **⌘+Delete** | Delete previous word. |
| **⌘+Shift+Delete** | Delete next word. |

**Moving Text.** To move text:

1. Select it.

2. Cut it (using the **Cut** command in the **Edit** menu). The cut text disappears from its present position and reappears on the **Clipboard.** (You can check this with the **Show Clipboard** command under the **Edit** menu.)

3. Position the cursor where you want the text to go and click.

4. Choose **Paste** from the **Edit** menu.

**Copying Text.**   To copy text:

1. Select it.

2. Copy it (using the **Copy** command in the **Edit** menu). The copied text remains in its position and a copy appears on the **Clipboard**.

3. Position the cursor where you want the text to go and click.

4. Choose **Paste** from the **Edit** menu.

**Replacing Text.**   To replace text:

1. Select it.

2. Type new text, or paste in text from the **Clipboard**.

## Undoing Edit Changes

The **Edit** menu's **Undo** command negates most editing operations. Select **Undo** immediately after you cut, copy, paste, or style text — even before you click in a new position in the text box — and the operation is undone. (The **Undo** command changes to tell you what it's about to undo. For example, after a cut change, it reads **Undo Cut**.) If you then decide you really did want the operation, select **Redo** (which will have replaced the **Undo** in the **Edit** menu, for undoing the undo, so to speak).

## Styling Text

Text in a design or layout is more than just the meaning of words and numbers; it's also the style and format (also known as the attributes) of those words and numbers. Basic attributes include:

- Font
- Size
- Type style
- Color
- Shade

Once you've created or imported your text, you can format it. There are four ways to set text attributes. In each case you start by selecting the section of text to format (by dragging the mouse across it or using one of the other selection commands described earlier on in this chapter). Then you use:

- The **Style** menu (pull down the menu, pop up a sub-menu, and select a particular style, as shown in Figure 3-2).

- The keyboard shortcuts (press the key combination for a particular format). These are listed in the appendices and within the **Style** menu.

- The **Character** attributes dialog box as shown in Figure 3-3. (Choose **Character...** from the **Style** menu or press ⌘+**Shift+D**, then select the attributes in the box and click on **OK**.)

- Or, the status section of the **Measurements** palette, as shown in Figure 3-4. Choose **Show Measurements** from the **View** menu, then click on the appropriate attribute in the palette. This is often the quickest route to a new format or style.

*USING QUARKXPRESS*

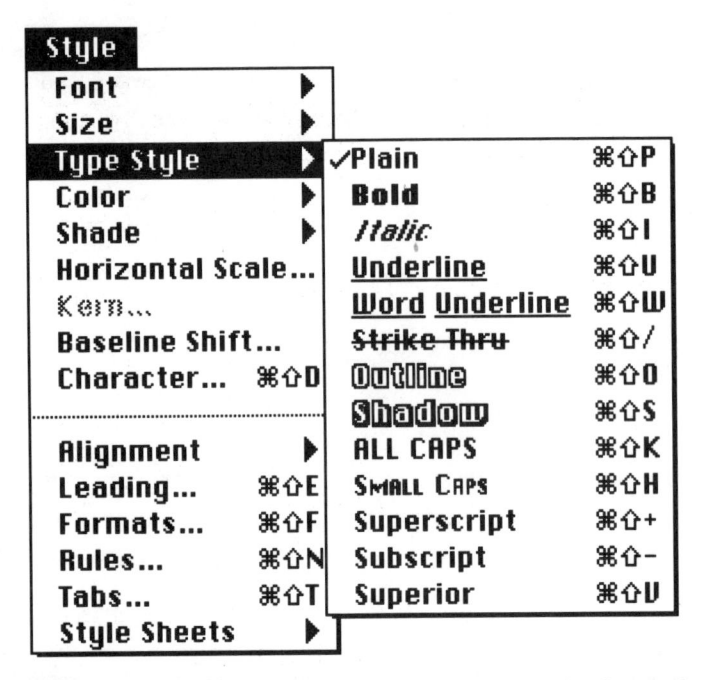

Figure 3-2. The Style menu's pop-up sub-menus for formatting text. The character sequences to the right of each command denote its keyboard shortcut (if available).

Figure 3-3. The Character attributes dialog box for formatting text.

82

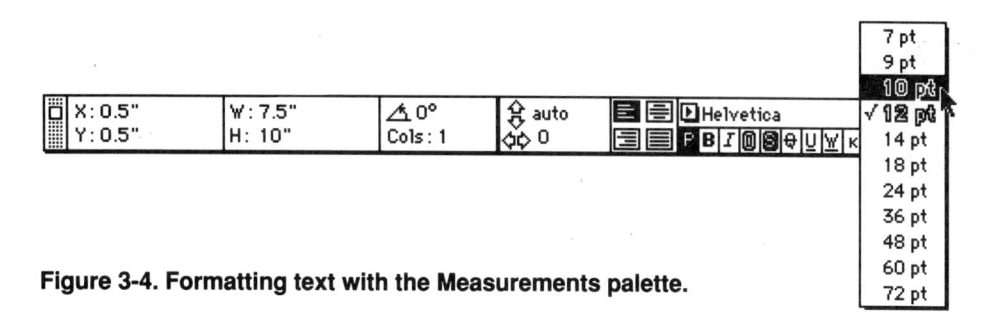

Figure 3-4. Formatting text with the Measurements palette.

## Formatting Text

Besides the style (color, size, shape) of the individual characters, text also has a format (a position setting that places it precisely within a text box). Familiar formats for anyone with word processing experience include margins, columns, gutters, tabs, and indents.

QuarkXPress offers all of these options. The margins, columns, and gutters are set when you create a new document, as described in Chapter 2.

Figure 3-5. The Paragraph Formats dialog box.

Paragraph formats such as tabs and indents are controlled through the **Paragraph Formats** dialog box (Figure 3-5) and the **Tabs** dialog box (Figure 3-6). The **Paragraph Formats** dialog box also controls such sophisticated typographical elements as drop caps, hyphenation, and leading. (Chapter 4 covers those topics.)

To use the **Paragraph Formats** dialog box:

1. Select a text box with the **Content** tool.

2. Select the paragraphs you want to format. (A paragraph will be affected if any of its characters are highlighted or if the **Editing** cursor is blinking within that paragraph.)

3. Choose **Formats** from the **Style** menu.

4. Specify the distances you want to indent text from the left and right edges of the text box by typing those values in the corresponding fields.

5. Specify the special indent for the first line of text. This will add to the left indent. If you choose a negative value, the first line will indent *less* than the following lines.

6. Click **Apply** when you're done to see if you like the results. (You can move the **Paragraph Formats** dialog box out of the way so you can see clearly.) If you are satisfied with the results, click **OK**. If not, enter new formatting values into the fields or click **Cancel** to abandon the whole thing.

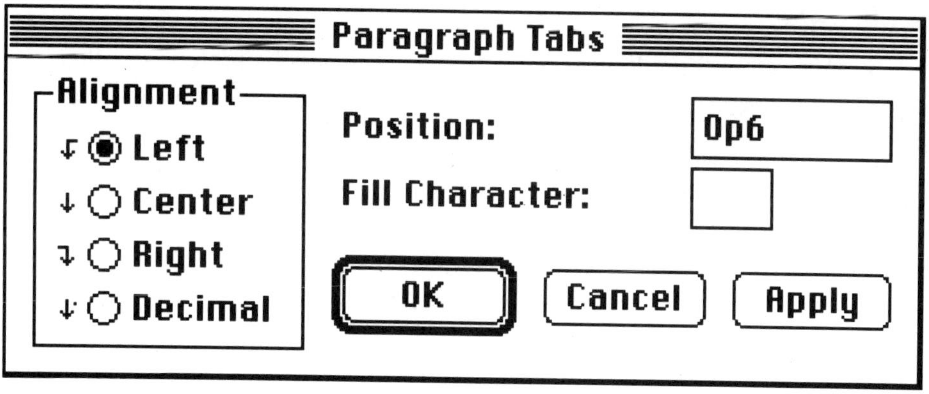

## WORD PROCESSING

```
┌─────────────────── Paragraph Tabs ───────────────────┐
│  ┌─Alignment──────┐                                  │
│  │  ↓ ● Left      │   Position:        │ 0p6  │      │
│  │  ↓ ○ Center    │                                  │
│  │  ↓ ○ Right     │   Fill Character:  │      │      │
│  │  ↓ ○ Decimal   │    ┌──────┐  ┌────────┐ ┌───────┐│
│  │                │    │  OK  │  │ Cancel │ │ Apply ││
│  └────────────────┘    └──────┘  └────────┘ └───────┘│
└──────────────────────────────────────────────────────┘
```

**Figure 3-6. The Tabs dialog box.**

To use the **Tabs** dialog box:

1. Select a text box with the **Content** tool.

2. Select the paragraphs for which you want to create tabs. (A paragraph will be affected if any of its characters are highlighted or if the **Editing** cursor is blinking within that paragraph.)

3. Choose **Tabs** from the **Style** menu.

4. Set your tab type by choosing **Left**, **Center**, **Right**, or **Decimal**.

5. Type a tab position number or click on the appropriate ruler position. (You can set up to 20 tabs.)

6. To delete a tab, click on it and drag it off the ruler. To delete all tabs, hold the **Option** key and click on the ruler.

## Style Sheets

Style sheets are predefined collections of text formatting choices that you can apply in one step. They're stored as parts of documents. You can reach any document's style sheet through a **Style** menu command pop-up menu (as in Figure 3-7), or through a keyboard shortcut that you define yourself. Style sheets are especially useful if you're working on long documents that must have consistent styles throughout. Then you don't have pull down half a dozen (or more!) menus each time you want to style a new section of text. Just select the text once and apply the style sheet.

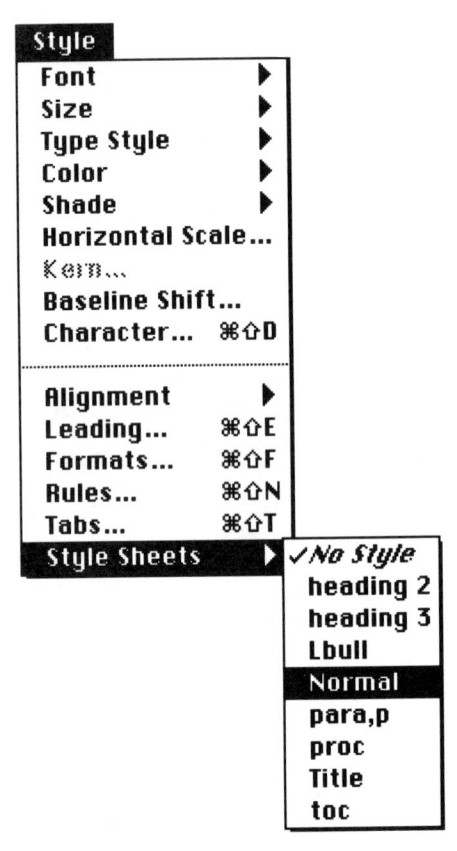

Figure 3-7. Style Sheet pop-up menu within the Style menu.

To define a style sheet:

1. Select a section of text.

2. Apply the attributes you wish to assign to the style sheet.

3. Choose **Style Sheets** from the **Edit** menu (*not* from the **Style** menu). The **Style Sheets for** dialog box appears (as in Figure 3-8), allowing you to create new style sheets or edit existing ones.

4. Notice the listing for style and format information that appears in the bottom of the **Style Sheets** dialog box, as in Figure 3-8.

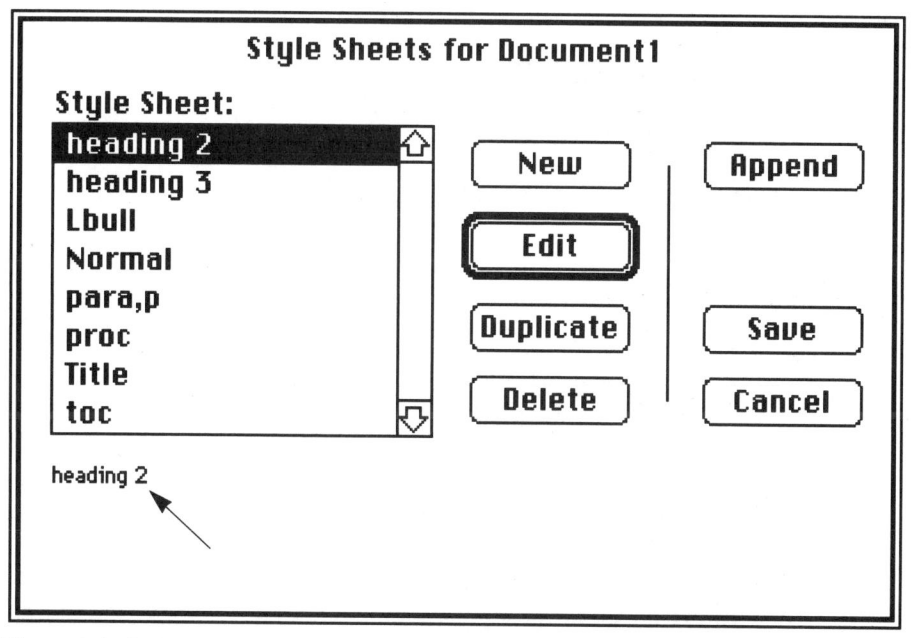

**Figure 3-8. Style sheets dialog box. The arrow is pointing to the listing for style and format information, as described above in Step 4.**

5. Choose **New** to create a new style sheet. Notice that all of your selected text's attributes are listed in the **Edit Style Sheet** dialog box (Figure 3-9).

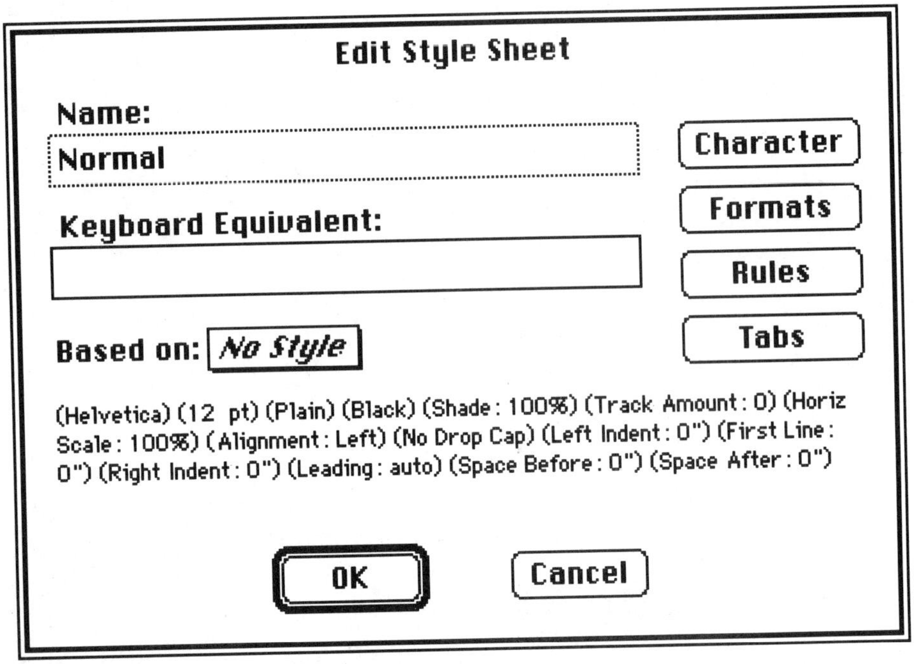

```
                    Edit Style Sheet
   Name:
   ┌─────────────────────────────────┐      ┌───────────┐
   │ Normal                          │      │ Character │
   └─────────────────────────────────┘      └───────────┘
   Keyboard Equivalent:                     ┌───────────┐
   ┌─────────────────────────────────┐      │  Formats  │
   │                                 │      └───────────┘
   └─────────────────────────────────┘      ┌───────────┐
                                            │   Rules   │
   Based on: │ No Style │                   └───────────┘
                                            ┌───────────┐
                                            │   Tabs    │
                                            └───────────┘
   (Helvetica) (12 pt) (Plain) (Black) (Shade: 100%) (Track Amount: 0) (Horiz
   Scale: 100%) (Alignment: Left) (No Drop Cap) (Left Indent: 0") (First Line:
   0") (Right Indent: 0") (Leading: auto) (Space Before: 0") (Space After: 0")

              ┌────────┐        ┌──────────┐
              │   OK   │        │  Cancel  │
              └────────┘        └──────────┘
```

Figure 3-9. Edit Style Sheet dialog box.

6. Type a name for the new style sheet and type a keyboard equivalent (the shortcut key combination you want to use to invoke it).

7. You can select the styles of some other style sheet as a base by selecting another sheet from the pop-up **Based on:** menu. Change any attribute by clicking on the appropriate button in this dialog box — **Character, Formats, Rules,** or **Tabs** — and then setting the attributes in the corresponding dialog box (these are shown in Figures 3-9 through 3-13). After setting attributes in one of these dialog boxes, click on **OK**, then click on **OK** in the **Edit Style Sheet** dialog box.

*WORD PROCESSING*

8. Finally, click on **Save** in the **Style Sheets** dialog box.

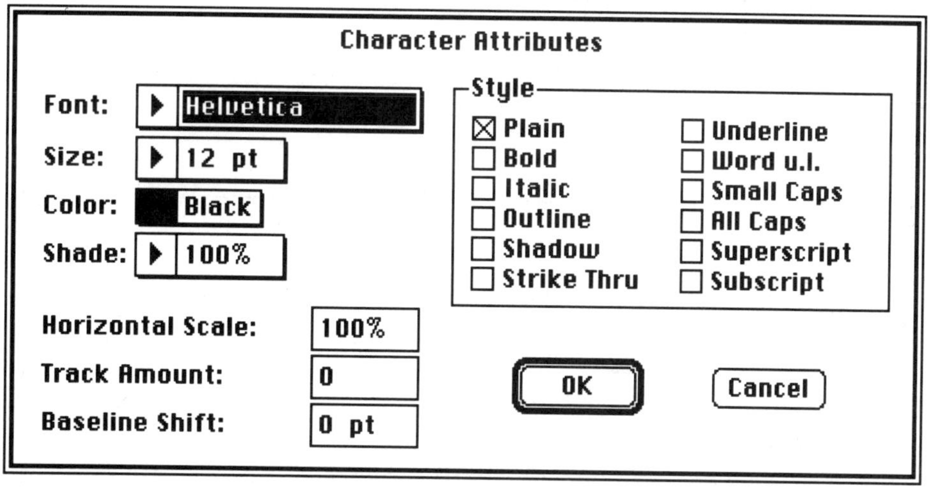

Figure 3-10. Character Attributes dialog box.

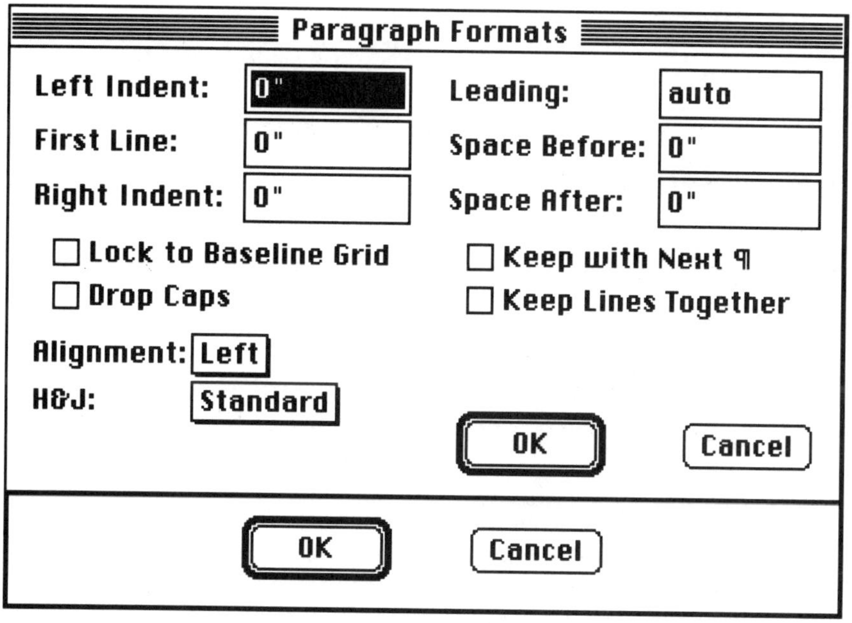

Figure 3-11. Paragraph Formats dialog box.

Figure 3-12. Paragraph Rules dialog box.

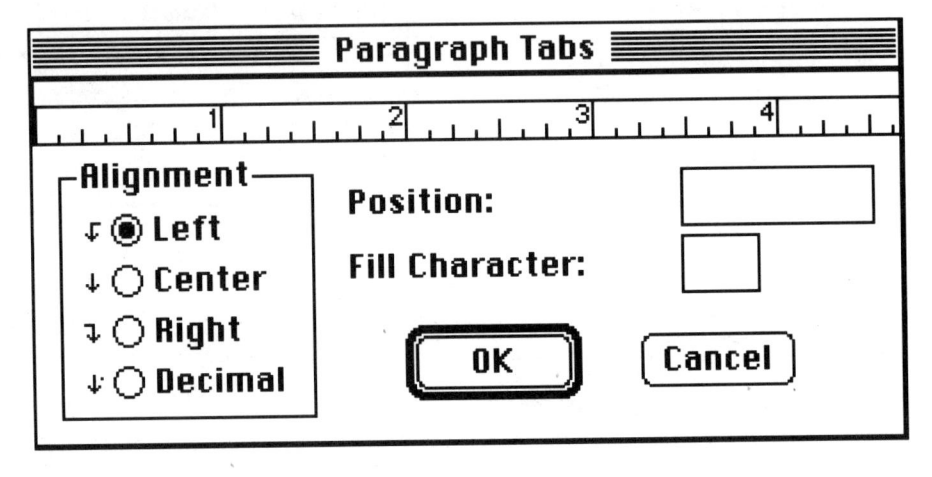

Figure 3-13. Paragraph Tabs dialog box.

Change (edit), duplicate, delete, or append style sheets using these same dialog boxes.

Change a style sheet's styles by clicking on **Edit** from the **Style Sheets** dialog box, setting the new styles, and saving the result.

Add the style sheets from any document to your current document by clicking on the **Append** button in the **Style Sheets** selection dialog box.

Eliminate an unwanted style sheet by selecting its name in the **Style Sheets** dialog box and then clicking on the **Delete** button.

> *Note:* when you're assigning keyboard equivalents, use any combination of the ⌘ key, **Option** key, or **Shift** key, plus any number from the numeric keypad to the right of your keyboard or, if you have an extended keyboard, the **F-5** through **F-15** keys. This gives you more than 164 keyboard-command combinations. It's a good idea to include at least one of the modification/command keys with a number. This keeps you from inadvertently changing paragraph styles when you enter numbers from the keypad.

Similarly, save yourself the trouble of recreating common style attributes in multiple style sheets by clicking the **Duplicate** button, changing the unwanted attributes, and renaming this new style sheet created from the old one. For example, if your design calls for several different style sheets for similar headline styles (each headline is Helvetica Extra Bold, and you need several different style sheets to accommodate italics, outlines, small caps, etc.), duplicate the same style sheet for each new style and change the character attributes accordingly.

### Stylesheet Adventure

1. Open a new document in QuarkXPress 3.0 by choosing **New** from the **File** menu. Click on **OK** when you see the **New Document Setup** dialog box.

2. Choose **Style Sheets...** from the **Edit** menu. Then click on the **New** button to create a new style sheet.

3. Click on the **Character** button and define some style attributes for your new style. QuarkXPress automatically selects 12 point plain Helvetica, 100% Black, as the starting styles.

4. Click on the **Bold** check box in the **Style** area, change the horizontal scale to 50% by double clicking on the **Horizontal Scale** entry field and type 50. (You can enter 50 by itself without adding the % sign.)

5. Click on **OK**.

6. Name your new style by typing **Helvetica Bold Head** in the **Name** field of the **Edit Style Sheet** dialog box, and click on **OK**. The results up to this point are shown in Figure 3-14.

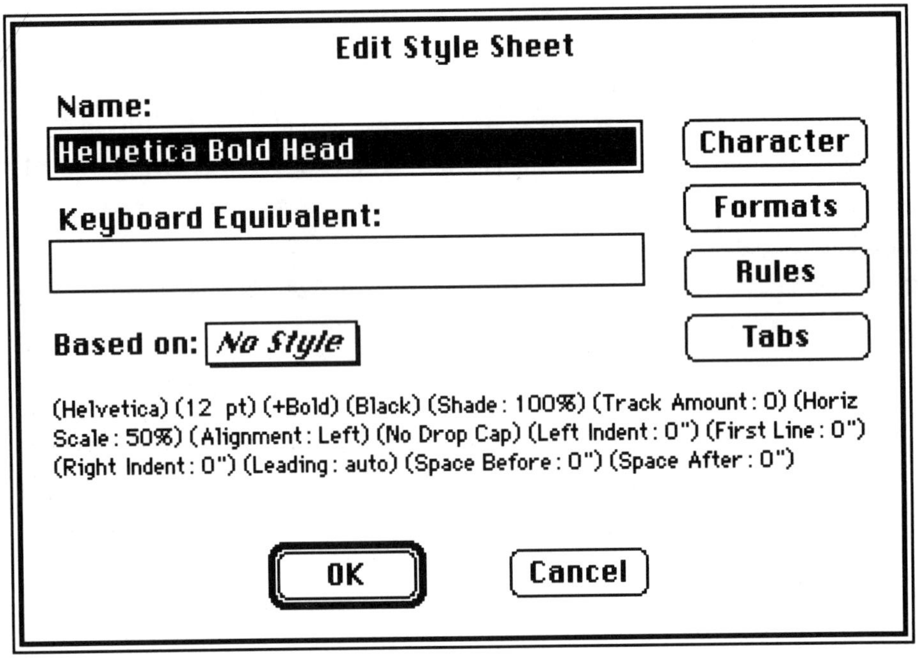

**Edit Style Sheet**

Name: Helvetica Bold Head

Keyboard Equivalent:

Based on: No Style

[Character] [Formats] [Rules] [Tabs]

(Helvetica) (12 pt) (+Bold) (Black) (Shade: 100%) (Track Amount: 0) (Horiz Scale: 50%) (Alignment: Left) (No Drop Cap) (Left Indent: 0") (First Line: 0") (Right Indent: 0") (Leading: auto) (Space Before: 0") (Space After: 0")

[OK] [Cancel]

Figure 3-14. The style sheet as of Step 6.

7. You'll see the name of your newly created style sheet in the **Style Sheet** menu in the **Style Sheets for Document 1** dialog box. If your new style sheet isn't already selected, click on it and then click on the **Duplicate** button.

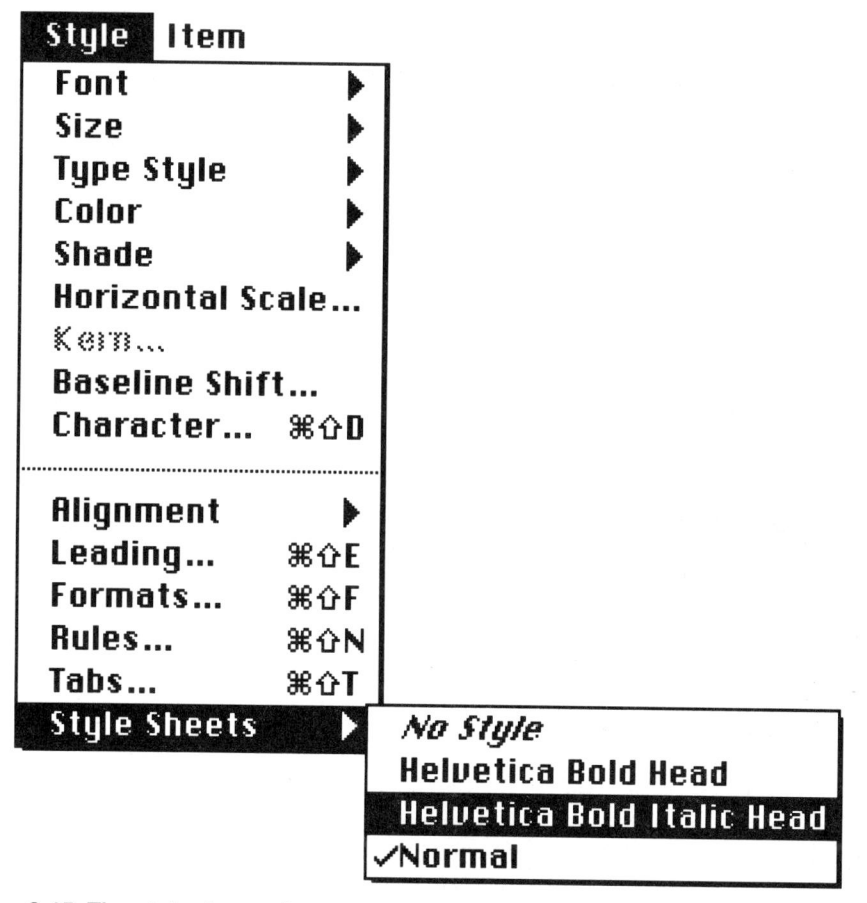

```
Style   Item
  Font              ▶
  Size              ▶
  Type Style        ▶
  Color             ▶
  Shade             ▶
  Horizontal Scale...
  Kern...
  Baseline Shift...
  Character...   ⌘⇧D
  ┄┄┄┄┄┄┄┄┄┄┄┄┄┄┄┄
  Alignment         ▶
  Leading...     ⌘⇧E
  Formats...     ⌘⇧F
  Rules...       ⌘⇧N
  Tabs...        ⌘⇧T
  Style Sheets      ▶   No Style
                        Helvetica Bold Head
                        Helvetica Bold Italic Head
                        ✓Normal
```

Figure 3-15. The style sheets that you've created through Step 10 appear in the Style menu.

8. The **Edit Style Sheet** dialog box appears with the words **Copy of Helvetica Bold Head.** Rename the new style sheet here (if you want).

Type in **Helvetica Bold Italic Head** in the **Name** field, because the next step shows you how to change the style attribute to italic.

9. Click on the **Character** category button, then click on the **Italic** check box of the **Style** area.

10. Click on **OK**, and when the **Edit Style Sheet** dialog box appears, click on **OK** again. Save your new style by clicking on the **Save** button when you see the **Style Sheets for Document 1** dialog box. This brings you back to the document window.

11. Now select your text box and pull down your **Style** menu to **Style Sheets**. You should see both **Helvetica Bold Head** and **Helvetica Bold Italic Head** in the pop-up menu, as shown in Figure 3-15.

## Finding or Replacing Text

As any self-respecting word processor should, QuarkXPress has a **Find/Change** command. As you can tell from its name, this command lets you search for any character or word in the text, or replace any character or word in the document. (It also works on numbers, symbols, and phrases — anything you can type into its **Find** blank.)

To find or change a simple letter, word, or phrase:

1. Place the cursor in the text box.

2. Choose the **Edit** menu and then the **Find/Change** command (or use the ⌘+F shortcut).

3. In the **Find/Change** dialog box that appears (see Figure 3-16), type the character, word, or phrase you want to find in the **Find what**: field.

4. If you're changing text, type the replacement character, word, or phrase

```
╔═══════════════ Find/Change ═══════════════╗
         Find what:              Change to:
     ┌Text─────────────┐      ┌Text─────────────┐
     │                 │      │                 │
     └─────────────────┘      └─────────────────┘
     ☐ Document  ☐ Whole Word  ☒ Ignore Case  ☒ Ignore Attributes
     ┌─────────┐ ┌──────────────────┐ ┌──────┐ ┌──────────┐
     │Find Next│ │ Change, then Find│ │Change│ │Change All│
     └─────────┘ └──────────────────┘ └──────┘ └──────────┘
```

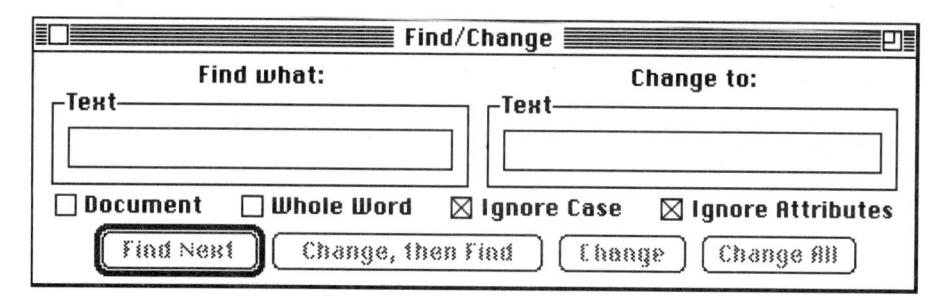

**Figure 3-16. Find/Change dialog box.**

in the **Change to:** field.

5. Select the options you want in the **Find/Change** dialog box by clicking (putting an X in the box) next to:

   a. **Document** — to search through all text in your document.

   b. **Whole Word** — to find only instances where your **Find what:** character, word, or phrase is independent of surrounding text.

   c. **Ignore Case** — to search for both uppercase and lowercase instances of your **Find what:** entry. (Without this option, it will only search for those instances that match whatever case you typed.)

   d. **Ignore Attributes** — to search for all instances of your **Find what:** entry, regardless of type style or size. (If you click to leave this box open, you can search for text with certain attributes or dictate the attributes of the replacement text. This is explained in the next section.)

6. Click on one of the action buttons:

   a. **Find Next** — to find the first instance of the **Find what:** text after the cursor's position. It's highlighted when it's found.

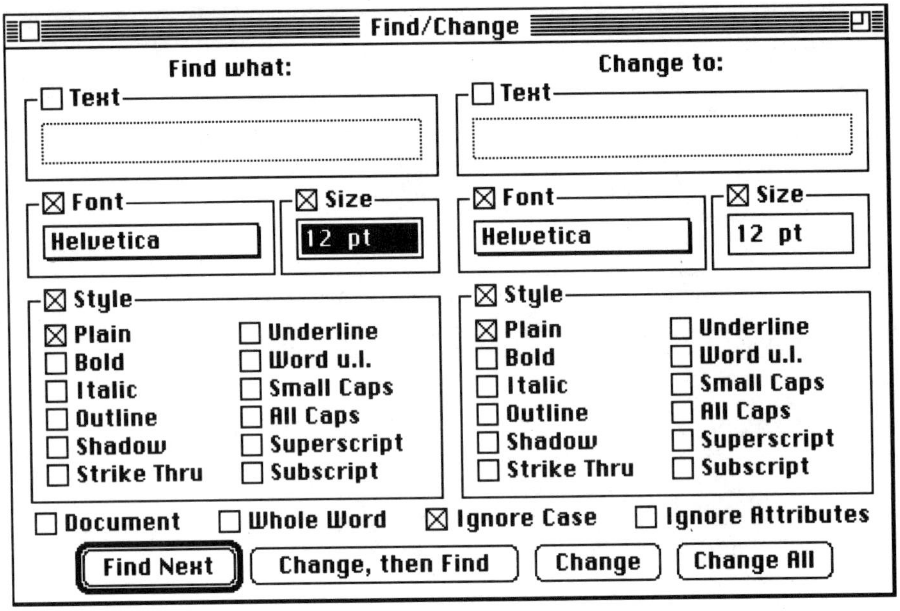

Figure 3-17. The expanded Find/Change dialog box — using Attributes.

    b. **Change All** — to find all instances of the **Find what:** text and change them to the **Change to:** text

7. If QuarkXPress can't find any instances of your **Find what:** text, it will beep (or make whatever sound is set on your Mac) once. Then you can:

    a. Choose some new text to search for by double-clicking in the **Find what**: field and typing the new text.

    b. Quit the find/change work by clicking on your document (outside the **Find/Change** dialog box) or by closing the **Find/Change** dialog box by clicking in the close box in top left corner.

8. If QuarkXPress does find an instance of your **Find what:** text, it highlights it. Then you can:

a. Edit it in any way you like by clicking on your document work area, then using normal editing commands.

b. Click on **Find Next** to move to the next instance of the **Find what:** text.

c. Click on **Change, then Find** to change this first instance to whatever text you have entered in the **Change to:** field, then to move on and highlight the next instance of the **Find what:** text.

d. Click on **Change** to change this first instance to whatever you have entered in the **Change to:** field.

e. Click on **Change All** to change this first instance and all others to the **Change to:** text.

## Find/Change with Attributes

**Find/Change** searches for or replaces any particular character, word, or phrase in the text. It also works with the typographic sophistication of a design program: It can limit its search to only those instances of text that have certain attributes, such as size, style, and font settings. It can replace text with new text having a particular set of attributes — even attributes different from the searched-for text. And it can also search for any text with particular attributes, no matter what the characters are. This can be very useful if you only want to change subheads of a certain type size, or if you want, for instance, to replace all **Strike Thru** text with **Underline** text.

### To Find or Change with Attributes:

1. Click on the **Ignore Attributes** box so that no X shows in the box. The expanded **Find/Change** dialog box appears, as shown in Figure 3-17.

2. Enter text for **Find what:** and **Change to:**. To enter text in either field, you have to first click in the field's selection box.

3. Select the attributes you want for the **Find what:** and **Change to:** text. (If you enter attributes without entering **Find what:** and **Change to:** text, you'll be searching for any text with those attributes.)

## Spell Checking

QuarkXPress comes with an 80,000-word dictionary of correctly spelled words and a built-in utility program that checks your text against the items in that dictionary (this isn't a conventional dictionary with definitions — it only contains the words themselves). If any word in your text can't be found in the dictionary, QuarkXPress lets you know so you can ignore the discrepancy or correct the word. You can also add the word and its spelling to an auxiliary dictionary.

You can check spelling in your document at three levels: you can check a single word; any continuous chain of text; or the entire document, even text in different and unconnected text boxes.

### Spell Checking a Word

To use the spelling dictionary to check a particular word:

1. Click on the word itself or click right next to the word.

2. Choose **Check Spelling...** from the **Utilities** menu and choose the **Word** selection. (The keyboard shortcut is ⌘+**W**.)

3. The **Check Word** dialog box appears (as shown in Figure 3-18) with a list of suggestions for the correct spelling of the selected word. Scroll through them by clicking on the arrows at top and bottom of the scroll bar on the right side of the list. (If there are multiple suggested corrections, QuarkXPress highlights the one it guesses is best.) Replace the word in your document with that selected suggestion by pressing **Enter**

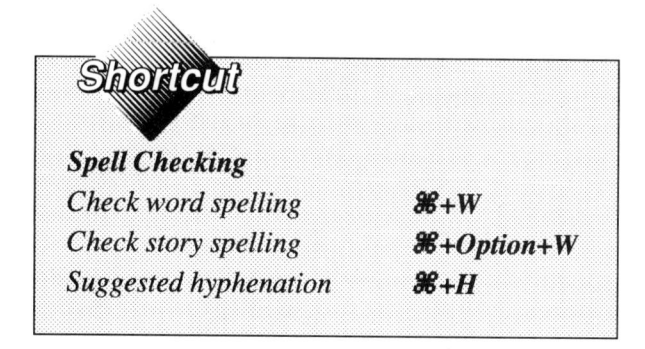

> **Shortcut**
>
> **Spell Checking**
> Check word spelling      ⌘+W
> Check story spelling      ⌘+Option+W
> Suggested hyphenation      ⌘+H

or **Return** or double click on any of the suggested spellings in the list to use it as the replacement. If none of the suggested words are right, click on the **Cancel** button and the dialog box disappears.

## Spell Checking a Story or Document

To check the spelling for an entire document or linked chain of text:

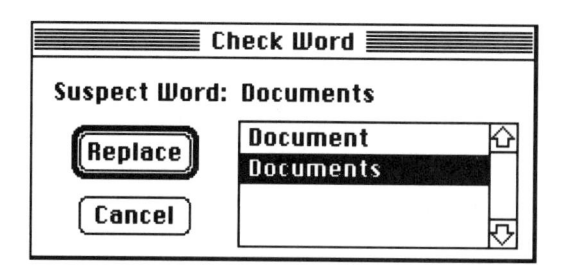

Figure 3-18. The Check Word dialog box for spell checking.

1. Pull down the **Utilities** menu, choose **Check Spelling**, and from the pop-up menu choose **Story** or **Document** (**Story** is for a single chain of text; **Document** is for all text in all chains in your document).

> **Shortcut**
>
> *Remember, the keyboard shortcut to select the cancel button without using the mouse is ⌘+"." (period).*

2. Whether you choose **Story** or **Document**, next you'll see a **Word Count** dialog box. This tells you how many words are in your story or document, how many are **Unique** (this counts each word the first time it appears only), and how many are **Suspect** (QuarkXPress thinks they may be spelled incorrectly). Click on **OK**.

3. The first suspect word is highlighted and the **Check Story** or **Check Document** dialog box (they differ only in title) appears with that word at the top. Figure 3-19 shows the **Check Document** dialog box. This dialog box offers a list of suggestions, if there are any, and a text entry field for you to enter the correct spelling if the dictionary does not list the word you are trying to spell.

The **Check Story** and **Check Document** dialog boxes each have a title bar across the top, which lets you reposition them on your screen.

In either the **Check Story** or **Check Document** dialog box, you can:

1. Type a correct spelling for the highlighted word in the **Replace with:** field and then click on **Replace** to replace the highlighted word.

2. Click on **Lookup** to see a list of possible correct spellings for the highlighted word, click on one of those spellings to select it, then click on **Replace** to replace the highlighted word.

3. Click on **Cancel** to end the spell checking or **Skip** to highlight the next suspect word. You can use **Cancel** or **Skip** at any time.

4. If you have an open auxiliary dictionary (as explained below), you can click on **Keep** to save the suspect spelling as a new correct spelling and prevent it from being tagged as suspect the next time you check spelling using that auxiliary dictionary.

it size reduces the number of **lnes** you can print on the
you change the font size in the mailing label documents for
you may need to remove paragraph marks (if you increase the
rt extra paragraph marks (if you decrease the font size) in

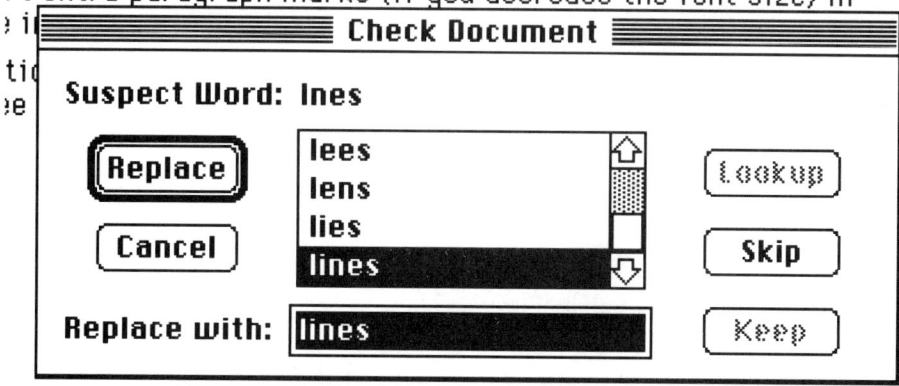

```
═══════════════ Check Document ═══════════════

Suspect Word: lnes

  ┌─────────┐    lees    ↑      ┌─────────┐
  │ Replace │    lens           │ Lookup  │
  └─────────┘    lies           └─────────┘
  ┌─────────┐    lines   ↓      ┌─────────┐
  │ Cancel  │                   │  Skip   │
  └─────────┘                   └─────────┘

  Replace with: │lines         │    ┌─────────┐
                                    │  Keep   │
                                    └─────────┘
```

Figure 3-19. The Check Document dialog box for spell checking.

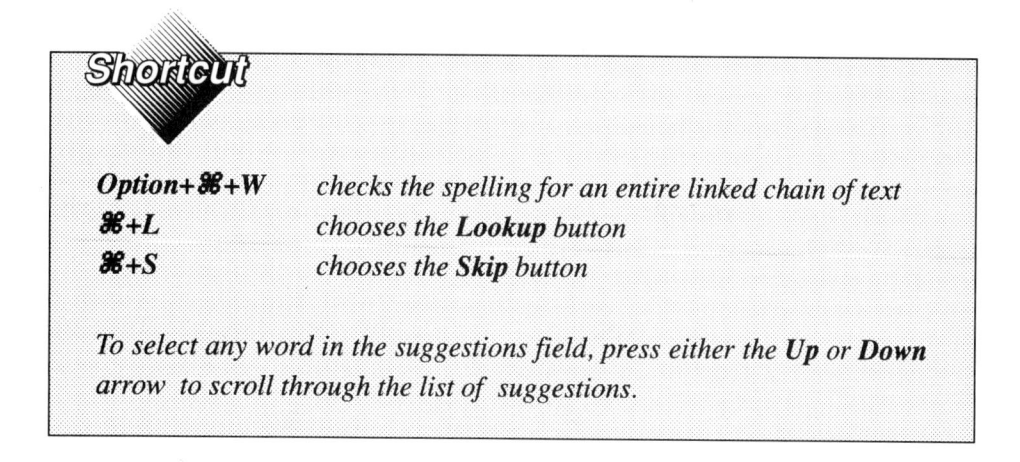

### Shortcut

**Option+⌘+W**   *checks the spelling for an entire linked chain of text*
**⌘+L**         *chooses the **Lookup** button*
**⌘+S**         *chooses the **Skip** button*

*To select any word in the suggestions field, press either the **Up** or **Down** arrow to scroll through the list of suggestions.*

## Auxiliary Dictionaries for Spell Checking

There may be words, symbols, and acronyms in your work or documents that aren't common enough to appear in the main QuarkXPress spelling

101

dictionary. These will appear as suspect words every time you check spelling, which will slow you down in finding genuine suspect words. Solve this by adding them to an auxiliary dictionary. If you open that dictionary before you run a spell check, QuarkXPress singles out those spellings. You can make as many auxiliary dictionaries as you like, keeping a large one for all of your work or opening separate ones for each type of document.

To open an auxiliary dictionary or to create a new one:

1. Choose **Auxiliary Dictionary...** from the **Utilities** menu.

2. From the dialog box that appears, either:

    a. Select a named dictionary from the disk and click on **Open.**

    b. Click on **New,** type a dictionary name, and click on **Save.**

To add spellings to or delete spellings from an open auxiliary dictionary:

1. Choose **Edit Auxiliary** from the **Utilities** menu.

2. The **Edit Auxiliary Dictionary** dialog box appears, as shown in Figure 3-20. Then make your changes:

    a. Add a spelling by typing it in the dialog box field above the command buttons (and below the list area), then click on **Add**. (You can also add spellings by using the **Keep** command while checking spelling, as mentioned above.)

    b. Delete a spelling by clicking on it in the list area, then click on **Delete**.

    c. Click on **Save** to keep your changes or on **Cancel** to toss them out.

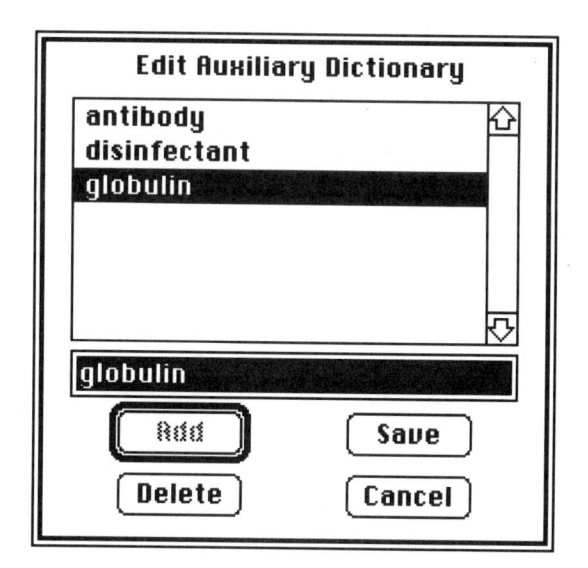

**Figure 3-20. The Edit Auxiliary Dictionary dialog box.**

## Save Text

When you've done everything you want to your text, you can save it to a file on your hard-disk drive. To do so:

1. Select the part of the text you want to save (unless you want to save all of the text in your document).

2. Choose **Save Text...** from the **File** menu.

3. In the **Save Text** dialog box that appears, click on the appropriate button to save either just the **Selected Text** or the **Entire Story**.

4. Choose a format for the saved file from the pop-up **Format:** menu. (You can choose from ASCII, MacWrite II, MacWrite 5.0, Microsoft Word 3.0/Write, Microsoft Word 4.0, and XPressTags.)

5. Type a name for the file you're saving.

6. Click on **Save**.

# CHAPTER 4

# Typography

If your only concern with text is to enter and edit it, to cut, copy, and paste sections of it until they are in order, and to check its spelling, you could use the simplest word processor on any personal computer. If you also care to add some style to that text's appearance, such as employing more than one font and putting different character sizes and styles to work, you could use just about any Macintosh word processing application. After all, the Mac sports such text style in just about every program — it's built into the basic Mac operating system software.

But if you need to control every aspect of the characters that make up text, and of the spaces between those characters, you care about "typography." For your work, the appearance of the characters is as important as their meaning.

Very fine control over type is a QuarkXPress trademark. It's one of the key features that often convinces designers or publishers with Macs to choose QuarkXPress over other desktop publishing and design programs. In fact, QuarkXPress allows precise type manipulation that previously was available only with specialized and expensive professional typesetting equipment.

QuarkXPress allows intricate manipulation of text within each text box. It lets you control kerning, tracking, leading, horizontal scaling, and vertical justification. In addition, the text boxes themselves can be rotated in increments of .001 degree and can be transparent, have background color, text color and shading, and borders (called "frames") of any width and style. The QuarkXPress 3.0 frame-editing utility lets you make your own frames and borders. (No more messy border tapes or hard-to-control dry transfer borders that plagued the old-fashioned design and publishing process!)

This chapter explains the theory and practice of typography with Quark-XPress. It begins with the terminology of type, then explains QuarkXPress' commands for type, and finally shows examples of type itself used as a design element.

## Terminology of Type

Since the development of the printing press, printers have been hard at work developing new words to describe and define terms unique to their science. Then the computer entered the world of type and printing, and more terms were needed. You'll need to understand some of these terms (or be able to flip back to their definitions) while working through this chapter.

**Point**: a unit of measurement used primarily to describe type sizes (see Figure 4-1). There are 72 points to an inch, 12 points to a pica.

**Pica**: a unit of measurement primarily used to describe line length. There are 6 picas to an inch and 12 points to a pica.

**Cicero**: a unit of measure from the Didot system used in continental Europe (except in Belgium). A cicero equals 12 "corps" (.178 inch) and a corps equals .01483 inch.

**En-space**: a unit of measure, typically one-half of an em-space.

**Em-space**: a unit of measure, one em is (typically) the space occupied by a capital "M" in any typeface or style. The physical measurement of an em is different for each size and style of type. In QuarkXPress, one em-space is the space occupied by two consecutive zeros.

# TYPOGRAPHY

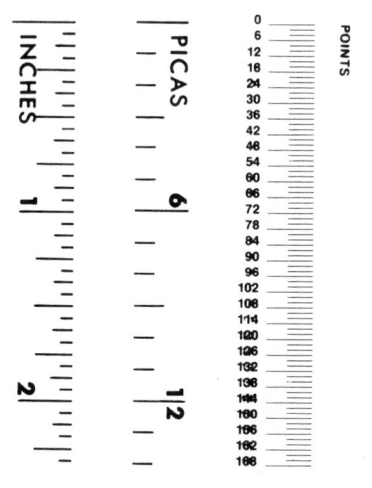

Figure 4-1. Typographical units of measure together for comparison.

**X-height**: the major proportion of a type size. The X-height is measured from the baseline of the text to the beginning of the ascender.

**Ascender**: the part of the letter that extends above the letter's main body.

**Descender**: the part of the letter that extends below the main body of the letter.

**Baseline**: the major axis on which the text is aligned.

**Font**: a complete assortment of one size and face of type. For example, Times Roman is a font. There are different styles of fonts, such as Times Roman Bold or Times Roman Italic.

107

**Kern**: the process of reducing or increasing the amount of white space that appears between individual letters.

**Track**: the process of reducing or increasing the amount of white space that appears between groups of letters.

**Lead** or **leading**: the spacing between lines of type, usually measured in points.

**Linespace**: the amount of space between individual lines of type.

**Letterspace**: the space between individual characters of text.

**User-definable**: a $35 word included here at no additional cost to indicate that a feature that the user can change. Marketing departments often believe "user-definable" sounds better on a spec sheet than "changeable."

Popular conjecture holds that these printing terms were created to keep the general public in the dark about how all of this magic really works. That theory may hold even more truth now that printing and publishing has become digital, except that with the advent of the computer and electronic design, even the printers are confused.

## Macintosh Screen Fonts

The Macintosh displays fonts on your screen with a bit-mapped representation of the font that is composed of pixels (dots, bits, tiny little points on the screen). The clean display of those fonts on your screen at larger sizes depends on having the corresponding sizes of that "screen" font installed to your system. (Read your Macintosh Owner's Manual.) Changing the font size to a size larger than you have installed in your system results in a very rough representation of that font on your screen.

# TYPOGRAPHY

In late 1990 or early 1991 Apple is scheduled to release its new System 7.0 system software for the Mac, which will make some changes in the Mac's approach to type. This will not significantly affect your QuarkXPress typography as explained in this book for some time.

## Macintosh Printer Fonts

Printer fonts are downloadable instructions to your printer to help it print fonts that are not resident in your printer's memory. If you haven't got the corresponding "printer" font in your system folder for a screen font you're using, your printer will print the same bit-mapped image of the font that appears on your screen. Currently, printer fonts must be present in your system folder to print correctly on your printer. (This may change with System 7.0.) This feature makes for a clean and accurate representation of the font on paper, even if it appears chunky and blocky on your monitor screen.

PostScript is a secret language of wizards, gnomes, and software engineers that helps your laser printer (or other high-resolution output device) produce such finely resolved images and fine typography. Some books spend chapters extolling and explaining PostScript. Not this one. The basics of the PostScript page description language are not required to use a Macintosh or QuarkXPress, just as a full understanding of the fuel injection system in your car is not a prerequisite to knowing how to drive. The only PostScript you need to know to manipulate and print beautiful type with QuarkXPress 3.0 is that your PostScript compatible printer needs to "download" a font to print any font that is not already resident (built-in) in the printer.

Every Macintosh system comes with a good collection of fonts. If you are printing your work on a LaserWriter II NT or NTX laser printer (both use PostScript), then some of these fonts will be resident (or permanently installed) in the printer's memory. These LaserWriter fonts make possible the very fine resolution of Macintosh typefaces.

## Font Usage

There is a utility built into QuarkXPress 3.0 that will list all of the fonts used in the active document. To see that list:

1. Pull down the **Utilities** menu.

2. Select **Font Usage:**.

3. From the Font Usage dialog box that appears (as in Figure 4-2), you can see the fonts and the styles used for those fonts.

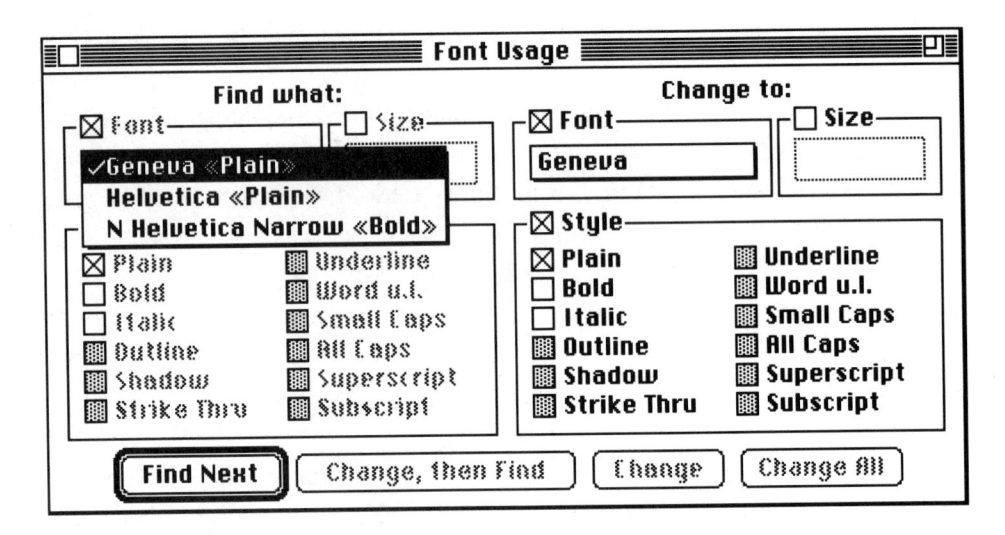

**Figure 4-2.** The Font Usage dialog box.

You can also put the **Font Usage** dialog box to work changing fonts in your active document. For any font and style that's selected on the left side — the **Find What:** side of the dialog box — select a replacement font, style, and size on the right side — the **Change to:** side of the dialog box. Then apply the **Find Next, Change,** then **Find, Change,** or **Change All,** buttons at the bottom of dialog box just as you would the same buttons in the **Find/Change** dialog box of the **Edit** menu (which is discussed in Chapter 3). This **Font Usage** dialog box is just a specialized version of that command, committed to finding fonts and not specific characters, words, and phrases.

When you're done with the **Font Usage** utility, just click in the upper-left corner box to close the dialog box.

> *It's always a good idea to restart QuarkXPress after making font changes.*

## Kerning and Tracking

The simplest character display systems for computers divide the display screen into little rectangles, typically fitting 80 of them across the screen and 25 down, to make 25 lines of 80 characters each. Then a single character (including the space character) can be displayed in each rectangle. This system makes it difficult if not impossible to display different size and style characters. It also ignores the differences between characters within the alphabet. The "i" for instance doesn't need as much room as the "w." What's more, an "o" that comes just after a capital "T" doesn't need as much room as an "o" that comes after another "o." The "o" after the "T" can actually fit under the top of the "T." And it looks better that way – look at magazines and books. They all use this variable spacing, this "kerning" of the letters. After inspecting them and look at evenly spaced computer printouts, you'll see that lack of kerning is one key factor in the obvious lower-quality appearance of conventional computer "hard copy."

QuarkXPress lets you choose your own inter-letter spacings, your own kerning and tracking. This is vital to both design and publishing projects.

Kerning and tracking change the amount of white space between letters in text. Kerning is the adjustment of space between two characters. Tracking is the adjustment of space between more than two characters.

QuarkXPress 3.0 can manipulate kerning and tracking of type in increments of .0005 em. This gives great precision and flexibility in manipulating large display and headline type. It also offers very subtle control over larger volumes of type.

Kerning adjusts the space between two letters. Tracking adjusts the space between all of the letters in a section of text. QuarkXPress can kern or track in fractions of an em-space — very small pieces indeed. That precision is critical when large characters are used in headlines or designs. It also helps you to fit text neatly into defined spaces and allows you to adjust the look of text to fit your own artistic and practical aims.

**Kerning.** To change the character space between two characters:

1. With the **Content** tool, select the text box holding the text you wish to edit. Place the cursor between the two characters you wish to manipulate.

2. Choose **Kern...** from the **Style** menu and, in the dialog box shown in Figure 4-3, enter a value to adjust the spacing between the two letters. Kerning can be adjusted in increments of .0005 em. A positive value will spread the letters farther apart; a negative value will bring them closer together. Experiment a bit to see how it works. (You can also set the kerning value in the **Character...** dialog box from the **Style** menu.)

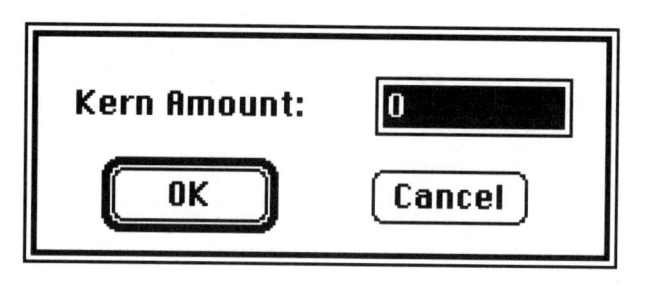

**Kern Amount:** 0
OK    Cancel

**Figure 4-3. The Kern... dialog box.**

Keep in mind that each style of each font can use different kerning values, and that you could fiddle with kerning until doomsday. (It's an art that keeps some typesetters and printers busy for a lifetime, building kerning tables of all the "best" values for various letter pairs.) If you want to do more than just kern individual character pairs that look like they need it badly, you should turn to QuarkXPress' Kerning Table Edit.

**Changing Kerning Tables.** You can kern a single pair of characters in a document, as mentioned above, or you can deal with the kerning for an entire font and style in one swoop by editing the kerning table for that font and style.

To do that:

1. Pull down the **Utilities** menu and choose **Kerning Table Edit....**

2. From the **Kerning Table Edit** dialog box as shown in Figure 4-4, click on the particular font/style for which you want to set kerning values, then click on **Edit**.

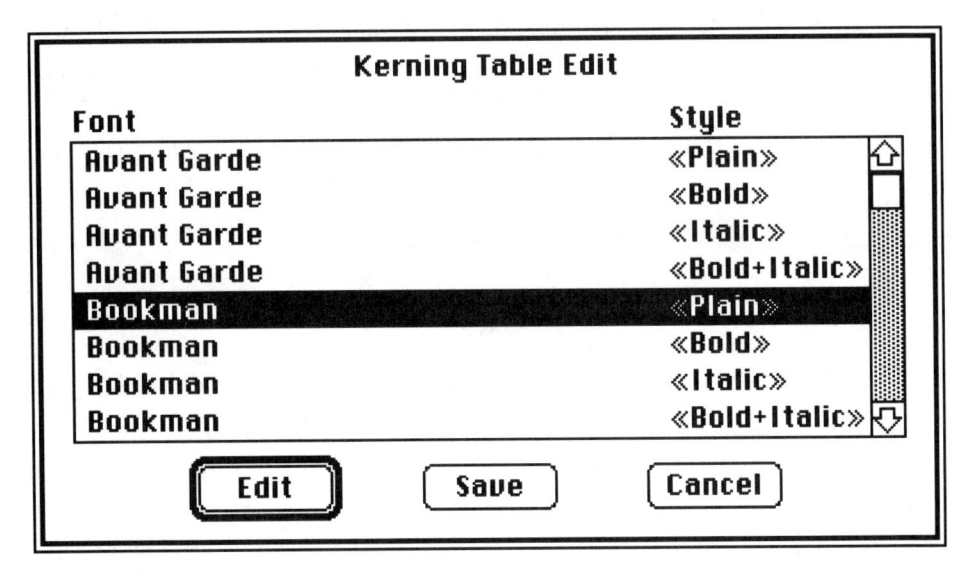

```
                    Kerning Table Edit
   Font                                   Style
   Avant Garde                            «Plain»
   Avant Garde                            «Bold»
   Avant Garde                            «Italic»
   Avant Garde                            «Bold+Italic»
   Bookman                                «Plain»
   Bookman                                «Bold»
   Bookman                                «Italic»
   Bookman                                «Bold+Italic»

          [  Edit  ]      [  Save  ]      [ Cancel ]
```

Figure 4-4. Kerning Table Edit dialog box.

### Kerning and Tracking Are Relative

*The value you set for kerning or tracking is relative to the typeface being used. This means that if you've spent ten minutes trying to get the letter spacing of a major headline using Helvetica just right, and the type style has been changed to Times, the kerning and tracking values remain in effect for the new typeface. You won't have to re-work all of that time-consuming type manipulation.*

3. Next you'll see the **Kerning Values for** dialog box as shown in Figure 4-5. Here you can:

   a. Delete a character pair from the table (select the pair and click **Delete**).

   b. Add a character pair to the table (type a new pair in the **Pair:** blank, then type a value in the **Value:** blank, and click **Add**).

   c. Edit a character pair in the table (select the pair or type it in the **Pair:** blank, then type a new value in **Value:**, then click **Replace**, which will replace the **Add** button).

   d. Recover the original kerning values for the font (click on **Reset**).

   e. Abandon your kerning work (click **Cancel**).

---

*Shortcut*

### Manipulating Characters

*1. With the **Content** tool, place the text cursor between the two characters you wish to manipulate.*

*2. Hold down the **Shift** and ⌘ keys and press the ] or [ key to move the characters closer together or farther apart, respectively. This keyboard command will move the characters together or apart in increments of .05 em. Move the characters in smaller increments of .005 em by holding down the **Option** key while performing the same keyboard command.*

Note: Whenever you select a pair or type a new pair with a value, the large box in the lower center of the **Kerning Values for** dialog box (Figure 4-5) will show you how that pair will appear with that kerning value. Compare the display in Figure 4-5 to that in Figure 4-6.

4. When you're done adding, deleting, and otherwise editing kerning pairs in the table, click on **OK**, then on **Save** in the **Kerning Table Edit** dialog box.

**Exporting and Importing Kerning Values.** You can export an ASCII text file with all of the kerning values by clicking **Export** in the **Kerning Values for** dialog box shown in Figure 4-6. This file could be useful for analysis by a typographer or as information for your service bureau or print shop.

Conversely, you can import kerning values into a table, by clicking **Import**. Imported data replaces what's already in the kerning table.

**Tracking.** You may be asking yourself, "What's the point of having such precision in kerning to be able to adjust characters in increments smaller than the human eye is able to perceive?" The answer is tracking. Tracking is kerning that has been applied to a range of text, like a line of type, a paragraph or series of paragraphs, or even a whole document. There are some very practical applications of such precision in almost any document you design.

Tracking at small increments allows for some very subtle copy fitting in any document. If you are creating a page holding a body of text that is not fitting precisely to the text boxes you've placed, you can correct for this by tracking the entire range of text in minute increments, without having to disturb the overall design of your page by manually extending or shortening the length of the text

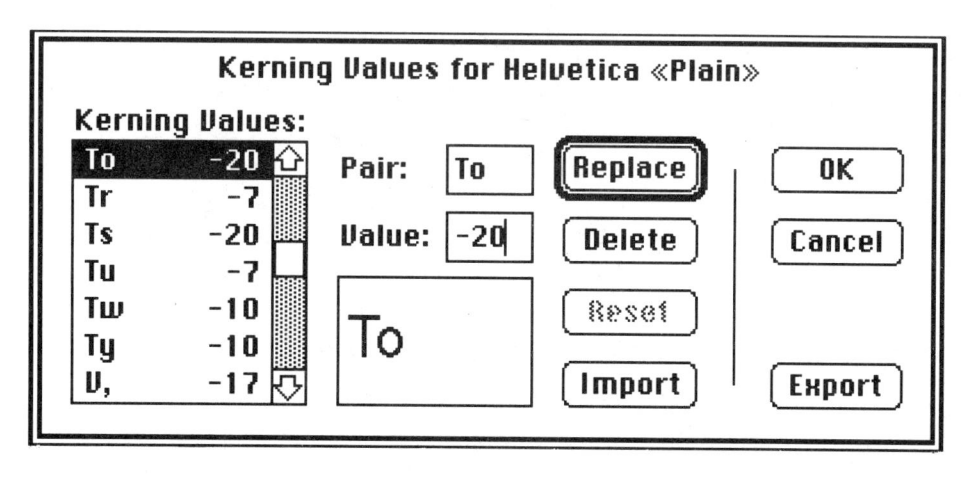

Figure 4-5. Kerning Values for dialog box (with -20 em kerning between T and o).

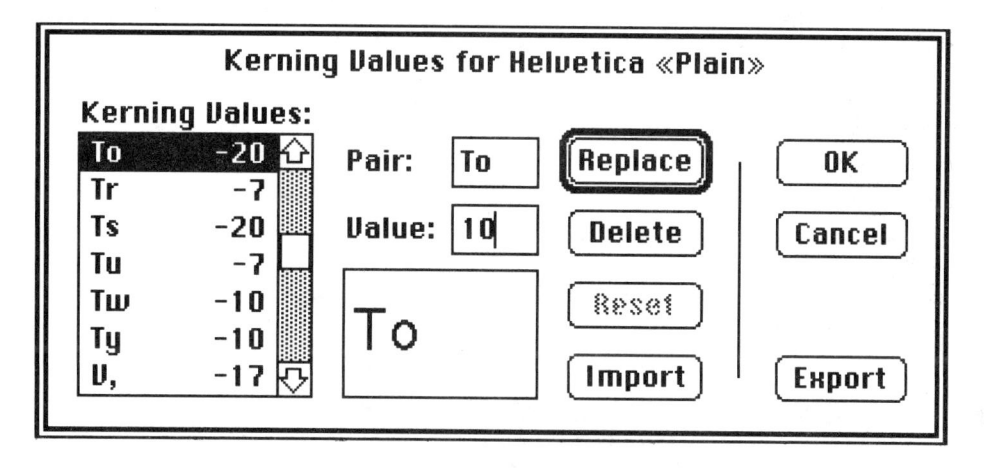

Figure 4-6. Kerning Values For dialog box (with 10 em kerning between T and o).

*USING QUARKXPRESS*

### Tip

***Kerning is Crucial to Headlines***

Because headlines often appear so large, kerning and tracking ability is crucial to good design. Most typefaces have automatic kerning pairs that contract at larger type sizes, but you can customize the spacing to make the text appear even better.

The very large headline in Figure 4-7 could benefit from some kerning finesse, as shown. The headline flows better and becomes more readable with the new kerning values applied to each pair of letters.

As with most matters of design, personal taste and design skill make the greatest difference when judging the appropriate kerning and tracking of text at larger sizes. Fortunately QuarkXPress gives you the capability to precisely control the spacing of your headline text in increments of 5/10,000 of an emspace. This level of precision is even more important larger text sizes, as the proportion of the type size is the unit of measure when kerning text.

# HeadLine
# HeadLine
-17  -5  -0  -7   -9  -5  -12

**Figure 4-7. The upper headline could benefit from some kerning finesse. The lower one has been kerned using the values specified.**

# TYPOGRAPHY

box. Tracking the text in smaller increments over an entire range of text can make up a lot of space without visually affecting the cadence of the body of text, as shown in Figure 4-8.

| You may be asking yourself, "What's the point of having such precision in kerning to be able to adjust characters in increments smaller than the human eye is able to perceive?" The answer is tracking. Tracking is kerning that has been applied to a range of text, like a line of type, a paragraph or series of paragraphs, or even a whole document. There are some very practical applications of such precision in almost any document | You may be asking yourself, "What's the point of having such precision in kerning to be able to adjust characters in increments smaller than the human eye is able to perceive?" The answer is tracking. Tracking is kerning that has been applied to a range of text, like a line of type, a paragraph or series of paragraphs, or even a whole document. There are some very practical applications of such precision in almost any document you design. |

**Figure 4-8. Copy fitted to a text box before and after tracking.**

*Tip*

*Changed font kerning tables and tracking tables are stored in the file on disk called XPress Data. (Hyphenation exceptions and frame editor specifications are also stored in this file.) If QuarkXPress cannot find this file in the QuarkXPress program's folder, it looks in the System folder. If it can't find it there, it makes a new data file, losing any changes you've made. Therefore, if you want a service bureau to accurately reproduce your QuarkXPress files, you must also provide them with a copy of this XPress Data file.*

Tracking is also very useful in fitting text between adjacent paragraphs in the same text box. Because QuarkXPress 3.0 lets you track in such subtle increments it is possible to tuck up stray words (widows and orphans) in paragraphs without creating a discernable difference between paragraphs.

You track a range of text in the same manner as kerning between characters.

1. Select the text to track.

2. Choose **Track...** from the **Style** menu, and in the **Track...** dialog box (shown in Figure 4-9), enter a tracking value. Just as with kerning, you can track in increments of .0005 em. A positive value will spread the letters farther apart, a negative value will bring them closer together. (You can also set the tracking value in the **Character...** dialog box from the **Style** menu.)

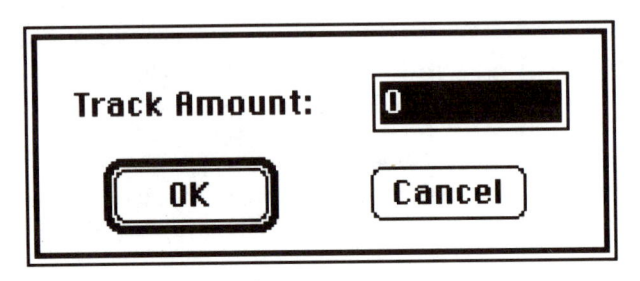

Figure 4-9. Track... dialog box.

It is possible to "over-track" characters of body text. If you're trying to fit text to a small area and it is not fitting after tracking to -20/200 em (as shown in Figure 4-10) you should consider changing your design to accommodate an additional line or two of text. Tracking most typefaces beyond -20/200 em will begin to make them unreadable (and unsightly). Use tracking with prudence.

> It is possible to "over-track" characters of body text. If you're trying to fit text to a small area and it is not fitting after tracking to -20/200 em (as shown in Figure 4-10) you should consider changing your design to accommodate an additional line or two of text. Tracking most typefaces beyond -20/200 em will begin to make them unreadable (and unsightly). Use tracking with prudence.

**Figure 4-10. Example of a horrendously overtracked paragraph.**

**Custom Tracking Tables.** You can track a selected area of text, or you can create custom tracking tables for entire fonts. These tables will then be used to space characters whenever those fonts are used. Any manual tracking you dictate, as described above, will add to the tracking from this table. (The table will be stored in the XPress Data file, as mentioned in the sidebar above.)

To create a custom tracking table:

1. Pull down the **Utilities** menu and choose **Tracking Edit....**

> *As with kerning, you can use the keyboard equivalent **Shift+⌘+[** or **Shift+⌘+]** to adjust tracking in .05-em increments. Also, holding down the **Option** key with either operation refines the increments to .005 em (relative to the typeface).*

121

2. From the **Tracking Edit** dialog box as shown in Figure 4-11, click on the particular font you want to set tracking values for, and then click on **Edit**.

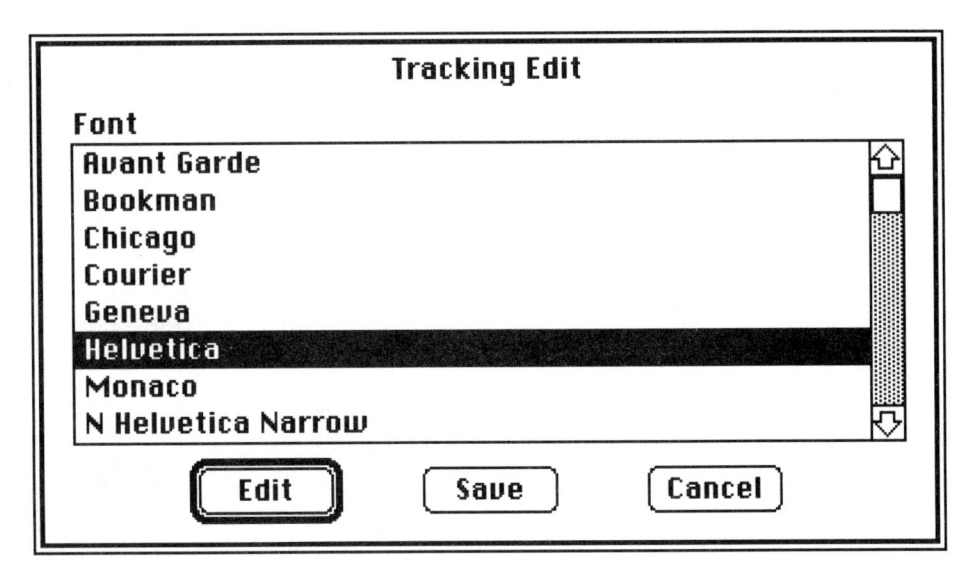

```
                    Tracking Edit
Font
  Avant Garde
  Bookman
  Chicago
  Courier
  Geneva
  Helvetica
  Monaco
  N Helvetica Narrow

        [ Edit ]    [ Save ]    [ Cancel ]
```

Figure 4-11. Tracking Edit dialog box.

3. Then you'll see the **Tracking Values for** dialog box as shown in Figure 4-12. This dialog box has a tracking value curve that sets different amounts of tracking for different size characters in the font. Initially it is set at 0 for all font sizes.

4. If you click anywhere on the line (which runs horizontally on the 0 of **Tracking Value**) a handle will appear (a tiny black rectangle). You can then drag this handle up or down to increase or decrease the tracking val-

ue at that particular font size, as shown in Figure 4-13. The top right corner of the dialog box will show you the current value and font size at the cursor's position. You can create up to four handles to move various points in the curve.

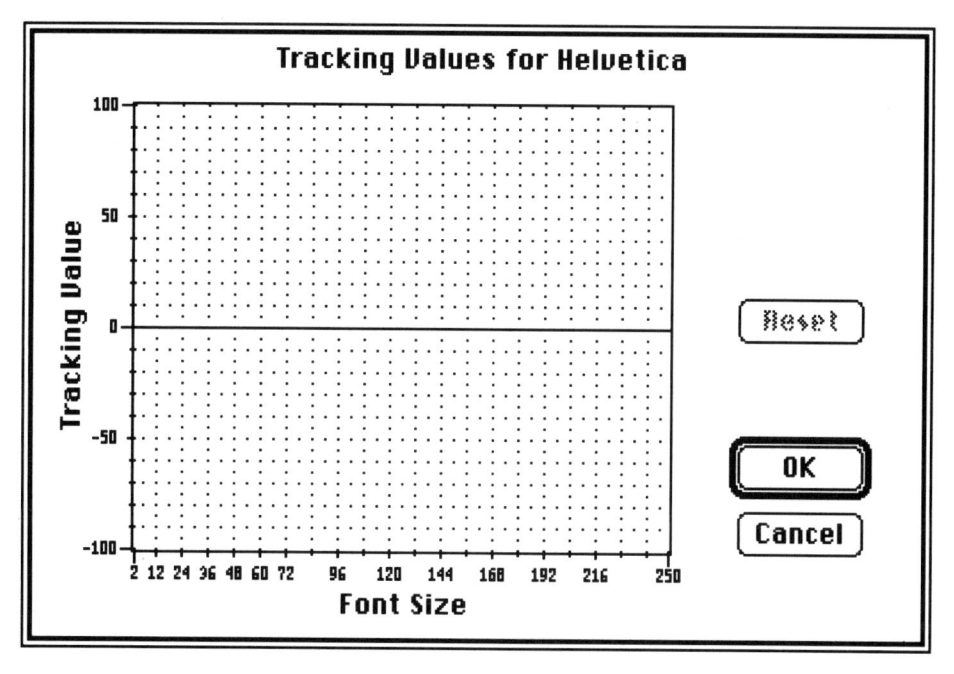

Figure 4-12. Tracking Values for dialog box with initial 0 tracking value for all sizes.

5. If you want to delete a curve, hold the **Option** key. The cursor will change into a small open rectangle with cross. Click this on a handle and the handle will disappear.

6. If you're not happy with the results, you can reset the values with the **Reset** button.

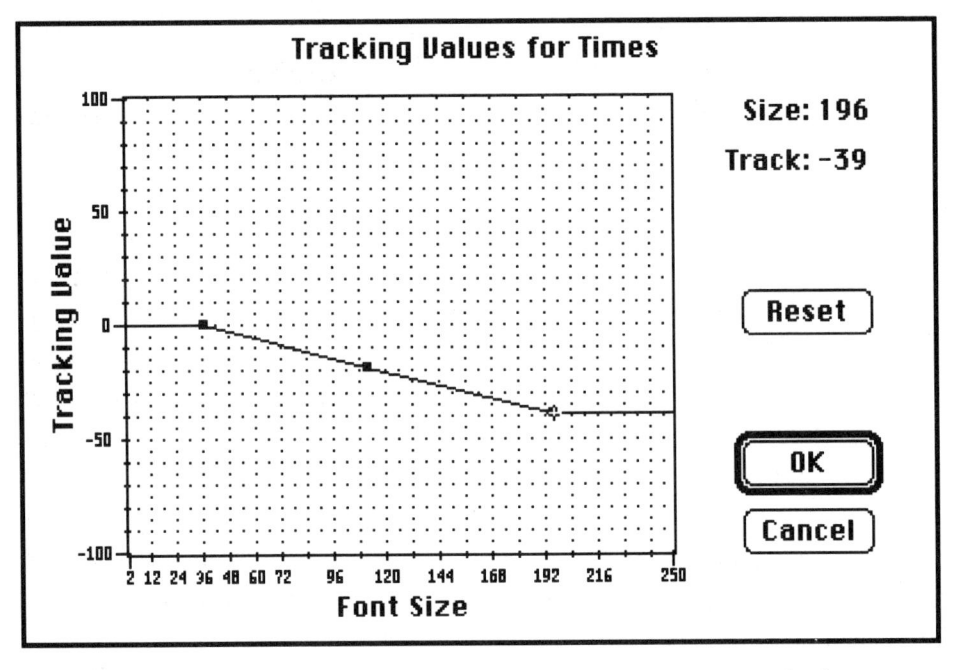

Figure 4-13. Tracking Values for dialog box with an example of a changed values curve.

## Horizontal Alignment

A column of text may be set to align along the right, left, or both margins or in the center of the text box by choosing **Left**, **Right**, **Centered**, or **Justified** in the **Alignment** pop-up menu under the **Style** menu, as shown in Figure 4-14. (Although "justified" is used in the menu to mean aligned to both sides at once, the word also is used as a synonym for "aligned" as in "justified to the right," "justified to the left," and so on. You can dictate some details of the justification decisions QuarkXPress makes in the H&J settings described in a later section in this chapter.)

Justified text (spacing it so that it is flush on both edges of the column margins) can sometimes become spaced oddly across each line because of the spaces added to plump lines out to meet the margins, as in Figure 4-15.

# TYPOGRAPHY

## Leading

Leading (pronounced ledding) is the white space that occurs between lines of type. Figure 4-16 shows some examples. Leading gets its name from the days of traditional hot metal type when lines of characters were manually assembled in racks and then mounted to large heavy steel plates. Solid strips of lead were used to space the lines of type apart.

Each typeface has its own optimum leading value relative to the length of its ascenders and descenders.

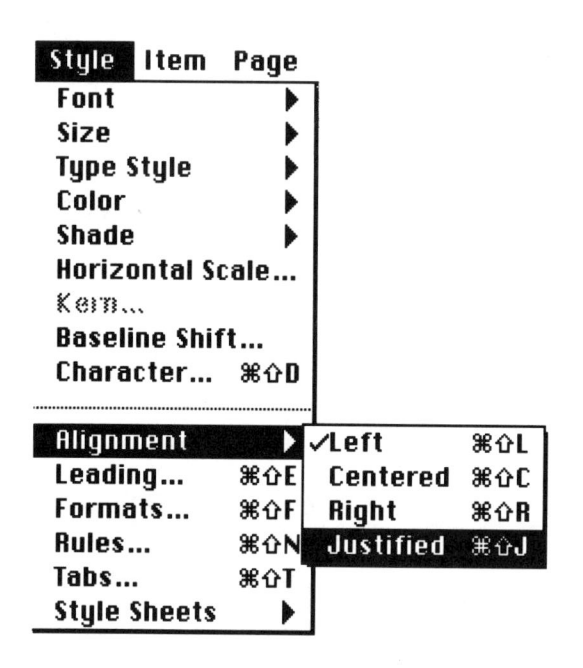

Figure 4-14. Alignment menu in QuarkXPress.

| You can dictate some details of the justification decisions QuarkXPress makes in the | H&J settings described in a later section in t h i s chapter.)Justified text (spacing it so that it is | flush on both edges of the c o l u m n margins) can sometimes become spaced oddly across | each line because of the spaces added to plump lines out to meet the margins, as in Figure 4-15. |

Figure 4-15. Example of unevenly spaced text in columns.

125

*Technique*

## Alignment to Irregular Text Margins

There are two easy ways to get text to conform to irregular margins. Both are effective and flexible. You can use a polygon picture box to create text that will conform to unusually shaped margins by choosing **Invert** from the **Runaround Specifications** dialog box. Or you can use a series of opaque lines to create irregular margins. These both depend on the runaround text wraparound commands explained in Chapter 5. Here is a quick example of their use.

1. Import some body text into your text box.

2. Select the **Line** tool (the angled line tool in the **Tool** palette, as explained in Chapter 5).

3. Click and drag a diagonal graphic line over your text. Lines are automatically drawn as transparent so you don't have to worry (yet) about displacing your type.

4. From the **Style** menu choose a new width for your line. Make it thick enough to be easy to click on with the **Cursor** tool.

5. You'll ultimately want this line to be "invisible" so it won't print. To do that, choose **White** as a color or choose to style the line as 0% shade of the default **Black**. Remember, even if you can't see the line itself, you can always tell if it is selected because the endpoint handles will be visible. (Another reason to make the line thick: it is easier to find, click and manipulate a wide invisible line than a narrow invisible line.) You can use another tactic here by choosing **Modify** from the **Item** menu and selecting the **Suppress Printout** check box. The line will still show on screen, but the page will print without the line.

6. Now choose the **Item** menu and select **Runaround**.

7. Select the **Item** pop-up menu from the **Runaround** dialog box.

8. Duplicate the line by choosing **Duplicate** from the **Item** menu.

Leading (pronounced ledding) is the white space that occurs between lines of type. Figure 4-16 shows some examples. Leading gets its name from the days of traditional hot metal type when lines of characters were manually assembled in racks and then mounted to large heavy steel plates. Solid strips of lead were used to space the lines of type apart.

Leading (pronounced ledding) is the white space that occurs between lines of type. Figure 4-16 shows some examples. Leading gets its name from the days of traditional hot metal type when lines of characters were manually assembled in racks and then mounted to large heavy steel plates. Solid strips of lead were used to space the lines of type apart.

Leading (pronounced ledding) is the white space that occurs between lines of type. Figure 4-16 shows some examples. Leading gets its name from the days of traditional hot metal type when lines of characters were manually assembled in racks and then mounted to large heavy steel plates. Solid strips of lead were used to

**Figure 4-16. Examples of different leading values.**

There is no one "right" leading value for all typefaces. Leading is measured from the baseline of the text. It is represented in the form of a fraction by showing the size of the text itself over the sum of the text size plus the amount of leading. Leading is usually measured in points from the baseline of one line of text to the baseline of the next line. (You can specify any unit of measure. If your preferences call for inches, the **Leading** dialog box will automatically measure leading in points; you can still specify leading in inches by typing " to designate the measure as a portion of an inch.)

Leading values may be specified using any measurement system that QuarkXPress 3.0 supports. No matter which method you have set in your **Preferences** dialog box, you can type in the values followed by the measurement definition. For example, even if your measurement preferences are set to inches, you can still specify a measurement in points by typing in **pt** after the number in any field.

**Specifying Leading in QuarkXPress.** QuarkXPress 3.0 lets you specify leading values in three different fashions.

- As an absolute value, by specifying a set value that remains the same no matter what size type face is specified in a line of text.
- Proportionally, as a percentage of the largest typeface size in a line.
- Incrementally, by adding a set amount of leading to the largest typeface size in a line.

To specify an absolute leading value, select the paragraph or any part of the paragraph whose leading you wish to adjust. Choose **Leading...** from the **Style** menu. Type a value in the dialog box that appears.

To specify leading proportionally, choose the **Edit** menu, the **Preferences** pop-up, and finally the **Typographic...** dialog box, as shown in Figure 4-17. There find the **Auto Leading** line and enter a percentage. If the value is set at 20% of the type size, 12 point text will be set with 2.4 points of lead, or 12/14.4. Eighteen-point text will be automatically set at 18/21.6 points, and so on.

To specify leading incrementally: Place your text cursor into any part of a paragraph, or select several paragraphs (or even a whole text chain) and choose **Leading...** from the **Style** menu. Then designate a relative leading value by typing in the dialog box that appears a numerical leading value preceded by a + or -, as shown in Figure 4-18.

Changing the leading value in any paragraph by selecting any part of the paragraph will specify the leading for the whole paragraph. That means you can adjust paragraph leading by selecting a word or series of words, or just by placing the text cursor anywhere in a paragraph.

# TYPOGRAPHY

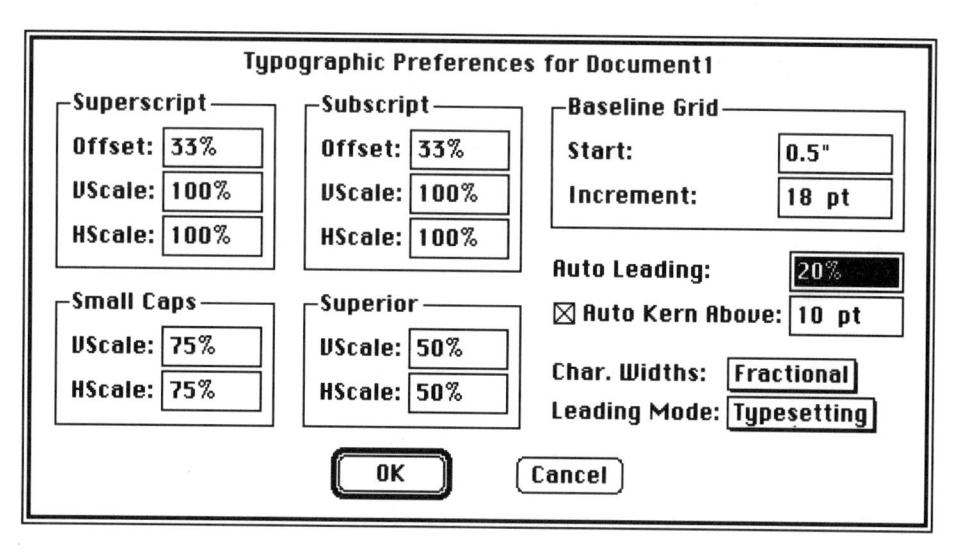

Figure 4-17. The Typographic... preferences dialog box for setting proportional leading.

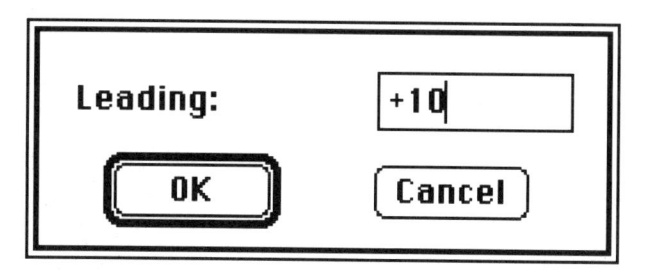

Figure 4-18. Specifying leading incrementally by entering a leading value with a + or -.

The "typewriter" and "word processor" modes for leading (in the **Typographic Preferences** dialog box) differ in how they measure. Typesetting measures upward from the baseline of one line of text to the baseline of the line above. Word processing mode measures downward from the top of the ascent on one line of text to the top of the ascent on the line below.

129

> ### Shortcut
>
> **Leading Shortcuts**
>
> *If your leading has been specified incrementally or as an absolute value, you can adjust it with these keyboard commands:*
>
> | | |
> |---|---|
> | ⌘+E | *calls up the **Leading Specifications** dialog box.* |
> | ⌘+Shift+: | *decreases leading in 1 point increments.* |
> | ⌘+Shift+" | *increases leading in 1 point increments.* |
> | ⌘+Option+Shift+: | *decreases leading in .1 point increments.* |
> | ⌘+Option+Shift+" | *increases leading in .1 point increments.* |

**Size Subheads Carefully and Reduce the Leading.** Subheads are a great way to enhance text by highlighting key topics and key words at the beginnings of paragraphs. But there's more to creating a subhead than just choosing a lead phrase and making the text bold. You also have to consider the subhead's text size as it relates to the size of the body text. Text sizes that are too large can overpower the body text and distract the reader. Text sizes too small can escape notice, defeating the subhead's purpose. A good rule of thumb is to keep the subhead text size no larger than 180% and no smaller than 120% of the size of the body text that follows. Figure 4-19 shows an example.

When making subheads to lead off important paragraphs in long, text-intensive documents, it's a good idea to keep the subhead close to the body text so their connection is more obvious. However, if your subhead text size is substantially larger than the text size, and you have the leading set to a proportional default (like 20%), then the larger text size will carry with it a larger leading value. Defeating this trait is easy. Figure 4-20 shows an example.

> **Subheads**
>
> Subheads are a great way to enhance text by highlighting key topics and key words leading off paragraphs. But there's more to creating a subhead than just choosing a lead phrase and making the text bold. You also have to consider the subhead's text size as it relates to the size of the body

> **Subheads**
>
> Subheads are a great way to enhance text by highlighting key topics and key words leading off paragraphs. But there's more to creating a subhead than just choosing a lead phrase and making the text bold. You also have to consider the subhead's text size as it relates to the size of the body

Figure 4-19. Example of sizing subhead text — between 120% and 180% of body text size.

Figure 4-20. Reduced leading for a subhead.

By creating a separate stylesheet for the subheads, you can control the subhead leading and adjust it to allow the body text to fall closer to the baseline of the subhead. You can then invoke this stylesheet for every subhead as you work.

## Baseline Shift

You can move characters up or down from their default "baseline" by adding a baseline shift. To do this:

1. Select the text.
2. Pull down the **Style** menu and select **Baseline Shift...**.
3. Enter a baseline shift value in the dialog box that appears, placing a plus sign (to move up) or minus sign (to move down) before the value. You

can shift the baseline up to three times the size of the highlighted characters. Figure 4-21 shows an example of a baseline shift.

4. Click **OK**.

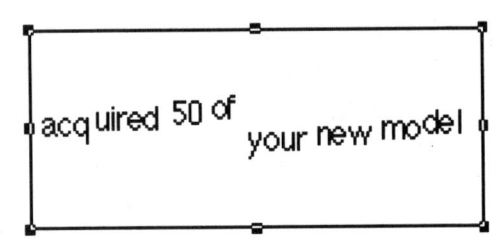

Figure 4-21. Baseline shift example.

## Text Inset

The text inset margin is the amount of space you define between the boundaries of the text box and the beginning of any character in your text. This value is set in the **Text Box Specifications** dialog box found when you choose **Modify** from the **Item** menu, as seen in Figure 4-22.

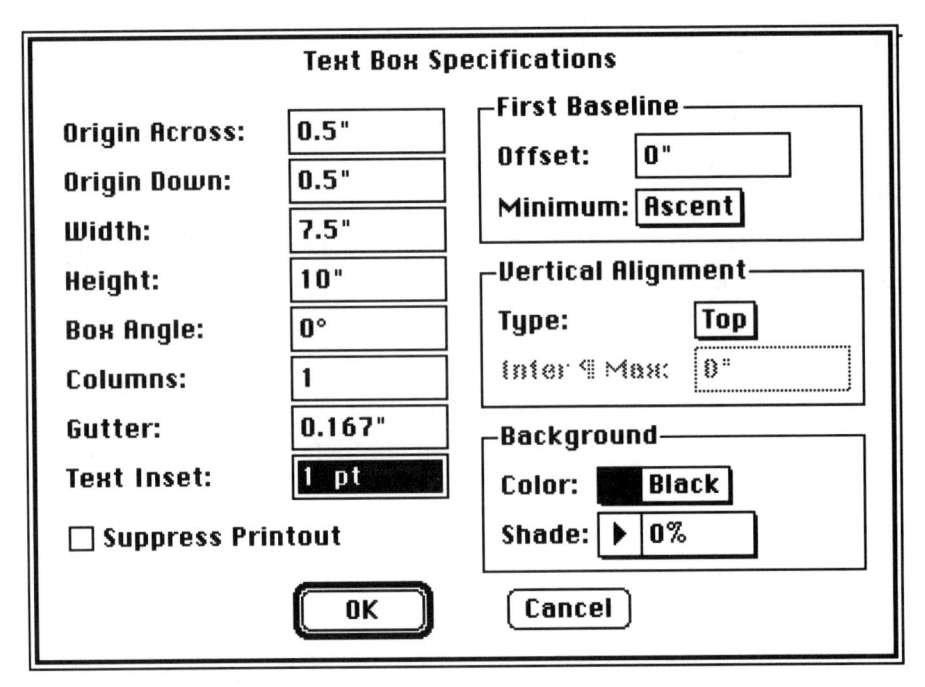

Figure 4-22. Text Box Specifications dialog with callout to text inset value.

# TYPOGRAPHY

The text inset can be set in increments of .001 of any unit of measure and is measured from all sides (the amount of space you specify as the minimum distance between the boundaries of the box and the start of any character will be for the top and bottom, as well as the sides). This value can also specify the distance from the top of the text box to the first baseline of the first line of text in that text box.

## Vertical Alignment

It's possible to align multiple columns of text along the top edge, bottom edge, center, or both top and bottom edges of columns of type. (This is analogous to horizontal alignment, mentioned above.) Figure 4-23 shows an example.

When columns of text are vertically aligned from the top of the text box, alignment is made from the defined first baseline distance from the top boundary of the text box. The first baseline is measured in any unit of measure and is placed according to any of the three styles available in the pop-up menu in the First Baseline area of the Text Box Specifications dialog box the area between the cap height and the tex inset boundary).

When columns of text are vertically aligned from the top of the text box, alignment is made from the defined first baseline distance from the top boundary of the text box. The first baseline is measured in any unit of measure and is placed according to any of the three styles available in the pop-up menu in the First Baseline area of the Text Box Specifications dialog box the area between the cap height and the tex inset boundary).

When columns of text are vertically aligned from the top of the text box, alignment is made from the defined first baseline distance from the top boundary of the text box. The first baseline is measured in any unit of measure and is placed according to any of the three styles available in the pop-up menu in the First Baseline area of the Text Box Specifications dialog box the area between the cap height and the tex inset boundary).

When columns of text are vertically aligned from the top of the text box, alignment is made from the defined first baseline distance from the top boundary of the text box. The first baseline is measured in any unit of measure and is placed according to any of the three styles available in the pop-up menu in the First Baseline area of the Text Box Specifications dialog box the area between the cap height and the tex inset boundary).

**Figure 4-23. Vertically aligned text — all four examples.**

To do this:

1. Choose **Modify** from the **Item** menu.
2. From the **Text Box Specifications** dialog box that appears, click on the **Vertical Alignment** pop-up menu and select the vertical alignment style you want, as shown in Figure 4-24.

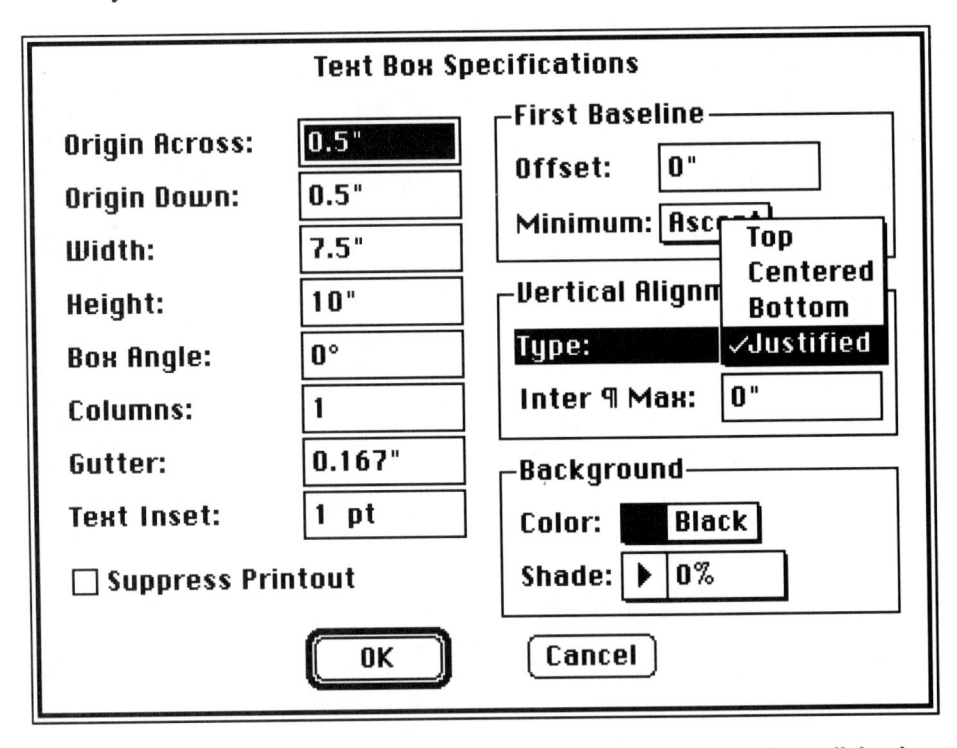

Figure 4-24. Vertical Alignment pop-up menu in Text Box Specifications dialog box.

**Top Vertical Alignment.** When columns of text are vertically aligned from the top of the text box, alignment is made from the defined first baseline distance from the top boundary of the text box. The first baseline is measured in any unit of measure and is placed according to any of the three styles available in the pop-up menu in the **First Baseline** area of the **Text Box Specifications** dialog box (see Figure 4-25). The minimum value is measured from the ascent (the top of the ascenders), cap plus ascent (the height of the capital letters plus the additional space required by punctuation that extends above the cap height), or cap height (the height of capital letter characters, meaning that any punctuation that appears above the cap height will appear in the area between the cap height and the text inset boundary).

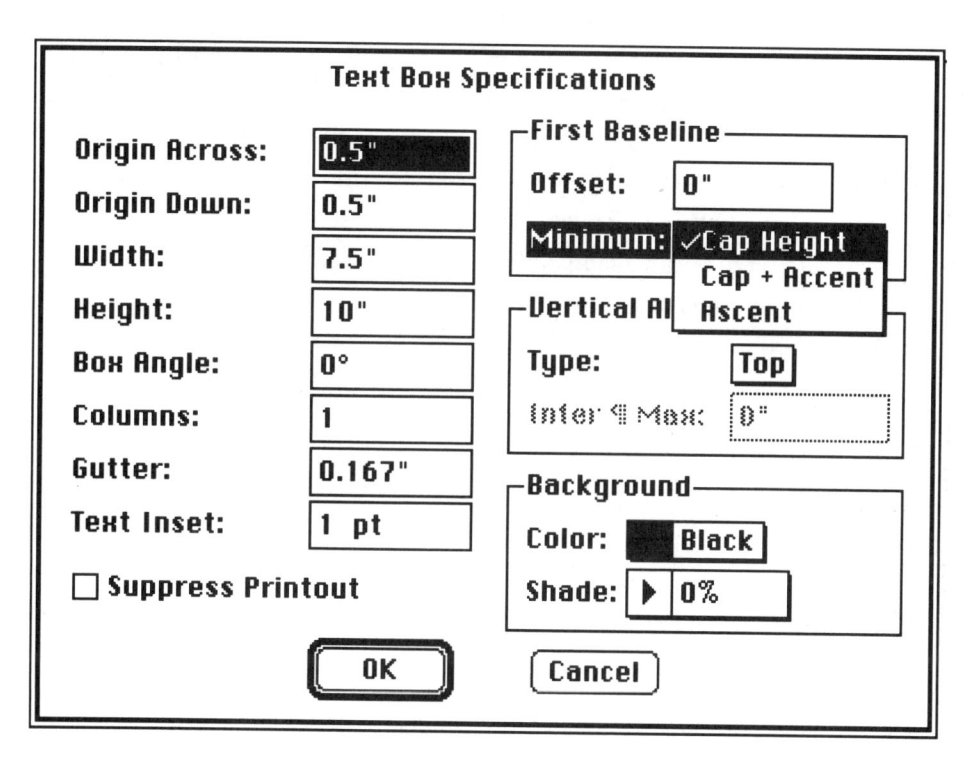

**Figure 4-25.** First baseline specifications for vertical alignment.

**Center Vertical Alignment.** When columns of text are vertically aligned from the center, lines of text are aligned along a center line that occurs between the first baseline measurement (as defined in the **Text Box Specifications** dialog box, see Figure 4-24) and the text inset value (defined at the bottom of the **Text Box Specifications** box). Lines of text are spaced according to the leading value you specify for the text.

135

**Bottom Vertical Alignment.** When columns of text are vertically aligned from the bottom, they are aligned with the descenders of the typeface flush with the text inset value, and will not occur above the text inset boundary inside the top of the text box.

**Justified Vertical Alignment.** When columns of text are vertically justified with the first line occurring on the first baseline as defined in the **Text Box Specifications** dialog box, the rest of the lines are evenly spaced between the first baseline and the text inset boundary along the bottom of the text box. In the **Text Box Specifications** dialog box the **Inter ¶ Max** field (this only appears when you choose **Justified Vertical Alignment**, as shown in Figure 4-24) will be enabled for you to define the maximum space between paragraphs. This value is important if you want the leading value to remain consistent with other non-aligned text. If the **Inter ¶ Max** field value is 0, the vertical justification will override the leading value and evenly space the lines to fill the column height, as shown in Figure 4-26.

Bottom Vertical Alignment. When columns of text are vertically aligned from the bottom, they are aligned with the descenders of the typeface flush with the text inset value, and will not occur above the text inset boundary inside the top of the text box.

Justified Vertical Alignment. When columns of text are vertically justified with the first line occurring on the first baseline as defined in the Text Box Specifications dialog box, the rest of the lines are evenly spaced between the first baseline and the text inset boundary along the bottom of the text box. In the Text Box Specifications dialog box the Inter ¶ Max field (this only

Bottom Vertical Alignment. When columns of text are vertically aligned from the bottom, they are aligned with the descenders of the typeface flush with the text inset value, and will not occur above the text inset boundary inside the top of the text box.

Justified Vertical Alignment. When columns of text are vertically justified with the first line occurring on the first baseline as defined in the Text Box Specifications dialog box, the rest of the lines are evenly spaced between the first baseline and the text inset boundary along the bottom of the text box. In the Text Box Specifications dialog box the Inter ¶ Max field (this only

**Figure 4-26. Example of columns of text evenly justified and with max ¶ value defined.**

## Hyphenation and Justification

Good typography has an even cadence across a line of text. Words and sentences don't appear bunched up, crowded, or spaced too far apart. Kerning and tracking control the spacing between pairs of characters. You can also control the spacing of words and characters in paragraphs the way you set hyphenation and justification values. You use the **Edit** menu's **H&J...** (hyphenation and justification) dialog box (shown in Figure 4-27) to handle this work. (A word is hyphenated when it is broken into two parts that are separated by a hyphen, as in high-light. Justification sets the number of spaces between characters and words.)

QuarkXPress 3.0 lets you create and edit your own hyphenation and justification guides for any text. Like setting leading values for a paragraph, specifying H&J values will affect any selected paragraph. These guides can be saved like a stylesheet and used as often as necessary or appended between documents to use the same hyphenation and justification guides in any documents.

Hyphenation and justification values can be set to automatically break words, with the break positions dependent on the word length, capitalization, and space from the column edges. Values may be set for minimum number of characters required to break a word, as well as for the smallest word to hyphenate. You can even specify the number of hyphens occurring in a row and set a hyphenation zone relative to the column margins. Automatic justification values may be set to control word spacing and character spacing defined as a percentage of word length. There is even a setting to control the flush zone in a paragraph.

***Remember**: H&J values don't apply to all text. Like style sheets and paragraph formats, they only affect paragraphs to which they are applied.*

You can create up to 127 different H&J guides for any document, and assign them to individual paragraphs as needed. To create a new hyphenation and justification guide for a document:

1. Choose **H&J...** under the **Edit** menu.

2. From the **H&J...** dialog box (as shown in Figure 4-27), click on:
   a. **New** to create a new H&J specification.
   b. **Edit** to change a selected H&J specification.
   c. **Duplicate** to create a new H&J specification that's based on a current spec.
   d. **Append** to pull in an H&J specification from some other document.
   e. **Delete** to eliminate an H&J specification.
   f. **Cancel** to get back to the menus without playing H&J games.

3. If you click **New** or **Edit**, the **Edit Hyphenation & Justification** dialog box (as shown in Figure 4-28) appears.

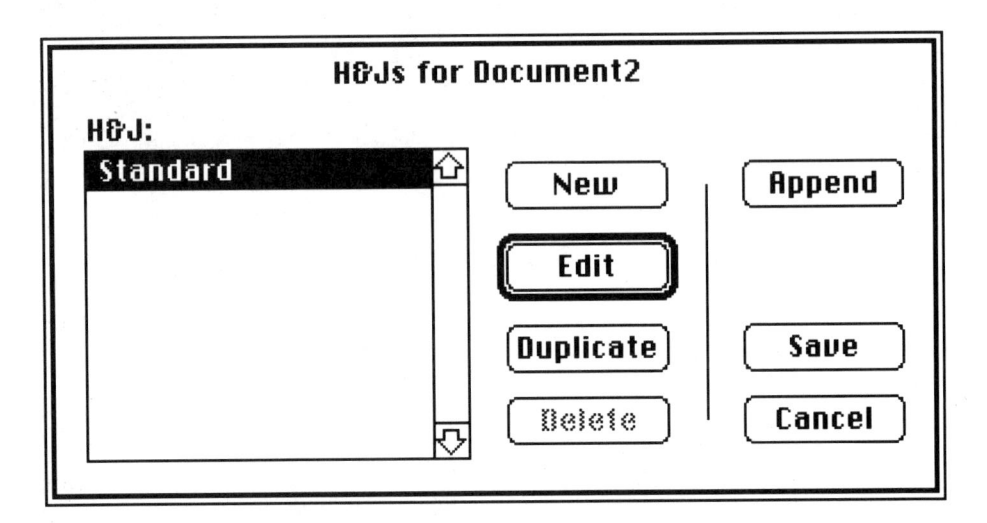

Figure 4-27. H&J dialog box.

4. Specify your hyphenation values.

   a. Click in the small box beside **Auto Hyphenation** to enable that feature. Then choose the details of auto hyphenation: the smallest word to hyphenate, minimum words before and after a hyphenation, and whether to hyphenate capitalized words.

   b. Set the maximum hyphens in a row and the maximum number of consecutive lines that can end with a hyphenated word.

   c. Enter a size for the hyphenation zone, the area measured from the right indent, where hyphenation can occur.

5. Set your justification values.

   a. You determine the maximum (up to 500%), minimum (down to 0%), and optimum amounts of space to add between words, in percents of the normal space for the font and size of the paragraph. QuarkXPress first tries to use the optimum value, then limits itself by the maximum and minimum values.

   b. You also set maximum (up to 100%), minimum (down to -50%), and optimum values for the space between characters.

   c. Set a size for the flush zone, measured from the right indent. (If the last line of a paragraph ends in this zone, the line will be justified. If it doesn't reach into this zone, the line won't be justified because the spread of the few characters and words in the line across the entire text box would look awkward.)

6. Give the new specifications a name.

7. Click the **OK** button and then save the specifications, giving them a name you'll recognize later.

Now, whenever you choose **Formats...** under the **Style** menu your new H&J specifications will appear in the pop-up **H&J** menu in the **Paragraph Formats** dialog box.

```
                Edit Hyphenation & Justification
Name:                         ┌─Justification Method─┐
┌─────────────────────┐        ┌─Word Spacing────────┐
│                     │        │ Minimum:  [100%]    │
└─────────────────────┘        │ Optimum:  [100%]    │
┌─⊠ Auto Hyphenation─────┐     │ Maximum:  [150%]    │
│ Smallest Word:    [6]  │     └─────────────────────┘
│ Minimum Before:   [3]  │     ┌─Character Spacing───┐
│ Minimum After:    [2]  │     │ Minimum:  [0%]      │
│ ☐ Break Capitalized Words │  │ Optimum:  [0%]      │
└─────────────────────────┘    │ Maximum:  [15%]     │
                               └─────────────────────┘
 Hyphens in a Row:  [unlimited]
 Hyphenation Zone:  [0"]        Flush Zone: [0"]

      ( OK )        ( Cancel )
```

Figure 4-28. Edit Hyphenation & Justification dialog box.

**Suggested Hyphenation and Hyphenation Exceptions.** In the **Utilities** menu you'll find two hyphenation commands: **Suggested Hyphenation** and **Hyphenation Exceptions.**

*Note:* Setting H&J specifications does not affect manual hyphenation. You can manually hyphenate any line of text at any time.

# TYPOGRAPHY

**Suggested Hyphenation** (with the shortcut of ⌘+H) simply displays the possible hyphenations of a selected word, as shown in Figure 4-29. The suggestion will be based on the currently applied H&J specification.

**Hyphenation Exceptions** offers a dialog box (shown in Figure 4-30) where you can create a list of exceptions to the H&J rules. When hyphenating, QuarkXPress will break these words as you show them hyphenated in the exceptions list, instead of as they would break by the rules of the H&J settings. For example, to restrict "disaffected" from breaking as shown in Figure 4-29, and leave it only the option of breaking in the middle, you could:

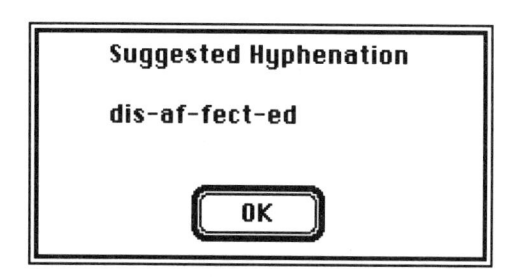

Figure 4-29. Suggested Hyphenation example.

1. Pull down the **Utilities** menu.
2. Select **Hyphenation Exceptions**.
3. Type *disaf-fected*.
4. Click on **Add**.
5. Click on **Save**.

Then QuarkXPress would only have the choice of hyphenating "disaffected" as "disaf-fected." You can add words to the list, delete them, and save your list of exceptions. You can also specify that words should *not* be hyphenated.

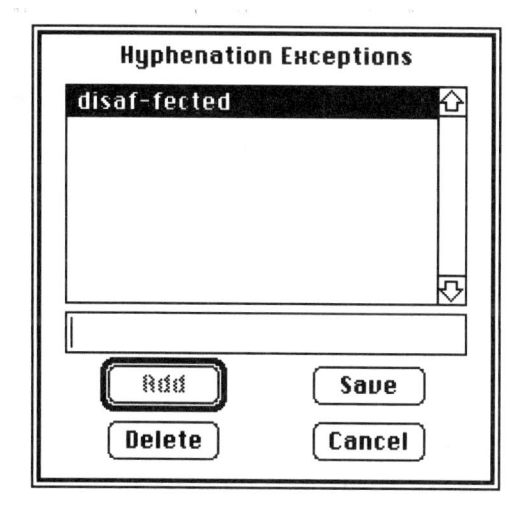

Figure 4-30. Hyphenation Exceptions dialog box.

141

## Widows and Orphans

Widows and orphans are "leftover" words hanging alone at the bottom of a paragraph, or leading into a new page. The first line of a paragraph that is on its own on the last line of a page is an orphan. The last line of a paragraph that is on its own at the top of a page is a widow. The macabre-sounding "control of widows and orphans" is actually an important subject to designers and publishers, because the viewer's or reader's eye will seize upon such isolated words, distracting from the overall design or content.

To make sure that a paragraph does not end with an orphan:

1. Select the text you wish to apply this constraint to (which usually means selecting all of the text).

2. Choose **Formats** from the **Style** menu to see the **Paragraph Formats** dialog box, as in Figure 4-31.

3. Click on the box beside **Keep with Next ¶** to keep the last line of a paragraph together with the first line of a following paragraph.

4. Check the **Keep Lines Together** box, the dialog box will expand as shown in Figure 4-31. This will offer you more options to control the way the last lines of a paragraph appear.
    a. Click on **All Lines in ¶** to prevent any paragraph from ever breaking.
    b. Specify at least 2 in the **Start:** and **End:** boxes (or use other, larger values) to tell QuarkXPress to keep together at least three lines from a paragraph at the top of a page and two lines at the bottom.

5. Click on **Apply** to see the results; click on **OK** to make them permanent. (You can save this control as part of a style sheet too.)

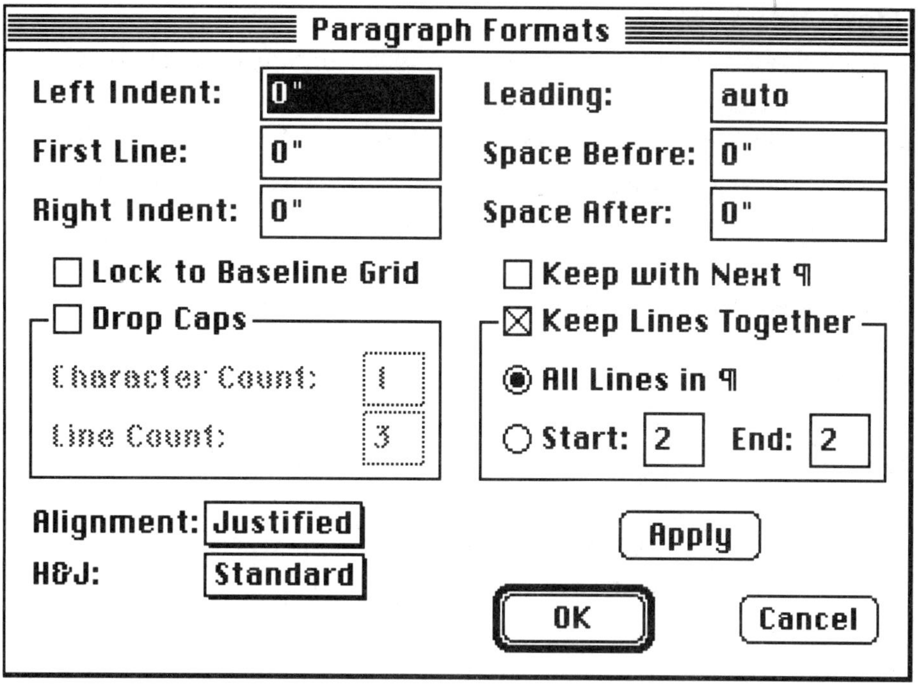

*TYPOGRAPHY*

Figure 4-31. Widow and orphan control with the Paragraph Formats dialog box.

### Technique

### Keeping Subheads with Their Paragraphs

*You can use the* **Keep with Next ¶** *check box in the* **Paragraph Formats** *dialog to dictate that subheads will be kept with their corresponding paragraphs. This will ensure that a column of text will not end with the subhead for the next paragraph.*

*To do this, select the paragraph subhead you wish to attach to the following paragraph, choose* **Formats** *from the* **Style** *menu, then check the* **Keep with Next ¶** *option.*

## Special Effects with Type

QuarkXPress 3.0 not only offers precise control of traditional publishing and design operations as kerning, tracking, and leading. It even packs some special commands you can turn loose on type, to stretch and squeeze it, to rotate it, to "reverse" it (against another color), and to automatically make drop caps (larger initial capital letters) of it. The remainder of this chapter covers these operations.

**Horizontal Scaling.** Another great feature of QuarkXPress 3.0 is the ability to change the horizontal scale of any typeface you're using. That is, it can stretch letters so they take up more space horizontally or squeeze them so they take up less horizontal space, where kerning and tracking affect only the space in between letters. So, for every typeface you're using in QuarkXPress you also have an entire range of condensed and extended versions of the same typeface! Figure 4-32 shows an example.

**Figure 4-32. Horizontal scaling: expanded lower case h (400% scaling), condensed upper case B (25% scaling).**

To change the scale of some text:

1. Select the text.
2. Choose **Horizontal Scale...** from the **Style** menu.
3. In the **Horizontal Scale...** dialog box that appears, enter a percentage value from 25% to 400%. Values less than 100% will condense the text, while values above 100% will extend it.

**Warning:** *Remember, though QuarkXPress 3.0 will condense and extend any typeface, to print these scaled versions at all well, you must have that typeface's corresponding "printer" font in your system folder for it to download correctly to your laser printer or other high-resolution output device.*

**Reversed Text.** Reversed text shows characters as holes in a shaded area instead of as shaded patterns on a blank area. Sometimes a lengthy "pull quote" or subhead will carry more impact if reversed. There are a couple of ways to do this in QuarkXPress. Some use graphics techniques described in Chapter 5, using anchored rules (lines). Here's how to reverse text in its own text box.

1. Create a new text box large enough to hold your text and place it somewhere away from your main body text.

2. Type or flow your text into it.

3. Choose **Select All** from the **Edit** menu (⌘+A is the shortcut when the **Content** tool is selected).

4. Pull down the **Style** menu and choose **Color**, then select **White** as your color.

5. While the text box is still selected, choose **Modify** from the **Edit** menu. (Or choose ⌘+M, the keyboard equivalent.)

6. Set the background color and shade to something in which the white text will appear clearly (such as Black, 80% shade), as shown in Figure 4-33.

**Figure 4-33. Reversing text in its own text box.**

7. Now place the reversed text box into your layout. Since you didn't adjust the text runaround attributes, it will displace any body text appearing around it.

**Text Box Rotation.** Text boxes (like picture boxes) may be rotated around an arbitrary point in increments of .001 degree. Some other design or desktop publishing programs let you rotate text, but not this precisely. All text in rotated text boxes is fully editable at any time. Just select the text with the **Editing** tool (as you would any other text you want to edit) and choose your style or text modifications.

You can rotate the text box manually, by choosing a value in the **Measurements** palette, or by choosing a rotation angle in the **Text Box**

**Specifications** dialog box that appears when you choose **Modify** from the **Item** menu. Figure 4-34 shows some text rotated at various angles.

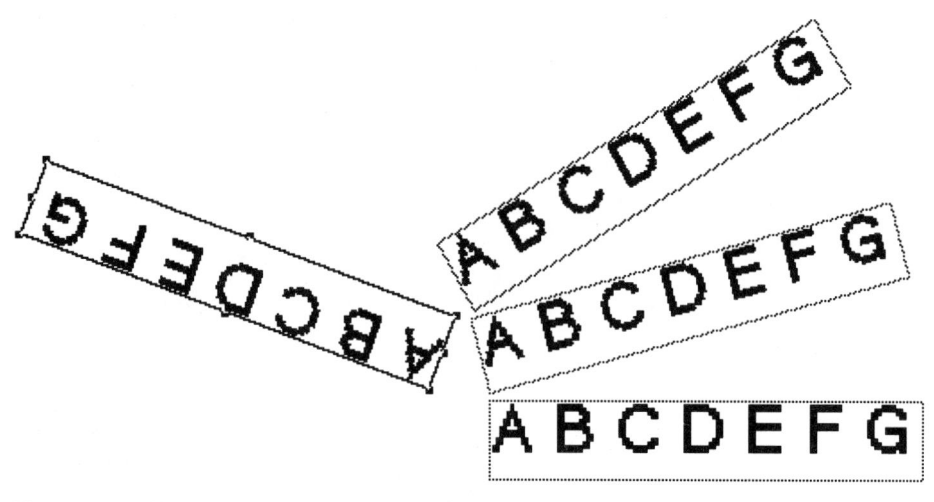

**Figure 4-34. Examples of rotated text boxes.**

To rotate a text box manually:

1. Choose the **Rotation** tool from the **Tools** palette at the side of your document window (as described in Chapter 2).

2. Select the text box you wish to rotate.

3. Click a center point around which you want the box to rotate, then drag the cursor away from the center point in the direction you want the box to rotate. A line will extend from the center point indicating the angle at which the box is being rotated. This line will help you roughly align boxes parallel to each other when rotating subsequent boxes.

4. See how the box angle value in the **Measurements** palette changes as the box rotates. This value can help you judge when two objects are parallel.

5. If the manual rotation doesn't quite place the box exactly at the angle you want, you can select that rotation value in the **Measurements** palette and change that value by typing in a new number. Also, choosing **Modify** from the **Item** menu will produce the **Text Box Specifications** dialog box, which contains an entry for box angle.

> **Extra!**
>
> *Add extra impact to your headline by using a very heavy compressed typeface and "bleed" it off of the edge of the page. QuarkXPress 3.0 accommodates bleeds automatically. Rotate your headline text box to your desired angle, then move the rotated text box so that part of the text begins to run off the edge of the page. Use discretion. Moving a word of text too far beyond the edge of the page can make it unreadable, or at least less recognizable.*

**Drop Caps.** Drop caps are larger initial capital letters that lead off a paragraph or section. Where some design and publishing programs only handle drop caps through a series of commands, QuarkXPress 3.0 makes drop caps an option in the **Paragraph Formats** dialog box under the **Style** menu. When you click the check-box by **Drop Caps**, the dialog box will expand to show options for the depth of the initial character in lines, and the number of initial characters to lead the paragraph, as you can see in Figure 4-35.

Remember, you are not limited to drop caps that simply drop to a specified line depth. You can also change the depth, height, width and margins of drop caps.

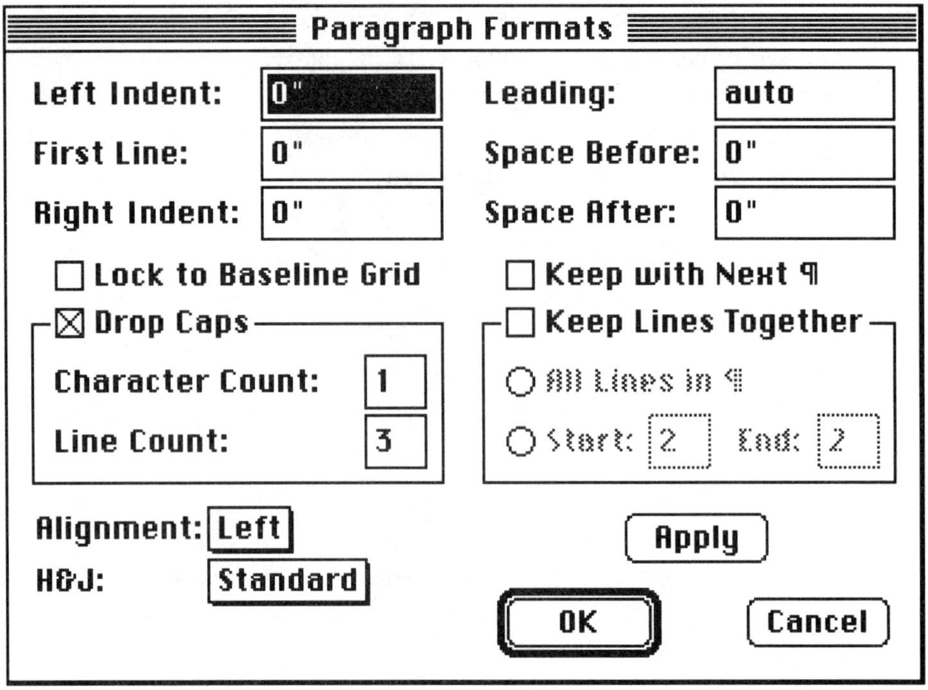

Figure 4-35. Paragraph Formats dialog box with Drop Caps option checked.

To create large initial drop caps:

1. Place your text insertion cursor anywhere in the paragraph you want to affect.

2. Choose **Formats...** from the **Style** menu.

3. Click the **Drop Caps** check box.

4. Specify the number of drop cap characters you want to lead the paragraph and the number of lines of text you want the characters to drop.

5. Click the **Apply** button to check that the changes you've selected are what you are expecting.

6. If the drop caps look all right to you, click the **OK** button to finish the change.

The initial letter will set itself at the baseline of the line you've specified as your cap depth, and will not extend above the ascent line of the first line of text. For example, if you've specified a three-line drop, the character will extend down to the baseline of the third line of the paragraph and be no taller than the tallest letter on the first line. Check Figure 4-36.

> The initial letter will set itself at the baseline of the line you've specified as your cap depth, and will not extend above the ascent line of the first line of text. For example, if you've specified a three-line drop, the character will extend down to the baseline of the third line of the paragraph and be no taller than the tallest letter on the first line.

**Figure 4-36. Drop Cap limits.**

You can specify that the initial cap extend above the ascenders of the first line of text by selecting only that letter and choosing **Size** and then **Other...** under the **Style** menu. You'll notice that the size designation is now measured as a percentage of the actual character's size. You can type in a larger size for the initial cap to extend it above the ascent of the first line of text. You can enlarge an initial cap up to 400% of its original size.

**Hanging Drop Caps.** Making hanging drop caps is easy (hanging drop caps "hang" outside of the margins of your paragraphs, as shown in Figure 4-37).

1. Create a paragraph with a large drop cap.

2. Then, while the paragraph is still selected, change the the left margin to allow as much space as the width of your initial cap letter.

3. Put that same amount of space as a negative value in the "First Line" field of the **Paragraph Formats** dialog box. You can see the amount of space the initial cap occupies by checking the ruler that appears at the top of the text box when the **Paragraph Formats** dialog is visible. If the margin doesn't quite line up with the edge of the letter, adjust the margin by changing the value in the **Paragraph Formats** box or by changing the kerning value for the space between the initial cap and the next letter of the text. Don't be afraid to experiment with the character width of the initial cap letter.

Subheads are a great way to enhance text by highlighting key topics and key words leading off paragraphs. But there's more to creating a subhead than just

Subheads are a great way to enhance text by highlighting key topics and key words leading off paragraphs. But there's more to creating a subhead than just

**Figure 4-37. Hanging drop caps.**

**Drop Caps with Drop Shadows.** You can make impressive drop caps with drop shadows. Shadowed text is a style option, but the shadow that ordinary typefaces place behind the character is not customizable. Here's how to create your own drop shadow to indicate more depth:

1. Place your text cursor (using the **Content** tool) anywhere in a paragraph of text.

# TYPOGRAPHY

2. Choose **Formats...** from the **Style** menu (or use the keyboard equivalent ⌘+Shift+F).

3. Click the **Drop Caps** check box.

4. You can choose to drop the cap as much as eight lines deep. Highlight the **Line Count** field and type 4. We want this letter to be moderately huge. Click **OK**.

5. Now select just the initial letter that leads your paragraph and choose **Other...** from the **Size** option under the **Style** menu. Type in 200%. The drop cap is now complete.

6. Next we add our own special drop shadow to complete the effect. Select only the initial cap letter and choose **Copy** from the **Edit** menu.

7. Create a new text box outside of the area of the original text box. Make sure it is big enough to hold the large drop cap letter. Select it using the **Editing** tool and choose **Copy** from the **Edit** menu. This will paste your initial cap letter into the new text box.

8. The letter will appear at 200% of its original 12 point size (assuming that's the size you started with), because it is set to drop four lines deep and be 200% of its original size as compared to the rest of the text in the paragraph. Since there is no other text in its box for it to be measured against, it is appearing at this size by default. To rectify this press the space bar once. This will insert a blank character that is the original text size, 12 points, allowing the initial cap to grow to its proper size.

9. Choose **Runaround...** from the **Item** menu and set the runaround specifications to **None**. This will allow you to move the text box to be placed near the original text box without disturbing the flow of the original text.

151

USING QUARKXPRESS

10. Select the original text box, the one with the body copy, and set its runaround specifications to **None**.

11. Before moving the smaller text box with the large initial cap back onto the page with the original text, select the huge initial cap letter inside and set its shade to 40% by choosing **Shade...** from the **Style** menu.

12. Now use the **Item** tool to move the new initial cap (which is now your drop cap shadow) onto your page but offset from the original initial cap. Since it was created after the original text box, it will rest on top of the original text box. Because you are using the **Item** tool, the new text box should appear transparent over the original text box, and the gray letter should cover parts of the image.

13. Move the new text box with the dropped shadow around until it is where you think it looks best, then select the text box with your new drop cap and choose **Send to Back** from the **Item** menu. This will place the new text box behind the original and have the effect of creating a custom drop shadow that the body text of the original text box will overprint. You can see the results in Figure 4-38.

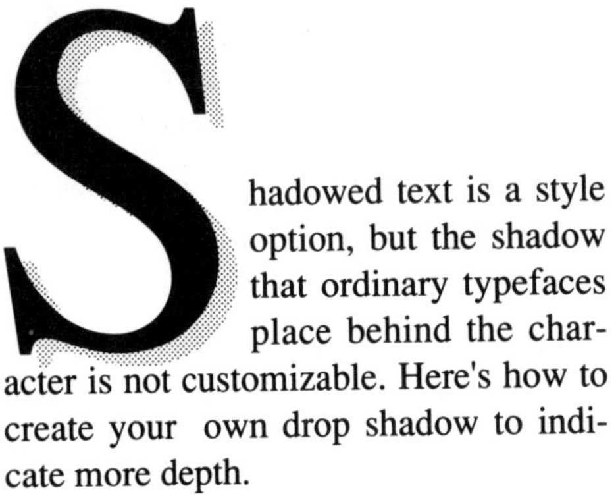

Shadowed text is a style option, but the shadow that ordinary typefaces place behind the character is not customizable. Here's how to create your own drop shadow to indicate more depth.

**Figure 4-38. Large drop cap with drop shadow.**

14. If the dropped shadow is not visible, chances are that you've left the **Runaround** of the original text box on **Item**. Change it to **None** to make it transparent. You should now be able to see the drop shadow through the original text box.

152

## TYPOGRAPHY

### Special Characters

Letters, numerals, and punctuation aren't enough to make most design or desktop publishing documents. You also need typographical "special characters," such as the ellipsis (...), that will not break a line the way three periods could. Most typefaces in QuarkXPress 3.0 include their own versions of these special characters.

Most of the special characters are available through a combination of the **Shift** and **Option** keys and characters on the keyboard. The following special characters are available with keyboard combinations (the + indicates that the keys are pressed simultaneously, and the hyphen key is the -).

| | |
|---|---|
| Breaking standard hyphen | **hyphen** |
| Nonbreaking standard hyphen (won't break to new line between words) | **⌘+=** |
| Discretionary (soft) hyphen | **⌘+hyphen** |
| Nonbreaking en-dash | **Option+hyphen** |
| Breaking em-dash | **Option+Shift+hyphen** |
| Nonbreaking em-dash | **⌘+Option+hyphen** |
| Indent here | **⌘+\\** |
| Discretionary new line | **⌘+Return** |
| New paragraph | **Return** |
| New line | **Shift+Return** |
| New column or new page | **Enter** |
| New box | **Shift+Enter** |
| Breaking standard space | **space bar** |
| Nonbreaking standard space | **⌘+space bar** |
| Breaking en-space | **Option+space bar** |
| Nonbreaking en-space | **⌘+Option+space bar** |
| Breaking half en-space | **Option+Shift+space bar** |
| Breaking punctuation space | **Shift+space bar** |

153

## Tips for Type

QuarkXPress makes possible some very interesting type effects that are easy to do and versatile.

**Type Reversed out of Type.** To create type reversed out of type:

1. Start by creating a text box to hold some large display type. Then type in a word and adjust its style to be 96 points tall and track the text so that all the letters are touching or are nearly touching.

2. Create another text box over the one holding your text and set its runaround attributes to **None**. Type in a phrase or word that you want to reverse out of the larger background text, select it, and change its color to **White**.

3. Before de-selecting the text and the text box, track the letters so they are spread out to fill the space better.

4. Select both boxes with the **Item** tool and choose **Group** from the **Item** menu.

Make sure that the background type is a very heavy and compressed type so you'll have plenty of area in which to reverse your foreground type.

Also make certain that the reversed letters are spaced properly so that they are all reversed out of a background color; white letters that are partially or entirely positioned over a white background will not show up when printed.

Some easy variations on this idea are:

1. Rotate one or the other text boxes before grouping them.

2. Try using different typefaces or styles for each text.

3. Try reversing the larger text out of a background color, then printing the smaller foreground type solid over the white background letters. See Figure 4-39.

**TYPOGRAPHY**

**Figure 4-39.** An example of white type reversed over black type.

**Upside-Down Type.** QuarkXPress' text rotation capabilities can make for some interesting and diverse type effects. This one is simple and can be varied.

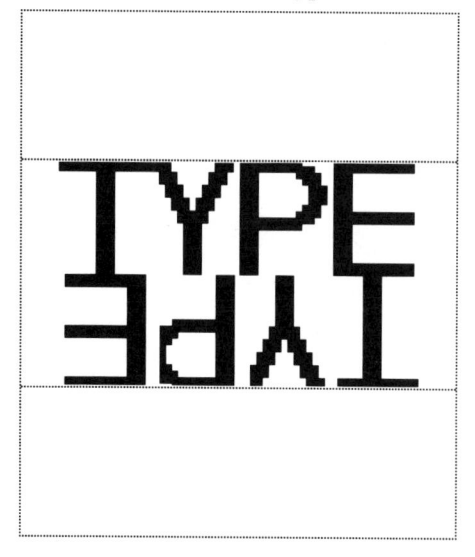

**Figure 4-40.** Upside-down type created by rotating and grouping text.

1. Create a new text box. Type in a word or phrase, make it extra large, center it, then make the text box transparent.

2. Now duplicate the text box and rotate it 180°. Move it so it lies directly beneath the original text box with the bottoms of its letters touching the bottoms of the original letters, as in Figure 4-40.

3. Group the two text boxes together.

155

# Graphics

There are basically two kinds of graphic elements in QuarkXPress 3.0: lines and pictures. Lines can be anywhere on a document; pictures must be in picture boxes. Both can add to or even be vital elements of a design or illustration. QuarkXPress lets you overlap and overlay text, lines, and pictures, showing one through the other, or wrapping text around graphics.

QuarkXPress 3.0 offers precise control over the graphic images that you import into your documents. You can control placement of images to within 1/1000 of a unit (pica, inch, cicero, or whatever you specify); rotation of images and/or the boxes containing them to within .001 degrees; borders, border styles, weights (thicknesses) to within .001 point; image color; background color; and most importantly, you can control how text runs around an image.

This chapter explains how to create and edit both lines and pictures.

## Lines

Lines are useful for organizing, decorating, or emphasizing parts of a design or publication. In such work, lines are often referred to as *rules*. Working with lines, or rules, in QuarkXPress 3.0 is just as easy as working with other items. You create and control them in the same manner as picture boxes and text boxes. You can set their **Runaround...** mode, duplicate them, step-and-repeat them, group them with other elements, or lock them from changes. But lines also come with some of their own styling considerations and menus, as explained in the following section.

## Line Types

There are two line types in QuarkXPress: orthogonal (also called "constrained") lines and conventional lines.

Both types are straight. If you want a curved line, you'll need to import it from some other graphics program as a picture into a picture box (as discussed later on in this chapter).

There's a tool in the **Tool** palette for each line type.

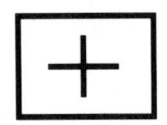

**Figure 5-1. The Orthogonal Line tool.**

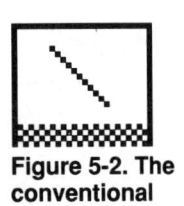

The **Orthogonal Line** tool, shown in Figure 5-1, can only draw vertical or horizontal lines. (Try it — regardless of which direction you drag the mouse with that tool, the line only stretches horizontally or vertically.)

**Figure 5-2. The conventional Line tool.**

The **Line** tool, shown in Figure 5-2, draws lines in any direction, though if you hold down the **Shift** key while drawing with the **Line** tool you'll only be able to draw horizontal, vertical, or 45-degree lines.

### Creating a Line

To create a new line in QuarkXPress:

1. Choose one of the line creation tools (as shown in Figures 5-1 and 5-2).

2. Click at one desired line endpoint in your document, then drag the mouse to the other endpoint.

### Changing Lines — Moving, Stretching, Shrinking

If a line isn't in precisely the right position, you can adjust it in several ways. First, select it by clicking on it with the **Item** tool. Then you can do one of the following:

1. Drag it to a new position.

*GRAPHICS*

2. Drag one of its endpoint handles to change the line's length and direction. The tool cursor is "smart;" it knows what part of the line it's over and changes to the appropriate tool to indicate what kind of change you can make to the line you selected. When the cursor is over the body of a line, it changes to the **Item** tool, letting you move the entire line without changing its orientation on the page. When the cursor is over an end point, it changes to the pointing hand cursor, letting you change the location of that end point.

3. Choose the **Modify** dialog box from the **Item** menu and use the **Mode** pop-up menu (as shown Figure 5-3) to select the line point — left point, right point, end points, or midpoint — you want to work on. Then enter the coordinates, angles, and lengths in the appropriate slots and click on **OK**.

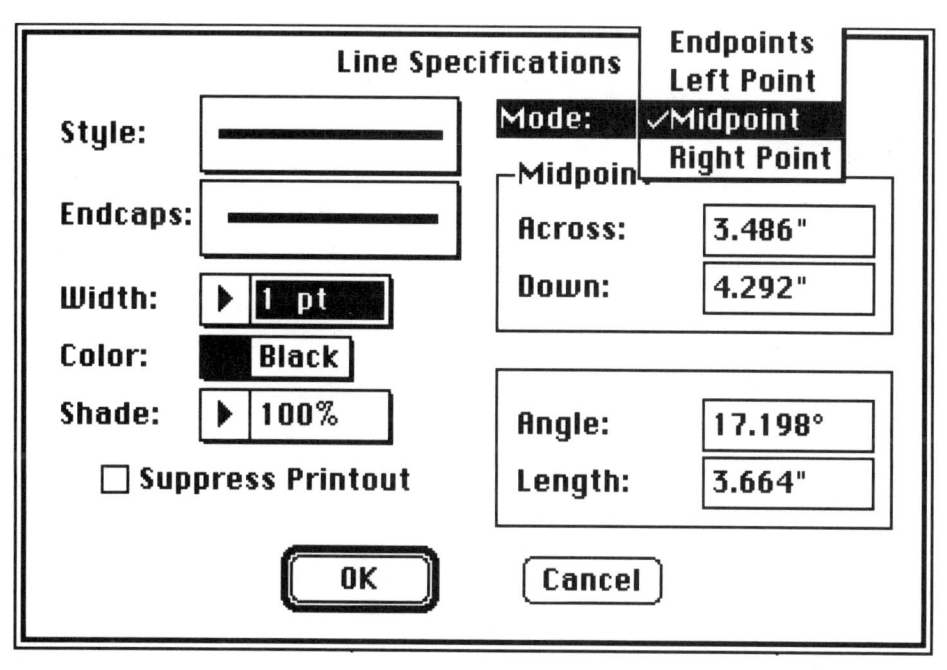

Figure 5-3. The Mode pop-up menu in the Modify dialog box for adjusting a line.

4. Double-click on the line with the **Item** tool. This brings up the same **Modify** dialog box from Option 3 (shown in Figure 5-3).

5. Use the **Measurements** palette. Click on its pop-up menu (as shown in Figure 5-4) to select from left point, right point, endpoints, or midpoint (as in the **Modify** dialog box option above). Then double-click on the coordinate, length, or angle you wish to change, type the new value, and press **Enter** (or click somewhere else on the pasteboard).

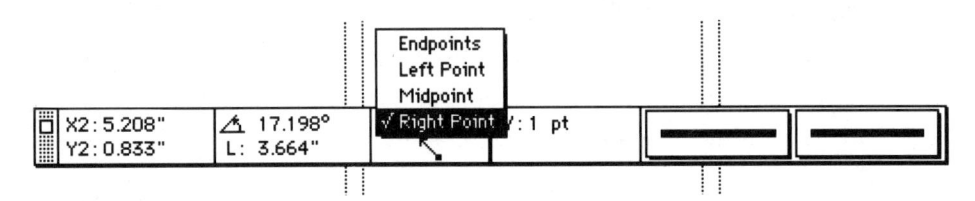

**Figure 5-4.** Using the Measurements palette to adjust a line.

## Line Styles

QuarkXPress 3.0 offers several style choices for your lines:

- 11 line styles (solid, dashed, etc.).
- 6 line endcap choices (arrowhead on left, arrowhead on right, and so on).
- 7 line width choices (plus a custom-width option).
- Colors (as many as in your palette).
- Shades (from 0% to 100%, in 1% increments).

To change the style of any selected line, you can do any of the following:

1. Pull down the **Style** menu and choose one of the sub-menus there (as in Figure 5-5).

*GRAPHICS*

2. Select the **Modify** dialog box from the **Item** menu (or double-click on the line to reach this dialog box). Then use its menus (as in Figure 5-6) to change the styles.

3. Use the pop-up menus of the **Measurements** palette (as in Figure 5-7).

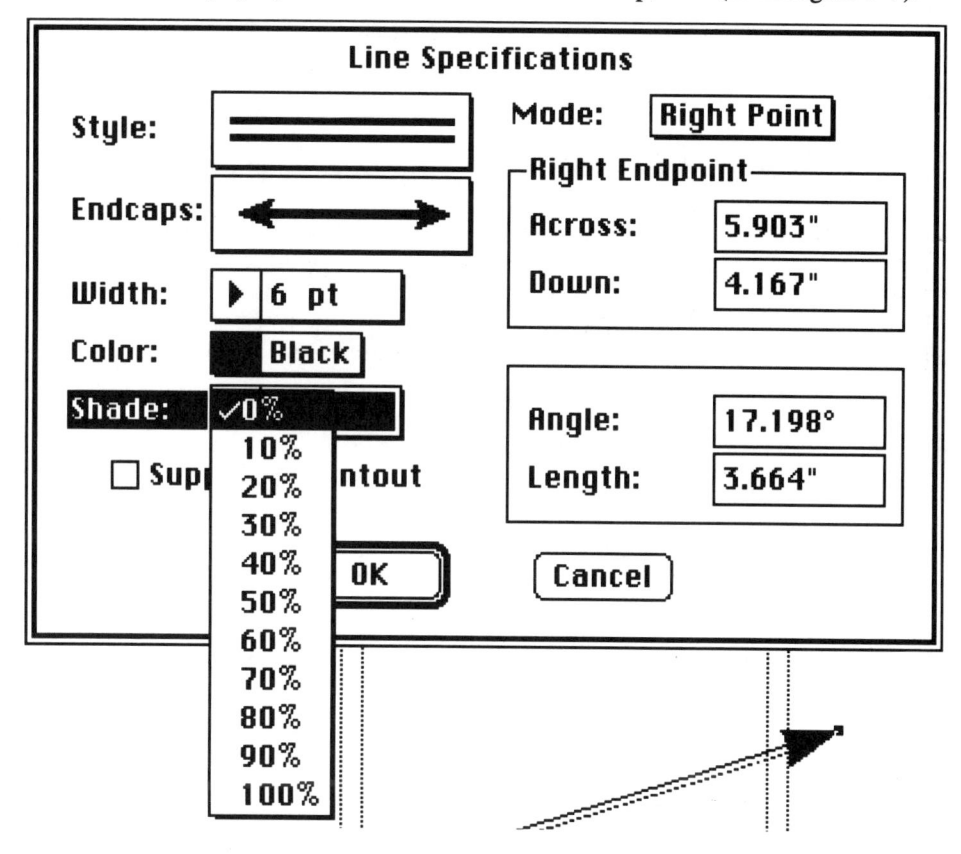

Figure 5-5. Line styles through the Style menu (using style as example).

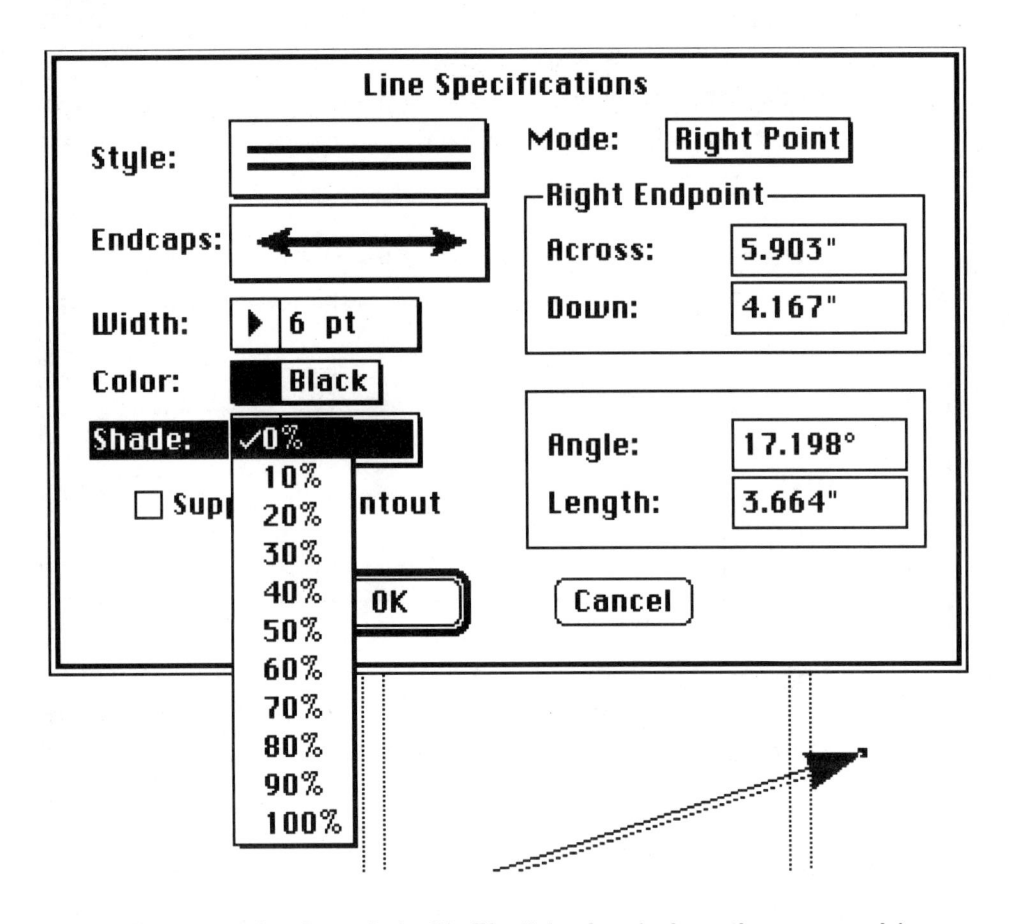

Figure 5-6. Line styles through the Modify dialog box (using color as example).

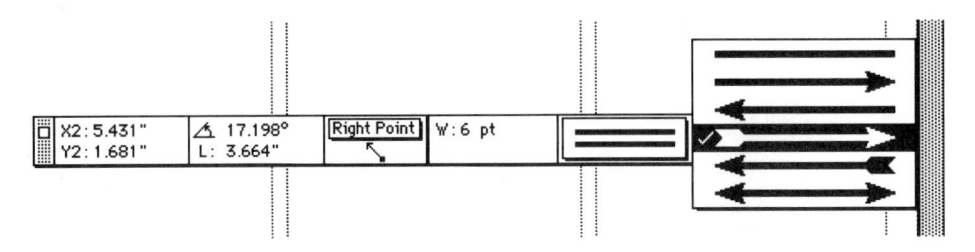

Figure 5-7. Line styles through Measurements palette (using ends as example).

When you're changing line color, remember that you're not limited to the eight colors appearing there. You can add colors to the palette by choosing **Colors...** from the **Edit** menu. (See Chapter 6 for details.)

## Anchoring Lines to Text

One of QuarkXPress 3.0's new features is the ability to anchor rules to text. When you anchor a rule to text, the rule travels with that text. If the text box it's in changes in width, the rule changes width accordingly.

To anchor a rule to text:

1. Select the text box in which you want to place the rules.

2. Place the text insertion cursor into the paragraph or paragraphs that you want to lead or follow with a rule.

3. Choose **Rules** from the **Style** menu (or use ⌘+**Shift**+**N**). You'll see the **Paragraph Rules** dialog box, as shown in Figure 5-8.

4. Choose the attributes you want from the **Paragraph Rules** dialog box.

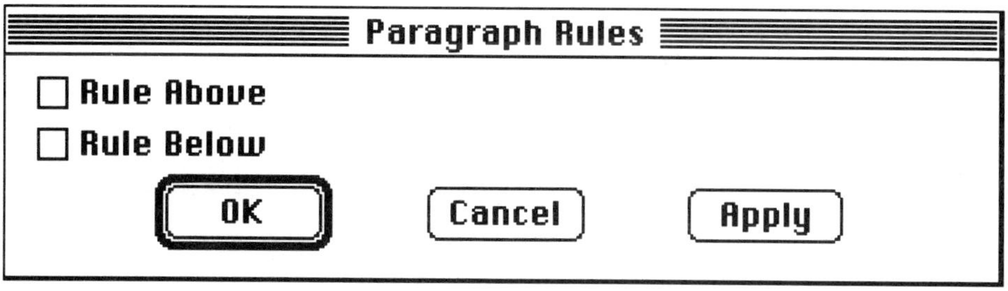

Figure 5-8. Paragraph Rules dialog box.

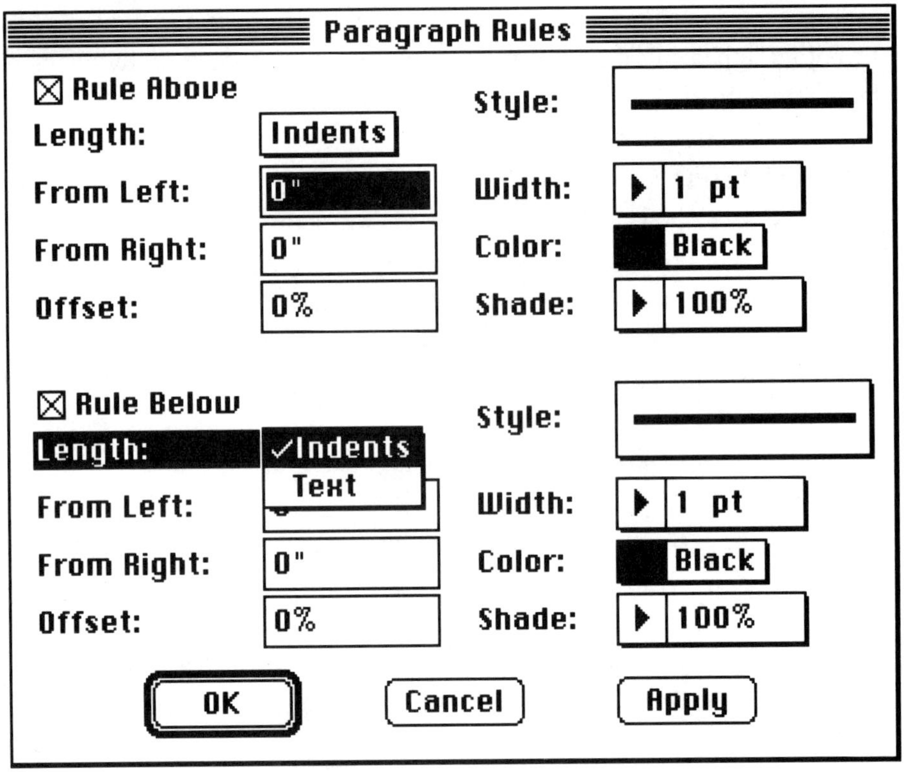

Figure 5-9. Expanded Paragraph Rules dialog box.

The **Rule Above** and **Rule Below** check boxes let you specify that a rule precede or follow the selected paragraph. When you click in the appropriate boxes to select **Rules Above** or **Rules Below**, you see the extra choices appear in an expanded version of the dialog box, as in Figure 5-9. The **Length** pop-up menu lets you define the actual length of the line relative to the column width. You can set a rule to extend from margin to margin or to any distance you specify between the right or left margins. The offset value is a percentage of the type size preceding the rule. Offset places the rule a distance away from the text. It may be defined in inches, points, millimeters, or ciceros, and it can be defined in increments of .001 of any unit of measure.

# GRAPHICS

**Extra!**

## Making Reversed Subheads with Anchored Rules
*Create your own reversed headlines or subheads with anchored rules.*

1. *Place the text insertion cursor anywhere in the line of text you want to reverse.*

2. *Triple-click to select the entire line of text in the subhead.*

3. *Choose **Color** from the **Style** menu and select **White**. (This demonstration assumes you want to reverse white out of a black rule.)*

4. *Choose **Rules...** from the **Style** menu. (The keyboard equivalent is **Shift+⌘+N**.)*

5. *Choose the **Rule Above** check box. The **Paragraph Rules** dialog box expands to show all of the choices for **Indents**, **Offset**, **Style**, **Width**, **Color**, and **Shade**.*

6. *Choose a width for the line that's at least as large, or larger, than the point size of the type you want to reverse, so that it covers the descenders and ascenders of the letters.*

7. *Select the field for offset distance. Offset lets you specify the distance from the midpoint of the rule to the baseline of the line of text as a percentage of the vertical distance from the ascent of the first line of text and the descent of the previous paragraph. You can also choose an absolute value for the offset. An absolute value can be a positive value of up to 15 inches and a negative value of up to half the width of the rule. Specify a negative value for the offset and include the value definition (" for inches, pt for points).*

> *(continued from page 165)*
>
> 8. Click on the **Apply** button to see if the head has reversed.
>
> 9. If it hasn't, try typing in a new value for the offset measurement and continue clicking on the **Apply** button until the rule is placed exactly where you want it.

## Pictures

Pictures are graphic images that you import from other programs. Each picture must fit into a picture box, just as text fits into text boxes. Within these picture boxes, you can size, clip, style, and perform other manipulations on the pictures. As with other items in QuarkXPress (lines and text boxes), you can overlap and overlay picture boxes so that they obscure, show through, or shape other items (for example, pictures can have text wrap around them).

### Creating Picture Boxes

Boxes are the building blocks of page layout with QuarkXPress 3.0. Like containers, they hold elements brought into or created in QuarkXPress. Picture boxes are easy to distinguish from text boxes: They're automatically marked with diagonal rules extending from corner to corner, whereas text boxes have only a fine dotted guideline around the edge. Picture boxes also come in a variety of shapes, from rectangular (such as text boxes) to rounded rectangles, ellipses, and polygons. Figure 5-10 shows the four kinds of picture boxes.

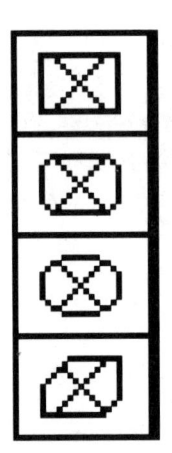

**Figure 5-10. The four picture box shapes.**

You can create new picture boxes at any time, using any of the four tools shown in Figure 5-11.

> *To create perfect square or circular boxes, hold down the **Shift** key while you click and drag. This constrains the box's shape to a square or circle.*

The first tool on the **Tool** palette creates square-cornered boxes for pictures, the second makes round-cornered shapes, the third makes circular and elliptical shapes, and the fourth makes free-form polygons. You can edit and modify each type of box and its contents at any time.

To create a new picture box or text box, select one of these tools from the palette, then click and drag from an origin point on your page.

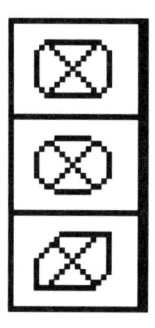

**Figure 5-11. Picture box creation tools.**

### Drawing a Polygon Picture Box

Creating polygon (free-shaped) picture boxes is slightly tougher than creating the other picture boxes. After you select the **Polygon Picture Box** creation tool in the **Tool** palette, click at each vertex (corner) of the box-to-be (these are called the control points). A line follows your cursor around, indicating the boundaries of your new picture box. To finish the picture box, click at the original starting point. You can also finish the polygon picture box by

> *You can create twisted picture boxes that show the same picture in what appears to be two frames. Simply cross the final picture-box boundary across any other picture-box boundaries.*

double-clicking at any point. The picture box connects a straight line from that point to the origin point.

## Reshaping Picture Boxes

Once the picture box is drawn, you can reshape it in several ways. First select it, then do one of the following:

1. Click on one of its handles and drag that handle to a new position.

2. Choose **Modify** from the **Item** menu, then change the box's width, height, or corner radius.

3. Click on and change a dimension in the **Measurements** palette.

4. Choose another shape from the **Picture Box Shape** pop-up menu of the **Item** menu. (Figure 5-12 shows this in action.) If you choose the polygon shape, you can then choose **Reshape Polygon** from the same menu and create a new shape by rearranging the handle points or adding new handle points to the polygon.

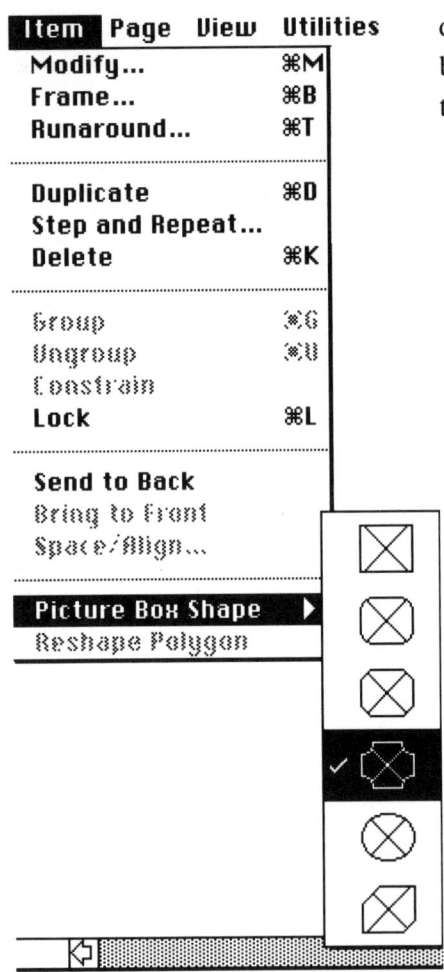

Figure 5-12. Picture Box Shape menu.

## GRAPHICS

**Extra!**

*How many times have you wanted to create cartoon balloons and had to quit QuarkXPress, go into your favorite PostScript drawing program, then waste time going back and forth between programs to get the shape just right? Here's a tip that helps you make your balloons quickly and easily without leaving QuarkXPress.*

1. *Make a circular picture box with the **Circular Picture Box** creation tool.*

2. *Choose **Polygon Shape** from the **Item** menu.*

3. *Choose **Reshape Polygon** from the same menu. A collection of control points then appears around the circle.*

4. *Click on one of the control points and drag it down to a point.*

5. *Voila! Homemade cartoon balloons, just like Mom used to make. (See Figure 5-13.)*

*A word of caution: The control points are always connected by straight lines. At larger sizes, these straight lines become more evident. Take this into account when deciding the size of your balloon and the thickness of its border.*

Figure 5-13. Making a cartoon balloon by reshaping a circle converted into a polygon.

## Moving and Positioning Picture Boxes

You can move the entire picture box around by using one of these methods:

1. Choose the **Item** tool and click and drag the box around on the page. (Use the **Measurements** palette to monitor the changes you make.)

2. Select the box, choose **Modify** from the **Item** menu, then change the position values in the **Picture Box Specifications** dialog box (see Figure 5-14).

3. Select the box and change the position values in the **Measurements** palette from the **View** menu (as shown in Figure 5-15). The values on the left side of the palette are for the box's position.

*GRAPHICS*

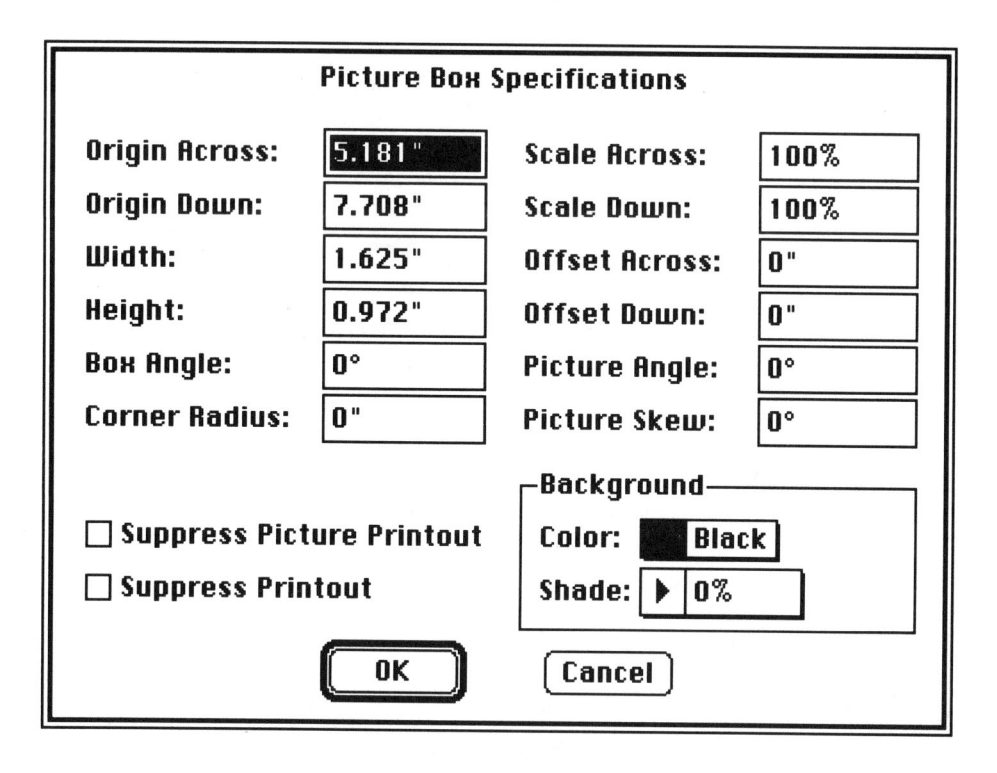

```
              Picture Box Specifications

   Origin Across:  [5.181"]    Scale Across:  [100%]
   Origin Down:    [7.708"]    Scale Down:    [100%]
   Width:          [1.625"]    Offset Across: [0"]
   Height:         [0.972"]    Offset Down:   [0"]
   Box Angle:      [0°]        Picture Angle: [0°]
   Corner Radius:  [0"]        Picture Skew:  [0°]

                              ┌─Background─────────┐
   ☐ Suppress Picture Printout │ Color: [ Black ]   │
   ☐ Suppress Printout         │ Shade: [▶] [0%]    │
                              └────────────────────┘
              ( OK )          ( Cancel )
```

Figure 5-14. The Picture Specifications dialog box settings for changing the position of a picture box.

```
X: 5.333"   W: 0.917"   ∠ 0°
Y: 6.278"   H: 1.139"   ⋉ 0"
```

Figure 5-15. The Measurements palette settings for changing the position of a picture box.

You don't have to keep your picture box on the page area. You can move the box off the edge of the page into the pasteboard area at the sides of the page. This allows images to bleed off any page edge.

171

> **Extra!**
>
> *If you're using the **Content** tool and want to quickly and temporarily switch to the **Item** tool without mousing over to the **Tools** palette, just hold down the ⌘ key while the cursor is over the picture box. The cursor turns into the **Item** tool for as long as you hold down the ⌘ key, allowing you to move the image around on the page without switching tools.*

### Framing a Picture Box

Each picture box can have a frame, or border. You can set the width, color, and shade of that frame. To do that, select the box, then:

1. Choose **Frame...** from the **Item** menu.

2. From the **Frame Specifications** dialog box that appears (as in Figure 5-16), choose:

   a. **style** — by clicking on one of the displayed styles

   b. **width** — by choosing from the pop-up menu, or typing a value in the **Width** field.

   c. **color** — by choosing from the pop-up menu

   d. **shade** — by choosing from the pop-up menu, or by typing a value in the **Shade** field.

   The color, shade, and style you choose are displayed on the title of the dialog box.

3. Click on **OK** when you're done.

You can also create custom frames, as explained in Chapter 2.

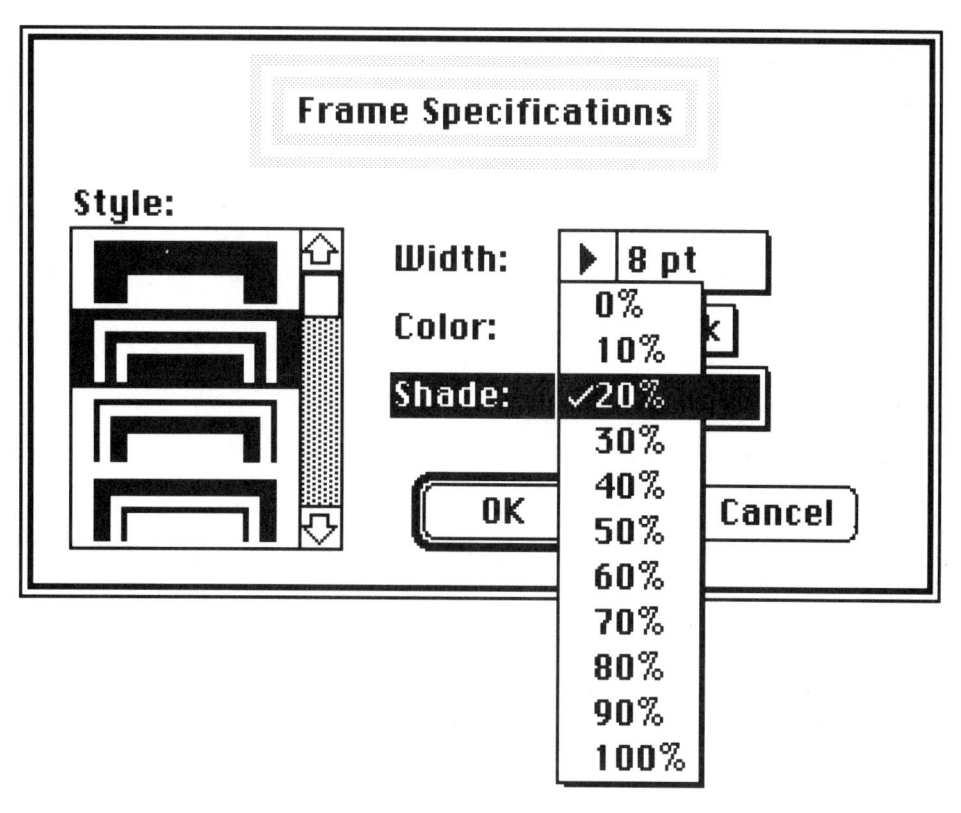

Figure 5-16. Frame Specifications dialog box.

## Picture Box Runaround

The **Automatic Text Runaround** feature is what really put QuarkXPress on the map when the program first appeared in 1986. Since then, this feature has been refined to include new capabilities and options.

Whenever you create a new picture box in QuarkXPress, it's opaque and text automatically runs around it. (This is also known as *wraparound* or *flowing text around*.) That is, the words and characters in the text move out of the way of an overlapping picture box, flowing down in their own box to fit around the picture. Figure 5-17 shows a simple example.

173

# USING QUARKXPRESS

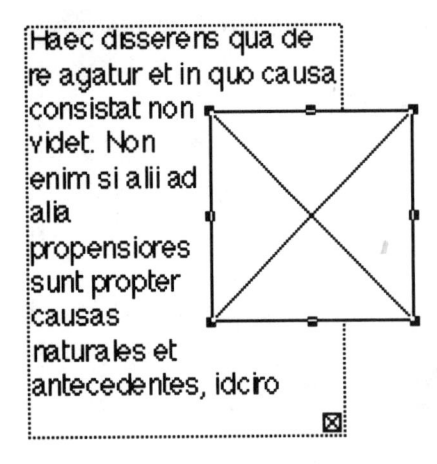

Haec disserens qua de re agatur et in quo causa consistat non videt. Non enim si alii ad alia propensiores sunt propter causas naturales et antecedentes, idciro

**Figure 5-17. Example of simple Runaround... for a picture box overlapping a text box.**

There are several kinds of runaround options. While the picture box is selected, you can change its runaround specifications by choosing **Runaround...** from the **Item** menu. You then see the dialog box shown in Figure 5-18. (The keyboard shortcut for this is ⌘+T.)

The **Runaround Specifications** dialog box lets you choose from four modes for text to runaround the image:

**None** makes the picture box and its contents transparent, allowing text to run over the image.

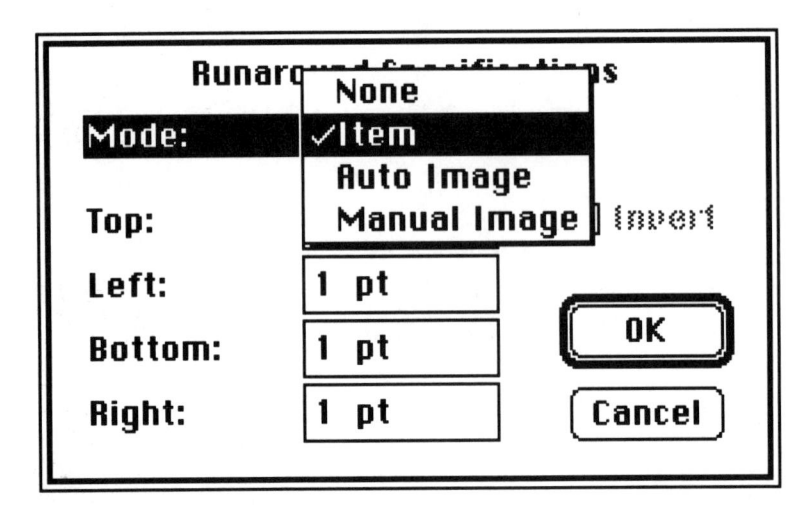

**Figure 5-18. Runaround... dialog box.**

174

**Item** makes the picture box itself opaque and causes text to runaround the boundaries of the picture box.

**Auto Image** causes the picture box itself to become transparent, but text runs around the image within it. You can define a minimum text outset space around the image.

**Manual Image** causes an invisible border to appear around the image, allowing you to customize the way the characters wrap around the image.

Examples of the four options are shown in Figure 5-19.

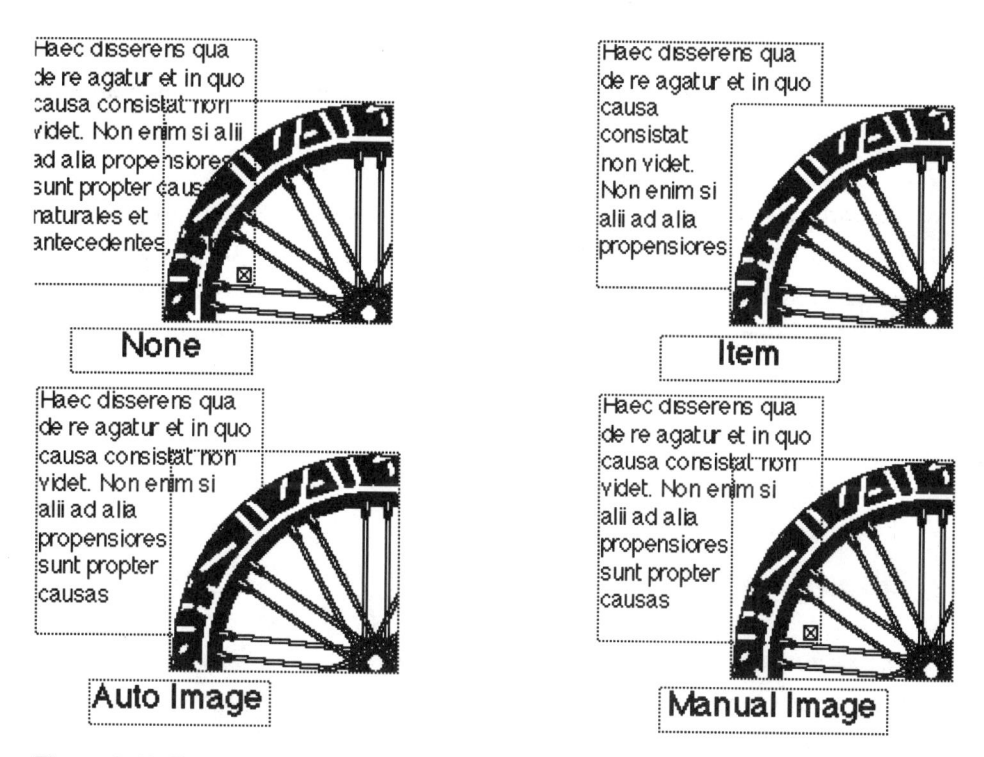

Figure 5-19. Examples of the four runaround modes.

> **Tip**
>
> *To save time when experimenting with **Manual Image** mode, hold down the **space bar** when you move the handles of the runaround polygon and release the **space bar** when you're finished. This way, you don't have to wait through a text flowing operation each time you move a single control point — the text won't reflow until you release the **space bar**.*

Customizing the character runaround or wrapping is easy — decide just exactly how close the text will come to the image. There are several ways to do this:

1. Use the **Manual Image** mode. This draws a runaround polygon around the image itself. When the cursor is over a polygon's control point, it changes into the pointing hand cursor, as shown in Figure 5-20, indicating that you can move that control point by clicking and dragging the point to its new location. The text then runs around this changed polygon. To create new control points, move the cursor over the control points, hold down the ⌘ key, and click when the cursor becomes a small hollow box pointer.

> **Tip**
>
> *QuarkXPress doesn't flow text around both sides of a picture or picture box within a text box. It only flows it down the side with the most horizontal space, as demonstrated in Figure 5-22. To get the effect of text on both sides, you can anchor your graphic in the text, as explained at the end of this chapter.*

*GRAPHICS*

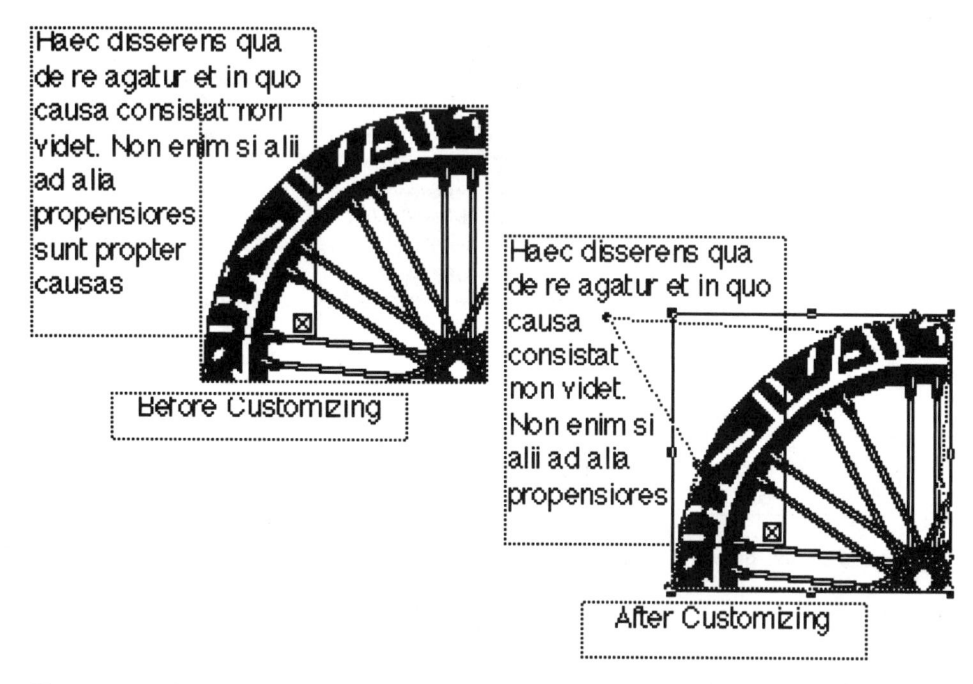

**Figure 5-20.** Customizing runaround by moving a control point in Manual mode.

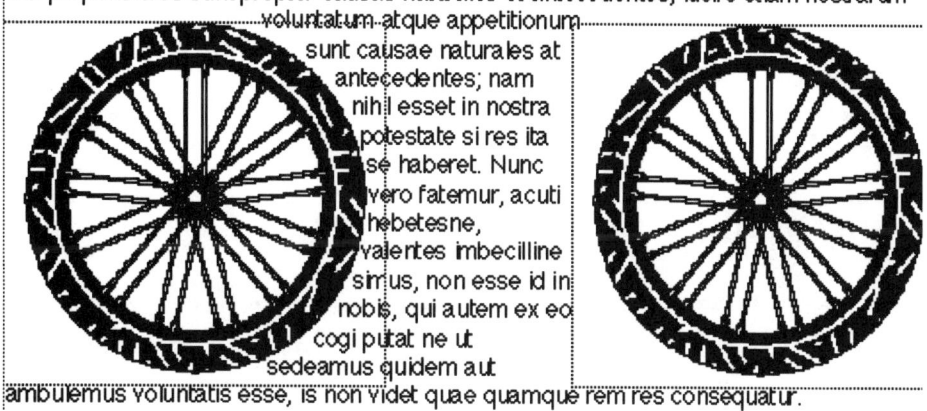

**Figure 5-21.** Using different Text Outset values to customize runaround in Auto Image mode.

177

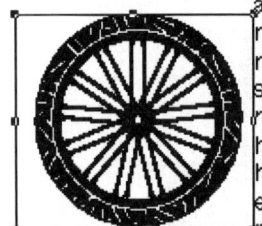

**Figure 5-22.** Text only flows down one side of a picture box within a text box.

2. In **Manual Image** or **Auto Image** modes, enter a value in the **Runaround Specifications** box for **Text Outset**: The larger the value, the farther text will stay away from the edge of the **Runaround...** polygon (in **Manual Image** mode) or the image itself (in **Auto Image** mode). Figure 5-21 shows an example of two outset values in **Auto Image** mode.

> **Tip**
>
> **Inverted Runaround:** *In the **Runaround Specifications** dialog box, you'll see a small checkbox called **Invert**. Click on this and surrounding text flows into the graphic, instead of around it, as shown in the inverted runaround of text into a circle in Figure 5-23. For you to be able to do this, the text box must be behind the picture box, and you must clear the image within the picture box.*

# GRAPHICS

Figure 5-23. Inverted runaround.

3. Use the **Item** mode and set the **Text Outset** (from the picture box) for **Top**, **Right**, **Bottom**, and **Left**.

## Runaround Pitfalls

If you've specified **Manual Image** for the runaround of a graphic object that's only partially visible in the picture box, and you then enlarge the picture box, the invisible border surrounds only the part of the graphic that was visible in the picture box. To change this, enlarge the picture box to show the entire image, then choose **Runaround...** and **Auto Image**. Then choose **Runaround...** again and **Manual Image**.

Be careful when you choose **Manual Image** for **Runaround...** mode and any part of your image extends beyond the picture box. Even though only part of the image is visible in the picture box, the part that is invisible still displaces type outside of the picture box. You can avoid this displacement by choosing **Auto Image** in **Runaround...** mode.

## Importing Images

It's simple to import images to QuarkXPress 3.0. Just select (or create) the picture box where you want the image to appear, select the **Content** tool (not the **Item** tool — this is important), and choose **Get Picture** from the **File** menu (the shortcut is ⌘+E). Then choose the image you wish to import. QuarkXPress

179

shows a thumbnail preview of the picture in the **Picture Preview** frame inside the **Get Picture** dialog box, as you can see in Figure 5-24.

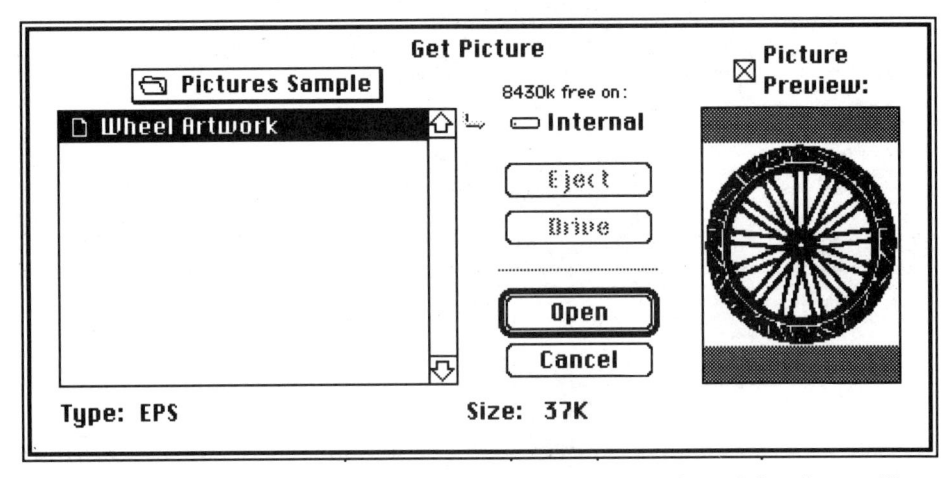

**Figure 5-24. The Get Picture dialog box with thumbnail preview of the chosen file.**

When QuarkXPress imports a high-resolution image (RIFF, TIFF, PICT, EPS) into a document, it displays only a "picture" of the image for placement. The graphic information for printing the image is stored with the image document itself, to save QuarkXPress document space. Whenever QuarkXPress prints the document, it looks for the graphic in that same place on your disk. If you've changed or moved the picture between the time it was first imported and the time it's printed, QuarkXPress beeps to alert you that the picture's been changed or can't be found. You can then tell QuarkXPress to print the document anyway, without the image information, at the resolution that the graphic appears on-screen, or to update the image information by telling it where the image is now stored.

QuarkXPress 3.0 has a feature, **Auto Picture Import**, that automatically updates any high-resolution images changed since you last saved the QuarkXPress document. You can enable this feature in the **General Preferences** dialog found under the **Edit** menu, as shown in Figure 5-25.

# GRAPHICS

```
┌─────────────────────────────────────────────────────────┐
│          General Preferences for Document2             │
│  Horizontal Measure: [Inches]    Points/Inch: [72]     │
│  Vertical Measure:   [Inches]    ☐ Render Above: 24 pt │
│  Auto Page Insertion:[End of Section] ☒ Greek Below: 7 pt│
│  Framing:            [Inside]    ☐ Greek Pictures      │
│  Guides:             [Behind]    ☐ Auto Constrain      │
│  Item Coordinates:   [Page]                             │
│  Auto Picture Import:│✓Off│                             │
│  Master Page Items:  │ On │  s    ( OK )   (Cancel)    │
│                      │On (verify)│                      │
└─────────────────────────────────────────────────────────┘
```

Figure 5-25. Auto Picture Import preference setting in the General Preferences dialog box.

You can enable **Auto Picture Import** to automatically update, or to update and verify whenever it finds that an image has been altered. Choosing **Verify** tells QuarkXPress to ask you about each individual image before printing so you can decide which images are appropriate to update. This saves you time if you're printing a few pages from a large document with plenty of pictures and you don't want to update every picture in the document.

> *When printing to any high-resolution printer, QuarkXPress must be able to retrace the path from the QuarkXPress document to the graphic-import document. If you're transporting your document to another device for printing, such as when using a service bureau, remember to include all of your graphic import files with your document files. These files must be in the same folder as your document files for them to print correctly.*

181

Enabling **Auto Picture Import** with the **Verify** option shows a dialog box with the names of files that are missing or altered, the pages where this occurs, and the type of image and its status (missing or altered). There's also a handy **Show Me** button to help you remember which picture belongs to which title.

## Import File Types

QuarkXPress 3.0 can't grab just any graphics file, but it does import most popular Macintosh file formats. These include:

- TIFF (Tag Image File Format)
- RIFF (Raster Image File Format)
- PICT
- PICT2
- Bit maps (MacPaint and one-color paint programs)
- EPS (Encapsulated PostScript)

Each type of graphic image file format has its own characteristics and capabilities within QuarkXPress 3.0. Knowing a bit about each of them will help you decide how to save and manipulate each type of image. All types of images may be adjusted for size, orientation and location; but some don't allow for certain kinds of manipulation, such as color, shade, or halftone screen characteristics. There's a complete chart of editing possibilities in your QuarkXPress 3.0 reference manual.

With the exception of EPS images, enlarging or reducing the size of any of these high-resolution images affects the resolution of the final output. If you enlarge a scanned TIFF image 400%, then each of the grayscale or color pixels that make up that image is also enlarged. This can have a negative effect on your output quality if you scanned the image at a coarse pixel resolution. EPS images, on the other hand, retain the highest resolution possible from your LaserWriter or other high-resolution printing device, no matter how coarse the images appear on screen.

**TIFF and RIFF Images.** TIFF and RIFF images are saved as color or grayscale and are usually imports from scanner documents or image-editing software. You can manipulate grayscale TIFF and RIFF images in QuarkXPress 3.0 to affect size, contrast, color, and halftone screen characteristics (dot frequency and dot shape).

**PICT Images.** You can usually edit grayscale PICT images for contrast, color, and halftone screen characteristics. You can only edit color PICT images for size, contrast, and location — not for color.

**EPS (PostScript) Images.** EPS images are imported with set instructions to the page-layout program for color, including separation information. You can only edit them for size, orientation, and location. You can't adjust them to enhance contrast, color, or halftone screen characteristics. EPS halftone screen information is controlled by the **Halftone Screen** setting in the **Page Setup** dialog box and shares the halftone screen values that you've set for any other non-editable halftone screens that appear in your document.

## Moving Pictures Inside a Box

QuarkXPress imports the entire image into the selected picture box. Even if the box is not large enough to display the whole picture, the entire picture is inside the picture box, ready for you to manipulate.

You can move the picture around within the box by any of these methods:

1. Use the hand cursor that appears when you select the **Content** tool and place the cursor over the image area. Just click and drag with the hand cursor.

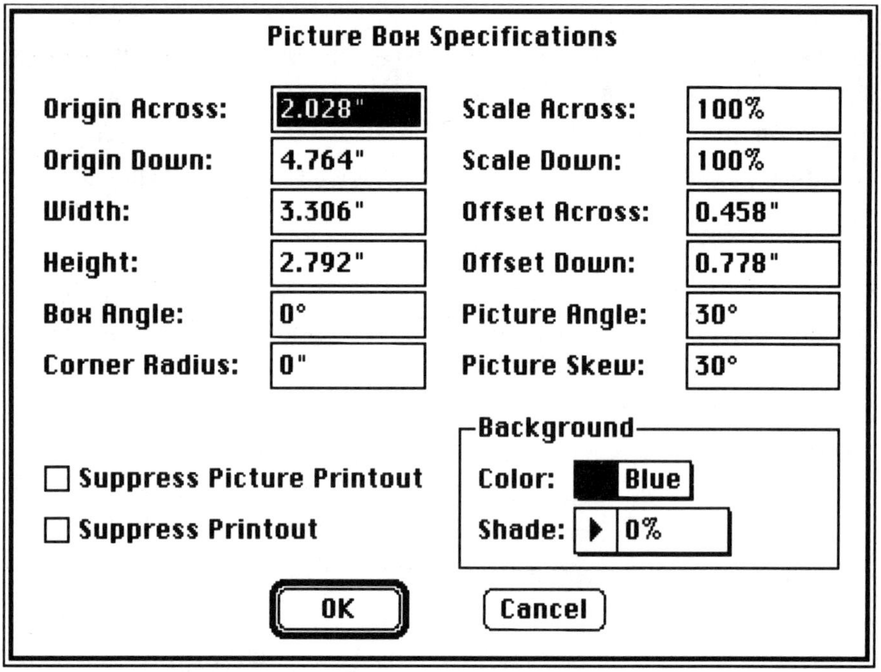

## Picture Box Specifications

| | | | |
|---|---|---|---|
| Origin Across: | 2.028" | Scale Across: | 100% |
| Origin Down: | 4.764" | Scale Down: | 100% |
| Width: | 3.306" | Offset Across: | 0.458" |
| Height: | 2.792" | Offset Down: | 0.778" |
| Box Angle: | 0° | Picture Angle: | 30° |
| Corner Radius: | 0" | Picture Skew: | 30° |

Background
Color: Blue
Shade: ▶ 0%

☐ Suppress Picture Printout
☐ Suppress Printout

[ OK ]   [ Cancel ]

**Figure 5-26. Picture Box Specifications dialog box and Measurements palette for moving a picture inside a box.**

2. Select the picture box, choose **Modify** from the **Item** menu (or double-clicking with the **Content** tool on the picture box), then type new values for **Offset Across** and **Offset Down** — the X and Y coordinates for the picture within the box, as in Figure 5-26.

3. Select the picture box, select the **Measurements** palette, then change the **X+** and **Y+** values in that box. These are the same as the **Offset Across** and **Offset Down** values you reached through **Modify**. They're on the right side of the palette; the **X** and **Y** values on the left are the picture box coordinates within the document, as in Figure 5-26.

# GRAPHICS

> ### Shortcut
>
> To fit an imported picture exactly to a box's dimensions, press **Shift+⌘+F** while using the **Content** tool.
>
> To fit an imported picture to the box dimensions and retain its aspect ratio (reduce or enlarge it proportionally to its original dimensions), press **Shift+⌘+Option+F**. The picture automatically reproportions itself to its original aspect ratio.
>
> If you've imported a picture and can't see it in the picture box window, use the **Content** tool to click and drag the hand cursor around in the box to look for the image. Or press **Shift+⌘+M** to bring the center of the picture to the center of the picture box.

## Styling and Formatting Pictures

When you select a picture box, the **Style** menu holds controls for picture color, shade, contrast, and halftone screen attributes — but only when these can apply to the type of picture selected. When an attribute is not appropriate for the kind of graphic image you've selected, the attribute selection in the pull-down menu is grayed and unavailable. Figure 5-27 shows the complete list of picture style choices.

**Figure 5-27. Style choices for Picture boxes.**

**Color** lets you replace shades of black in the picture with colors from the color palette.

185

**Shade** lets you set the saturation of color in a picture.

**Negative** produces a true negative image of the picture (you can reverse this operation just by choosing it again), as shown in Figure 5-28.

**Normal Contrast** dictates that a picture be displayed and printed with its original contrast (tonal values — the relationship between black, various shades of gray, and white), as in Figures 5-28 and 5-29.

**High Contrast** changes the image to black and white (Figure 5-29). Any gray shade below 50% becomes white; any above 50% becomes black.

**Posterized** changes the image to have only six levels of gray (black, 80%, 60%, 40%, 20% gray, and white) or color (if it started as a color image), as shown in Figure 5-30.

**Other Contrast** shows a dialog box where you set the contrast curve for the image to dictate the changes in contrast from input to output. This dialog box has a set of icon commands of its own for adjusting the curve and is explained in depth in the QuarkXPress reference manual. If you're working on the contrasts in a color picture, you can also choose which color model to work with — HSB, RGB, CMY, or CMYK — and alter the component colors of your image (color models are explained Chapter 6). Change the curve to what you like, then click on **Apply** to preview the effects. When you're sure, click on **OK**.

**Screen** options let you choose to print pictures at various screen angles. The default is **Normal Screen** and is determined by the value you enter in the **Halftone Screen** field in the **Page Setup** dialog box (see Chapter 2). Here you can choose from three common screens (60-line line, 0 degrees; 30-line line, 45 degrees; 20-line dot, 45 degrees) or make a custom screen with **Screen**, **Angle**, and **Pattern** settings of your own. Using these options, you can create special

*GRAPHICS*

**Figure 5-28. Positive and negative images.**

**Figure 5-29. Normal contrast and high contrast.**

**Figure 5-30. The effects of posterization.**

screen effects. For example, if you change the shape of the halftone dot, it will enhance the contrast.

### Editing Picture Boxes and Pictures

QuarkXPress 3.0 makes it easy to control several other attributes of both the picture box and the picture within, including picture rotation and skew, and box angle, radius, and background color. Just select the box with the **Content** tool, then choose **Modify** from the **Item** menu. Figure 5-26 shows the **Picture Box Specifications** dialog box with its options. This list tells you what each of those options can do:

**Origin Across**, **Origin Down** defines the location of the top left corner of the picture box.

**Width**, **Height** determines the dimensions of the actual box area.

**Box Angle** indicates the rotation angle of the box relative to the page.

**Scale Across**, **Scale Down** indicates size of the image relative to its original size.

**Offset Across**, **Offset Down** defines the location of the image relative to the top left corner of the picture box.

**Picture Angle** defines the angle of the picture within the picture box, relative to the picture box.

**Picture Skew** slants the image, distorting it from 75° to -75°, relative to the picture box.

**Background Color** and **Shade** set background color and shade for any picture box. Available colors are limited to what has been appended to the **Color** palette (see Chapter 6).

**Suppress Picture Printout** suppresses the individual picture printout to speed up printing of larger documents. When you select this option, a picture's border still prints, but the picture itself does not.

**Suppress Printout**: suppresses the printing of both the picture and its border.

Some of the attributes also appear in the **Measurements** palette, where they're less clearly labeled but easier for experienced folk to access. Double-click the cursor on that attribute, then type a new value. If you want to change other attributes, press **Tab** to advance the selection to the next attribute and type in new numbers to replace the selected values.

## Anchoring Graphics to Text

Graphic images can be anchored to text in a text box. The image is inserted in the text box as a text character. It travels with the text and is displaced by the addition or deletion of words in that text box.

To paste a graphic image into text:

1. Select the picture box while using the **Item** tool.

2. Choose **Cut** from the **Edit** menu.

3. Select the **Content** tool.

4. Select an insertion point in your text. The text editing cursor blinks at the insertion point.

5. Choose **Paste** from the **Edit** menu.

Figure 5-31. Example of anchored picture within text box.

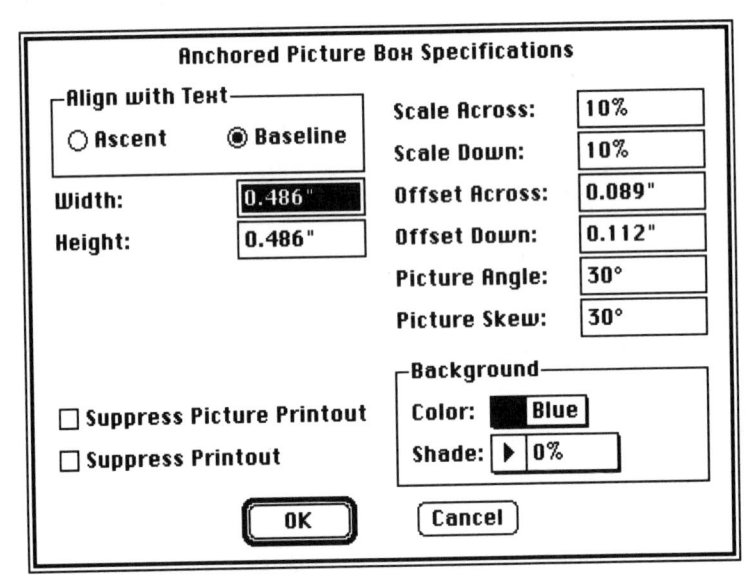

Figure 5-32. Anchored Picture Box Specifications dialog box.

The picture box and its contents will appear in the place you've selected. Figure 5-31 shows an example.

You can modify the picture and the picture box almost as you would any other picture box. Figure 5-32 shows the **Anchored Picture Box Specifications** dialog box. Most of the attributes available for editing in a regular picture box are available here except the location, picture-box angle, and corner-radius fields.

The only way you can move an anchored picture box after you've placed it is to move the text around it. You can't place the location of the picture box relative to the page, as you would any other item. It's a character like the rest of the text and is placed relative to the characters that directly precede and follow it.

To delete an anchored picture box, place the text insertion cursor directly after the anchored picture box in the text (as if it were one big letter) and press the **Delete** key. Remember, QuarkXPress considers this graphic image a character like the rest of the text. You won't be able to choose **Delete** from the **Item** menu.

## Save Page as EPS

Naturally, you can save graphics along with your QuarkXPress documents in QuarkXPress' own file format. But you can also save any single page as a PostScript graphic file on its own. This file contains all of the text, layout, and pictures on the page. (This may be necessary for using a QuarkXPress page in some other program. Many programs can import files saved in the EPS format.)

To save a page as a PostScript file:

1. Activate a document.

2. Choose **Save Page as EPS** from the **File** menu.

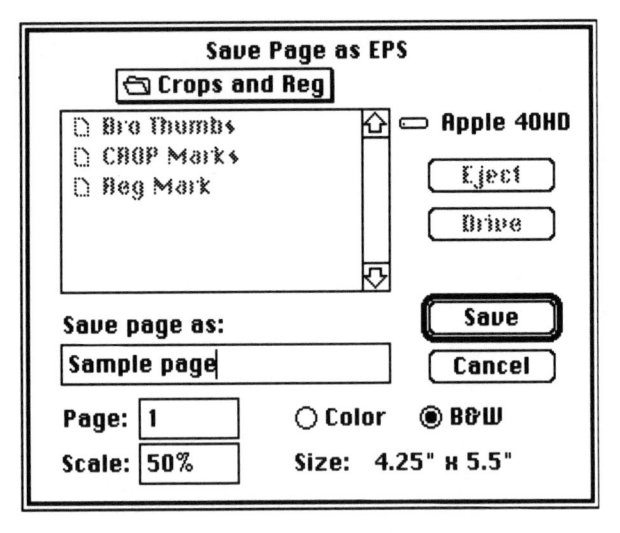

Figure 5-33. Save Page as EPS dialog box.

3. When the **Save Page as EPS** dialog box appears, as in Figure 5-33, type a name for the file-to-be.

4. Click in the **Page:** field and type the number of the page you want to save.

5. If you want anything other than 100% scaling on the saved page, click in the **Scale:** field and type the scale factor there (you'll see a note to the right on how large this will make the page).

6. Decide if you want to save the file in color or black and white, then click on either the **Color** or **B&W** (black and white) button.

7. Click on **Save.**

### The Library

Chapter 2 mentioned the **Library**. This is a special file in which you can store items for easy access and use later. You can have any number of libraries stored on disk, though you can only have seven documents, templates, and libraries open at a time. Pictures are items, and so are text boxes and lines, so you can store pictures, text boxes, and lines in the **Library** for use in the same document or in other documents. This is especially helpful if you've created a complex conglomeration of items that you can group into a single item and move into the **Library** to use again later.

# GRAPHICS

To use the **Library**:

1. Choose **Library** from the **Utilities** menu.

2. From the **Library** dialog box, start a new library or select a library by name from the disk directory list.

3. Once the **Library** window appears, as shown in Figure 5-34, you can drag or cut and paste items from the document to the library or from the library to the document.

4. Locate items in the **Library** by scrolling or by pulling down the **Labels** menu.

5. Label items by double-clicking on them and typing a name in the dialog box.

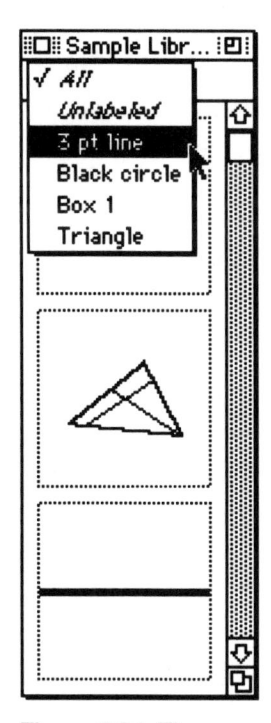

**Figure 5-34. The Library window (with graphic display of items and pop-up menu for selection by label).**

## Picture Usage

In the **Utilities** menu, you'll also find a special feature that lists all of the high-resolution pictures used in your document (it doesn't list bit-map images). The **Picture Usage** command tells you the picture name, page it's used on, picture type (EPS, PICT, TIFF, etc.), and status (**OK** means it can be found, **Modified** means it's been changed since it was imported, **Missing** means it can't be found).

The **Picture Usage** window has two commands:

1. **Update.** Use this if you need to find a missing picture. The **Find** dialog box lets you search through directories to find and reimport the picture.

2. **Show Me.** Use this to view the selected picture in the list. When you click on **Show Me**, the document scrolls to the picture and displays it on the screen.

## Halftone Advice

Scanned images can be a blessing or a curse in QuarkXPress 3.0, depending on the circumstances. If you apply some general rules, you can enhance the look of your work and maximize the time spent processing your document when it prints.

If you're using an image simply as a placement guide (position stat) for one that your printer will later strip in, as in a four-color image or high-quality halftone image, scan the image at a lower resolution, such as 75 dots per inch. You'll still get an accurate guide for placement, and your printer won't have to spend so much time processing a denser, more finely resolved image.

If you're scanning an image to be used in the final camera-ready artwork, be sure to check the halftone screen density of the output in the **Other Screen...** option under the **Style** menu. Make sure the screen density and direction are set to provide maximum quality for contrast and reproduction. For example, if it is a larger-quantity print run on paper or ceramic plates, make the halftone density a little coarser because the halftone dots may tend to close up toward the end of the run as the plate degrades.

A good way to research the different effects is to create a page full of images with different densities and styles (be sure to label each one) and run it as an extra page on your next print job. This will give you a reference guide to better decide what effect to specify on a particular job.

If you are printing regular LaserWriter output as camera-ready art to print and aren't going to strip in higher-quality halftones, you can get more dramatic effects that will reproduce better on press by changing the halftone screen attributes to a coarser density using lines instead of dots to create the image. Lines are easier for the camera to see than dots on a standard LaserWriter output and have a more "artsy," dramatic effect.

If you are using scanned images as placement guides only, you can speed up processing and printing time even more by saving them as simple bit maps instead of grayscale images. A simple bit-mapped MacPaint image is much easier for QuarkXPress to digest than the grayscale image, which has more information packed into every pixel of the image. If you're using Apple's Scanner, then it came with an application called HyperScan that uses HyperCard as a front end to the scanning application. It scans and saves images exclusively in a bit-mapped format, eliminating the need to convert the image with your regular scanning software.

**The Split Fountain Effect.** You can get a nice "split fountain" effect using a grayscale image created in any image-editing software, imported into a picture box with a different color as a background color. For example, changing the color of a graduated fountain to red, making the background of the picture solid yellow, will produce a picture box that will change smoothly from solid yellow to solid red. This can save you some money at the printer in the stripping department.

## Using What You've Learned

Here are some ideas and suggestions for using QuarkXPress' graphics features.

**The Starburst Outline.** This is a simple graphic that you can create to add some excitement to a layout.

1. Create an elliptical picture box and give it a 2-point border. Create another, smaller one inside the original.

2. Select the original picture box, choose **Picture Box Shape** from the item menu, change the selection to the polygon shape, and choose **Reshape Polygon**. This will give the ellipse many more control points around the border that you can then change by dragging them around.

3. Drag every other point into the ellipse to the border of the smaller interior ellipse.

4. After you've finished moving all the points, choose **Reshape Polygon** from the item menu to deselect it. Then delete the interior ellipse. You're now ready to place a text box in the shape (see Figure 5-35). Then group the two boxes so they'll transport together. Move the group into your library palette and name it **Flash**.

**Variation:**
1. Try rotating the group to add impact.

2. Try extending some of the points to add variety to the shape.

**The Variable Drop Shadow for Any Object.** You can create drop shadows of any depth by duplicating any object, then repositioning it using the **Item** tool.

This one's simple.

1. Select any object for which you want to create a drop shadow.

2. Add a screen value and remove the border of the new object to make it appear as a shadow (see Figure 5-36).

**Figure 5-35.** Starburst outline with text added.

3. Choose **Step and Repeat** from the **Item** menu. Remember: since QuarkXPress 3.0 automatically places new copies on top of the old ones, make sure the numbers you enter will move the new copy in the direction you desire. If you want the new object above and to the left of the shadow, type in negative numbers. This will keep you from having to move it with the **Item** tool or nudge it with the arrow keys after it's duplicated.

**Figure 5-36. Starburst with a drop shadow.**

# Chapter 6

# Color

Color is becoming more possible and more important in desktop publishing and design projects. Now that personal computer hardware can handle the large files and complex calculations necessary for color work, software has been developed to put that hardware to work. Not all designs need color, but some require it and most can profit from it. This chapter explains the general theory of color design and layout while focusing on QuarkXPress' color capabilities.

Fortunately for you, QuarkXPress 3.0 is prepared to meet the increasing demand for color publishing and design because it:

- Can color text, box frames, lines, and just about any other element.
- Lets you build your own color palette.
- Lets you build a different color palette for each document.
- Offers four color models for specifying color.
- Can automatically print color separations.

## Why Color Is Important in Design

Color can make a big impression in a graphic design, and you can use it in lots of ways to achieve different effects. The eye is naturally attracted to sharp contrasts in color — add contrasting shades in your design. Bright colors attract attention even from a distance — take advantage of this in your posters and other display materials. Subtle color changes add a touch of sophistication that can enhance the look of any printed piece. Color also sets a mood for your piece: brighter colors create a festive and active atmosphere, while subdued colors present a calm and sedate feeling.

Any printer will tell you that using colored ink instead of plain black ink, your publication will see a 40% increase in readership. These readers will remember your piece 60% longer because of the impact of the color.

## Planning Color

It's important that you plan for color when you begin designing your printed work. If your budget can afford a second or third color in printing, figure in this aspect from the start. Printed work always looks best when colors are planned as a part of your design element, rather than added as an afterthought.

Start your color planning by thinking about the goal, audience, and medium of your design or publication. Discuss color ideas with editors, authors, artists, and your viewers or readers. Remember that colors can mean different things in different contexts: red is a negative to bankers, blue has a special meaning to IBM employees and customers.

Once you've decided on the colors you want to use, talk to your printer to find out the most cost-effective color-production method for your job. If your budget won't support a six-color printing job, you could match those colors using process-color screen builds. If your job requires only two colors, it may not be necessary to print it with the four-color process method; you can save money by printing those two colors as spot colors.

Desktop publishing and QuarkXPress make it much easier to play and experiment with colors than it was with older technologies. Try something. If you don't like it, save it (in case it turns out better than your other experiments) and try some other color combination. You don't have to change your design's shape and appearance when you change its colors.

## How to Use Color in QuarkXPress

There are three steps to using color in QuarkXPress:
- applying colors.
- creating a color palette.
- printing the results.

## Applying Colors

Applying colors to items is much like applying other style and format attributes. Select the item first, then find the menu, dialog box, or tool that lets

# COLOR

> **Extra!**
>
> *Whenever you're beginning a project that involves a new technique or employs a new feature you haven't tried yet, such as some color trick, it's a good idea to allow a couple of extra days in the design schedule and enough in the project budget to re-run parts (or all) of your project in case the-worst-that-can-happen happens. If it doesn't, then you're both time and money ahead.*

you choose a new color. To set a color you must choose a color name and specify a shading percentage.

## Coloring Selected Text Elements

Colored text can be effective when it's used on large initial caps that lead off a paragraph or page layout, or to emphasize key words or phrases.

It's easy to change the color of a text element. Just select it with the **Content** tool and choose a new color from the **Style** menu (see Figure 6-1) or from the **Character** dialog box (see Figure 6-2). In both cases, you can also select a color and a shade.

You're probably used to seeing examples of this colored-text technique in your daily junk mail: "You may have ALREADY won MILLIONS in Cash Prizes!"

Color can also be effective as a background for reversing text. Try adding some drop shadows and initial caps (the exercises in Chapters 8 and 9 use this technique). See Figures 6-3 through 6-5 for examples.

## Coloring Body Text

Another handy trick for coloring type is to change the body-text color from black to a complementary color that reflects the overall feel of your piece. Darker grays and warmer, neutral grays work especially well with this technique. It adds a level of sophistication that says, "This work was designed, not just thrown together in a hurry."

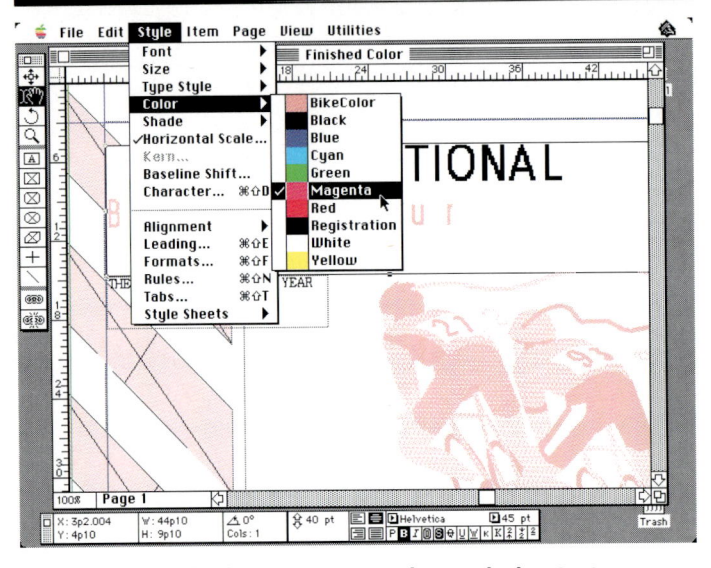

Figure 6-1. The Style menu approach to coloring text.

## Coloring Lines

It's easy to color lines made with the line tools — this creates a nice effect. You can use these colored lines as a background for colored text if the text box is transparent and on top of the line. Just follow these steps:

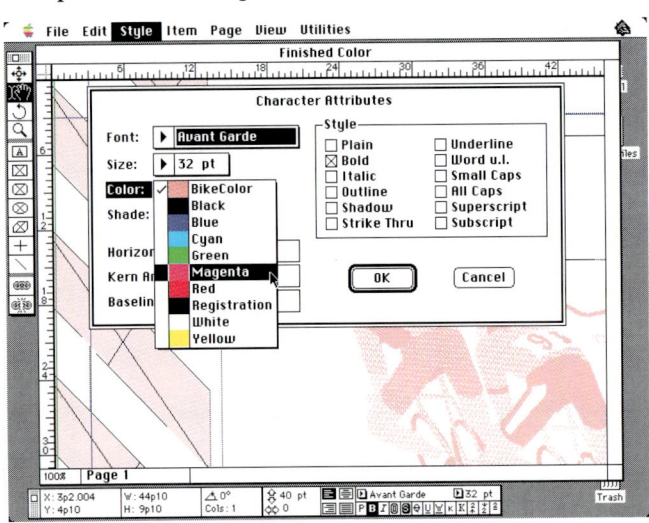

Figure 6-2. The Character dialog box approach to coloring text.

*COLOR*

1. Create your text.

2. Change the **Runaround**... attribute to **None.**

3. Create your line.

4. Specify the line's color (from the **Style** menu, as in Figure 6-6; or from the **Modify** dialog box of the **Item** menu, as in Figure 6-7).

5. Send it to the back (select the object and use the command from the **Item** menu).

6. Select both items and group them.

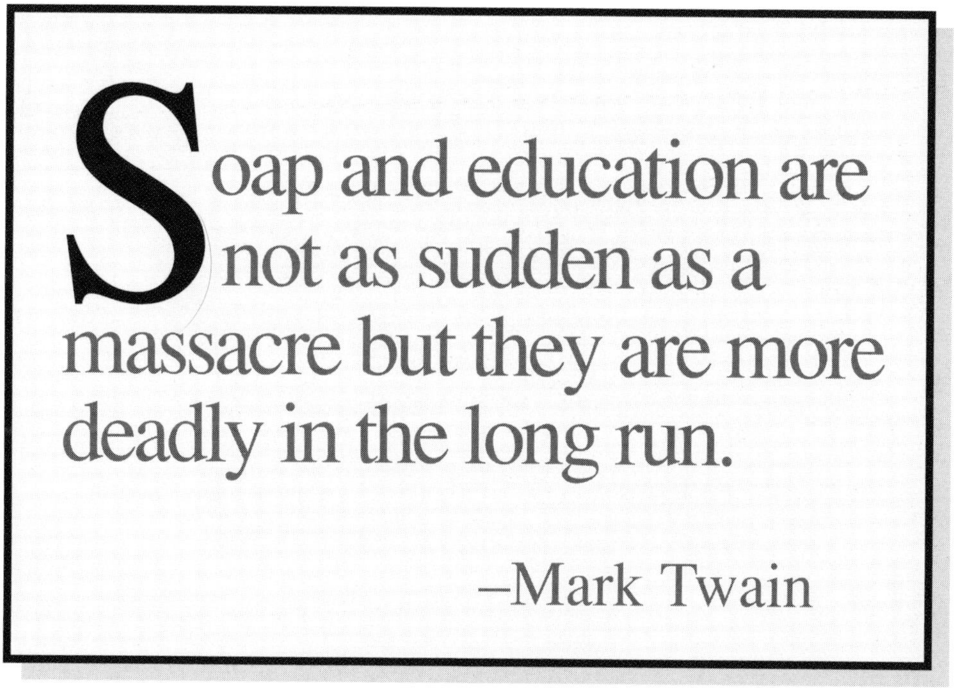

> Soap and education are not as sudden as a massacre but they are more deadly in the long run.
>
> –Mark Twain

**Figure 6-3. An effective use of color in a text object.**

203

USING QUARKXPRESS

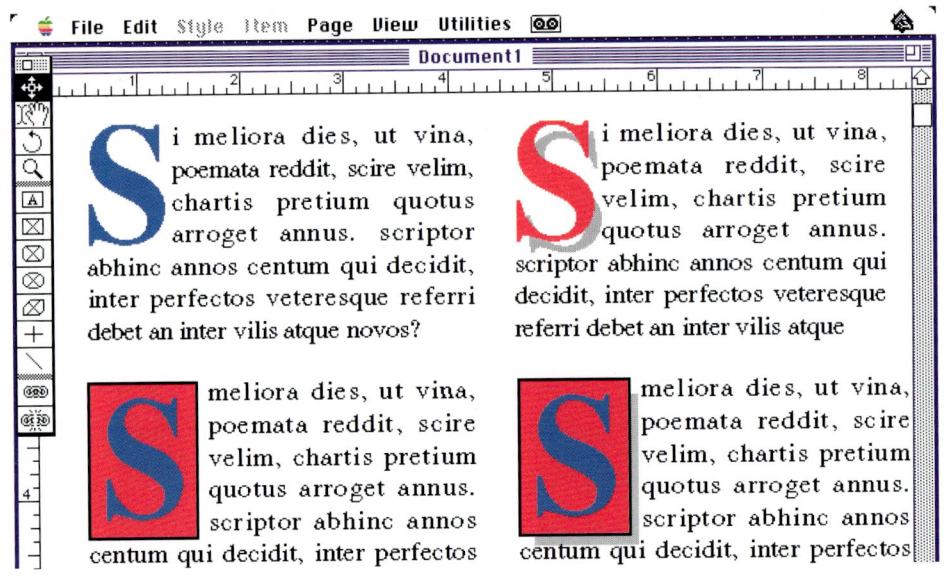

Figure 6-4. Some ways color can enhance the impact of large initial caps.

Figure 6-5. Color as a background for reversed text or shape.

## Coloring Frames

Just as you can color independent lines, you can color the frame lines that border boxes. Choose a color that contrasts or complements the background color of the box or the colors of the box contents. To color a frame:

1. Select the box.

2. Choose **Frame** from the **Item** menu.

3. In the **Frame Specifications** dialog box (shown in Figure 6-8), choose a color and a shade for the frame.

## Coloring Graphic Images

You can also color certain kinds of graphic images, such as grayscale TIFF, RIFF, and PICT images, and one-color bit maps. You can easily convert them to color and separate them from their backgrounds. You cannot separate color PICT, TIFF, and RIFF images, although in most cases, you can change their contrast. As with other items, select the item and use the **Style** and **Item** menus for their

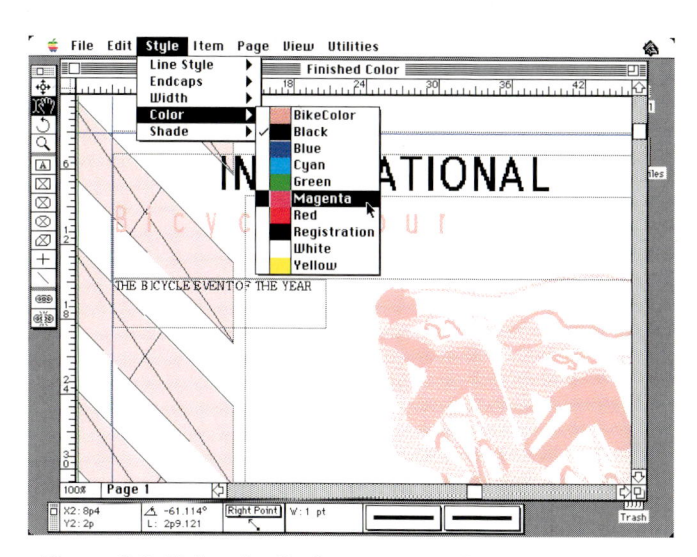

Figure 6-6. Using the Style menu to color a line.

USING QUARKXPRESS

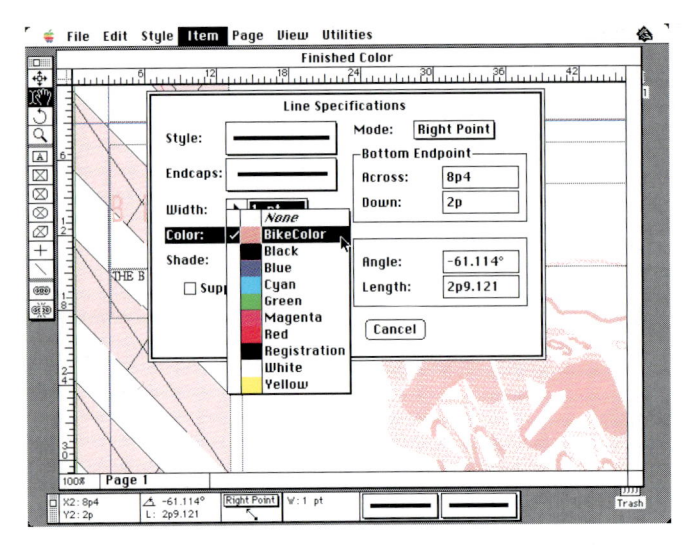

Figure 6-7. Using the Modify dialog box to color a line.

Color and Shade choices. See Figures 6-9, 6-10, and 6-11 for examples of graphic-image coloring.

## Creating a Color Palette

QuarkXPress packs its own color palette containing all of the colors you can use in its text, frames, boxes, and other elements. The palette colors are those that appear in the various pop-up menus from both the **Style** and **Item** menus. You can create a color palette for each document that supercedes QuarkXPress' main palette.

You determine which colors are in these palettes, both for QuarkXPress' default palette and for each document's dedicated palette. You can accept the colors that are in the palette when you open a document (or when you create a new document), add new colors to a palette, delete colors from a palette, and save a palette with a document or template to use later.

206

*COLOR*

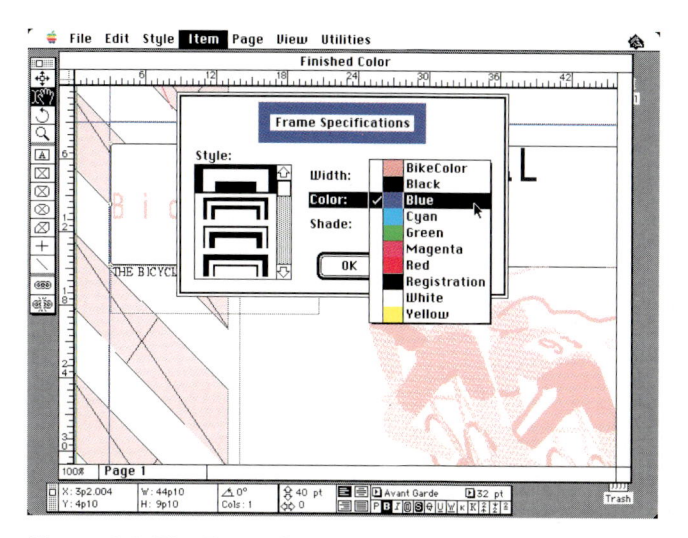

**Figure 6-8.** The Frame Specifications dialog box for coloring a box border.

**Figure 6-9.** This grayscale RIFF image was colored red and placed into a picture box with a 100% green background color. When printed, the image will automatically separate into the green and red plates as shown here.

207

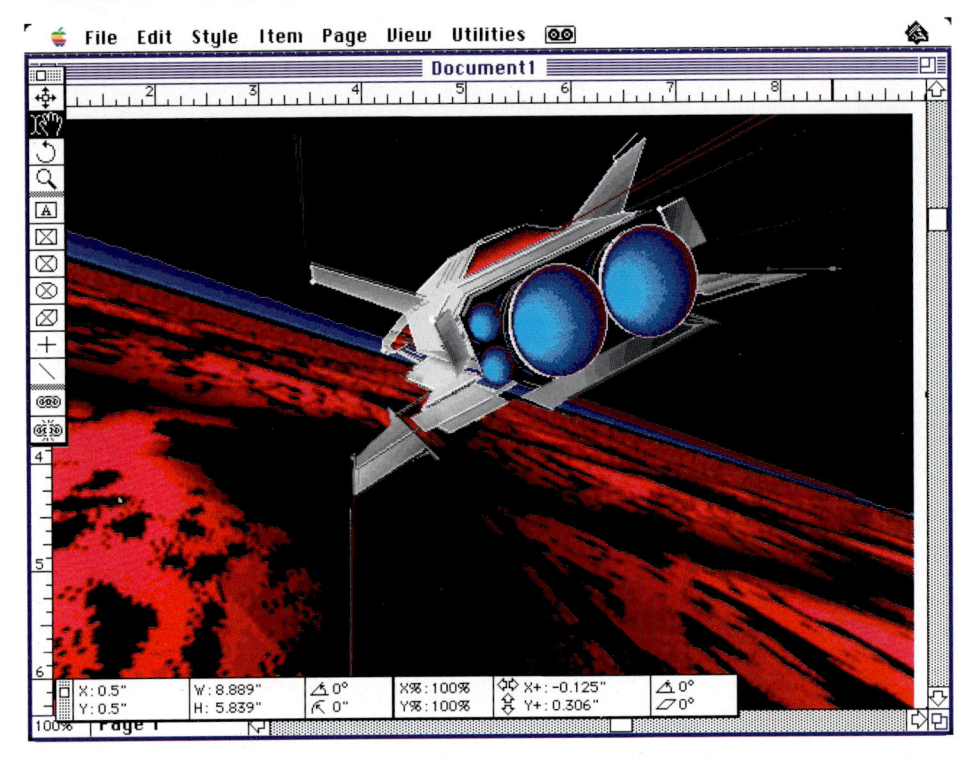

Figure 6-10. This image won't separate into its component color plates but will be printed as a halftone (if you select Print Colors as Gray in the Printing Specifications dialog box).

Any palette work you do without opening a document changes QuarkXPress' main palette. Any palette work you do after opening a document changes that document's palette.

### Technique

*You can't edit any of the fundamental process colors (CMYK), white, or registration colors. There is a trick, however. You can select any of the unchangeable colors and click on* **Duplicate**. *This creates an exact duplicate that you can then edit and save under a different name.*

*COLOR*

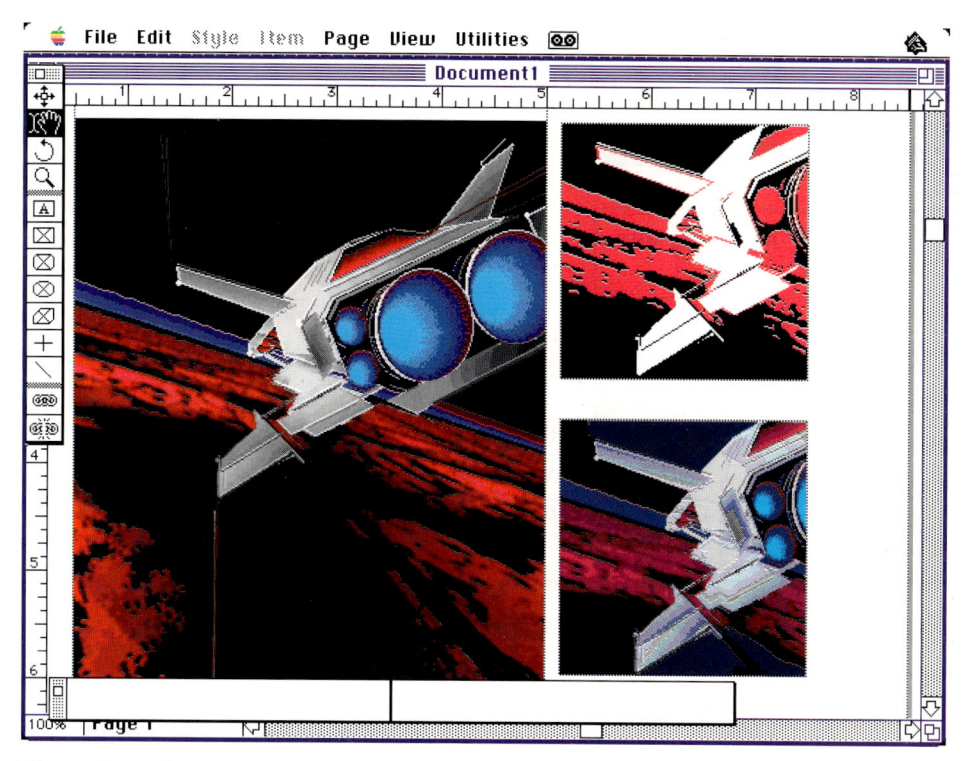

Figure 6-11. Contrast.

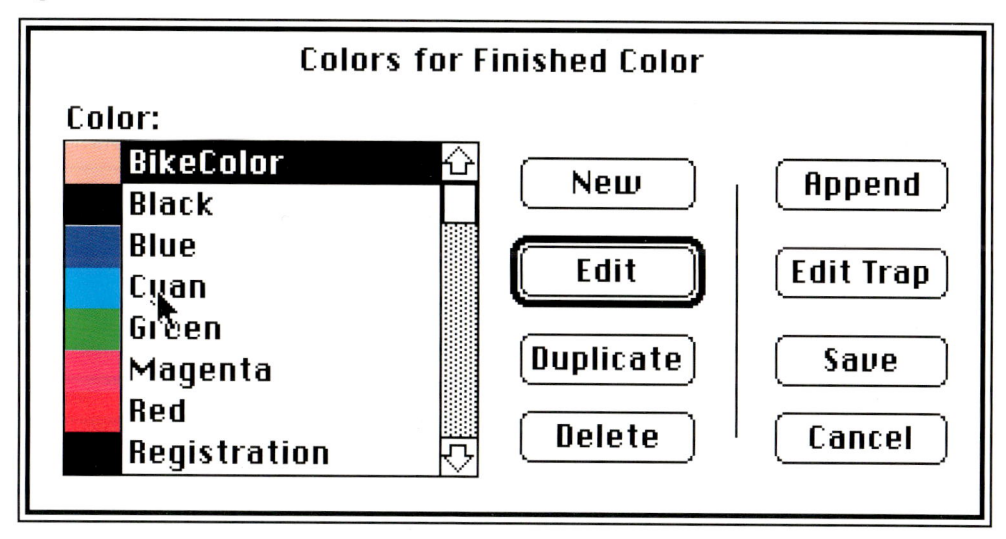

Figure 6-12. Colors dialog box.

209

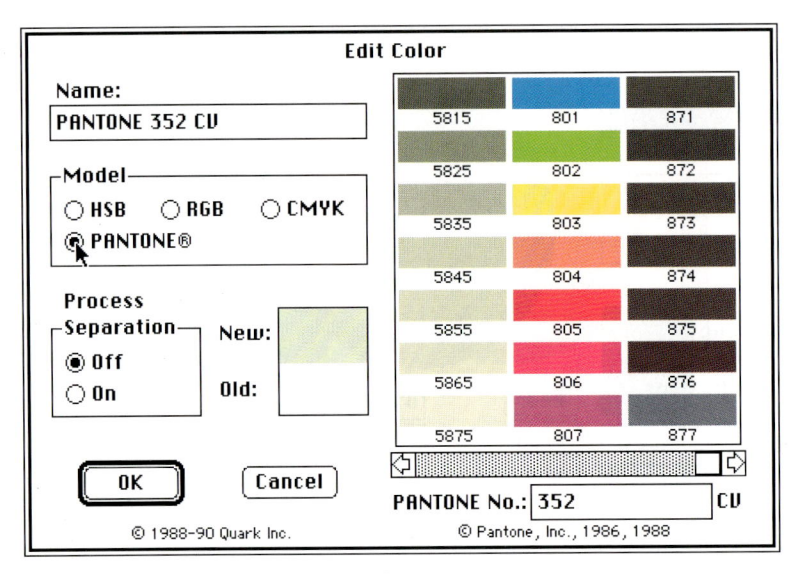

Figure 6-17. The Color Picker with the Pantone model selected.

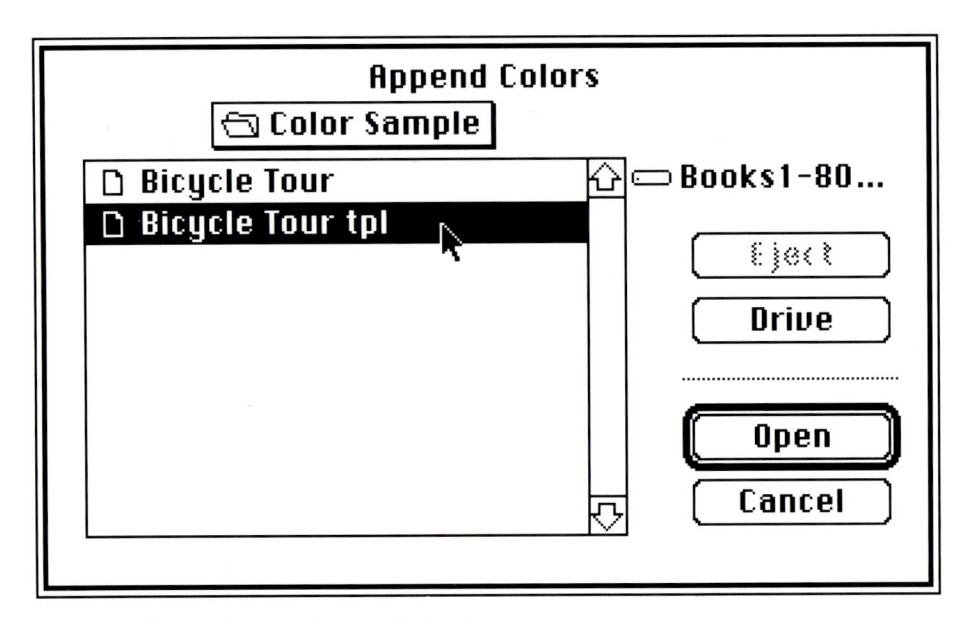

Figure 6-18. The Append Colors dialog box.

*COLOR*

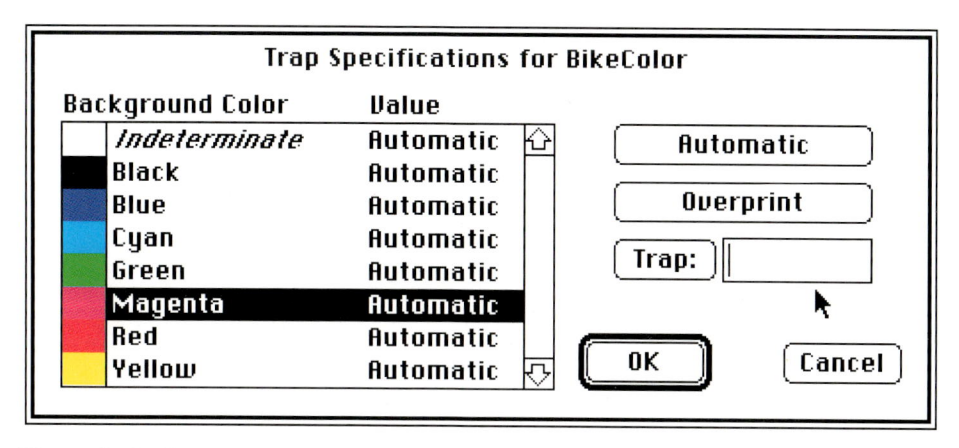

Figure 6-19. Trap Specifications dialog box.

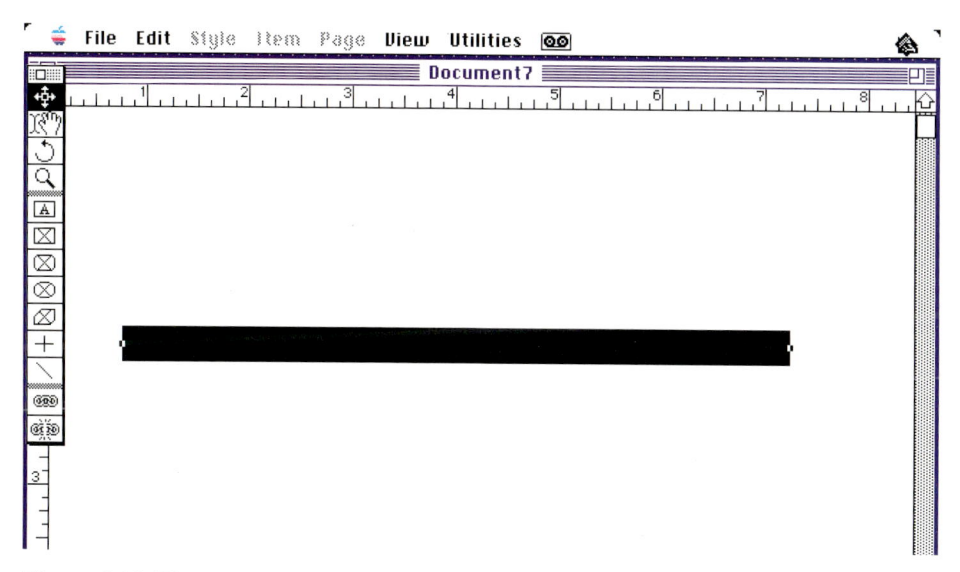

Figure 6-20. The widened line.of

213

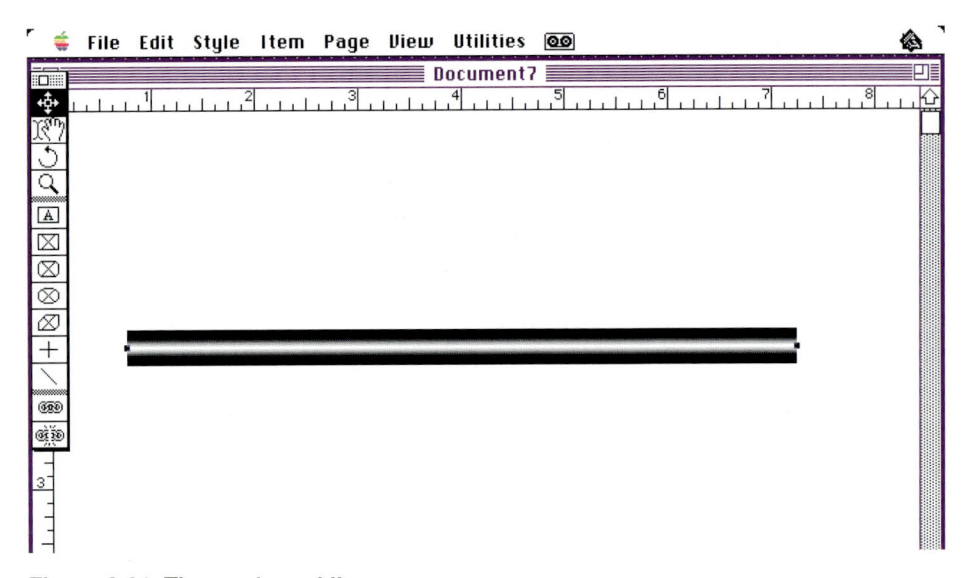

Figure 6-21. The graduated line.

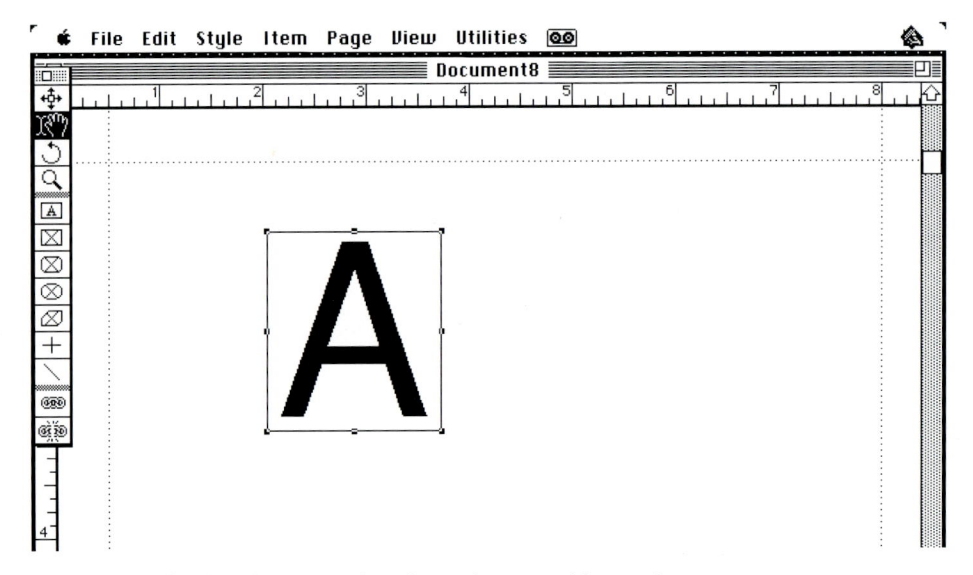

Figure 6-22. Capital A centered and evenly spaced in text box.

214

*COLOR*

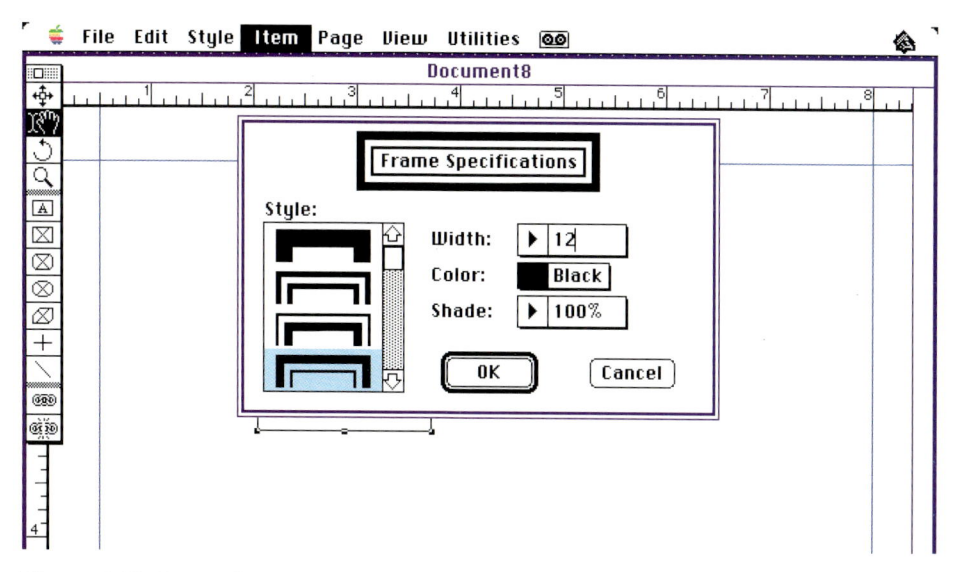

Figure 6-23. Frame Specifications dialog box.

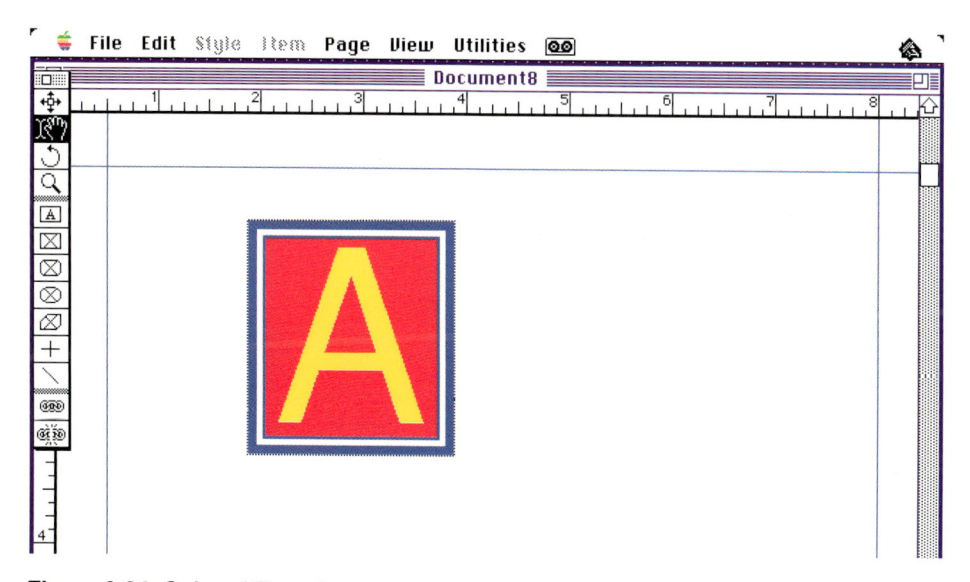

Figure 6-24. Colored Text character, box, and frame.

215

## Viewing the Palette

You can see the colors in your current palette by selecting an item on-screen and choosing the **Color** pop-up menu from the **Style** or **Item** menus, or you can just pull down the **Edit** menu and choose the **Color...** selection. This raises the **Color Palette** or **Colors** dialog box, as shown in Figure 6-12.

The palette's first eight colors are shown and named in the window to the left of the box. You can scroll down to see any more that didn't fit in the window.

> **Tip**
>
> **Color PICT Images.** *You can't change the color of color PICT images because each pixel has already been assigned a color for its display. These colors can't be altered. This includes scanned color images in TIFF, PICT, or EPSF formats.*
>
> **Scanned Color Images.** *QuarkXPress won't separate scanned color images. You can change the component contrast of color images using any of the four-color models, but they won't be separated in the final output.*
>
> **Grayscale PICT and TIFF Images.** *You can change the color of grayscale PICT and TIFF images. When specifying a PMS color for a grayscale image, enable the* **Process Separation** *button in the* **Color Specifications** *dialog box.*
>
> **Color EPSF Images.** *You can't change the colors of a color EPSF image because these colors are already set in the code that generates the image. If your color EPSF image uses any Pantone colors, make sure those colors are a part of your document's color palette so it separates properly.*

# COLOR

Some of the buttons on the right of the dialog box have obvious functions:

**Delete** throws out the selected color.

**Duplicate** copies the selected color.

**Save** saves the palette as it is.

**Cancel** tosses out any palette changes you've made since the palette was last saved.

**Append** adds the colors from another document's palette to this palette.

**Edit** lets you change a color in the palette.

**New** lets you add a new color to the palette.

**Edit Trap** lets you dictate printing effects between the selected color and other colors (this is explained in more detail below).

---

**Extra!**

### Color Work on Monochrome Screens

*A Mac with a monochrome or grayscale monitor has the same dialog boxes and color choices as a color monitor does. It's more difficult to choose colors accurately, however, because you'll only see various shades of gray. Read the section describing the PMS (Pantone Matching System) color model. This is the best model for you because the PMS ink color standard uses numbered colors that are easy to check and compare against the PMS color guide.*

217

# USING QUARKXPRESS

## Adding or Changing (Editing) Colors

You add a new color to the palette or change (edit) a color that is already in the palette as follows:

1. Select the color you want to edit.

2. Click on either **New** or **Edit**. This shows the **Edit Color** dialog box, as in Figure 6-13.

    a. New. If you're working on a new color, no color appears in the **New: Old:** box and no **Name:** appears in the slot at the upper left.

    b. Edit. If you're editing a color, that color's name appears at the upper left, its color fills the **New: Old:** box, a cursor point marks it on the color wheel (or its Pantone position shows), and its constituent values are listed (or its Pantone number is displayed).

3. Choose a color model (as explained in the next section).

4. Select a color by clicking on a color in the wheel or by adjusting the scroll bars (for HSB, RGB, or CMYK colors). To lighten or darken a color, scroll the bar on the far right. To select a Pantone color, click on the Pantone radio button, then scroll through the available colors or type a color number in the field at the bottom right. When you're satisfied with the new color (for editing a color, you can compare your new choice to the old choice in that very box), type its name in the blank at the upper left.

5. Set **Process Separation** to **On** or **Off**.

6. Click on **OK**.

7. You'll be back to the **Color Palette** dialog box. If the palette is now complete and the way you want it, click on **Save**. (If you want to dump your changes, click on **Cancel**.)

## Duplicating a Color

This one's easy. If you've spent some time creating a nice color and you want to recreate it but just make it a little darker (or lighter, or cooler, or warmer), you can duplicate that color and make changes to the duplicate. To do this:

1. Select the color you wish to duplicate in the **Color Palette** dialog box.

2. Click on the **Duplicate** button. A copy of the selected color will be added to the palette and named **Copy of** (whatever the color name).

3. Make changes (as described in the previous section on editing a color).

4. Type a new name in the **Name:** field.

5. Click on **OK** and then on **Save.**

## Color Models and the Color Picker

QuarkXPress 3.0 uses four color models to express color: HSB, RGB, CMYK, and PMS. Each model is best suited to a particular aspect of working with colors: seeing, printing, showing, and making colors. This chapter explains how the models can all work together and how you can use each to its best advantage.

The models show up in the **Color Picker**, which is part of the **Edit Color** dialog box (Figure 6-13). This picker shows up in many Macintosh programs, though not in exactly this form. It lets you choose the colors you're going to use in your document.

## Seeing Color: HSB

HSB stands for hue, saturation, and brightness. It refers to the way the eye perceives color. The best way to demonstrate this is to use QuarkXPress itself to show HSB's characteristics.

1. Choose **Colors**... from the **Edit** menu and click on the **New** button to see the **Edit** dialog box with the **Color Picker.**

2. Click the **HSB** radio button to change the current color-definition model to HSB, as shown in Figure 6-14. Now position the cursor on the color you want to pick from the color wheel and click to pick a color. Try picking some other colors. Each color you choose appears in a swatch in the **New:Old:** color area.

3. Now play with the percentages of **Hue**, **Saturation**, and **Brightness**. Scroll through each by clicking on the arrows at the end of each scroll bar or by clicking on the box within the scroll bar, just as you do the scroll bar for scrolling the page. This demonstrates the effects of increasing and decreasing each of HSB's values and their corresponding effects on what you see on-screen.

### Showing Color: RGB

Your computer monitor (or even your color television) shows color with the RGB model. RGB stands for red, green, blue. A computer monitor or video screen creates its images and colors by combining different intensities of red, green, and blue phosphors on the screen. If you look very closely at a video display, you'll see each of the red/green/blue pixels making up every image.

1. Change your color model selection in the **Edit Color** dialog box to **RGB**, as in Figure 6-15.

2. Notice how the **Red**, **Green**, and **Blue** percentage values change as you select different locations on the color wheel.

3. Experiment with the scroll bars for **Red**, **Green**, and **Blue**, choosing different component values to see how they add up to a final color.

> **Extra!**
>
> *A note of caution regarding choosing PMS colors (and any other color selection you make in QuarkXPress): It's a good idea to get a PMS color selector and have it handy when choosing colors in QuarkXPress 3.0. The on-screen representation of the color is rough at best and should not be held as an accurate interpretation of the true color. Always choose the color you want from the PMS color selector book before choosing its corresponding screen representation from the QuarkXPress on-screen color library.*

## Printing Color: CMYK

If you intend to have several colors throughout a printed piece, then printing them all as spot colors can be expensive because each spot color requires a separate plate.

Most color is printed on paper through process-color printing. Process color mixes separate halftones of each of four colors — cyan, magenta, yellow, and black (CMYK) — to simulate a whole range of colors. This is also how full-color photographs are simulated in printing. In fact, if you look closely at the cover of this book with a magnifying glass, you'll see that the color images there are made from a combination of all four process colors.

You can use different combinations of halftone screens of each of the four process colors to closely match almost any color. Most printers will give you a screen color guide/selector to help you match a process color to any color you've chosen. QuarkXPress 3.0 has this matching capability built-in.

1. Change your color model selection in the **Edit Color** dialog box to CMYK, as in Figure 6-16.

2. Try the same experiments with the **Color Picker** using the CMYK color model as you did with the other models. This time, you have four scroll bars. Change a CMYK color selection by changing the percentages of each of these component colors. Try scrolling the CMYK color-percentage fields. Notice how the color selection dot changes location to reflect the color change you specify when you change the values in those fields.

The CMYK technique of specifying colors is convenient only if you know the exact percentages of the component process colors needed to create the color you want. Even if you have a process-color selection guide with all of the available combinations, it's still tedious to specify color this way. Read the next section on PMS for the best way to select color accurately in QuarkXPress 3.0.

## Making Color: PMS

The simplest way to print in color is to mix up the colored ink you've chosen and apply each with a separate plate on the press. This is known as spot-color printing. It's easy and effective if you're printing only two or three colors on a piece. (As mentioned earlier, it's less expensive to use process color or process separations when you print a piece with several colors.)

PMS stands for Pantone Matching System, and it's a proprietary color standard developed by the Pantone Corporation. It consists of thousands of individual colors that are mixed using standardized ink-mixture formulas accepted all over the world. When you design and produce art for any graphic or publishing project and specify a certain PMS ink color, you can print the piece anywhere in the world and be confident that the printed color that comes back will be the same color you chose when you created your piece.

You can get Pantone color-selection guides at any art supply store or through your local printing rep. The guides come in small swatch books or in a huge library with several volumes and thousands of tear-off swatches, making it easy to compare the colors on your monitor screen to the actual colors in the guide.

As QuarkXPress 3.0 incorporates the PMS color library into its software, it's the easiest and most accurate model to use when choosing color.

1. Choose the **Pantone** option in the **Edit Color** dialog box. The standard color wheel becomes the Pantone library of ink colors, as shown in Figure 6-17.

2. If you're working with a PMS color that's part of a corporate graphics standard, type the PMS color number. The color library display jumps to that color, highlighting it and putting its name into the **Name** slot.

3. Choose any PMS color from the Pantone library, then choose the CMYK option radio button. You can see QuarkXPress 3.0 building this color, using different percentages of the four process colors.

## Hardware's Effects on Color Models and Matching

You can always expect the on-screen representation of any color to be different when it's shown on different monitors or different machines, or even on the same machine at different times. It's easy for the monitor's calibration to change from day to day, owing to sunspots, solar flares, elves, gnomes, wizards, demons, and bodily humors.

If you're using a large-screen monitor and card combination with enhanced color-display capabilities, such as 24-bit or 32-bit color, your color representation on-screen will be much more accurate and consistent from day to day.

**Extra!**

*To select more than one background color when you're specifying trapping amounts, hold down the **Shift** key while you select sequential background colors on the menu list. Hold down the ⌘ key while you individually click each color to select colors that aren't sequential.*

This solution is somewhat expensive, but it's worth it if you need that kind of accuracy and consistency. Check with your local dealer for information.

## Back to Creating a Color Palette

Now that you're clear on color models, you can turn back to some of the other **Edit Color** choices for your color palette.

**Appending Colors.** If you've created a document with a special color palette and then have to create another document using the same colors, you can transfer the colors from an existing document to a new one (or from any document to any other document) by appending the color palette.

1. Find another QuarkXPress document with a palette you like (do this by keeping notes on which documents have valuable palettes or by opening the documents on-screen and inspecting the palettes until you find one you want).

2. Open a new document and choose **Colors** from the **Edit** menu.

3. Click on the **Append** button in the **Default Colors** dialog box.

4. In the **Append Colors** dialog box (shown in Figure 6-18), select the document you chose in Step 1. Click on **Open** (this won't actually open the document but will add its palette to your new document's palette).

5. Scroll through your new palette to see the combined palettes.

**Specifying Traps, Spreads, and Chokes.** You can select an individual color or group of colors in your palette and specify the amount it will spread, choke, or trap against or over a background color. However, you need to know some printing terms before you can understand traps and how to set them.

**Spot color:** requires that separate plates be created for each color that's printed.

**Process color:** colors that are created by mixing halftones of different densities of four process colors (cyan, magenta, yellow, and black).

**Separations:** the individual plates that together make up composite colors or images in printing.

**Registration:** the method that ensures all composite plates and colors are aligned properly for accurate printing.

**Spread:** a slight enlargement of items on a color plate to overlap another color when printing.

**Trap:** a minute overlapping technique that allows for a slight misregistration on the press to keep color integrity.

**Knockout:** a colored area that has been removed so another color can be printed in that area; this keeps the first layer of ink from overprinting the other.

**Choke:** the slight reduction of items from which color is knocked out of a background color.

**Over Print:** when one color is printed directly onto another color.

**Screen-build:** when a color is created, or built, by mixing halftone screens with the four process colors.

## Setting Trap Values

1. Open the document where you want to set trap values.

2. Choose **Colors**... from the **Edit** menu.

3. From the palette, select the color you want to set the trap for.

4. Click on the **Edit Trap** button. You'll see the **Trap Specifications** dialog box, as shown in Figure 6-19.

5. Set the trapping relationship between your selected color and any of the

other background colors that appear in this menu. (The name of your background color will be part of the dialog box title.) You can set trapping values to **Automatic, Overprint,** and **Numeric** value — to ±5 points in increments of .001 point (or any other unit of measure you're using).

6. Click on **OK** when you set your trap, then click on **Save** to store the new trap values with your document.

It's easiest to leave all of the settings on **Automatic** unless there are special conditions and you know what you're doing.

**Automatic Trapping Specifications.** QuarkXPress 3.0 has automatic trapping based on the amount of black in the object's color and background. If an object's color is darker than its background color (as measured by the amount of black in either color), then the background is choked to trap the colors. If an object's color is lighter than its background color (as measured by the amount of black in either color), then the background is enlarged, or spread, to create the trap.

**Custom Trapping Values.** Though you'll probably use the automatic trapping option, sometimes you may want to customize the trapping values yourself, as in the following, or other situations:

1. Larger format jobs. When your image area is very large on a sheet and there is a greater chance that the paper sheet will stretch, it's a good idea to create a little more trapping area to allow for paper stretch.

2. Multicolor jobs running on single-color presses. When a print job is being run several times through a press, there is greater chance for misregistration and paper stretch. In these situations, it might be appropriate to increase slightly the trapping values. This is especially true if the color covers large areas of the paper.

3. Smaller multicolor jobs being run on multicolor presses. When working with small image areas where colors are adjacent to each other and registration is not a problem (such as business cards), it's probably a good idea to edit the trapping values so they're a little lower.

Some situations might call for customized trapping values for specific colors. When customizing any trapping relationship, it's always a good idea to consult your printer.

## Tips on Printing Color

After you've set your palette and done some designing with its colors, you need to get those colors out of QuarkXPress and onto a hard copy somewhere.

However, there are a few tips you should keep in mind when preparing color production with QuarkXPress.

Tight registration is important to have but difficult to get. In fact, highly accurate registration of the images and separations on your work is absolutely crucial. If you have already created and output a project and want to make changes to some items, colors, or information so that you have to rerun some or all of the job, it's best to rerun all of the separations for each changed page.

In fact, you should rerun them at the same time, on the same day, because the age and temperature of the developing chemistry, the air temperature and humidity in the room where the processor is running, the temperature and age of the photosensitive paper or film on which the project is being imaged, and other magical forces of nature (or even the mental attitude of the operator) can have small but very significant effects on your output's quality.

These effects may take the form of almost invisible changes to such things as screen density, location of trim lines, and image stretching. These may be imperceptible when you view them alone, but when they're brought together on press they can have disastrous effects on your final output, such as a moire pattern (a visual effect of pattern lines where there shouldn't be any) that completely ruins an image.

For example, if you have a four-color project that uses process colors and there you make a late change to some text on the black plate, your first reaction might be to re-run only the black plate with the text changes. Don't do it. Small changes and possible misregistrations can cause unsightly moire patterns in every image that appears on this page. Depending on how far along the project is toward completion, this can destroy your schedule and budget.

Also, if you're going to produce your work using process colors and you've chosen PMS colors as some of the colors in your palette, you must remember to select the **Process Separation** option for QuarkXPress to make the separations needed. Otherwise, QuarkXPress will print your PMS colors as spot colors.

Finally, remember that experience is your best education. You should budget time and money for a few experiments each time you try a new technique. The few dollars more you spend to test the output will be worth every cent. It is certainly better than having to reprint an entire job.

> **Tip**
>
> *Take care when you reverse colored text from a background color. It's easy for smaller-sized text to misregister on the printing press. Consult with your printer to make sure it can calibrate and control its presses to the precision your design demands. Overprinting text onto a halftone screen or process-color background can also create problems if the halftone screen is coarse enough to interfere with the small serifs and thin lines of small text. In these instances, make sure you specify a fine line-screen value for the halftone or that the type is large enough so that the type won't fight with the halftone dots.*

## Some Special Tricks with Color

Here are some special tricks you can perform with colored items in QuarkXPress.

**Graduated Lines.** This first trick is possible because QuarkXPress lets you group objects together and save them as a group so you can use them later on. It is a good idea to perform this trick on an open part of the page or on the pasteboard area to keep the background clear of any extra objects that might be in the way.

1. Start by creating a new constrained horizontal or vertical line.

2. Change its attributes to make it wider. Make it 24 points wide by changing the Width field in the **Measurement** palette, as shown in Figure 6-20.

3. Choose **Step and Repeat** from the **Item** menu to make five copies of this widened line, but make sure that the offset values (the distance between each successive copy) are both 0. This creates all of the copies of the line right on top of each other. Because they all occupy the same location on the page, you won't see any change.

4. Select the top line by clicking on it. Don't change its location or angle yet, but change its weight to 2 points and its color to **White.**

5. Send it to the back by choosing **Send to Back** from the **Item** menu. It will appear to have disappeared or changed into a fatter black line because it has been moved behind the other five 24-point lines.

6. Select the next line (it will have automatically become the topmost line in the order). Change its weight to 4 points and its shade to **20%** of **Black**, then send it to the back.

229

7. Select the next line, change its weight to 6 points and its shade to **40%** of **Black**, then send it to the back.

8. Relax. Every time you change one of the lines and then send it to the back it will appear to change back into a 24-point line. Don't worry: the selected line is being moved to the back, so it's hidden by a wider line in front of it.

9. Select the next line by clicking on it and changing its attributes to 8 points and **60%** of **Black**. Send it to the back.

10. Select the next (fifth) line by clicking on it and change its attributes to 10 points and **80%** of **Black**. Send it to the back as it is.

11. Select the last 24-point black line and send it to the back.

12. The result of all this work is that you should see a graduated line like the one in Figure 6-21.

13. The final step: Use the **Item** tool to draw a selection rectangle around all six lines, thereby selecting all of them, and choose **Group** from the **Item** menu. This will save the group as a single element for use anywhere you want. Remember you can duplicate it and rotate it as often as you want, wherever you want.

You can change the length of the graduated line by ungrouping it and sequentially changing the length of each component part and sending it to the back. You can use this trick to create graduated lines of any color, but the smoothness of the gradation will depend on how many steps you use to make the gradation. A wide line with a smooth transition will take a lot more steps than the one in this exercise. Try it with different combinations and gradations of colors.

When you're finished, you can select the grouped lines and move them into your library palette for use later.

**Alphabet Blocks.** The second trick lets you create your own set of alphabet blocks to use as large ornaments to open paragraphs. You can make them as complex as you want and group them and save them as library items to use whenever you want.

1. Start by creating a new text box anywhere on a blank page. Then type in the capital letter **A**. Select it by highlighting it and change its size to 160 points. If the text box is not big enough to hold the letter, the letter disappears and you see the text overflow symbol in the lower right-hand corner of the box. If that happens, just enlarge the box to fit loosely around the letter.

2. Choose **Modify** from the **Item** menu and change the text box's **Text Inset** field to 6 points. This automatically forces the letter in from any edge by that amount. Click on **OK.** Now arrange the box so the letter is centered along both axes and looks evenly spaced, as shown in Figure 6-22.

3. Now go to the **Preferences... General** dialog box and make sure that you specify borders (**Framing**) to grow **Outside** from boxes. Then select your text box and place a 12-point double-line border around it, as in Figure 6-23.

4. Change the background color of the text box to whatever color you want, then select the character and change its color to a contrasting color. Finally, add some variety by changing the border color. Figure 6-24 is an example, though you may choose different colors.

This alphabet-block object may be stored as a library item for use anytime, anywhere. You can change the letter inside the block by selecting it and typing a new letter. If the new letter doesn't fit (if you get the overflow symbol and the letter disappears), just choose **Select All** from the menu and change the character width with your keyboard shortcut.

**CHAPTER 7**

**Sample Assignment #1**

# Creating a Newsletter Format

In this chapter, you'll create a four-page, three-column newsletter with linked text boxes, automatic page numbering, pictures, lines, borders, headlines, and special halftone effects. Talk about easy — you're going to love this stuff!

You'll produce this newsletter with the QuarkXPress 3.0 sample and tutorial files that came with your software, so the pictures and text are the same in this book as they are in your software.

The design follows a generic three-column layout grid. It throws in some unique QuarkXPress 3.0 enhancements that will really make your design stand out in the crowd.

Ready? Here we go . . .

Before you start on your computer layout, it's always a good idea to sketch out a few rough ideas on paper. This helps you visualize the layout while you're working.

1. To start, choose **New** from the **File** menu. When QuarkXPress 3.0 displays the **New Document** dialog box, put in attributes that match the ones shown in Figure 7-1.

2. Choose **Show Document Layout** from the **View** menu. This displays the **Document Layout** palette that shows the master-page layouts.

```
                              New
┌─Page Size──────────────────────────┐  ┌─Column Guides──────────┐
│  ○ US Letter   ○ A4 Letter   ○ Tabloid │  │ Columns:    [ 3 ]      │
│  ○ US Legal    ○ B5 Letter   ● Other   │  │                        │
│  Width:  [9"]      Height:  [12"]      │  │ Gutter Width: [0.375"] │
└────────────────────────────────────────┘  └────────────────────────┘

┌─Margin Guides──────────────────────────┐     ☒ Automatic Text Box
│  Top:    [1"]     Inside:  [1"]        │
│  Bottom: [1"]     Outside: [1"]        │        ┌────┐   ┌────────┐
│            ☒ Facing Pages              │        │ OK │   │ Cancel │
└────────────────────────────────────────┘        └────┘   └────────┘
```

Figure 7-1. New Document dialog box with attributes for Chapter 7 exercise.

## Creating the Layout

3. Now create a master-page format, or layout, by adding format lines and design elements that will be common to all the pages. Items you place on a master-page layout appear on every page you use the master to create. Start to create a master-page layout by double-clicking on the default **Master Page** icon. This shows you the default master-page layout.

> *Extra!*
>
> *Remember the shortcut to making your own thumbnail view: Reduce the size of the document window and choose **Fit in Window**. The advantage to this method over choosing **Thumbnails** from the **View** menu is that you can easily zoom in and out of the reduced view using the keyboard shortcut, without having to make a menu selection. It's also easier to move items in the layout.*

4. Choose **Fit in Window** from the **View** menu (the keyboard shortcut is ⌘+0 [zero]). This fits your master page layout view into your document window. Because you created this document in Step 1 with the **Facing Pages** option enabled in the **New Document** dialog box, the **Master Page** icon has turned-down corners, indicating that it accommodates a two-page spread layout. When you reduce this view to fit into the document window, it shows both pages of a spread. The spread page design involves master pages with shared design elements, so you'll create a format with this feature.

5. Now you can begin adding design elements to the master page. Start by creating a bold format line that stretches across the top of both pages. Click once on the **Constrained Line** tool to select it, then click and drag it across the top of the left page to place the line at the top margin and extending all the way over to the left page's boundary edge. Choose **Runaround** from the **Item** menu and choose **Item** in the pop-up **Mode** menu, then click on **OK**. This ensures that no text appears over the line. Create another line across the top of the right page by choosing **Step and Repeat** and typing 8" in the **Horizontal Offset** field and 0" in the **Vertical Offset** field. This creates an exact duplicate of the right page's format line. Figure 7-2 shows this action.

6. To make the line thicker, select it and choose a suitable line weight from the **Weight** pop-up menu under the **Style** menu. For this demonstration, choose the 12-point line weight. You can also perform this step by selecting the **Line Weight** field on the **Measurements** palette and typing in a new line thickness (see Figure 7-3).

7. To make the layout symmetrical, add another line at the bottom of the page. Before using the **Constrained Line** tool again, select only the line on the left page (handles should be visible at each end of the line) and choose **Step and Repeat** from the **Item** menu. Enter the values shown in

USING QUARKXPRESS

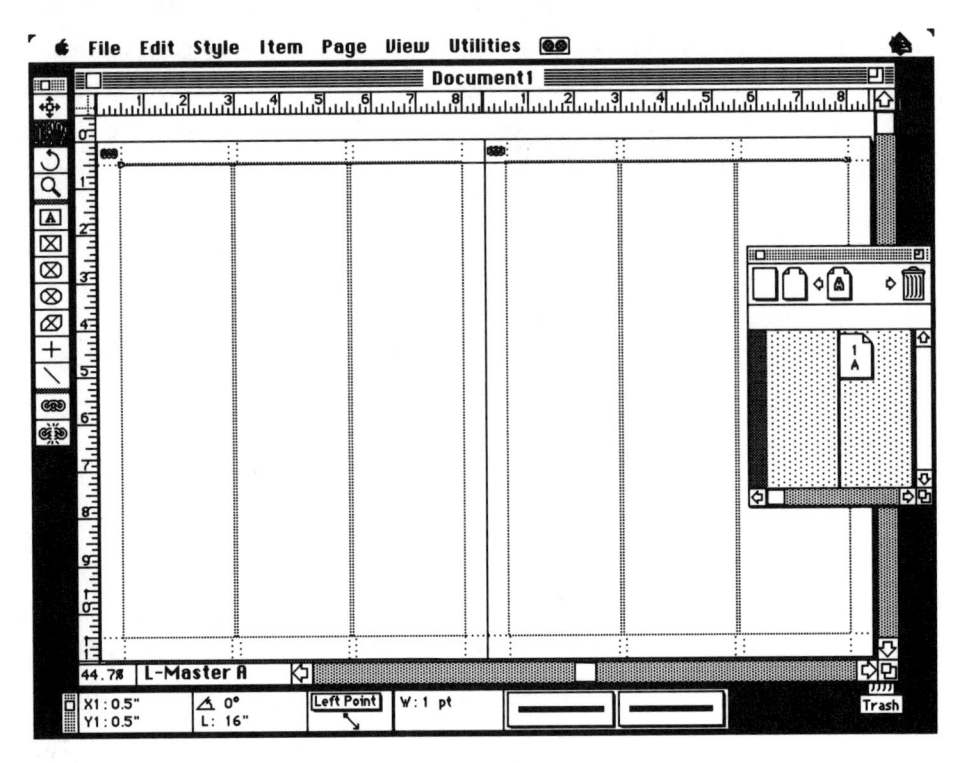

**Figure 7-2. Drawing Lines on both pages — Step 5.**

Figure 7-4 to repeat the line exactly 10 inches down from the original line: **0"** for the **Horizontal Offset** and **10"** for the **Vertical Offset**, with only **1** for the **Repeat Count.**

Click on **OK** and repeat the action for the line on the right page. Your layout should now look like Figure 7-5.

**Figure 7-3 Line weight field highlighted on the Measurements palette — Step 6.**

Figure 7-4. Step and Repeat dialog box with values for Step 7.

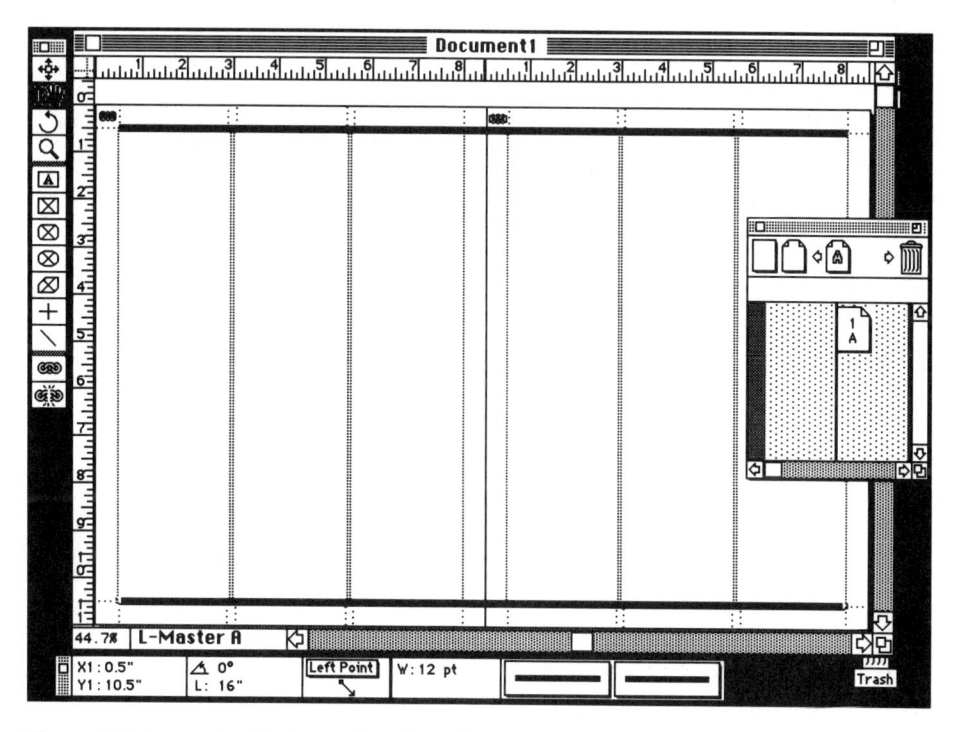

Figure 7-5. Layout with lines after Step 7.

USING QUARKXPRESS

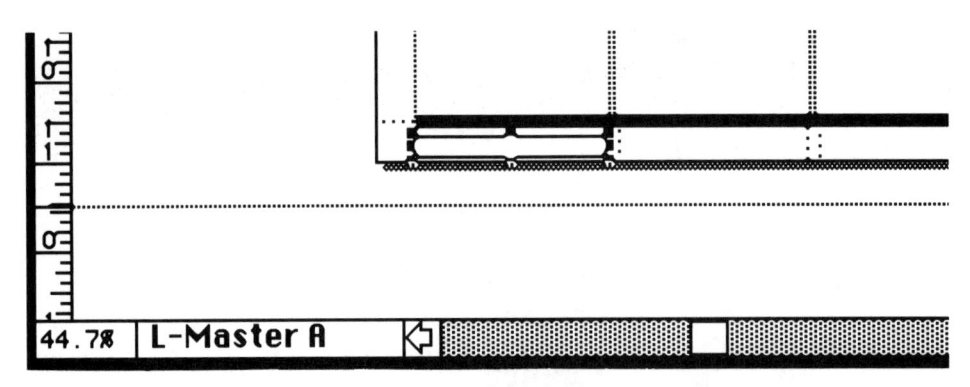

**Figure 7-6. Small text box for smart page numbering — Step 8.**

8. Add your "smart" page numbering by creating a new small text box and placing it in the layout's lower left outside corners, as shown in Figure 7-6. Zoom in for a closer view of this text box with the **Magnifying** tool. Click and drag the area until it fills the document window so that you can clearly see the page-numbering text as you add it. Or choose **200%** from the **View** menu and scroll to the area to get a closer look at it.

9. Now add the automatic page numbering text box. This text box is created on the master page layout, and anything you type into it automatically shows on each page created from this master.

   Click on the **Content** tool, then press ⌘+3 Spacebar and type **Newsletter.** This puts the automatic page number (which appears as <#>) and the word **Newsletter** on each of the left-facing master pages. The results should look like Figure 7-7. It appears like this on-screen, but it reads as the correct current page number when you finish making your master page layout and return to the document window.

10. Select the text and use the appropriate settings on the **Measurements** palette to change the character attributes to **10 point Times Italic**. You can also specify these attributes by choosing **Character...** under the **Style** menu.

238

**Figure 7-7.** Automatic page numbering text highlighted — Step 7.

11. Move the text box with the page number closer to the format line. Choose the **Item** tool, click on the text box and drag. Or select the **Vertical Location** field (the **Y** value, as shown in Figure 7-8) in the **Measurements** palette and change the number there to **10.625"**.

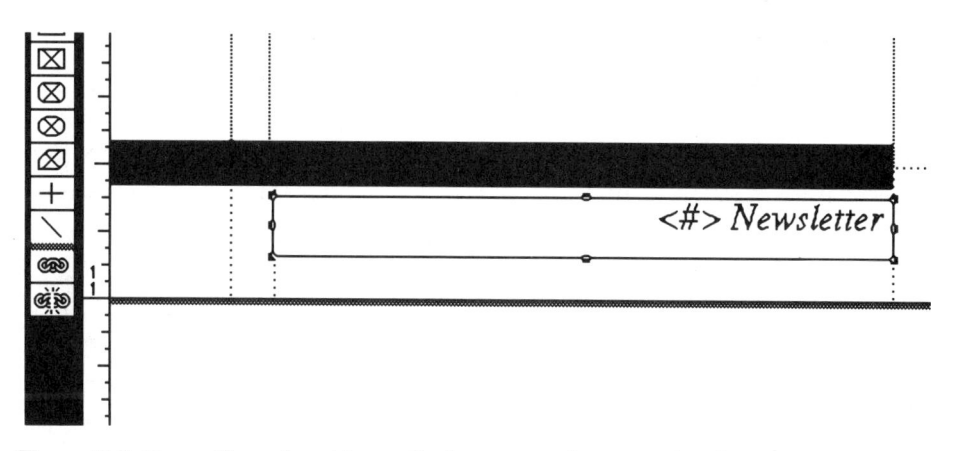

**Figure 7-8.** Repositioned and formatted page-number text after Step 11.

12. Now step-and-repeat this text box to the other side of the spread. Change your view to **Fit in Window** (in the **View** menu). As you did with the format lines, select the text box and choose **Step and Repeat** from the

Item menu. This time, tell the item to repeat itself horizontally about 10". This puts it close to the part of the area where you'll want it on the right page. Position it more accurately after duplicating it by selecting the **Item** tool and dragging this new text box to the right. Put the right edge of the text box flush with the right-page margin. If you want, change your view to 200% to clearly see the page margin and the text box.

13. Change the alignment of the text itself to flush right by selecting the **Content** tool and clicking on the **Flush Right** icon in the **Measurement** palette. This balances the page-numbering format in the spread so that the page numbering hugs the outside margin on both pages.

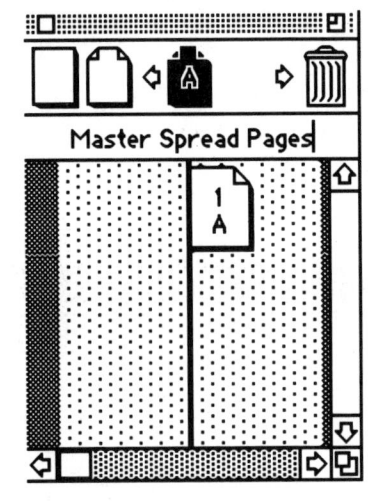

**Figure 7-9. Master Page icon selected and new name typed in — from Step 14.**

14. Your master page layout is complete. Give it a name by selecting the **Master Page** icon in the **Document Layout** palette and typing in a new name, as shown in Figure 7-9.

15. To return to the document window, double-click on the **Document Page** icon in the **Document Layout** palette.

16. Now to create the rest of the layout pages. As there is only one master page, use it to create the rest of the layout. Select the **Master Page** icon in the **Document Layout** palette and drag it down to the document page icons, as in Figure 7-10.

# NEWSLETTER FORMAT

## The Masthead

17. How about a snazzy masthead? Start by creating a new text box to hold your masthead type. Make it fairly large to accommodate a large type treatment. Stretch it across the top of the page, as shown in Figure 7-11.

18. Use the keyboard shortcut to center the masthead text (**Shift+⌘+C**). Then type in the title of your newsletter **SpokeS** (note the style effect of capitalizing the second S). Increase the view size by choosing **Actual Size** from the **View** menu (or use the keyboard shortcut ⌘+1), as shown in Figure 7-12.

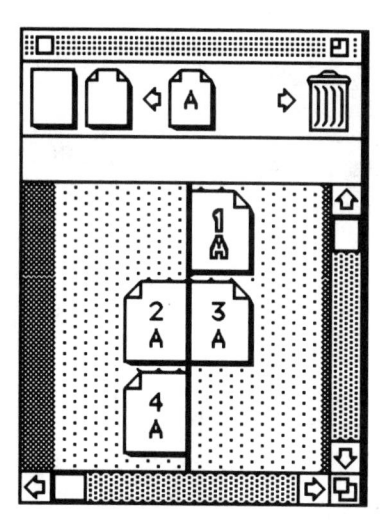

**Figure 7-10.** Results in Document Layout palette of creating four document page icons — from Step 16.

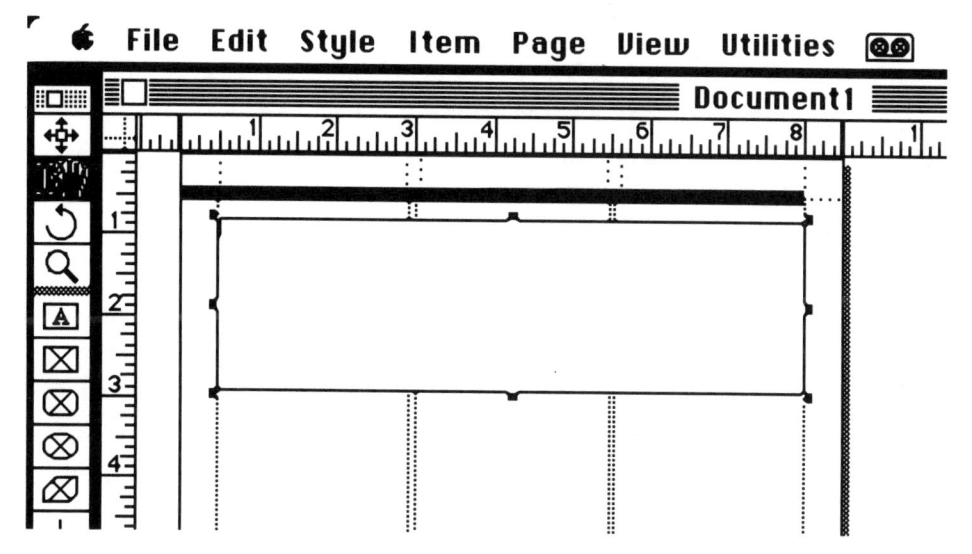

**Figure 7-11.** Large Masthead text box.

241

USING QUARKXPRESS

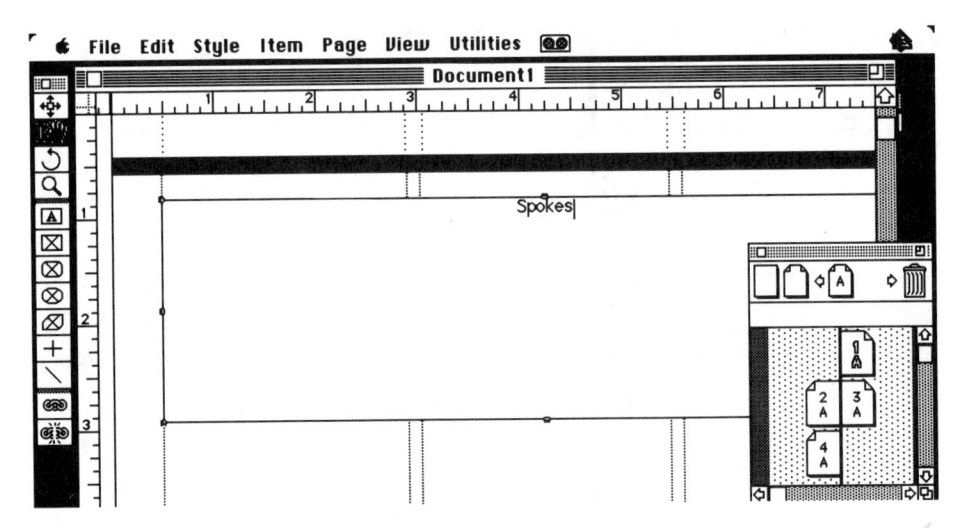

Figure 7-12. Actual Size view of text in Masthead box.

19. The default text-style selection is always Helvetica, which is fine for this project. Select all of the text in the masthead text box by double clicking on **SpokeS** or by choosing **Select All** from the **Edit** menu. Increase the text size by selecting the text-size field and choose some style attributes from the **Measurements** palette. For this demonstration, make the text size 144 points and choose the **Bold, Italic,** and **Small Caps** icons. You can also play around with the character spacing at this size. Try using your keyboard equivalents, **Shift+⌘+[** or **Shift+⌘+]**, to individually adjust each letter.

20. Change your text-inset value in the **Modify** dialog box to adjust the space between the top of the text box and the top of the tallest letters. You can also do this by placing your text-insertion cursor before the first letter, changing the text size to 2 points, and inserting blank line returns before the first letter. This creeps the text down in the box in 2-point increments. Be wary of your leading values, though: Your 144-point type still has 20% leading enabled. If you want to force the type to appear closer to the bottom of the text box, change the leading to a negative value, such as -24.

21. To give this masthead more impact, reverse the text out of a black background by selecting all of the text and choosing **Color** from the **Style** menu. Then choose **White** from that pop-up menu.

22. Now choose **Modify** from the **Item** menu and change the background color of the masthead text box to **100% of Black**. Do this either by choosing the **Background Color** pop-up menu or by using the **Tab** key to advance from field to field until you highlight the **Background Color** shade. Then you can type in any percentage up to 100% (in 1% increments).

23. Now for the fun part. To give your newsletter real impact, use QuarkXPress' powerful rotation feature to place the masthead vertically on the front page. Start by changing your view to **Fit in Window**. As the rotation value in the **Measurements** palette is measured around the center of the masthead text box, use the **Item** tool to move it to the center of the page so it has plenty of room to rotate. Double-click on the **Box Angle** field on the **Measurement** palette and type in **90º** to rotate the box 90º to the left.

24. Click and drag the box handles on either edge of the box to extend the length of the box up to and down to both format lines. Then use the **Item** tool to move the box over to the right edge of the page margin, as in Figure 7-13.

25. Now for a box within a box. If you want to add information, such as the newsletter volume number and publication date, create a new text box near the top of the masthead text box and type in your volume and date information. Make sure that the box you create is transparent by choosing **None** from the **Runaround...** dialog box (in the **Item** menu). Then select all of the text inside it and change its style and color to **Bold** and **White**, just as you did with the original masthead.

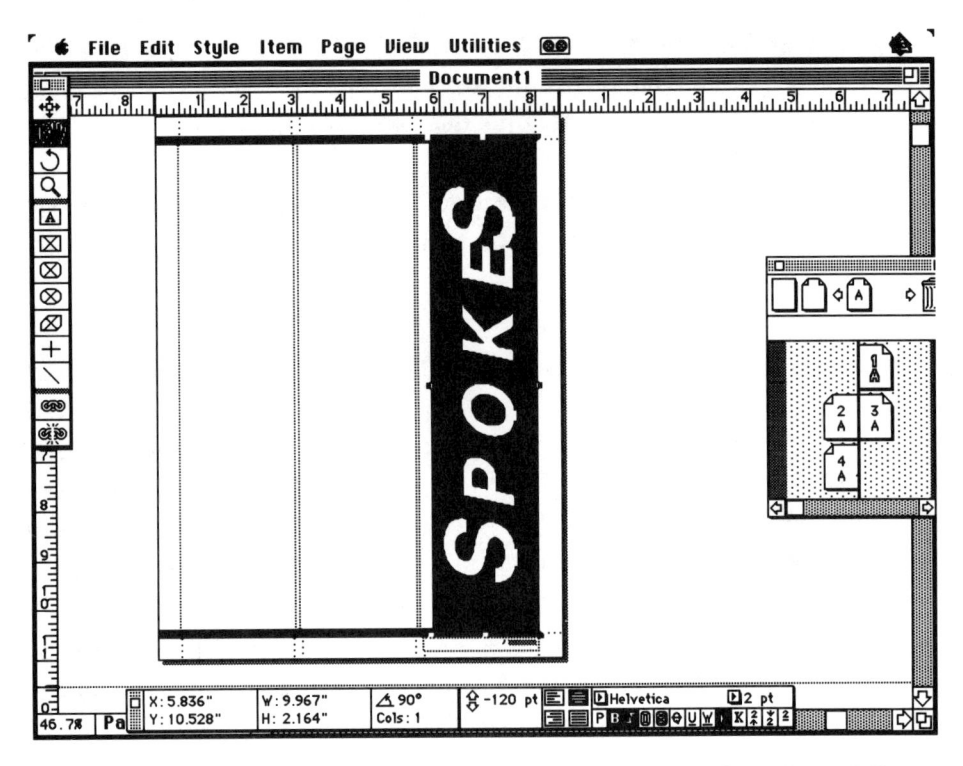

**Figure 7-13.** Masthead box rotated and moved to right page margin — through Step 24.

Group the masthead text box and the volume and date information box together by using the **Item** tool and selecting both boxes while holding down the **Shift** key. Then choose **Group** from the **Item** menu (the keyboard shortcut is ⌘+G). This ensures that the volume and date information text boxes go wherever the masthead goes. If you lock them both into their current position by choosing **Lock** from the **Item** menu, you can type new information into either box using the **Content** tool, but you won't be able to change their positions without using the **Measurements** palette.

244

## Flowing the Text

Now you're ready to start flowing your text into the main text boxes. Start by selecting the main text box on the first page with the **Content** tool.

26. Choose **Get Text...** from the **File** menu (the keyboard shortcut is ⌘+E). Select the text file called **Sample ASCII Text**. The text then flows into both front-page columns.

27. Select all of the text by choosing **Select All** from the **Edit** menu or by clicking anywhere within the text five times quickly. This highlights all the text in the active text chain. Change the text style to **Times** by selecting the **Font Selection** pop-up menu in the **Measurements** palette. Then double-click to select the leading value field and change that value to 18 points. This spaces your lines apart to make the text appear less dense.

You may also want to create more space at the top of the columns by selecting the text box and choosing **Modify** under the **Item** menu. Specify here where the first baseline occurs.

For this demonstration, type **1"** (notice that the default measurement has the " designation after the number — any number you type is measured in inches unless you define it as another unit of measure by typing **pt** for points, **p** for picas, **mm** for millimeters, etc.). This keeps a uniform 1-inch space between the boundary of the text box and the first baseline of the text. This also gives you space to create a bold subhead to lead off the text.

## The Bold Subhead

28. Create a new text box for your bold subhead and put it at the top of your main text box on page 1. Create a new text box because the subhead will extend across both columns of text in the main text box, as shown in Figure 7-14.

USING QUARKXPRESS

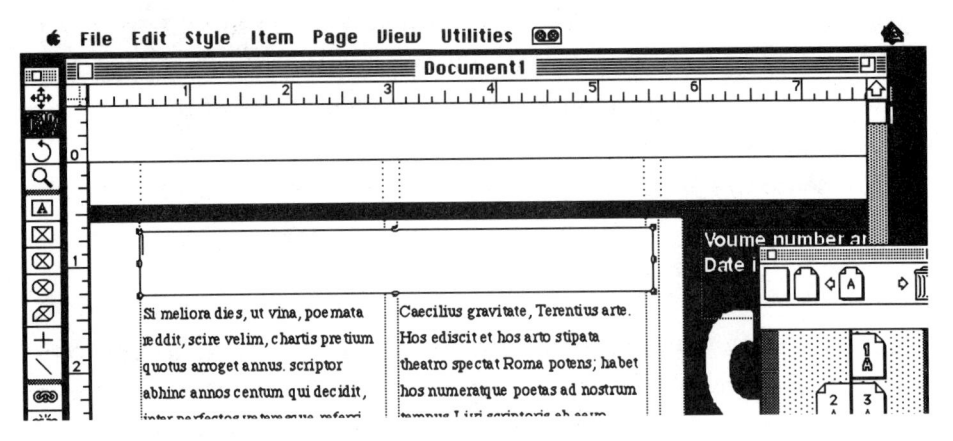

Figure 7-14. Subhead text box drawn across two columns of text.

29. Type in an appropriate headline, such as **Biking with the Best in 1990**. Select all the text and make it **Times Bold**, **30 points**, using the **Measurements** palette. Part of the subhead text should disappear and the overflow icon should appear, as in Figure 7-15.

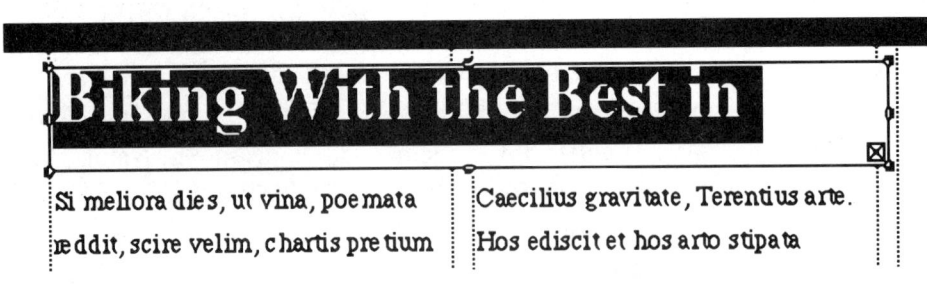

Figure 7-15. Formatted subhead text with overflow icon in text box — from Step 29.

While the subhead text is still selected, finesse the letter spacing to reduce the spacing between all of the characters by using your keyboard equivalent — **Shift+Option+⌘+[**. This tracks the text in increments of .005-em. All of the text should fit with a tracking value of -4. If it doesn't, continue tracking until it fits. Remember to follow the dictates of good taste. If you choose another subhead

246

# NEWSLETTER FORMAT

of your own that doesn't fit without excessive tracking, enlarge the text box to accommodate two lines of text. (See Chapter 4 for an explanation on tracking.)

## Smart Page Numbering

Create a **Continued On...** page number at the bottom of this text column to show where the text continues.

30. Change your view to 200% and zoom into the area at the bottom of the text box on page 1. Create a new text box and type: **This text is continued on page ⌘+4** (the keyboard shortcut command for indicating the next page number is ⌘+4). The results appear as in Figure 7-16.

**Figure 7-16. Text box with reference to page for text continuation.**

It reads **<None>** because the text box with the main text chain is not yet linked to any other text boxes.

31. To link this text box to the next text box, change your view to **Fit in Window.** Then select your **Text Chain Linking** tool and click on the text box holding your story. You'll see it highlighted with Apple's famous "marching ants" marquee. Now click on the main text box on page 3, which is where you want the text chain to continue. You'll see an arrow extending from the bottom of the text box on page 1 to the top of the text box on page 3, as in Figure 7-17. Whenever the text from the

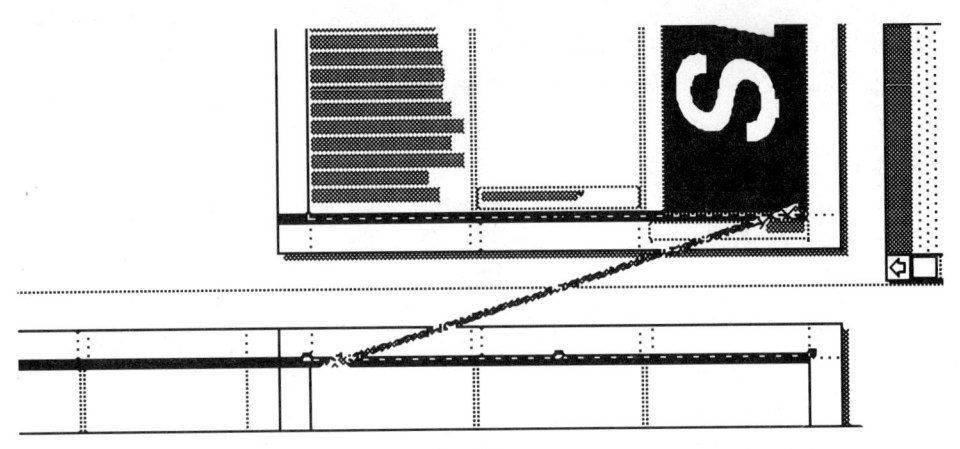

Figure 7-17. Text linking arrow from step 31.

text box on page 1 overflows that text box, it automatically flows to the text box on page 3.

Change your view to 200% again and zoom in on the "continued on..." statement. It should now read **Continued on page 3**.

32. To balance this statement, scroll down to page 3 and place another text box, such as the one you just placed on page 1, at the top of the first column of page 3. Type: **Continued from page ⌘+2**. (⌘+2 is the keyboard command for listing the previous page text chain.)

## Adding the Pictures

33. Change your view to **Fit in Window** and scroll back to page 1. Add a picture to page 1 by selecting one of the **New Picture Box Creation** tools and clicking and dragging it into position in the text box. Notice in Figure 7-18 how the new picture box displaces the text in the text box.

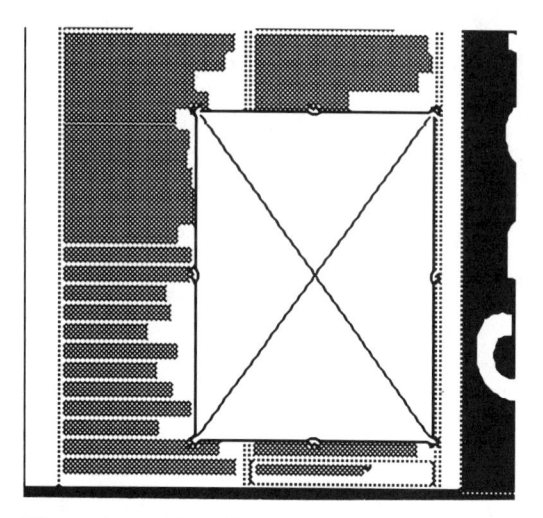

**Figure 7-18. New picture box displacing text, as in Step 33.**

**Figure 7-19. Text reflowing around a rotated picture box, from Step 35.**

34. While the new picture box is still selected, select the **Content** tool (if it isn't already selected) and choose **Get Picture** from the **File** menu. Select **Mt. Biker.TIFF** from the **Sample Pictures** folder that came with your QuarkXPress 3.0 package. Click on **Open.**

35. Reposition the image within the picture box by dragging it with the **Content** tool. After you've placed the image within the picture box, select the **Rotation** tool and drag the picture box from one of its corners to an interesting angle. The text in both columns automatically re-flows around the image, as shown in Figure 7-19, and even spills to page 3 if necessary.

**Figure 7-20. Text box for table of contents.**

## The Table of Contents

36. Create a new text box in the center of page 1 (column 2). This will hold a table of contents of your newsletter's major feature stories. (See Figure 7-20.)

37. Type or flow some contents listings into the new text box. Select all of the text and set the attributes, as shown in Figure 7-21.

While the type is still selected, choose **Formats** from

**Figure 7-21. Character attributes for table of contents text box.**

## Paragraph Formats

| | | | |
|---|---|---|---|
| Left Indent: | 0.25" | Leading: | +0 pt |
| First Line: | -0.15" | Space Before: | 0.125" |
| Right Indent: | 0.25" | Space After: | 0" |

☐ Lock to Baseline Grid  ☐ Keep with Next ¶
☐ Drop Caps  ☐ Keep Lines Together

Alignment: Left
H&J: Standard

[Apply] [OK] [Cancel]

Figure 7-22. Formats for table of contents.

- Change A Flat In 30 Seconds Flat
- More Of Your Favorite Recipes

Figure 7-23. Stray text between new table of contents box and rotated TIFF image.

the **Style** menu and set the style formats of Figure 7-22 for the table of contents.

38. Now put a frame around the table of contents box by choosing **Frame** from the **Item** menu and typing in 6 points for the weight. Wasn't that easy?

39. You may have some stray type between the table of contents box and the TIFF image, as shown in Figure 7-23.

If this happens on your layout, change the runaround characteristics of the picture box. As you know, runaround specifications are customizable for all four sides of your picture boxes. If you increase the text-outset values for the top and bottom edges of the picture box, you can force the stray text away from the picture box. To do this, select the picture box and choose **Runaround...** from the **Item** menu.

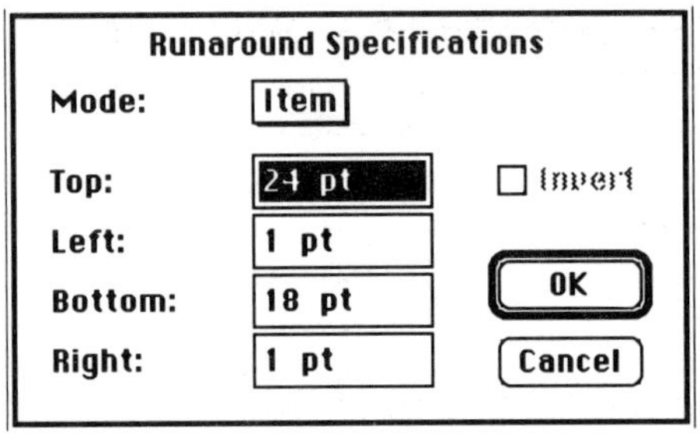

**Figure 7-24. Experimenting with the Runaround... specifications to move stray text away from the TIFF image.**

Add more space to the **Top** and **Bottom** fields, as in Figure 7-24. You might have to try a few numbers to get it right.

## The Innards

The inside front page has space for a brief advertisement of upcoming sales events and an article.

40. Go to page 2 (use the keyboard shortcut ⌘+J) and select the main text box with your **Content** tool.

41. To keep the format consistent, choose **Modify** from the **Item** menu and change the **First Baseline** value to **1"**, as you did with the main text box on page 1. (You can also do this when establishing formats in the master page display.)

42. Choose **Get Text...** from the **File** menu and select the same text file you did for page 1. Make sure to select the **Include Style Sheets** option. This flows the same text file into the first two columns of the text box.

43. This text will be your **Change a Flat** story, and it employs anchored rules, drop caps, and special formatting options. First choose **Modify** from the **Item** menu and change the **First Baseline** value to **1/2"**.

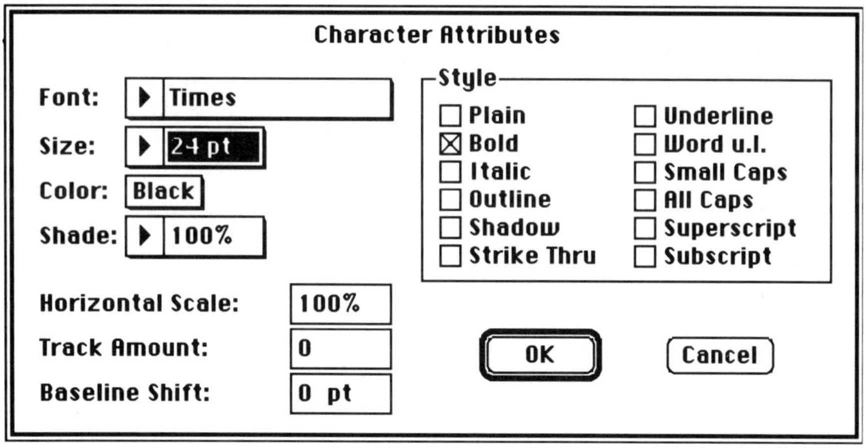

# LETTER FORMAT

Figure 7-25. Character attributes for subhead of Step 44.

44. Place your text-insertion cursor at the beginning of the text and type in a large subhead, **30 Seconds Flat.** Select it and change its attributes to match Figure 7-25.

45. Now select the rest of the text. Use the keyboard shortcut, **Shift+ Option+⌘+Down arrow,** to select all of the text from the insertion cursor to the end of the current text chain. Now format the selected text to include spaces between paragraphs, anchored rules, and drop caps by following Figure 7-26. Click on the **Apply** button before clicking on **OK,** to make sure everything fits.

46. Separate the paragraphs with rules. While the text is still selected, choose **Rules...** from the **Style** menu. Set paragraph rules to precede each paragraph by setting the **Offset** value and the **Width** value to the settings shown in Figure 7-27.

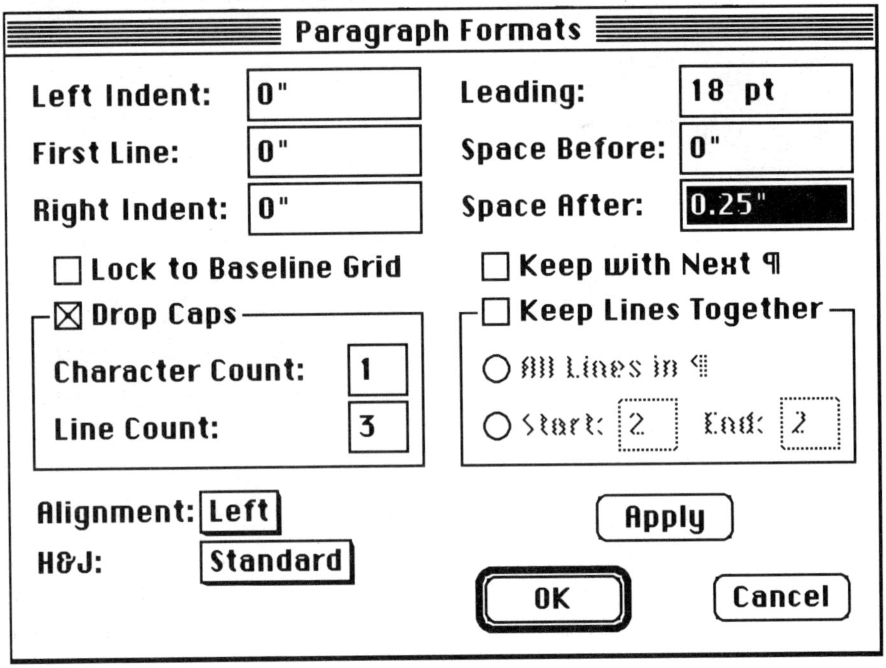

USING QUARKXPRESS

### Paragraph Formats

| | | | |
|---|---|---|---|
| Left Indent: | 0" | Leading: | 18 pt |
| First Line: | 0" | Space Before: | 0" |
| Right Indent: | 0" | Space After: | 0.25" |

☐ Lock to Baseline Grid    ☐ Keep with Next ¶

☒ Drop Caps                ☐ Keep Lines Together

Character Count: 1         ○ All Lines in ¶
Line Count: 3              ○ Start: 2  End: 2

Alignment: Left            Apply
H&J: Standard              OK    Cancel

Figure 7-26. Paragraph formats for text — from Step 45.

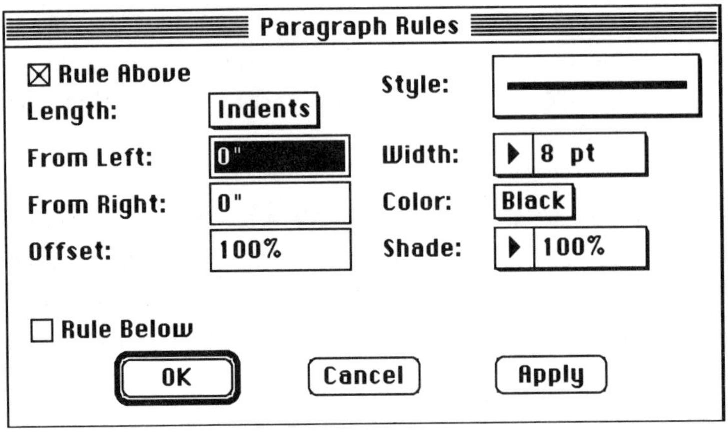

### Paragraph Rules

☒ Rule Above        Style: ─────────
Length: Indents
From Left: 0"       Width: ▶ 8 pt
From Right: 0"      Color: Black
Offset: 100%        Shade: ▶ 100%

☐ Rule Below

OK    Cancel    Apply

Figure 7-27. Offset and weight values for rules of Step 46.

## NEWSLETTER FORMAT

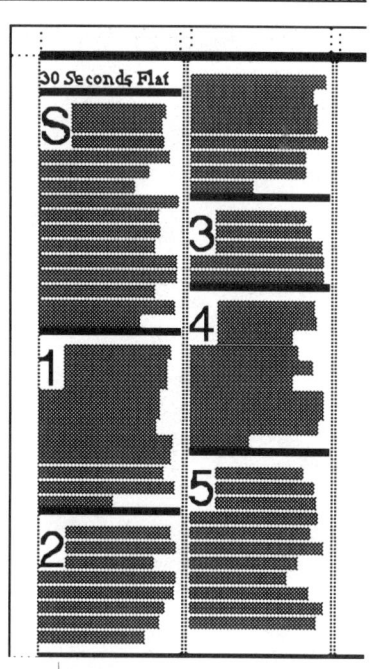

**Figure 7-28. Replacing initial paragraph letters with numbers — Step 47.**

47. Change the initial letters of each paragraph to numbers to better fit the article's premise. Change the page view to **Fit in Window** to make these changes easier. Select the initial caps by dragging the text cursor across them individually. Type a replacement for the initial cap in the same size and style as the rest of the word. Then type in a number to replace the letter. Take a look at Figure 7-28.

48. If you're going to illustrate the "30 Seconds Flat" story with diagrams or illustrations, place a square picture box at the top of the third column, then step-and-repeat it to fill the area. To make a square picture box, select a picture box creation tool, then hold down the **Shift** key while you drag in the area where you want the box.

49. Give the box a 1-point border by choosing **Frame** from the **Item** menu, then type **1** in the **Width** field.

50. Step-and-repeat the picture box vertically down the length of the column as many times as will fit the size box you've created. If you've followed this demonstration closely, you should be able to fit two copies of the box, about 3.25 inches apart, leaving plenty of space for captions. See Figure 7-29. Then import or paste pictures into each box to represent diagrams that would illustrate the story.

255

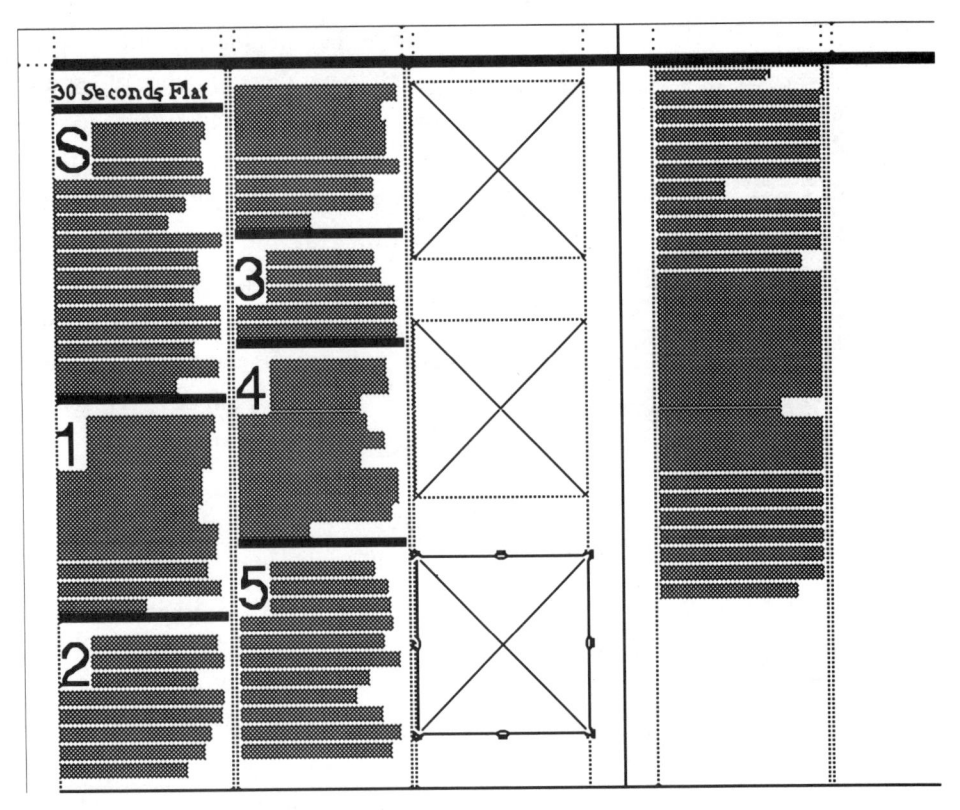

Figure 7-29. Square picture box after step-and-repeat operation — Step 50.

## The Advertising

Now you can add a special box on page 3 to hold advertising information. This will be a text box with an illustration, rotated text, and opposing tabs for prices.

51. Start by creating a new text box on page 3. Select the **Text Box Creation** tool and drag the cursor to create the box so it covers most of the extra space on page 3. Compare this to Figure 7-30.

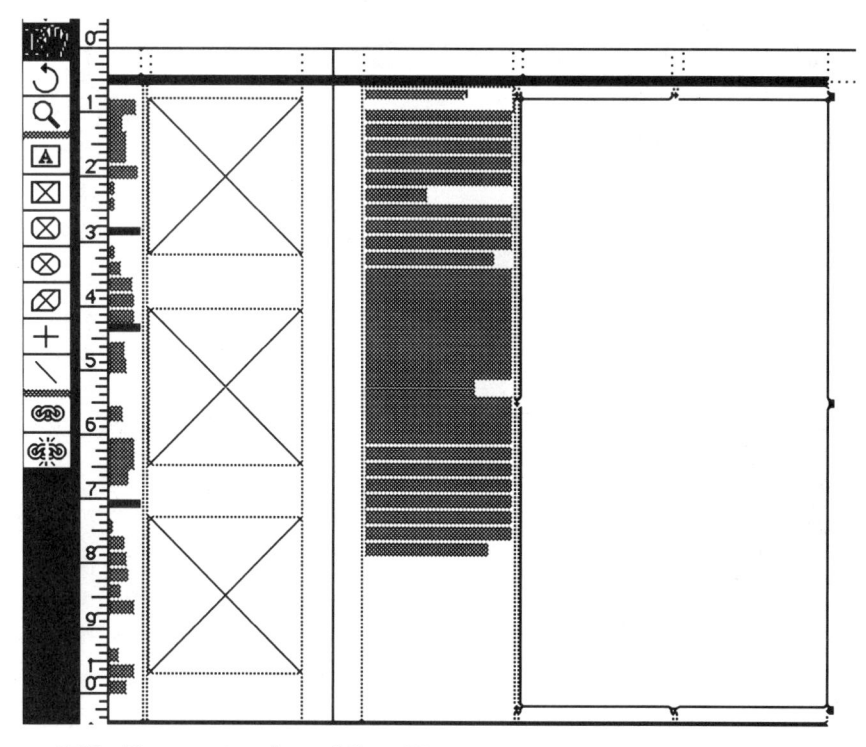

**Figure 7-30.** The new text box of Step 51.

52. Give the box a bold border by choosing **Frame** from the **Item** menu. Type 8 points for the **Width** field. Try choosing a different border style.

53. Create another text box within this one to hold the headline copy. Then type the headline copy: **SALE! SALE! SALE!**, and a smaller subhead that reads: **Savings and Value**.

54. Make the text of your subheads very large and bold so they capture the reader's attention, as in Figure 7-31.

55. Select both the headline text box and the surrounding bordered text box by using the **Item** tool and holding down the **Shift** key. Then choose **Space/Align...** from the **Item** menu. Click on the appropriate buttons and pop-up menus to align the two boxes horizontally along their center points, as shown in Figure 7-32.

Figure 7-31. Large, bold, attention-grabbing subhead from Step 54.

56. De-select the bordering box by holding down the **Shift** key while you click on it once. The headline box should still be selected. Now select the box angle measurement in the **Measurement** palette and change it to 10º. This tilts the entire text box to the left by 10º.

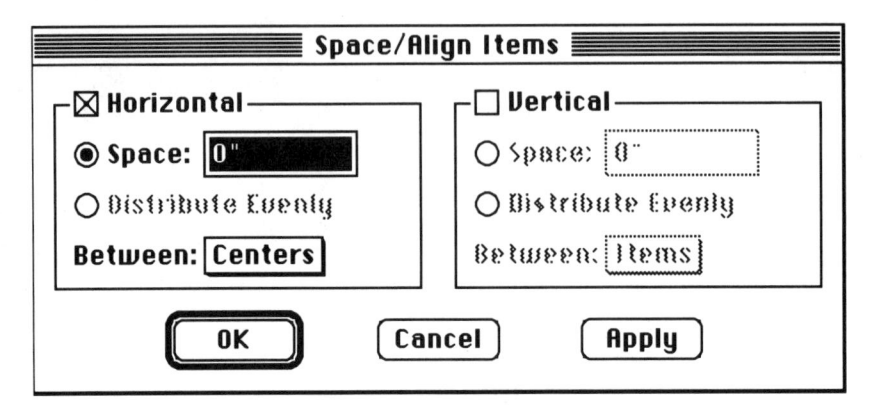

Figure 7-32. Spacing and alignment settings for Step 55.

57. Now for an extra format line to give the ad some pizzazz. Draw a new line under the headline by selecting the **Constrained Line** tool and dragging horizontally across the ad to the edge of the bordering box. Then change its angle to 10º.

**Figure 7-33. New picture box with imported Bicycle image — Step 58.**

58. Draw another new picture box about 1.25 inches square. Give it a 2-point border and import the picture **Bicycle** from the **Samples** disk that came with your QuarkXPress 3.0 package, as in Figure 7-33. (The **Bicycle** file is in the **Sample Library** folder.)

59. To make the design more consistent between the illustration and the headline, rotate the picture box 10º. Then rotate the picture inside by changing its rotation angle to -10º. This keeps the image inside the picture box perfectly horizontal while the border of the picture box rotates 10º.

60. Now step-and-repeat that picture box twice vertically on the page about 1.5 inches apart.

61. To create the opposing tabs for pricing information, select the large bordered text box with the **Content** tool and press **Return** until the cursor comes down to a point near the first bicycle illustration.

62. Choose **Formats** from the **Style** menu and specify 1/2" indents on the left side to give room between the illustration and the text margin. Change your text style to **18 point Helvetica Bold.** Type in a model name, press the **Tab** key once, and type in a price with a dollar sign, decimal point, and cents.

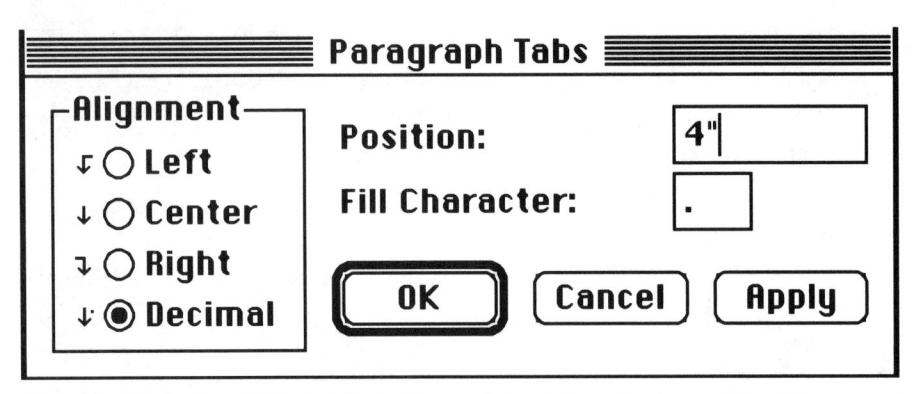

```
┌─────────────────────────────────────────────┐
│          ≡≡≡ Paragraph Tabs ≡≡≡             │
│ ┌─Alignment──┐                              │
│ │ ↲ ○ Left   │  Position:    ┌────────┐    │
│ │ ↓ ○ Center │               │  4"    │    │
│ │            │  Fill Character: ┌───┐      │
│ │ ↳ ○ Right  │                  │ . │      │
│ │ ↓ ● Decimal│  ┌──────┐ ┌──────┐ ┌──────┐ │
│ └────────────┘  │  OK  │ │Cancel│ │Apply │ │
│                 └──────┘ └──────┘ └──────┘ │
└─────────────────────────────────────────────┘
```

Figure 7-34. Decimal Tab to locate the model name and price — Step 63.

63. Select the line of text that has your model name and choose **Tabs...** from the **Style** menu. Set your decimal tab for a location of 4" with a period for a fill character. Click on the **Apply** button to see if your tabs space properly and there's enough room for the whole price number, as shown in Figure 7-34.

64. Type in paragraph returns to space the next number near the next picture box. Move the number to approximately the same position as the first number in relation to the picture box.

65. If you use the **Item** tool and the **Shift** key, select all of the items in this text box, and choose **Group** from the **Item** menu. You can preserve this group of objects for use in another publication by adding it to the library. Choose **Library...** from the **Utilities** menu. It asks you which library you would like to open, giving you the option of creating and naming a new library of your own. Use the **Item** tool and drag the group onto the **Library** palette appearing on-screen.

66. Create new text boxes to hold other information such as store hours, telephone numbers, and even descriptive product copy, or simply type and re-format it to fit the existing text box.

67. Now take a clearer look at your work. Choose **Fit in Window** from the **View** menu, then choose **Hide Guides** from the **View** menu. QuarkXPress shows the page without all the invisible guidelines. Your layout should look like the one shown in Figure 7-35.

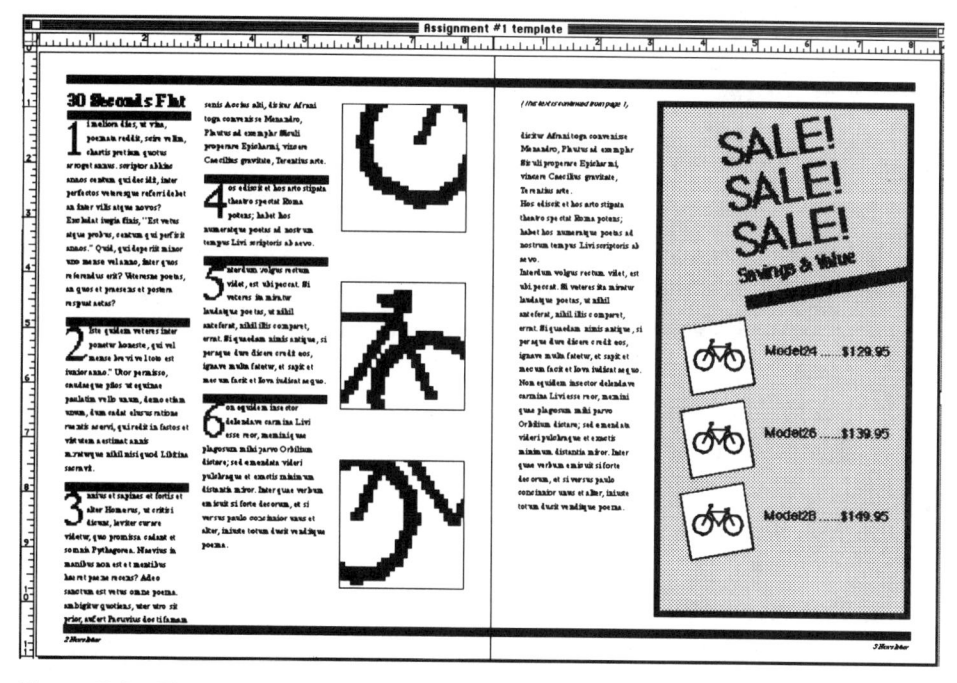

Figure 7-35. Finished layout.

## Saving Your Work

68. If you haven't saved your work (and you should do so every few minutes to avoid the wrath of the evil demons and trolls living inside of all computers), do it now. Name your file **This Month's Issue**.

69. If you're planning to use this layout for future issues, choose **Save As...** from the **File** menu (the keyboard equivalent is ⌘+Option+S) and click on the **Template** radio button. Give it another name, such as **Next**

**Month's Issue.** This saves your layout as a template that you can open, edit, and save as future documents. Templates retain all of the style sheets, colors, and formats that you establish for the original document. After you've opened and changed a template, QuarkXPress 3.0 asks you to save and name it as a new document before it allows you to close a template.

## Enhancements

You can enhance the look of your publication by adding a few simple extra goodies.

**Justify the text.** To make the text runaround on page 1 follow more closely the contours of the picture box boundaries, format the text to be justified. This causes the text to flow exactly to the boundaries of the picture box.

70. Select all of the text in the main text box. Choose **Alignment** and then **Justify** from the **Style** menu.

**Set the Text Outset.**

71. This should also push the text right up to the edge of the picture box. Use the **Runaround...** command to make more text-outset room around the picture box. Select the picture box and choose **Runaround...** from the **Item** menu (or use the keyboard equivalent, ⌘+T). Then select each text-outset field and increase the text-outset space to 12 points (or choose 1/6th of an inch or a more familiar unit of measure — QuarkXPress knows how to convert it).

**Enhancing the Image Output.** If you're printing your newsletter for final output on a LaserWriter, you can change the type of halftone screen that the picture prints to modify its appearance.

> **Extra!**
>
> ***Lino Notes:***
> *Linotronic paper output from an L-100, L-200, or L-300 imagesetter is 12 inches wide with a maximum length of 100 feet. This allows you to print a complete 8-1/2 x 11 inch page and gives you room for all of the trim lines and registration marks outside the page area.*

72. Select the picture box with the **Content** tool and choose **Other Screen...** from the **Style** menu (you can also choose one of the preset screen styles). Generally, a 30- to 40-line screen will reproduce the cleanest on a LaserWriter or other laser printer. This is an important consideration if you're mass-producing your newsletter with a copier instead of a printing press.

**Color.** If you're reproducing your newsletter at a print house and have the opportunity to use a second color, you can select and specify some of your design elements to be in the second color.

73. When you print your final output, choose the **Make Separations** option in the **Print...** dialog box. Select the **Registration Marks** option as well. QuarkXPress 3.0 will then print all plates with registration marks and plate labels.

Remember, if your page size is 8-1/2 x 11 inches and you specify separations and registration marks, QuarkXPress 3.0 will want to "tile" the pages (setting the final image out on separate pages with trim marks to help you assemble the pages later). That means a lot of unnecessary work. It's a good idea to consider sending your file to a service bureau for higher-resolution output. It'll cost a few dollars more, but it saves you from having to assemble the tiles of all the pages for the printer.

### CHAPTER 8

## Sample Assignment #2:
# Creating a Two-Color Magazine Ad

This assignment will go a little faster than the last one did. It'll be easier too. This time, you'll create a two-color magazine ad for a bicycle messenger service. You'll place a PostScript logo and fitted text — all in two glorious colors.

The hypothetical company's name is CityWheels Courier Service. You'll create its logo from some of the artwork that came with your QuarkXPress 3.0 software and store it as a **Library** document. Then you'll create reversed type, bleeds, format lines, and a huge initial capital letter.

Ready to start? Here you go . . .

### Getting Ready

1. Start by creating and setting up a new document. Set the page size to 8-1/8" x 10-7/8" in the **New** dialog box. Also set some parameters for the document by choosing **General Preferences** from the **Edit** menu. (The keyboard shortcut is ⌘+Y.) Set your preferences as shown in Figures 8-1 and 8-2. Turn off the **Auto Page Insertion** feature, and specify **Guides** to fall **In Front.**

2. Set up the display so it's easy to work on. Change your page view to **Fit in Window** so you can get a good overall look at the whole page. Since you won't have to create any master page formats, hide your **Document Layout** palette by clicking its close box or by choosing **Hide Document Layout** under the **View** menu. Select the default text box and make it transparent by choosing **Runaround...** from the **Item** menu and specifying **None** by clicking on the **Mode** pop-up menu, as shown in Figure 8-3.

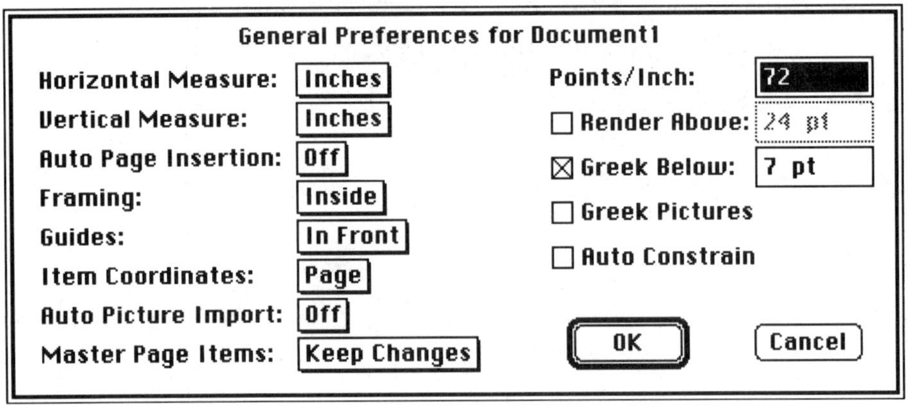

## USING QUARKXPRESS

```
General Preferences for Document1
Horizontal Measure:    [Inches]          Points/Inch:        [72]
Vertical Measure:      [Inches]          ☐ Render Above:     [24 pt]
Auto Page Insertion:   [Off]             ☒ Greek Below:      [7 pt]
Framing:               [Inside]          ☐ Greek Pictures
Guides:                [In Front]        ☐ Auto Constrain
Item Coordinates:      [Page]
Auto Picture Import:   [Off]                  [  OK  ]   [ Cancel ]
Master Page Items:     [Keep Changes]
```

Figure 8-1. Settings and preferences for the document.

```
                              New
┌─Page Size──────────────────────────┐  ┌─Column Guides────────┐
│ ○ US Letter  ○ A4 Letter  ○ Tabloid│  │ Columns:      [1]    │
│ ○ US Legal   ○ B5 Letter  ● Other  │  │                      │
│ Width: [8.125]  Height: [10.875]   │  │ Gutter Width: [0.167"]│
└────────────────────────────────────┘  └──────────────────────┘
┌─Margin Guides──────────────────────┐
│ Top:    [0]      Left:  [0]        │    ☒ Automatic Text Box
│ Bottom: [0]      Right: [0]        │
│        ☐ Facing Pages              │       [  OK  ] [ Cancel ]
└────────────────────────────────────┘
```

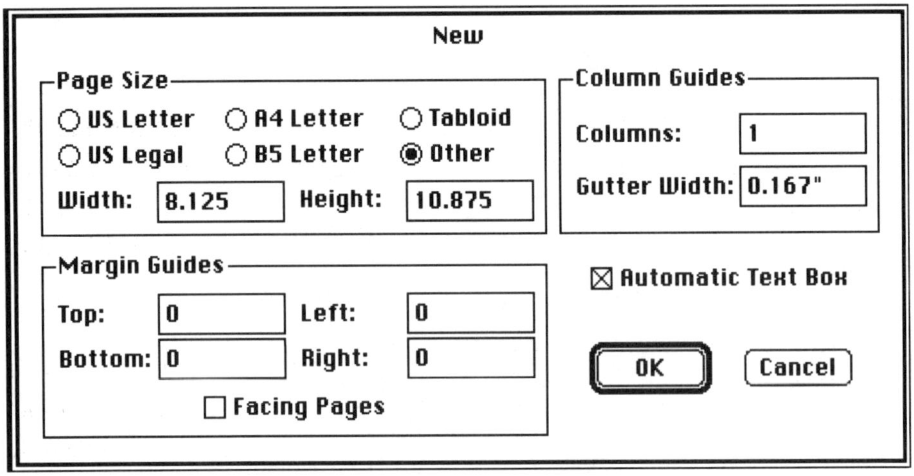

Figure 8-2. More settings and preferences for the document.

3. Then create a new picture box at the bottom of the page. (Click on the rectangular picture box icon and drag a box on the page.)

4. Next Choose **Colors...** from the **Edit** menu and add a new color to your palette: PMS 805. (Click on **New** in the **Colors** dialog box, click on the

*MAGAZINE AD*

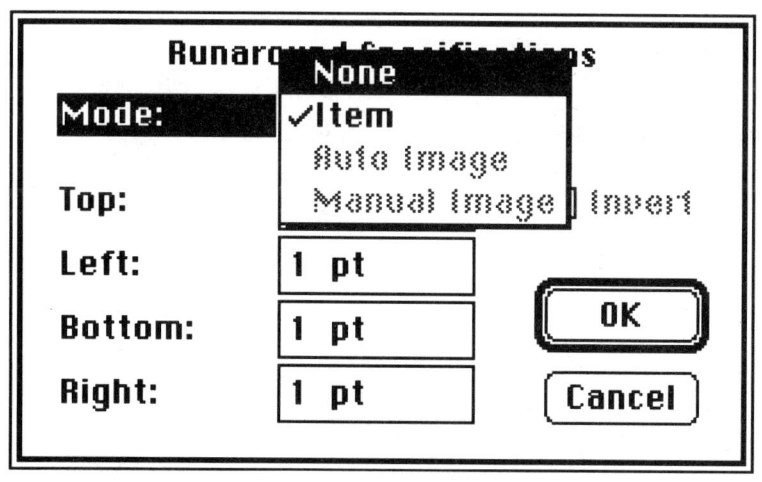

Figure 8-3. The Runaround Specifications box with the Mode pop-up menu — Step 2.

**Pantone** model button, click on the **Pantone No.:** field at the bottom right, type the number **805**, make sure **Process Separation** is set **Off**, and click on **OK**. See Figure 8-4.) This color is one of Pantone's brightest colors. Its **Process Separations** option is left **Off** because you'll want **PMS 805** to print as a spot color. Choose **Save** when you're done.

5. Choose **Get Picture...** from the **File** menu (the keyboard equivalent is ⌘+E) and choose **Yesteryear Cyclist.PICT** from the sample files that came with your QuarkXPress 3.0 package (it is in a folder called **Sample Pictures**). Make it transparent by choosing **Runaround...** from the **Item** menu and choosing **Auto Image** from the pop-up menu there. Change its size to 125% of its original size by clicking on the **X%** and **Y%** fields on the **Measurements** palette and typing the number **125** in each, or by choosing **Modify** from the **Item** menu and changing both percentages there (in the **Scale Across** and **Scale Down** slots) as shown in Figure 8-5.

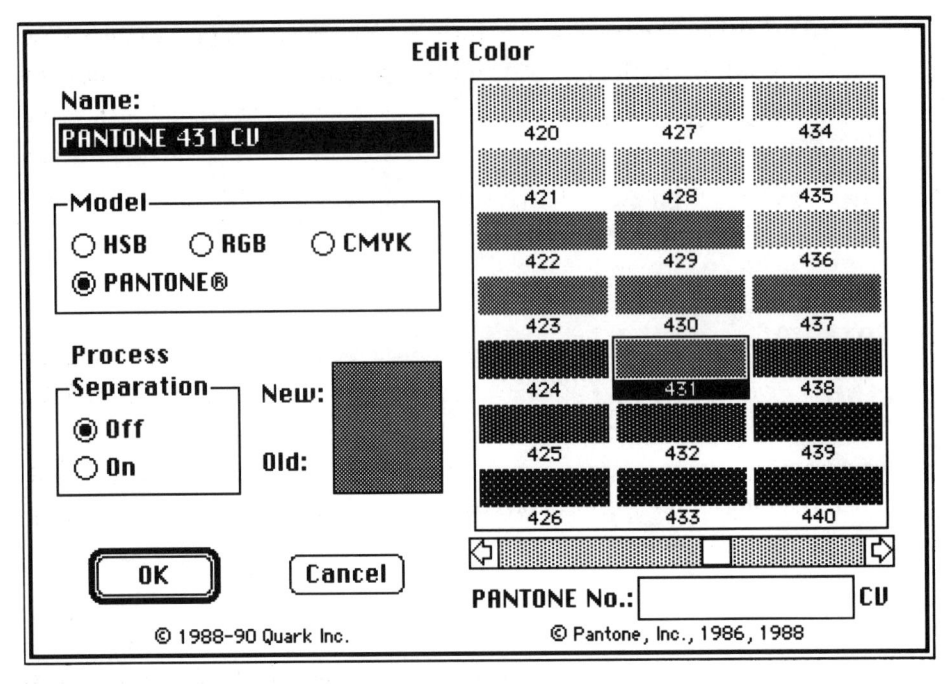

Figure 8-4. Setting the colors — Step 4.

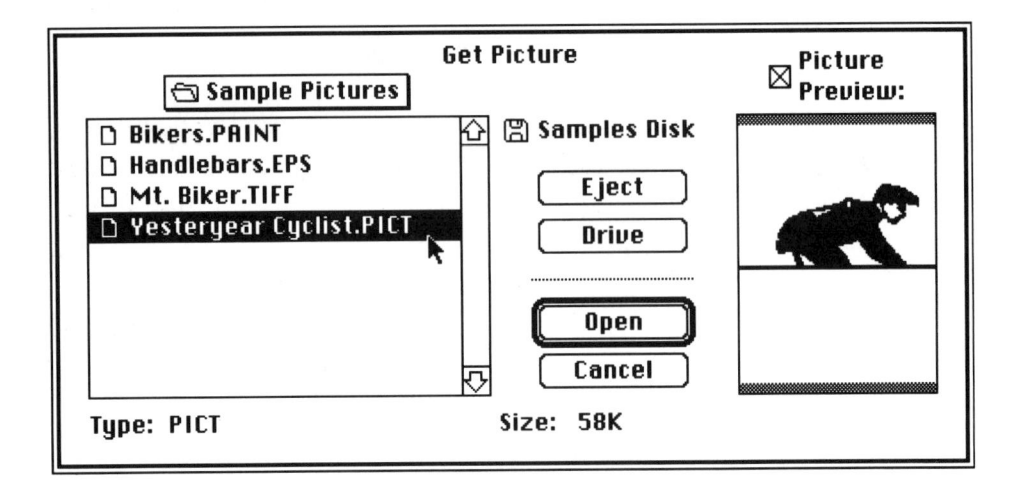

Figure 8-5. Importing the picture — Step 5.

6. QuarkXPress lets you place arbitrary guidelines that graphic elements can snap to anywhere in your publication. Create some guidelines now by clicking on the horizontal ruler and dragging down to the 1/2-inch mark. Watch as you drag: The **Measurements** palette shows you exactly where on the page the guideline appears. Now drag two more guides from the vertical ruler to a position 1-1/2 inches from the left margin and 1-1/2 inches from the right margin.

QuarkXPress measures the position of any item on the page from the top left corner of the page — unless you've changed the zero point for this document by clicking on and dragging the zero-point marker somewhere else on the page. (If you've done this, it's easy to fix. Hold down the **Option** key and click on the zero-point marker in the corner.) For example, your right guideline will fall 1-1/2 inches before the 8-1/8 inch page margin, so the right guideline should be positioned at 6-5/8 inches, or 6.625 inches.

If you miss the mark with your first attempt at placing the guides, just click on them and move them again. You can also remove them by dragging them back to the ruler at any time. The guidelines you just placed will help you position your text boxes and other graphic elements in this layout.

7. Now it's time to place your headline. Create a new text box at the top of the page, drawing it within the constraints of the guidelines you just placed (see Figure 8-6). Notice how the boundaries of the text box naturally snap into place, adhering to the guides.

8. Next, create the text box for your body copy. Create a new text box and start dragging it below the headline text box, but within the two vertical guidelines. Choose **Runaround...** (⌘+T) and specify **None**.

USING QUARKXPRESS

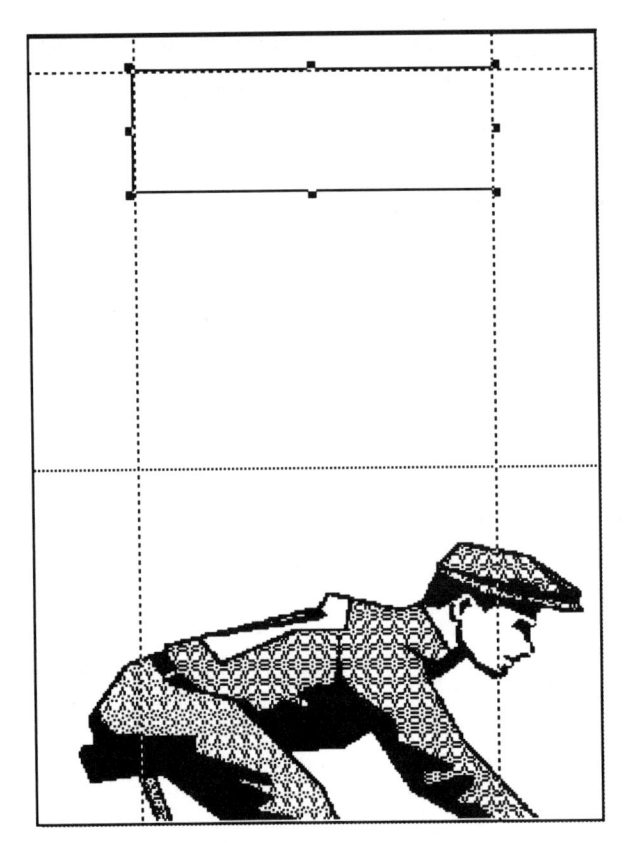

Figure 8-6. Headline text box and body copy text box in place — Steps 7 and 8.

**Extra!**

*If another item is in front of the guidelines and keeps you from clicking on the guideline, just move it out of the way before moving the guideline. Be sure to note its location before moving it, so you'll know exactly where to replace it when you're done.*

9. This text box will hold the body copy in two columns, so you need to specify your own gutter space. Choose **Modify** from the **Item** menu to specify the number of columns and the amount of gutter space.

   Change the **Columns** field to **2** and change the **Gutter** field to **18 pt** (or **.25"**) as shown in Figure 8-7. Then click on **OK**.

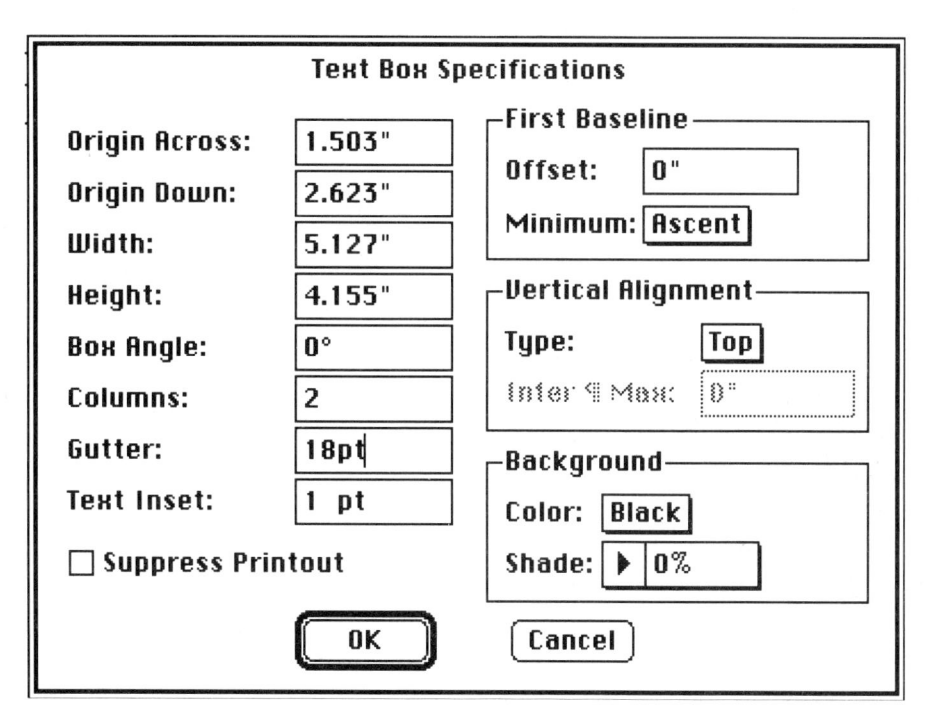

```
                    Text Box Specifications
                                    ┌First Baseline─────────
Origin Across:   1.503"             
                                     Offset:    0"
Origin Down:     2.623"
                                     Minimum:  Ascent
Width:           5.127"
                                    ┌Vertical Alignment─────
Height:          4.155"
                                     Type:     Top
Box Angle:       0°
                                     Inter ¶ Max:  0"
Columns:         2

Gutter:          18pt               ┌Background─────────────

Text Inset:      1 pt                Color:   Black

☐ Suppress Printout                  Shade:   ▶ 0%


              ( OK )      ( Cancel )
```

Figure 8-7. Setting the number of columns and the gutter space for body text — Step 9.

10. Flow your sample text into the text box by choosing **Get Text...** from the **File** menu. Choose **Sample Text** from the samples that came with your QuarkXPress 3.0 package. This text should overflow the text box (it's more than the text box can hold, so the bottom right of the box will show an overflow icon — a tiny box with an X in it). Don't worry about that now.

271

> **Shortcut**
>
> *If you selected the **Item** tool, you can get directly to the **Modify** dialog box by double-clicking on the item you want to modify.*

11. Change your view of the document to **Actual Size** (use the keyboard shortcut ⌘+1) so you can clearly see all the characters in the text. Use the **Content** tool (or ⌘+A) to select all of the text and change the text attributes in the **Style** menu to **Palatino** (the **Font** pop-up menu), **10 pt** (Size), **Justified (Alignment)**. Change the leading to an absolute value of 15 points (choose **Leading** in the **Style** menu, type **15** in the field of the **Leading** dialog box, and click on **OK**). Finally, specify 12 points of space after each paragraph (choose **Formats...** from the **Style** menu, then type **12 pt** in the **Space After** slot — be sure to type **pt** or you may end up with 12 inches or some other amount). You can also reach all of these choices without pulling down the **Style** menu by pressing ⌘+Shift+D to set **Character** attributes and ⌘+Shift+F to set **Paragraph Format** attributes.

12. Now place the text-insertion cursor anywhere in the first paragraph. Press Shift+⌘+F to display the **Paragraph Formats** dialog box and click on the **Drop Caps** option, as shown in Figure 8-8. Then click on **OK.** This creates your initial cap.

13. Now select just the first initial capital letter in the paragraph and press ⌘+Shift+\ (that's a backslash key) to specify its size. If you have selected only the initial cap letter, then the **Size Definition** dialog box will show that letter's size as a percentage instead of in points.

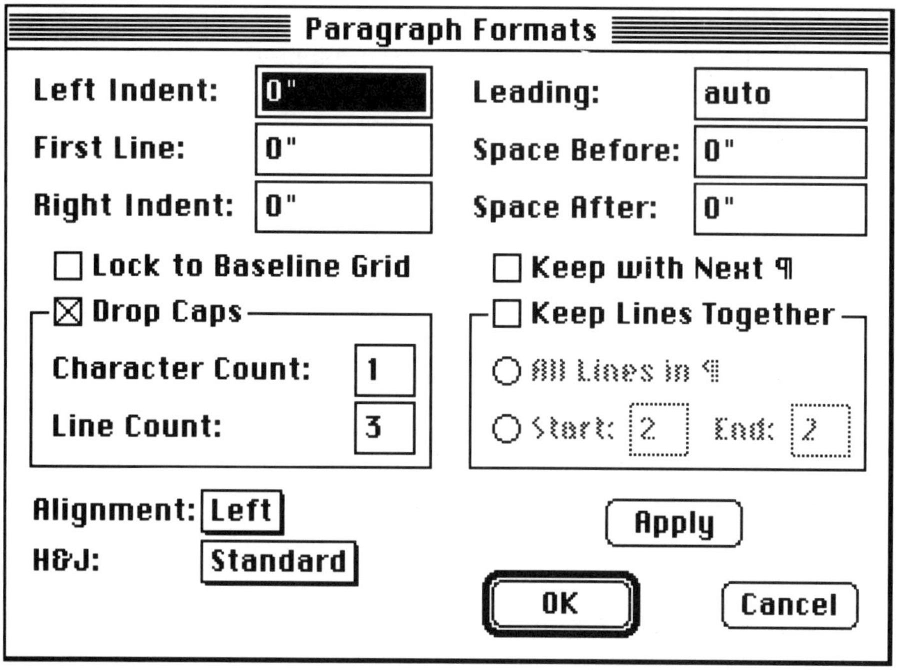

*MAGAZINE AD*

**Figure 8-8.** Selecting Drop Caps in the Paragraph Formats dialog box — as in Step 12.

Type in **150%** and click on **OK** (or press **Return**). This will enlarge the initial cap letter and extend it above the text's ascent line. Remember, this won't work unless you have specified an absolute leading value and have selected only the first initial cap letter.

14. Now to balance the two columns of text against each other. Press ⌘+M (or double click on the box using the **Moving** tool) to display the **Text Box Specifications** dialog box. In the **First Baseline** field for **Offset**, type **.5"** (**1/2"**). Click on **OK**. This will drop the first baseline of each column to 1/2" from the top boundary of the text box. Since that space is enough to accommodate the height of the initial cap letter, both baselines will align perfectly in the text box — Voila!

15. Click on the **Content** tool and place your text-insertion cursor somewhere near the end of the text in column two. (You may have to scroll with the vertical scroll bar, the one to the right of the pasteboard working area, to get there.) Hold down ⌘+**Shift+Option+Down arrow key** to select all of the text from that point to the end of the text chain. Then press **Delete** once to get rid of all the extra text that didn't fit in the box. (The extra-text icon in the bottom right corner of the text box should disappear.)

## The Headline

16. Now for the headline text. Select the headline text box you made earlier with the **Content** tool (you may need to scroll back up there to get at it), choose **Runaround...** (⌘+T), and specify **None** for **Mode**. You should see the blinking text-insertion cursor at the top left-hand corner of the text box.

17. Type in a catchy headline phrase, such as **Faster than a Speeding Mail Truck!** Select all the text and specify the text attributes as **56 point Palatino Bold, Small Caps, -10 points of leading, Centered alignment**, and the color as **100% of PMS 805**. Because the main body text box and the headline text box are transparent to each other (no runaround — that is, **Runaround... Mode** set to **None**), neither displaces text in the other, making it easy to adjust the sizing and spacing attributes. (Note: If you try to use the **Character** dialog box-size pop-up menu to set the point size, you'll be disappointed. That pop-up doesn't offer the odd size of 56 points. For that, you'll have to use the pop-up menu's **Other** option.)

## The Flag

18. Create a new text box to the left of your initial cap letter and extend it off the page. Make it transparent and send it to the back. This box will be a flag for the initial cap. (Choose the **Item** menu, then the **Runaround...** dialog box, and then the **Mode** pop-up menu to select **None**. Then use the **Item** menu's **Send to Back** command.) Extend the new text box to cover

your initial cap letter. (Place the cursor on the box handle in the middle of the side next to the drop cap, then drag that handle across to the right side of the drop cap.) Then change the box's background color to **100% of PMS 805** (use the **Style** menu pop-up menus). Since the text boxes on top of the initial cap are also transparent, the letter should disappear against the background of the new text box.

19. Change your view to **200%** or use the **Magnifying** tool to select and zoom into the area of your initial cap (scroll after zooming, if necessary). Select just the initial cap letter with the **Content** tool and change its color to white. (Click inside the main text box and outside of the new text box that covers the initial cap. Then drag the cursor across the initial cap. Choose **White** from the **Color** pop-up menu of the **Style** menu.) Now it will reverse color and appear against the darker flag. If your flag text box is not positioned properly, use the **Item** tool to select it and creep it into position using your keyboard's arrow keys (moving items with the arrow keys only works when the **Item** tool is selected). Compare your results to those in Figure 8-9.

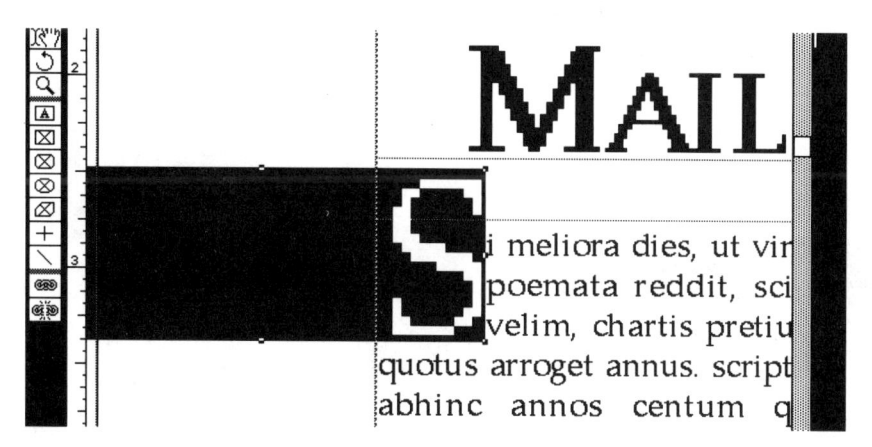

Figure 8-9. Flag box and initial cap with inverted coloring, from Step 19.

## The Logo

20. Use the **Magnifying** tool to zoom into the area of the page between the illustration and the bottom of the body-copy text box.

21. Create a small picture box here and make it transparent by setting its **Runaround... Mode** attribute to **None**. Select the **Editing** tool and import the PostScript art called **Wheel Artwork** from inside the **Picture Sample** folder (with the Tutorial files that came with QuarkXPress 3.0).

22. Reduce the size of the artwork to 25% of its original size by changing the size attributes in the **Measurement** palette or by using the **Modify** command under the **Item** menu. Position it to the far left of the picture box, as shown in Figure 8-10.

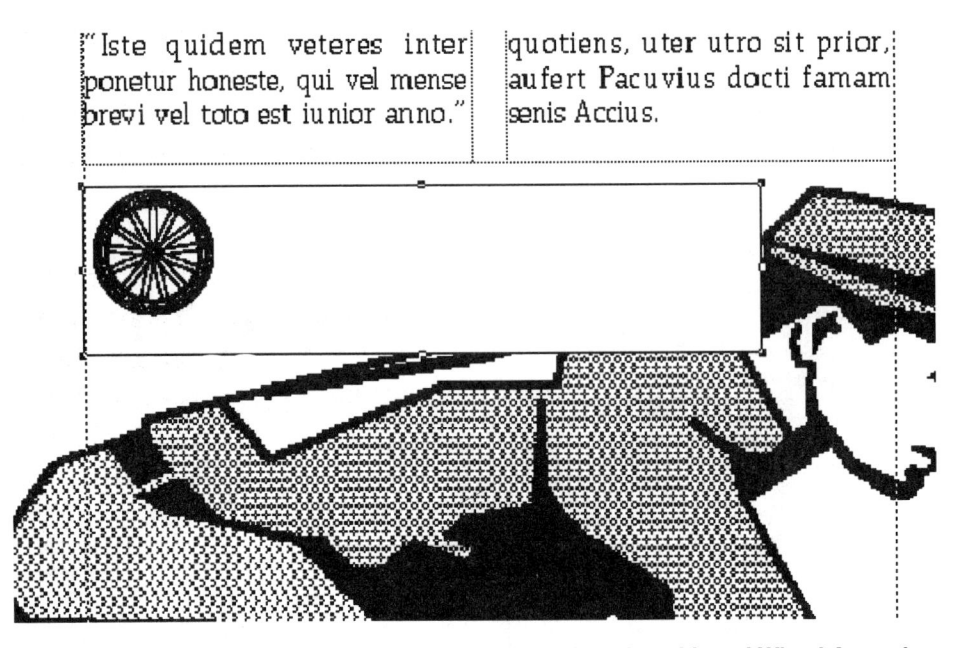

Figure 8-10. New picture box with imported, reduced, and positioned Wheel Artwork.

23. Now create a new text box inside the picture box holding the wheel artwork. Make it transparent, then type in the company name, CityWheels, and its slogan, **Faster Than Mail**. Use the **Measurements** palette to change the size and style of the logo type to **36 point Helvetica Bold Italic** with **8 points of leading** and the slogan to **18 point Helvetica Italic**. Adjust the tracking of the slogan text to space the letters apart so they are the same length as the logo type. (This is only practical with the **Measurements** palette. If you used the **Tracking** dialog box, you wouldn't be able to see the changes as you made them — you'd have to keep switching back and forth between the dialog box and the text on screen. To use the **Measurements** palette, click on the tiny arrows that point right and left, sitting just to the left of the justification icons. Adjust the tracking value here until the slogan and logo are about the same length.) Compare the results of all these changes to Figure 8-11.

24. One more special touch: Select the picture box holding the wheel artwork with the **Content** tool and change the **Picture Skew** value on the **Measurements** palette to **10°** (the icon in the bottom right with the skewed parallelogram). This will slant your wheel art to give it a hint of motion. Figure 8-11 shows the results.

25. Finally, use the **Item** tool to select the logo/slogan text box and the wheel picture box. (Hold down the **Shift** key while you select each item individually and choose **Group** from the **Item** menu. The keyboard equivalent is ⌘+G.) Now that these two items are grouped, they can be copied to and from the library for use in any other CityWheels printed material. Your ad should now look like the one in Figure 8-12.

277

"Iste quidem veteres inter ponetur honeste, qui vel mense brevi vel toto est iunior anno."

quotiens, uter utro sit pr aufert Pacuvius docti fan senis Accius.

**Figure 8-11. Logo and slogan styled and tracked, picture skewed, from Steps 23 and 24.**

## Printing the Ad

26. Try printing the ad for a proof. Choose **Page Setup...** from the **File** menu (keyboard shortcut: **Option+⌘+P**) and make the following changes to the LaserWriter **Page Setup** (shown in Figure 8-13): Disable **Font Substitution**, **Text Smoothing**, and **Graphics Smoothing** (click on the associated check box of each function to remove the X). Then click on the **Options** button and specify **Larger Print Area**. These changes will speed up printing for your proof and ensure that most (or all) of the image area will print on a standard page on your LaserWriter. Click on **OK**.

**Figure 8-12.** The finished ad.

To see how the page will look before printing, be sure to select **Hide Guides** (and **Hide Rulers** if you want) under the **View** menu. This gives you a clean preview of the page before it prints. (You may also need to zoom out, or select **Fit to Window** to see the entire page on screen.)

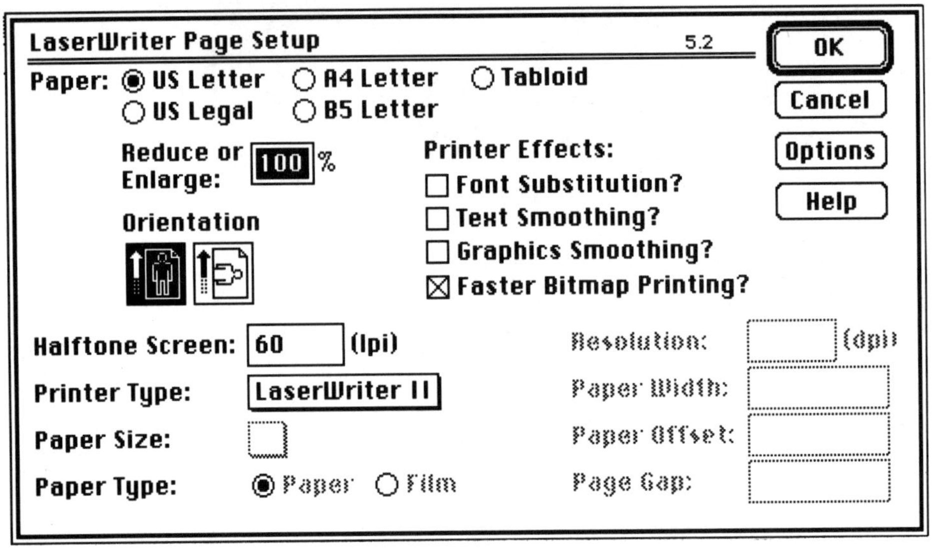

**Figure 8-13.** Page Setup.

27. When you're ready to print to your high-resolution output device — such as a typesetter or laser printer — remember to select **Make Separations** in the dialog box that appears when you choose the **Print...** command. This makes your printer output a separate page for each color plate. If you're printing with a high-resolution output device with a larger page size, enable the **Registration Marks** option (click in the check box).

## Enhancements

You can enhance this project by adding a few extra touches here and there, like adding a third color. There's a color PostScript image of the bicyclist included with your sample files. Use that as the illustration and specify your PMS color as a process separation. This changes your two-color ad to a four-color ad and includes the separations for all of the color on the page.

Was that fun? Was it too easy? The next chapter will be more of a challenge. Go to bed early tonight and get plenty of rest before starting it.

**Chapter 9**

**Sample Assignment #3**

# Color Corporate Brochure

This 12-page corporate brochure assignment leads you through creating multiple master page formats, style sheets, anchored rules, anchored graphic objects, multiple-page spreads, automatic page numbering, and process color separations. It's a lot to swallow, but when you're done, you'll be a certified QuarkXPress 3.0 wizard of wonder.

Ready? Take a deep breath. Clear your mind of fear and anxiety. Remember, may The Force be with you always as you confront:

- Setting up the format pages.
- Creating the document layout.
- Automatic page numbering.
- Adding new colors to the document palette.
- Creating style sheets and using them.

## First Step: On Paper

The first step of any design project is the thumbnail sketches. That's where all of the creative inspiration takes its first form. Once you've got your ideas on paper (even in rough form), the actual production process smooths out considerably. The paper roughs are not just an aid for visualization; they're also a help in planning production. Once you have a rough idea of the number of pages, common master pages, and so on, that are in a new project, you can really zip through production, endearing yourself to clients or profit-conscious supervisors and managers.

A good pre-starting place within QuarkXPress is at the **Preferences** dialog boxes. For this document, choose **Typographic Preferences** from the **Edit** menu and establish an 18-point baseline grid. This comes in handy later when you're flowing and formatting text.

1. To begin, create a new document by choosing **New...** from the **File** menu and assign your new document the page specifications shown in Figure 9-1.

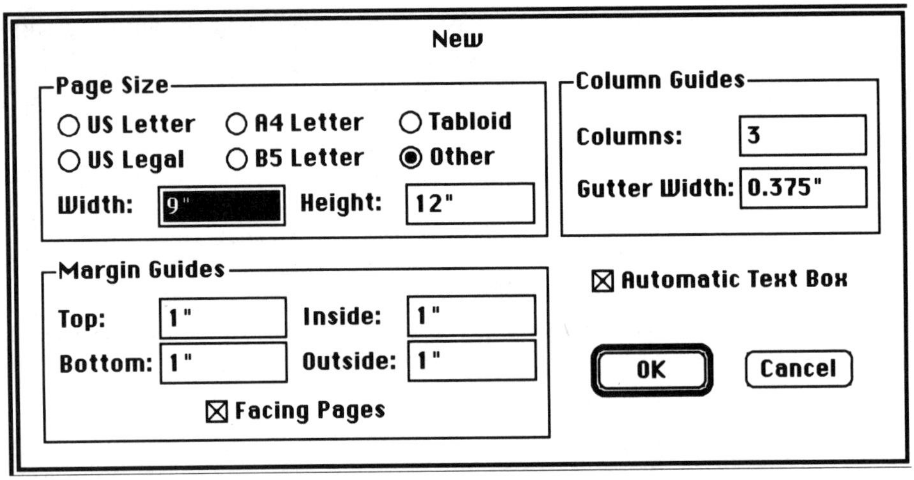

```
┌─────────────────────────────────────────────────────────┐
│                         New                             │
│  ┌─Page Size──────────────────────┐ ┌─Column Guides─────┐│
│  │ ○ US Letter  ○ A4 Letter  ○ Tabloid │ Columns:    3  ││
│  │ ○ US Legal   ○ B5 Letter  ● Other   │                ││
│  │ Width: 9"    Height: 12"            │ Gutter Width: 0.375" ││
│  └─────────────────────────────────────┘                ││
│  ┌─Margin Guides──────────────────┐   ☒ Automatic Text Box│
│  │ Top:    1"   Inside:  1"       │                      │
│  │ Bottom: 1"   Outside: 1"       │    [  OK  ] [Cancel] │
│  │        ☒ Facing Pages          │                      │
│  └────────────────────────────────┘                      │
└─────────────────────────────────────────────────────────┘
```

Figure 9-1. New Document dialog box with Page Specifications for Step 1.

2. Choose **Colors...** from the **Edit** menu and use the **New** command to add new colors to this document's palette.

   a. Use the Pantone color model by clicking on its button, as shown in Figure 9-2. (You'll be adding Pantone colors **PMS 430**, **PMS 327**, and **PMS 431** to the color palette.)

*CORPORATE BROCHURE*

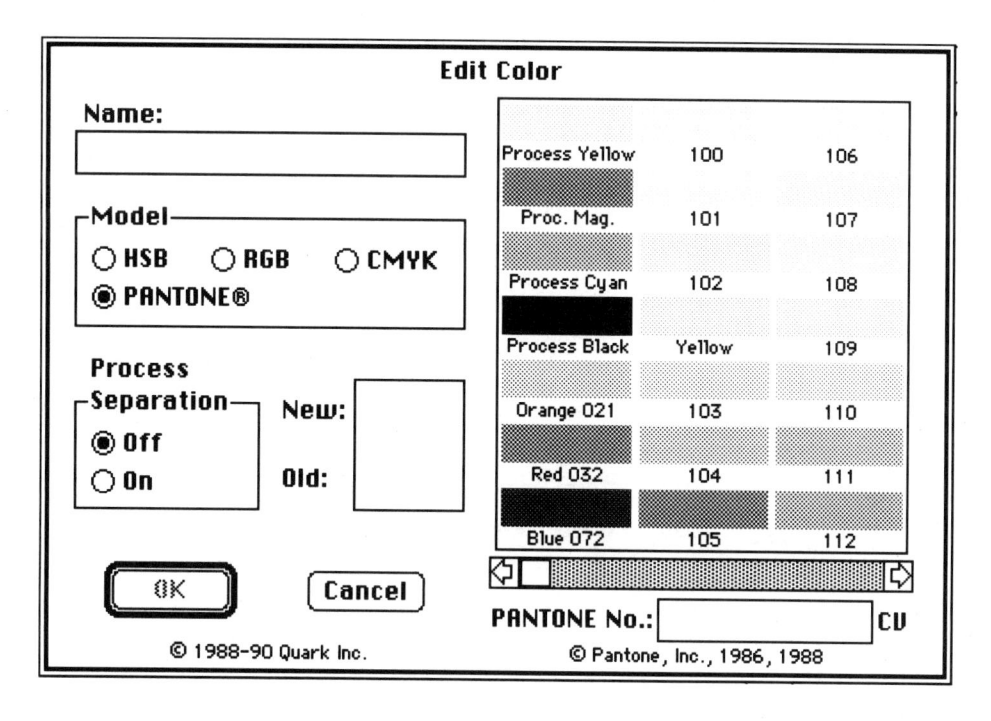

```
┌─────────────────────────────────────────────────────────┐
│                        Edit Color                        │
│  Name:                                                   │
│  ┌──────────────────────────┐  Process Yellow  100  106 │
│  │                          │                           │
│  └──────────────────────────┘  Proc. Mag.       101  107│
│  ┌─Model──────────────────────┐                         │
│  │                            │  Process Cyan   102  108│
│  │  ○ HSB   ○ RGB   ○ CMYK    │                         │
│  │  ⦿ PANTONE®                │  Process Black  Yellow 109│
│  └────────────────────────────┘                         │
│   Process                        Orange 021     103  110│
│  ┌Separation┐  New:  ┌──────┐                           │
│  │ ⦿ Off    │        │      │   Red 032         104  111│
│  │ ○ On     │  Old:  │      │                           │
│  └──────────┘        └──────┘   Blue 072        105  112│
│                                                          │
│  ┌────────┐  ┌────────┐                                 │
│  │   OK   │  │ Cancel │   PANTONE No.: ┌──────┐ CV      │
│  └────────┘  └────────┘                └──────┘         │
│       © 1988-90 Quark Inc.      © Pantone, Inc., 1986, 1988│
└─────────────────────────────────────────────────────────┘
```

**Figure 9-2. Edit Color dialog box — Step 2.**

b. Click the mouse in the **PANTONE No.:** field, then type **PMS 430**. The color display window above the blank jumps to show that color, and its name appears in the **Name** field at the upper left of the dialog box.

c. Click next to **On** in the **Process Separation** area at the left of the dialog box. This enables the **Process Separation** option.

d. Click on **OK** and that color becomes part of the palette.

e. Click on **New** again in the **Edit Color** dialog box and repeat the process (Steps b through d) for each color. When you come to **PMS 431**, make sure **Process Separation** is set to **Off**; it will be fifth color used just for text.

f. After choosing the PMS colors, choose the standard blue in the palette, click on **Edit,** and change its model to CMYK by clicking on the **CMYK** button. Select **Process Separation** for it too. Repeat the process for the standard red. Set it to **CMYK** and **Process Separation On.** These are the colors you will be using to create this brochure. Choose **Save** when you're finished choosing all of the colors.

3. Display the **Document Layout** palette by choosing **Show Document Layout** in the **View** menu. (This prepares you for creating the master page formats.)

4. Create the four different master-page formats that make up the brochure by dragging the facing **Master Page** icon (the icon with the turned-down corners) over into the palette's active area four times (the active area is just to the right of the first **Master Page** with the A in the middle, just to the left of the **Trash**). This procedure can be tricky — you need to move each new page just to the left of the small right-pointing arrow beside the **Trash** and above the line that holds the page's name. (See Figure 9-3.)

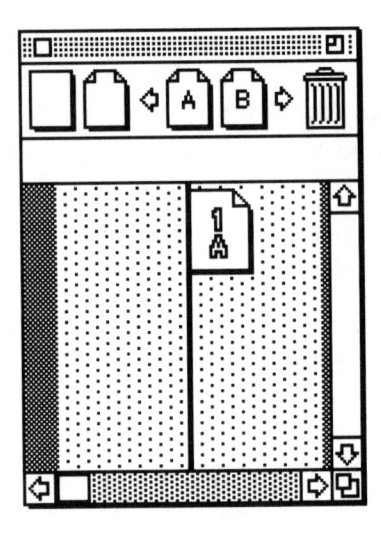

**Figure 9-3. Document Layout palette — Steps 4 and 5.**

284

QuarkXPress 3.0 names the master pages sequentially — A, B, C, and D — but you can give them names of your own that are easier to recognize. After you've created all four new master pages, name them one-by-one:

a. Select a master page (by clicking on a **Master Page** icon — A, B, C, or D).

b. Type a new name in the name field directly below the icon (where it says **Master A, B, C,** or **D**). See Figure 9-3 for an example.

c. Select the next master page and repeat the process. (If you can't see the one you need, click on either the small right-pointing arrow or the small left-pointing arrow to scroll through the **Master Page** icons.) Change names on the master pages thusly: **A** to **Marketing, B** to **Product, C** to **Capability,** and **D** to **Financial.**

5. To start creating the first master page format, click on the arrows in the **Document Layout** palette until you see the **Marketing** icon. Double-click on this icon to display that master page.

6. This page format sets a general format for the rest of the master pages. Create this master and duplicate it to create your other master pages. You know you're editing the master page by the **Text Chain** icon that appears at the top left corner of the document page. This default **Text Chain** icon indicates that text flowing in this document automatically flows from page to page via the default text box that appears on every page.

This master page layout is somewhat complex, but because you're duplicating it to create the other masters, that complexity makes creating each new master page a simple matter.

Choose **Fit in Window** from the **View** menu for your page view. Bring in and create your design elements in this view, then adjust them in the **Actual Size** view.

## Building the Pieces

7. Start your first master page by creating a narrow text box to hold the page subheads. Check the box's size by comparing the dimensions shown in your **Measurements** palette against the ones shown in Figure 9-4.

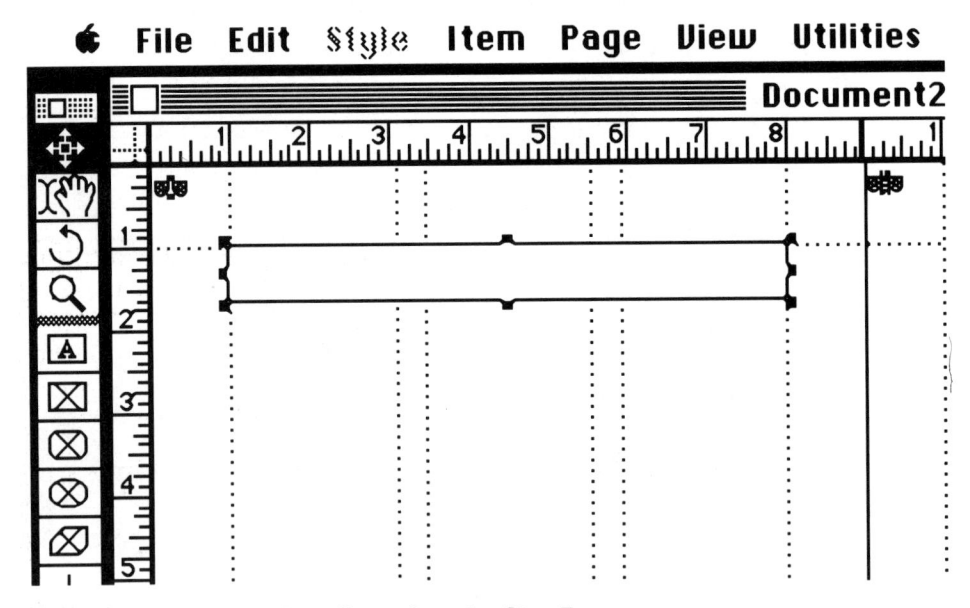

**Figure 9-4. Narrow text box dimensions for Step 7.**

To best proportion this text box, set it to be about as long as your three-column text margin.

CORPORATE BROCHURE

8. Type **Marketing** and set your text attributes to **24 point Helvetica Bold Italic, All Caps, 90%** of **Horizontal Scale**, with **Maximum Tracking (+100)**.

By now, you should be able to set all of those attributes using keyboard equivalents. (Don't feel bad if you haven't memorized all the keyboard commands yet — they're always listed in the menus.) You can also adjust all of these attributes at once using the **Character...** command in the **Style** menu.

9. Make a polygon picture box to hold this text box. The picture box is shaped like a banner and should enclose the whole text box. Create the shape shown in Figure 9-5.

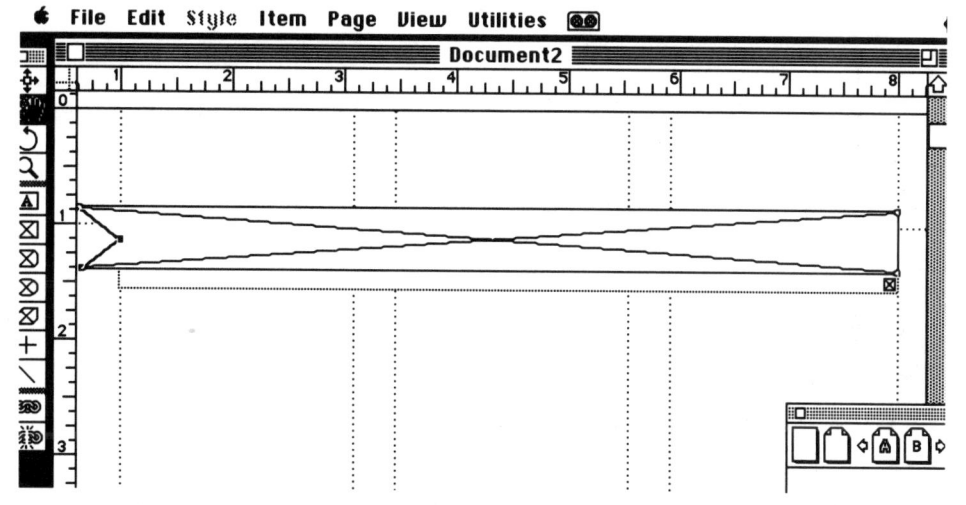

**Figure 9-5. Polygon picture box overlaying the text box — Step 9.**

Zoom in and try to position the polygon picture box so **Marketing** appears in the middle of the flag. Make the picture box transparent by setting its **Runaround...** attribute to **None**. If you have trouble shaping

287

the picture box accurately, don't worry. Finish the picture box, even if the edges are not perfectly straight — you can always adjust the individual points of the boundary after it's finished by choosing **Reshape Polygon** under the **Item** menu, then clicking on the individual control points and moving them.

10. While using the **Content** tool, select the text box and highlight the text, then make the text **100% White** by choosing it from the **Color** pop-up menu of the **Style** menu. While the text box is still selected, make it transparent by changing its **Runaround...** attributes to **None**. Choose **Bring to Front** from the **Item** menu.

11. Select the picture box and change its background color to **100% Blue** by choosing **Modify** under the **Item** menu.

12. Select both items using the **Item** tool and **Shift** key combination and choose **Group** under the **Item** menu. (The keyboard equivalent is ⌘+G). Now the two items are grouped together and can be manipulated as one item. See Figure 9-6.

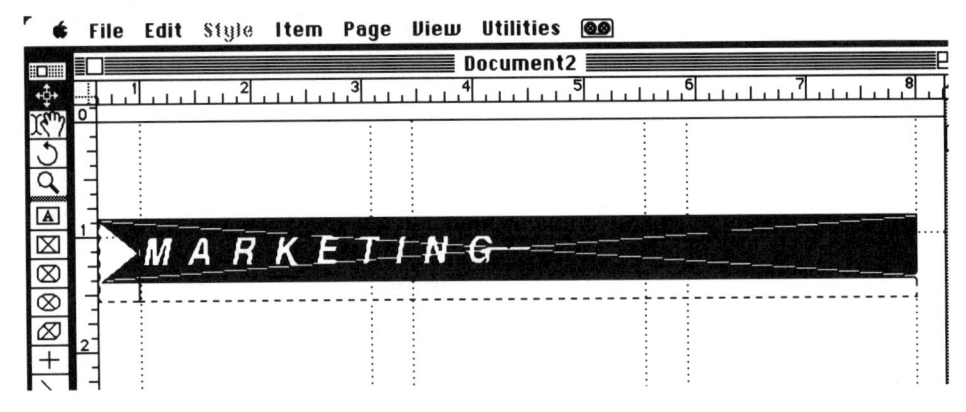

Figure 9-6. Grouped boxes, the result of Step 12.

288

13. Change your page view to **Fit in Window** and scroll to move the grouped items to the center of the page. This gives the group room to rotate so you can position it on the vertical edge of the page.

Notice that the **Measurements** palette only shows information pertinent to both objects. One of the options available is the box angle field. Double-click there and change it to 90º. Then change the X-location to 0" and the Y-location to 7" to position the box right on the edge of the page. Press **Return** to see the result and compare it to Figure 9-7.

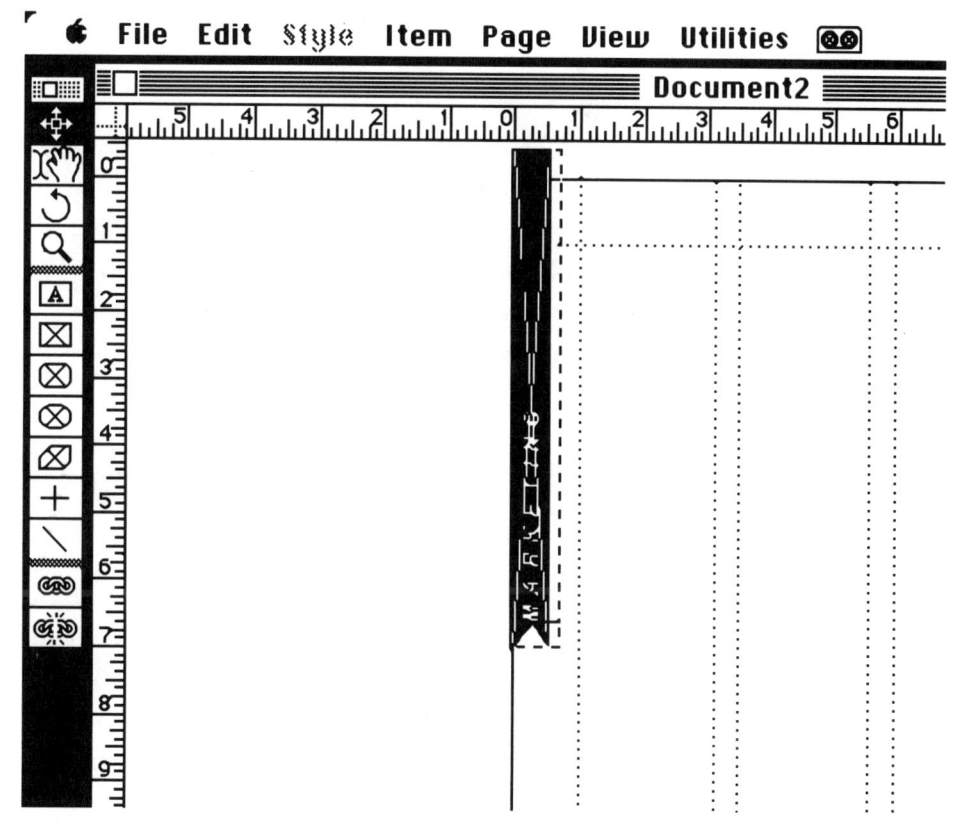

Figure 9-7. The moved and rotated group of Step 13.

14. You need to duplicate this rotated and positioned box to the other side of the page spread; so while it's still selected, choose **Step and Repeat** from the **Item** menu (the keyboard equivalent is **Option+⌘+D**). Set the **Horizontal Offset** to 18" and the **Vertical Offset** to 0" (that's approximately how far the elements must travel to be positioned on the other side of the spread). You can adjust the position more precisely after the duplication. Scroll over to the right side of the spread to see where the duplicated flag landed. It's probably resting just off the edge of the page, so you can move it with the mouse to get it close to where it belongs, then change your view to actual size and use the arrow keys to creep it over to its final position.

## Other Graphic Elements

15. Now create a repeating element that occurs on both pages but in different locations. Again, use a polygon picture box to create an odd shape and then step-and-repeat it across an area of the page. Start by making sure your page view is **Actual Size** (the keyboard equivalent is **⌘+1**). Then select your **Rectangle Picture Box** tool and create a narrow vertical box using the column gutter guidelines to help you proportion it correctly, as in Figure 9-8.

16. Change the box's shape by choosing the **Polygon Picture Box** option from **Picture Box Shape** under the **Item** menu, as shown in Figure 9-9.

17. Select **Reshape Polygon** from the same menu. This lets you select corner points on the rectangle so you can reshape it. Use the next column's column gutter guidelines to help keep the proportions equal, and compare it to the example in Figure 9-10. When you've done this, choose **Modify** from the **Item** menu to specify its background color as **100%** of **Red**.

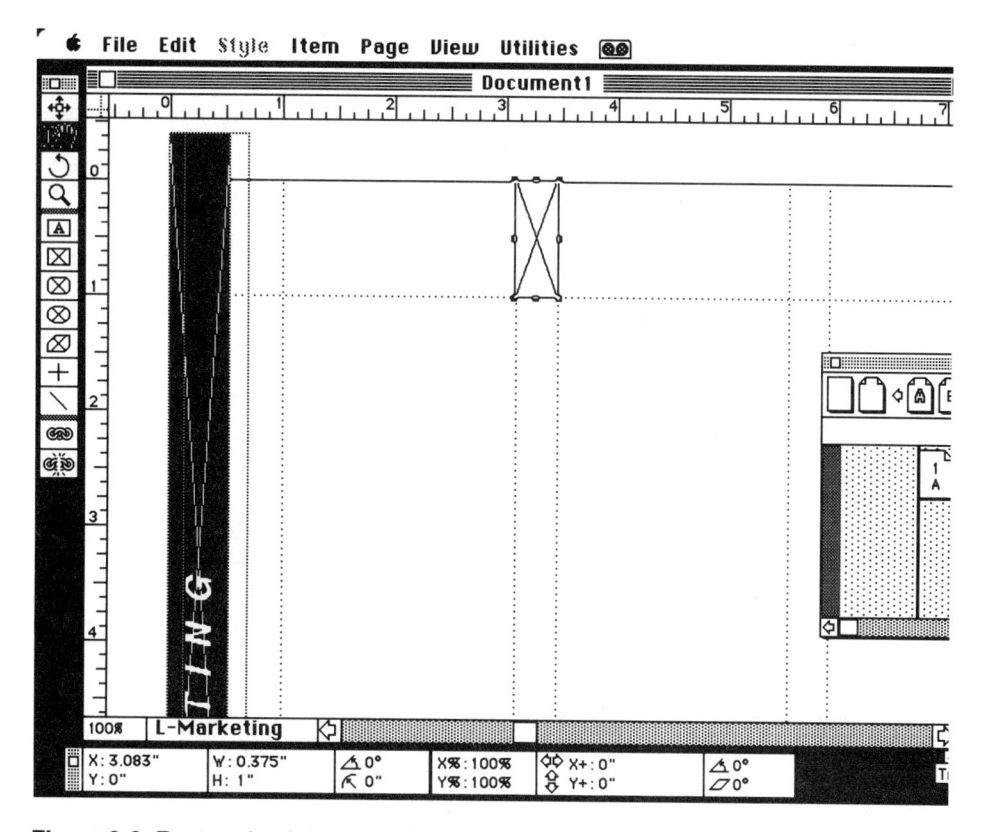

Figure 9-8. Rectangle picture box from Step 15.

18. Use the **Measurements** palette to change the vertical (Y) location of the box. Type in a negative number to draw the edge of the box off the page so it bleeds and lifts the bottom edge of the box away from the top of the default text box.

19. Change your view to **Fit in Window** (⌘+0 [zero]) and step-and-repeat the slanted picture box four times, horizontally, at 1-inch intervals. Then select the boxes and group them together. As there are no other graphic elements close to them, try using the **Item** tool to drag a selection rectan-

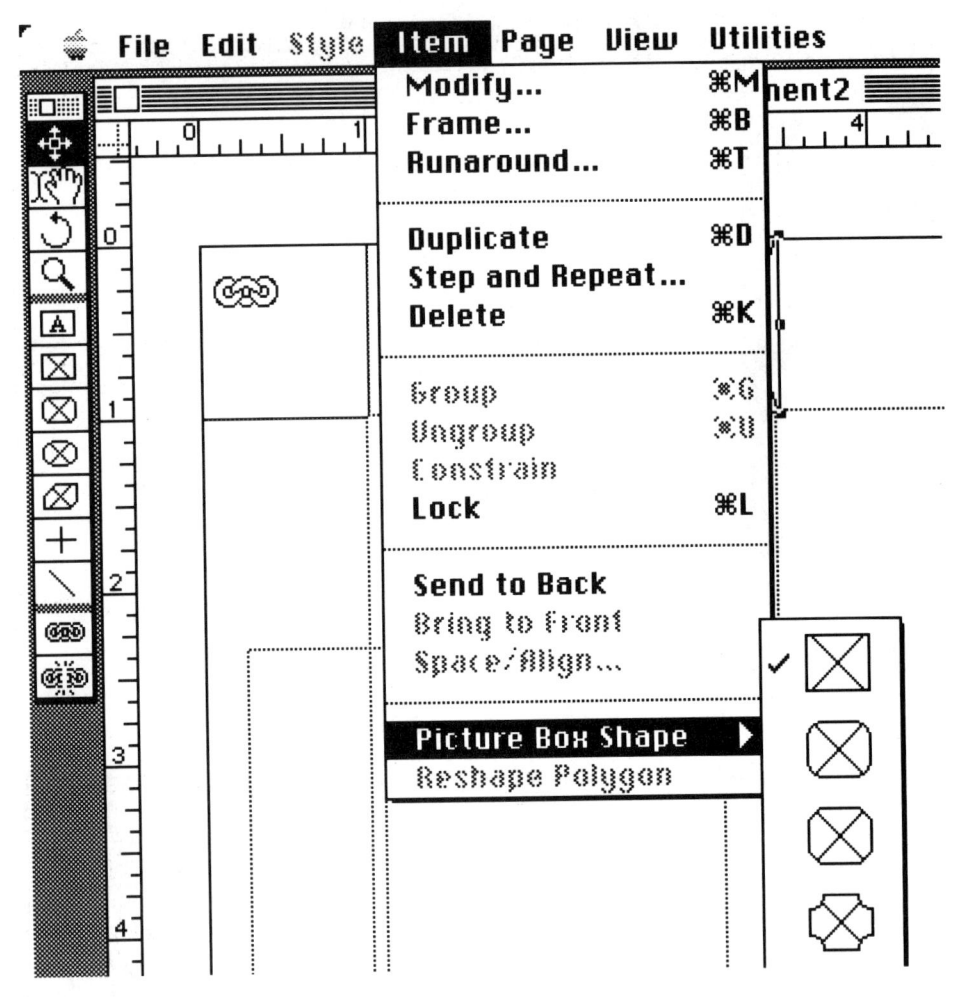

Figure 9-9. Choosing polygon picture box from the Item menu — Step 16.

gle around the group (or press **Shift** while clicking the **Item** tool on each) and choose **Group** from the **Item** menu (or press ⌘+G). Then move the boxes over to the top right edge of the page and position them so they bleed off the top and right edges of the page, as shown in Figure 9-11.

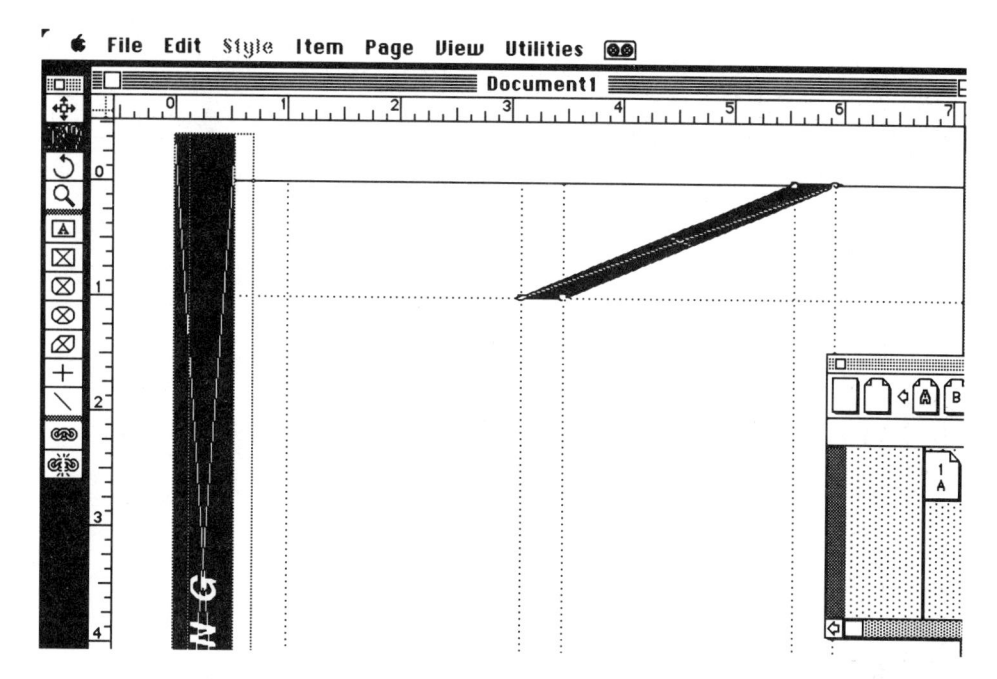

Figure 9-10. Reshaped, slanted picture box from Step 17.

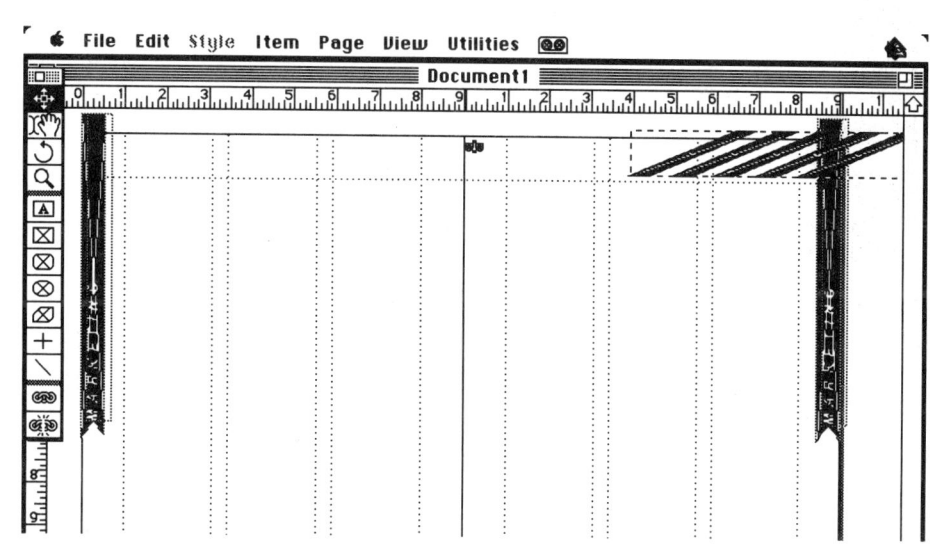

Figure 9-11. Grouped picture boxes bleeding off the top and right edges of the page, from Step 19.

Fine-tune the placement by setting the **X** and **Y** locations on the **Measurements** palette to **X: 4"** and **Y: -.125"**.

20. Now choose **Step and Repeat** again while the group is still selected and set the repeat distances to **Horizontal 9"** and **Vertical 9.375"**, which should give you the results seen in Figure 9-12.

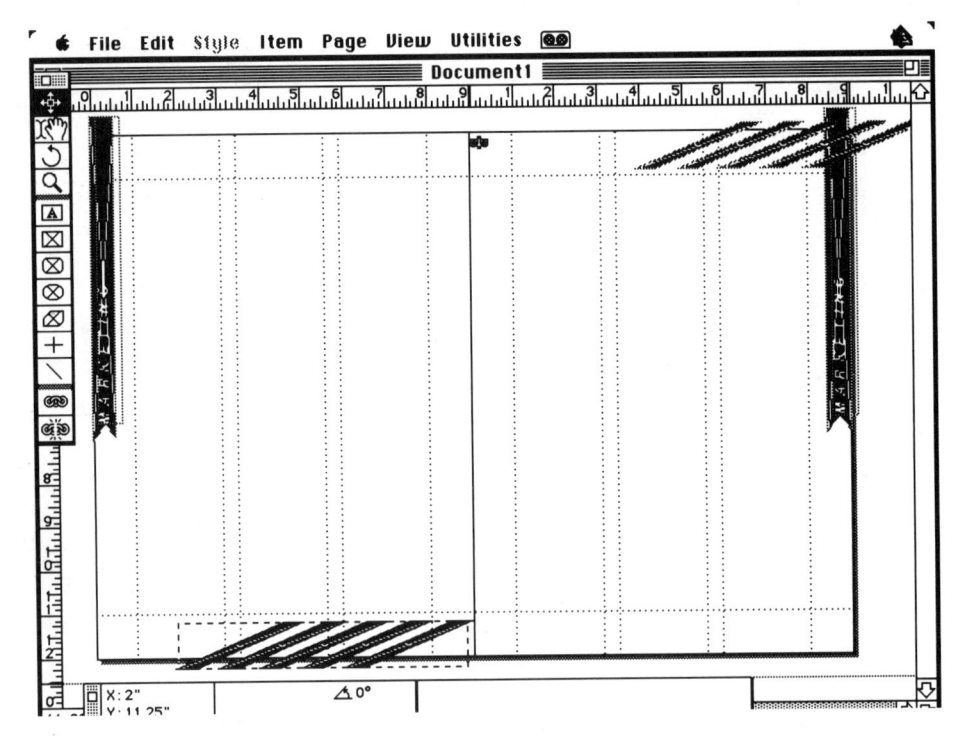

Figure 9-12. Results of Step 20.

## Page Numbering

Remember automatic page numbering? This time, we'll be a little more creative.

294

21. Create a new text box near the bottom left corner of the left page. Press ⌘+3. Remember, you have to have the **Content** tool selected before you can type anything into the text box. You may find it helpful to change your view to **Actual Size** or **200%**.

22. Align the automatic page number to the right and size the text box so that it extends beyond the left edge of the page and isn't much taller than the automatic page character as shown in Figure 9-13. Set the character attributes to **10 point Helvetica Italic** and color it **White.**

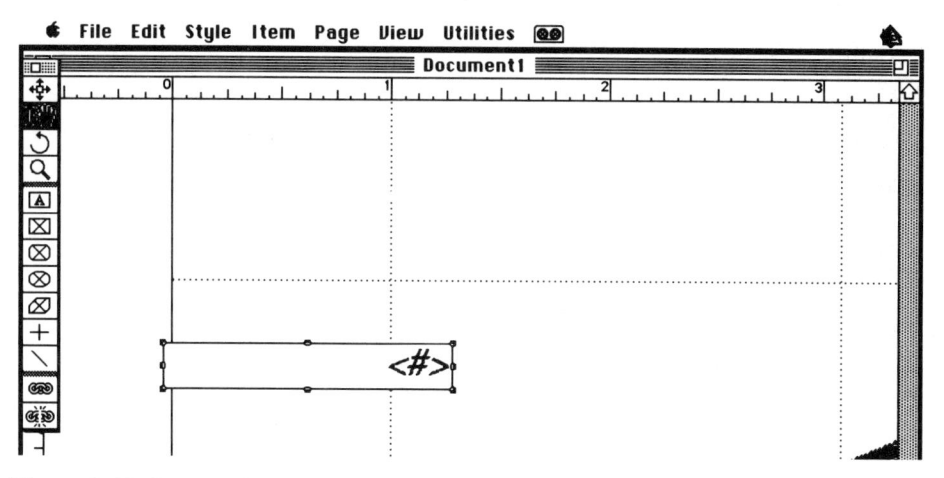

**Figure 9-13. Automatic page numbering box.**

Then change the background color of the text box to **100% Blue**.

23. Do the same step-and-repeat trick you did before to copy this text box to the other page. Remember to set the **Vertical Offset** to **0**, as you don't want the copy to travel vertically. Then position the text box exactly using the cursor keys.

24. Set the alignment to **Flush Left** so the page number rests under the corner of the third column. Place a default text box on each side of the spread (if there isn't one there already). Set it to have three columns with a .375-inch (3/8-inch) gutter between each column by choosing **Modify** from the **Item** menu. Do it this way instead of specifying the number of columns in the **Measurements** palette because the **Modify** command lets you designate a gutter space and the **Measurements** palette doesn't.

25. Place column lines between each column as dividers. Specify the first one as .5 point width, extend it from the top of the column to the bottom, then step-and-repeat it once to divide the other two columns.

26. Group the text box and its lines, duplicate it, and place it in position on the other page.

Done! Your first master page format is finished. Use this format as a guide to creating the rest of your page formats. Use the same elements, changing their attributes and locations for the other three page formats.

Ready to start the second master page format?

27. This one's easy. To create a duplicate of the **Marketing** master page layout, click and drag the **A Master Page** icon (which is now labeled **Marketing**) onto the **B Master Page** icon (which is now labeled **Product**). A dialog box appears to ask if you want to completely replace B with A. As there's nothing on B yet, click on **OK**. You now have two identical master page formats. To view it in the document window, double-click on the **B Master Page** icon.

28. Start by choosing **Actual Size** from the **View** menu (or click with the **Zoom** tool until the percentage value in the lower left corner of the document window reads 100%).

29. You don't have to ungroup any of the items to change their locations or the contents of their boxes. Choose the **Content** tool and select the rotated text box with **Marketing** in it, then choose **Select All** from the **Edit** menu. Your text is selected and ready to edit, even though the box and its contents are rotated.

30. Type **Product** to replace **Marketing.**

31 Select the polygon picture box behind it and change its background color to **Red.** As the two boxes are grouped together, you won't be able to modify any attributes that aren't common to both boxes. Select the picture box using the **Content** tool and choose **Modify** from the **Item** menu (or press ⌘+M) to display the **Picture Box Specifications** dialog box. Set the background color to **100% Red.**

32. Now start adding your graphics. Create a new picture box anywhere on the page and import the picture **Bicycle** from the **Library Samples** folder. Reduce the image size to 44% and reduce the size of the box so that it's just large enough to display the image. Then use the **Item** tool to select it and choose **Cut** from the **Edit** menu. Place it into the text after the last paragraph on each page by using the **Content** tool to select an insertion point, and choose **Paste** from the **Edit** menu. Do this at the end of every page of text to add an accent to the layout.

USING QUARKXPRESS

### Technique

*Save your work! (Save your sanity!) Remember to save your work every few minutes so you won't lose much if the little goblins living inside your computer cause a system crash.*

33. Select the slanted bars at the bottom of the page with the **Item** tool. The bars are grouped together, but they share the common attribute of their background color, so you can edit that attribute. Double-click on the

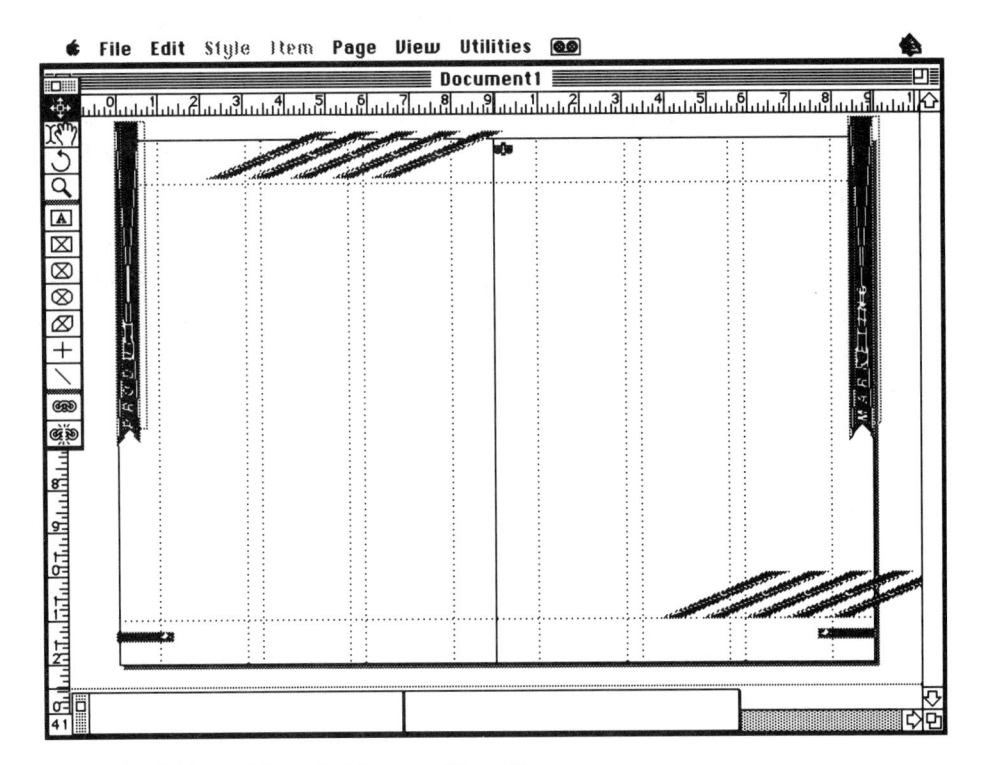

Figure 9-14. Repositioned stripes — Step 35.

298

grouped bars to display the **Picture Box Specifications** dialog box. Change the bars' background color to **PMS 430**.

34. Change the corresponding element colors on the spread's right facing page as you did on the left facing page. Leave the page numbers the same blue. They're consistent throughout the piece.

35. Time to get some diversity in your layout by moving the elements around. The page flags and page numbering flags should remain consistent throughout the publication, so leave them where they are. Move the stripes to new positions on the page, as shown in Figure 9-14.

## The Third Layout Spread

36. Now you're ready to perform the same trick to make your third master page spread. Drag the **B (Product) Master Page** icon over onto the **C (Capability) Master Page** icon. Double-click on the **C Master Page** icon to display its window.

37. Just as you replaced **Marketing** with **Product,** replace **Product** with **Capabilit**y in their respective text-box page flags. Remember, you must use the **Content** tool to make changes in the text boxes.

*Extra!*

*QuarkXPress 3.0 won't let you save the document if any whole element of a grouped item is completely off the master page boundaries. You'll get an error message, as shown in Figure 9-16.*

*USING QUARKXPRESS*

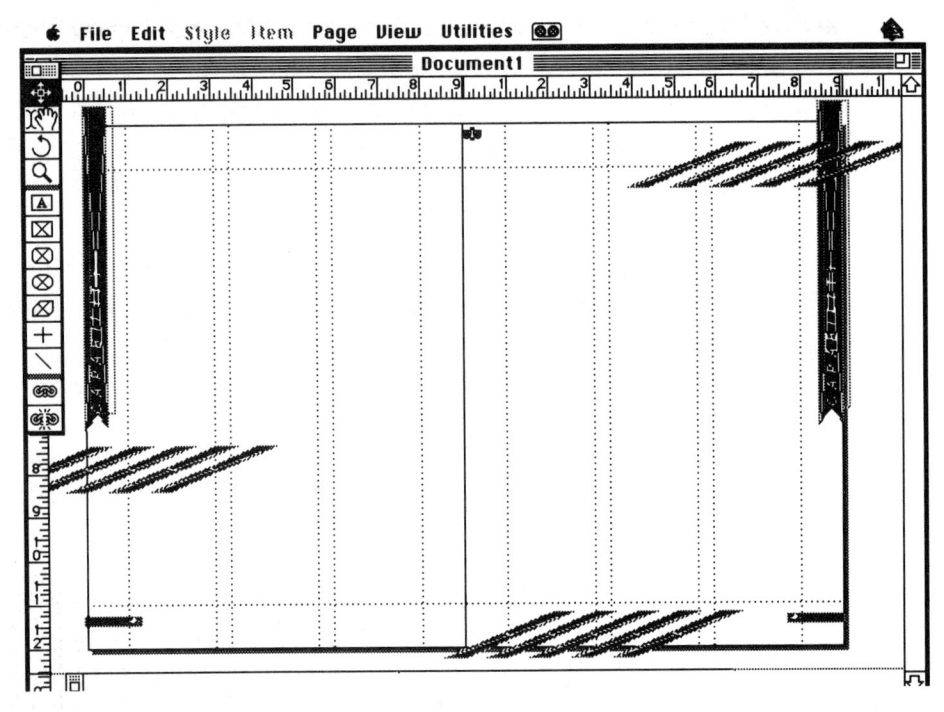

Figure 9-15. Results of Step 38.

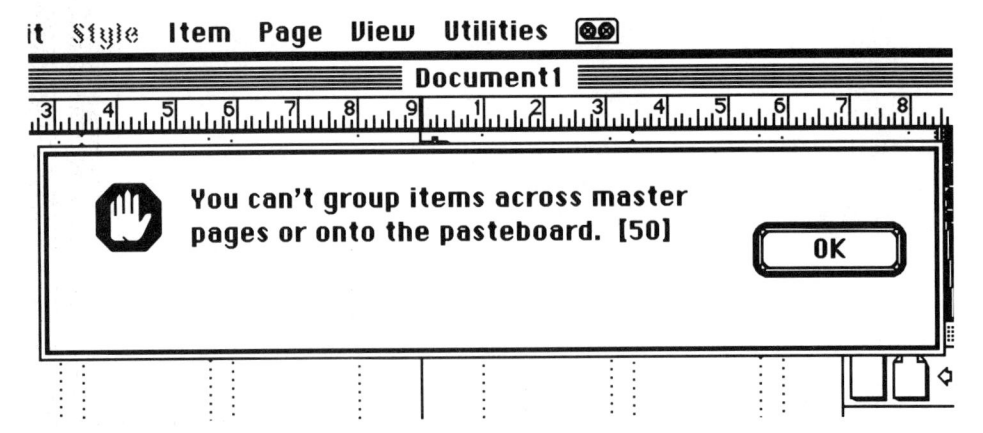

Figure 9-16. Error message when trying to save a document with item off master page boundaries.

38. Now change the background colors of the picture box page flags to **PMS 430**. After that, change the background colors of the stripes to **PMS 327** and move them to new locations on the spread. Duplicate one of them and place it somewhere on the right-facing page of the spread, as in Figure 9-15.

39. This is getting easier and easier, isn't it? Now drag the **C (Capability) Master Page** icon onto the **D (Financial) Master Page** icon to make your last master page format.

40. Make the same changes to the same elements as you did last time. Change the word **Capability** to **Financial**. Change the background color

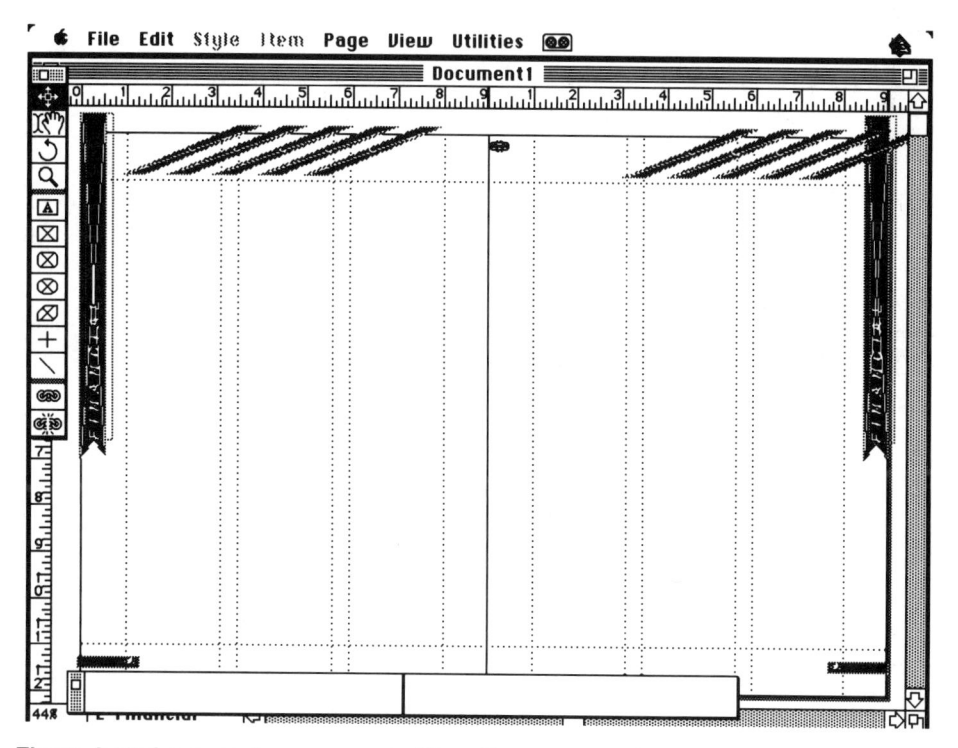

Figure 9-17. Last master page, as in Step 40.

of the page flag picture boxes to **PMS 327**. Change the background color of the stripes to **Blue**. Your result should look like Figure 9-17.

41. Save it! You're done with the master pages. Go back to the document. Double-click on the icon labeled **1A**. As this is page 1, and page 1 is always on the right, the page displayed is the right-facing half of the spread.

## Putting It Together

Now it's time to lay out the whole brochure using the master pages you've already created.

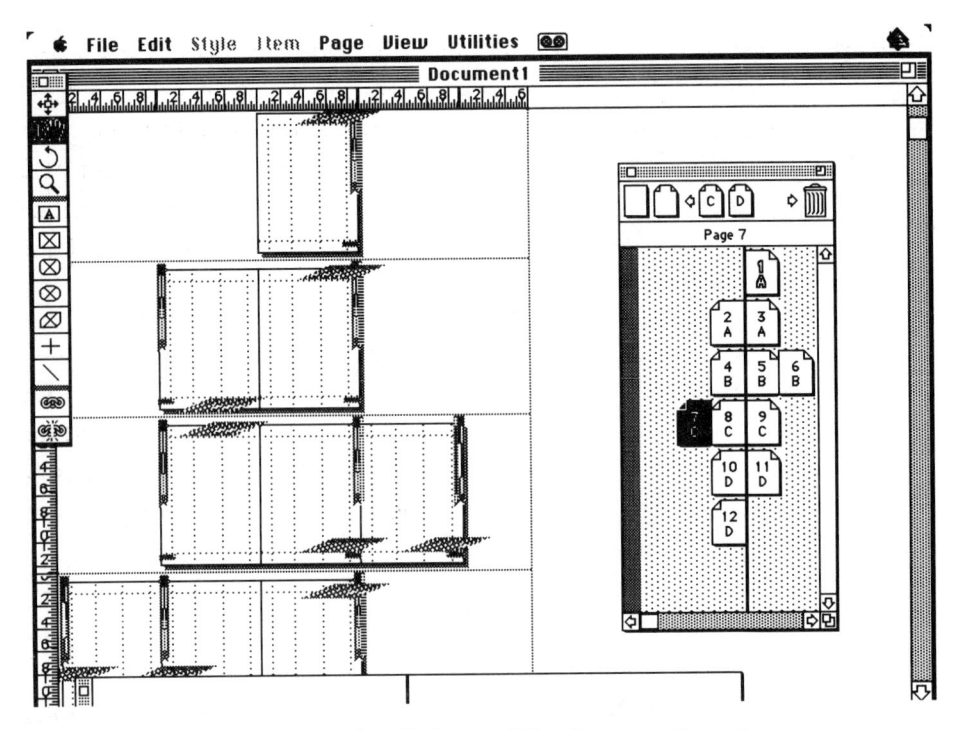

Figure 9-18. Pages in the thumbnail view and the document layout.

42. Drag each type of master page format icon down into the **Document Layout** palette in the way they appear in your brochure. As there are four sections and 12 pages, pull down three copies of each master page. Remember, you can always rearrange the order of the pages and even remove and edit any of the master page items.

43. Try setting up a couple of three-page fold-out spreads as the **Document Layout** palette shows in Figure 9-18. Choose **Thumbnails** from the **View** menu to see how the actual pages lay out.

    Enlarge your **Document Layout** palette by dragging the "size corner" to enlarge it. By the way, you can rearrange the layout in the **Document Layout** palette at any time while you're producing your brochure.

44. Start placing your graphics and text, starting on page 1. Draw a new picture box across the bottom of the page and import the color EPS file you used in the previous chapter (Old Time Biker). Enlarge it to **150%** of its original size and set its **Runaround...** characteristics to **Auto Image** with a text outset distance of 6 points. As you won't be needing the Marketing flag or the page number flag on page 1, select them both with the **Item** tool and delete them.

45. You're using the same sample-text file as you did in the previous assignments, so select the text box with the **Content** tool and import the sample-text document **Sample ASCII Text**. Notice that it automatically wraps around the illustration and comes no nearer to the image than 6 points, as in Figure 9-19.

## Setting up Style Sheets

46. To set up your first style sheet, change your view of the page to **Actual Size**.

**Figure 9-19.** Text imported and wrapping around illustration, with outset of 6 points (from Step 45).

47. Choose **Style Sheets** from the **Edit** menu. Click on the **New** button. Name your first style sheet **Body Text**. (If you want to give it a keyboard equivalent, remember that the keyboard equivalents you define should include the **Option** or ⌘ keys so you avoid inadvertently changing styles when you enter numbers from the keyboard.)

48. Click on the **Character** button and set the character attributes to **12 point Palatino Plain**, with no tracking or baseline shift, and leave the horizontal scale at **100%**. Choose **PMS 431** for the color. Then click on the **Formats** button and establish the paragraph formats as shown in Figure 9-20.

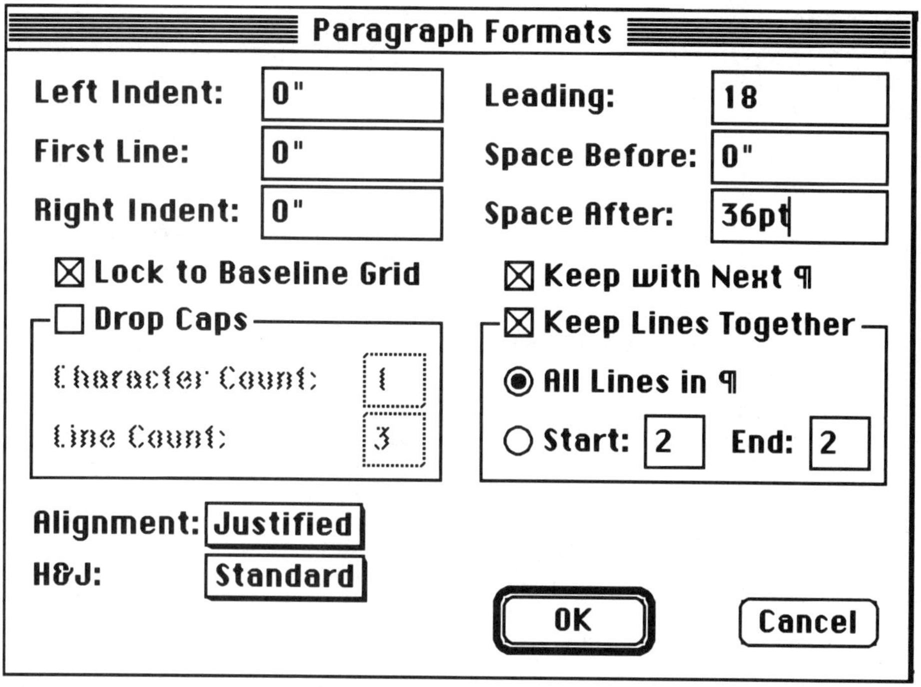

```
┌─────────────════ Paragraph Formats ═══─────────────┐
│  Left Indent:    [0"]      Leading:       [18]      │
│  First Line:     [0"]      Space Before:  [0"]      │
│  Right Indent:   [0"]      Space After:   [36pt]    │
│    ☒ Lock to Baseline Grid    ☒ Keep with Next ¶    │
│    ┌─☐ Drop Caps─────────┐  ┌─☒ Keep Lines Together─┐│
│    │ Character Count: [1]│  │ ⦿ All Lines in ¶      ││
│    │ Line Count:      [3]│  │ ○ Start: [2] End: [2] ││
│    └─────────────────────┘  └───────────────────────┘│
│  Alignment: [Justified]                             │
│  H&J:       [Standard]         ( OK )    ( Cancel ) │
└─────────────────────────────────────────────────────┘
```

Figure 9-20. Paragraph formats for Step 48.

Don't change any of the rules or tab attributes for this style. Note that the different style attributes are all listed in the description area of the dialog box. Click on **OK**.

49. The next style is an edited duplication of the **Body Text** style. This variation is used as a lead paragraph that starts each page and has a dropped initial cap. Select the **Body Text** style listed in the menu and click on the **Duplicate** button. This shows the **Edit Style Sheet** dialog box with **Copy of Body Text** highlighted in the **Name** field. Re-title this one by typing in the new name, **Lead Paragraph**. Change the **Formats** attributes to set it apart from the **Body Text** style. Click on the **Formats** button and enable the **Drop Caps** option by clicking its check box in the **Paragraph Formats** dialog box. Leave the **Character Count** at 1 and change the **Line Count** to 2.

50. The next style you'll create is a subhead style that begins sections of text. Start by clicking on the **New** button in the **Style Sheets** dialog box and then click on the **Character** button to display the **Character Attributes** dialog box. Set the attributes to the ones shown in Figure 9-21.

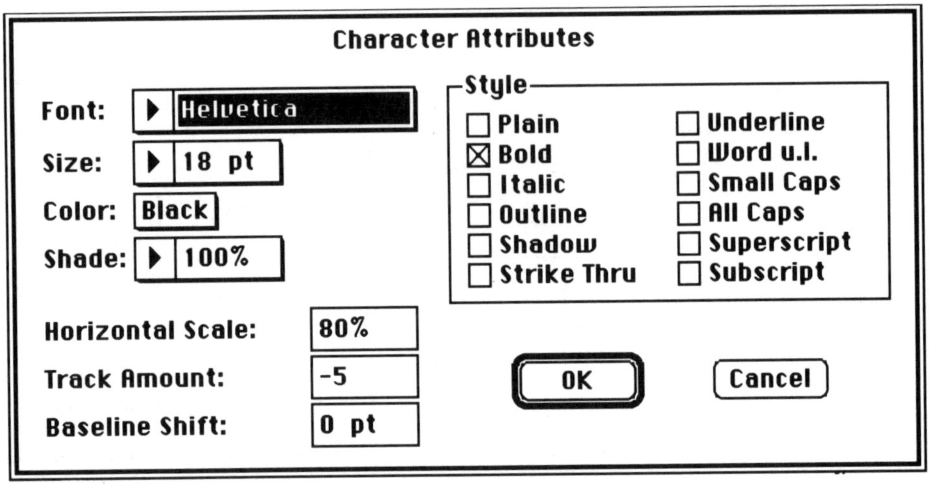

```
                        Character Attributes
                                    ┌Style─────────────────────┐
    Font:  ▶ Helvetica              │ ☐ Plain     ☐ Underline   │
    Size:  ▶ 18 pt                  │ ☒ Bold      ☐ Word u.l.   │
                                    │ ☐ Italic    ☐ Small Caps  │
    Color: Black                    │ ☐ Outline   ☐ All Caps    │
    Shade: ▶ 100%                   │ ☐ Shadow    ☐ Superscript │
                                    │ ☐ Strike Thru ☐ Subscript │
                                    └─────────────────────────┘
    Horizontal Scale:  80%
    Track Amount:      -5              [  OK  ]    [ Cancel ]
    Baseline Shift:    0 pt
```

Figure 9-21. Character Attribute settings for Step 50.

51. Next, you need a caption style for illustration and photograph captions. This also springs from an edited duplicate of the **Body Text** style, so select **Body Text** in the **Style Sheets** dialog box and click on the **Duplicate** button. Change the name to **Captions** and click on the **Character** button to change the **Character Attributes.** Once there, change the style to **Italic** and the size to **9 point**. This is your caption text style. Change the leading value in the **Paragraph Formats** to **+0** points (solid leading).

52. Finally, you'll need a general headline style. This style sheet is based on a duplicate of your subhead style. Select **Subhead** from the menu and

## CORPORATE BROCHURE

click on the **Duplicate** button. Change the name to **Heads** and change the **Character Attributes** size field to **36 points**. Leave everything else the same and click on **OK**.

Now you've finished setting up your style sheets. The next step is placing graphic images throughout the publication.

53. Make your own custom thumbnail view by reducing the size of the window and choosing **Fit in Window** from the **View** menu. Once you're able to view a few pages at a time in the document window, you can easily create and move graphic images around your document. The regular thumbnail view doesn't allow you to move items between document pages; it only lets you move the pages themselves.

    Start placing picture boxes throughout your document. Begin with page 2 and import the graphic document **Mtn Biker.TIFF** into a small box at the top left corner of the text box on page 2. Then make a new picture box that covers the middle and bottom half of the spread, import the file **Handlebars.EPS**, and enlarge the graphics to fill the whole box (200%). Then set the **Runaround...** to **Auto Image**, as shown in Figure 9-22.

54. The next spread is one of the three-page fold-outs. You will place a few smaller graphic images and later set the text-flow vertical alignment to **Bottom.**

    Place five new picture boxes at various locations across the spread and import the graphic files **Bikers, Gears, Wheel Artwork, Pedal,** and **Yesteryear Cyclist**. Use the keyboard shortcut **Shift+Option+⌘+F** to automatically size each image to fit each box. Then set the **Runaround...** to **Auto Image** for each and set the text outset to 12 points for each. Figure 9-23 shows the result.

USING QUARKXPRESS

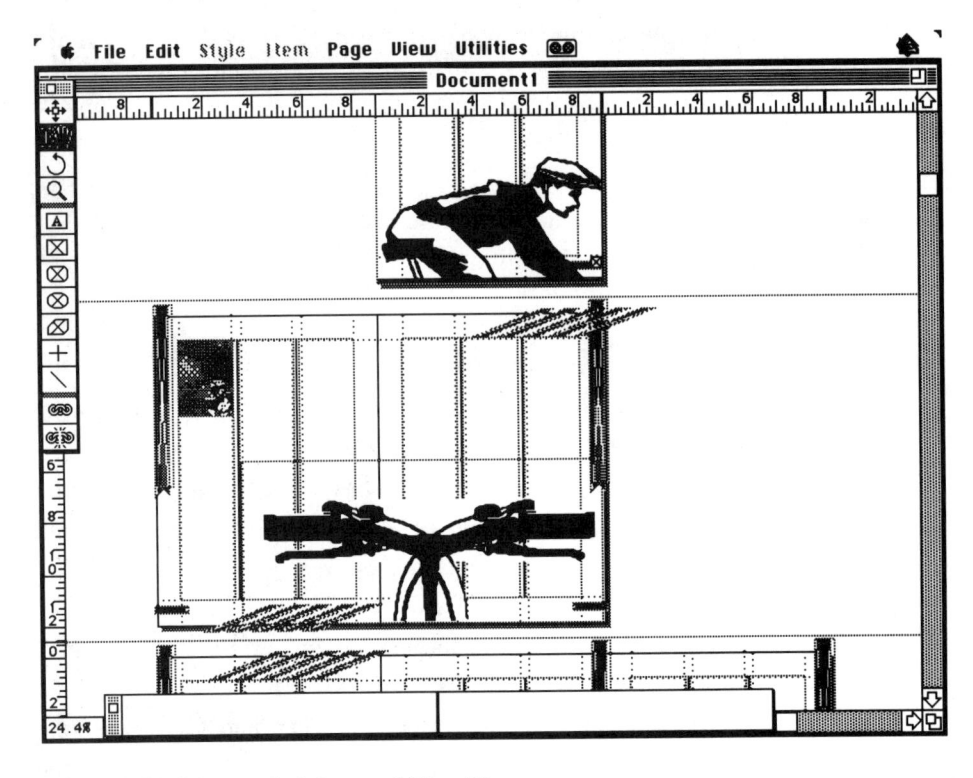

Figure 9-22. Imported pictures of Step 53.

55. For the next spread, step-and-repeat the same picture across the length of the page and rotate it sequentially 40% each time. Create a new text box at the bottom right-hand corner of the spread about 2 inches by 2 inches. Import the file **Bicycle** from the **Sample Library** folder. Enlarge it to fit by pressing **Shift+Option+⌘+F**. Leave the **Runaround...** set to **Item,** then step-and-repeat it eight times across the bottom of the page. Select each one and change its image-rotation angle using the setting in the **Measurements** palette (shown highlighted in Figure 9-24).

308

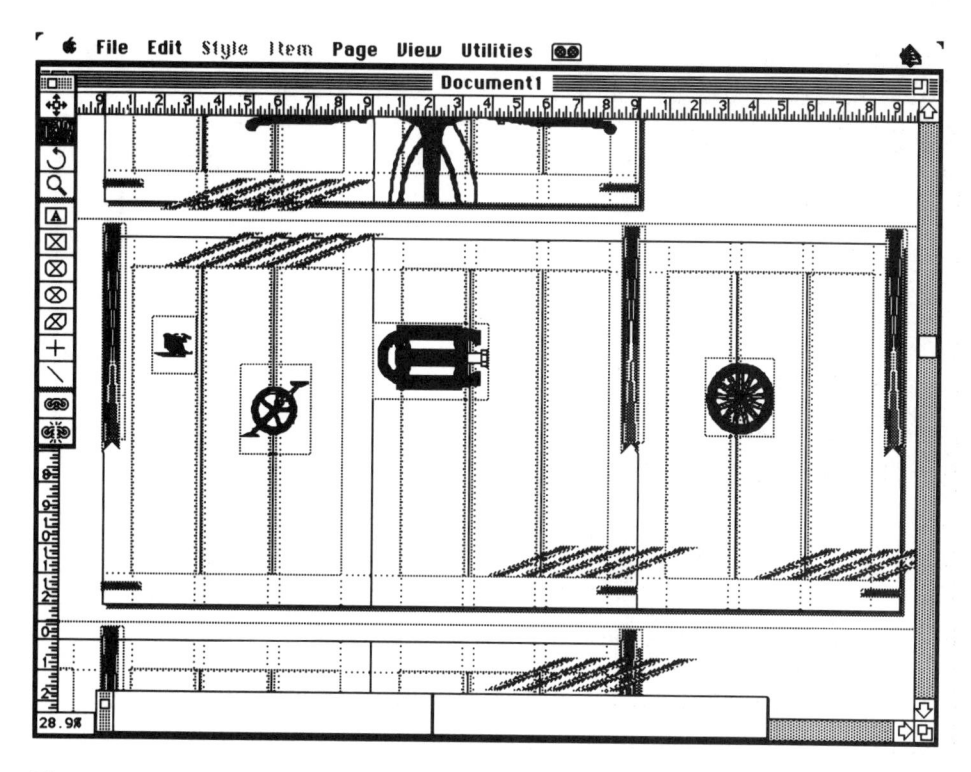

**Figure 9-23. Results of picture importing in Step 54.**

56. This is the last spread, pages 10 and 11. Create a new picture box in the lower left-hand corner of the left facing page and import the file **Handlebars** from the tutorial folder **Page Layout Sample**. Then step-and-repeat it on to the next page and import the file **Wheel Artwork**. Set the **Runaround...** of each to **Auto Image** with a 12 point text outset. Figure 9-25 shows this handiwork.

57. This is the last page. Create a small picture box near the center of the page and import **Bikers.PAINT**. Size it to fit and leave the **Runaround...** set to **Item**.

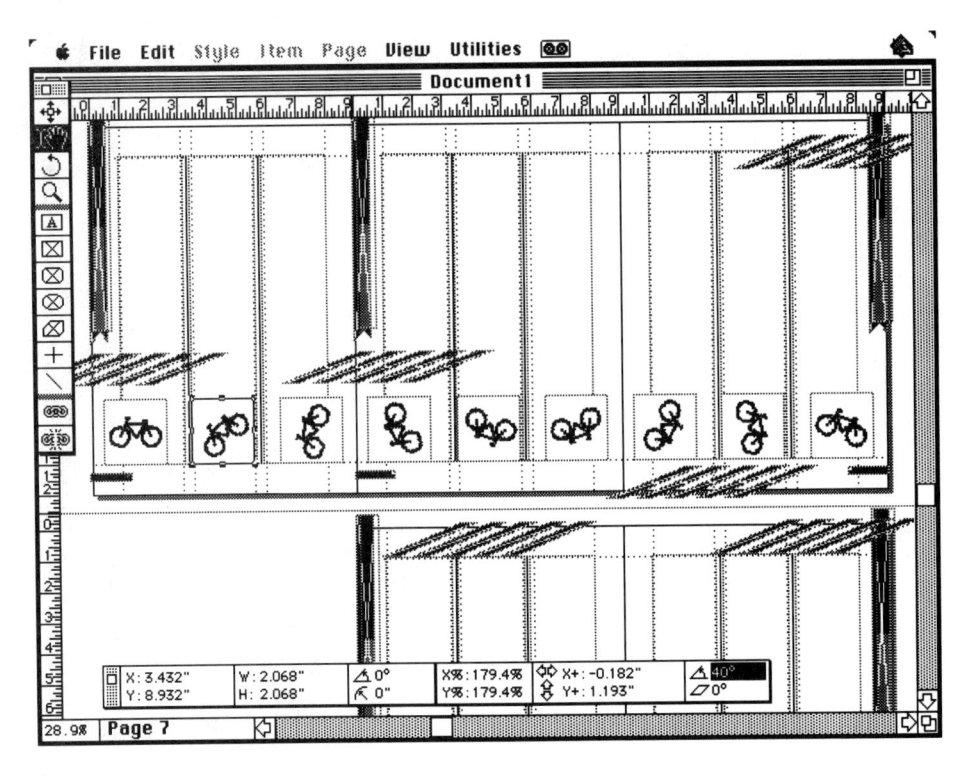

Figure 9-24. Rotating the bike images using the Measurements palette.

## Now for the Text

58. Jump back to page 1 by pressing ⌘+J and typing a **1** in the dialog box that appears.

59. Import the text file as many times as necessary to fill this document and change the style and alignments throughout. Select the first text box with the **Content** tool and import the text file **Sample ASCII Text**.

60. Select all of the text and choose your **Body Text** style at the bottom of the **Style** menu. As page 1 leads off the document, change the **First**

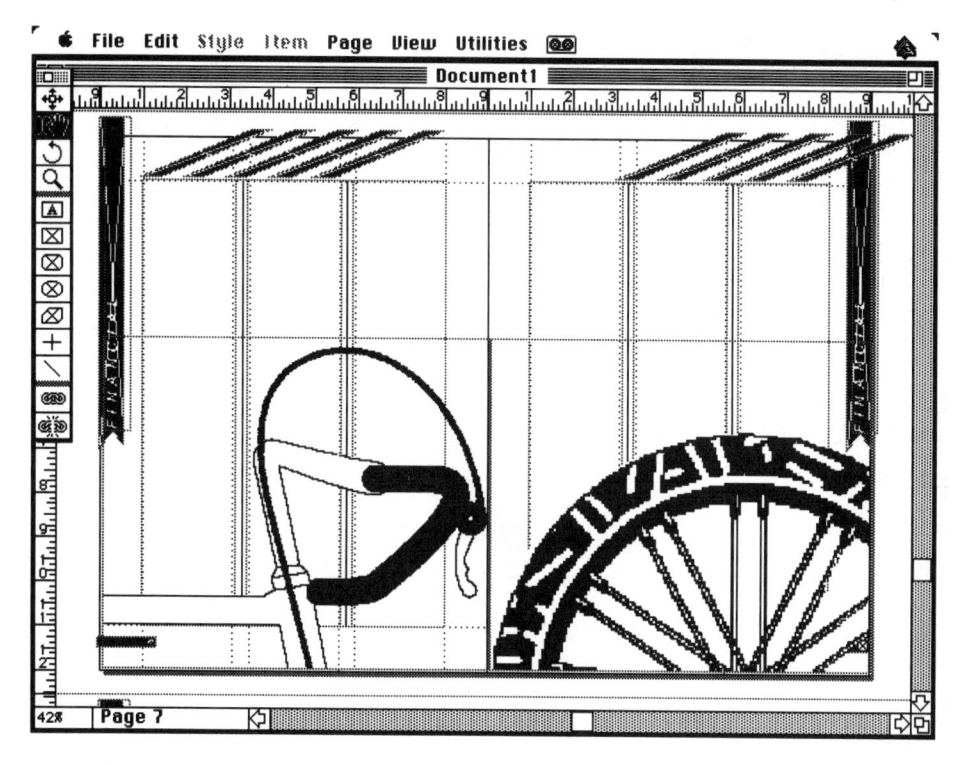

Figure 9-25. Pages 10 and 11 with pictures imported during step 56.

**Baseline** field in the **Text Box Specifications** dialog box to 1" to leave some room at the top of the text box for your headlines. With the new space at the top of the text box, your body text should have flowed into a totally different position, as you specified the **Keep with Next ¶** and **Keep Lines Together** options in the **Paragraph Formats** dialog box when you defined your styles.

61. Place a wide and shallow text box at the top of the page to hold your headline. Type an inventive headline, such as **Big Noticeable Headline**, and place it above the main body of text.

311

62. If you have some stray text hanging around anywhere on the page that isn't with the main body of text — such as that in Figure 9-26 —place the text insertion cursor at the end of what should be the last paragraph on the page and press **Enter** to force the stray text onto the next page or column.

**Figure 9-26. Stray text illustration for Step 62.**

63. On page 2, your lead paragraph should begin in the second column to emphasize the TIFF image in the first column. Use your **Lead Paragraph** style sheet to format the first paragraph on this page. For consistency throughout your document, change the first paragraph on every page to the **Lead Paragraph** style.

Separate text at the end of a column or page by pressing **Enter** at the end of paragraphs where you want the next paragraph to begin in the next column.

64. Choose **Get Text...** from the **File** menu, import the same ASCII text file, and flow it into the document to fill more space. Repeat this step as often as you need to as you progress through the document.

65. When you get to pages 9, 10, and 12, select all of the text on those pages and change the **Paragraph Formats** for that selected text to disable the

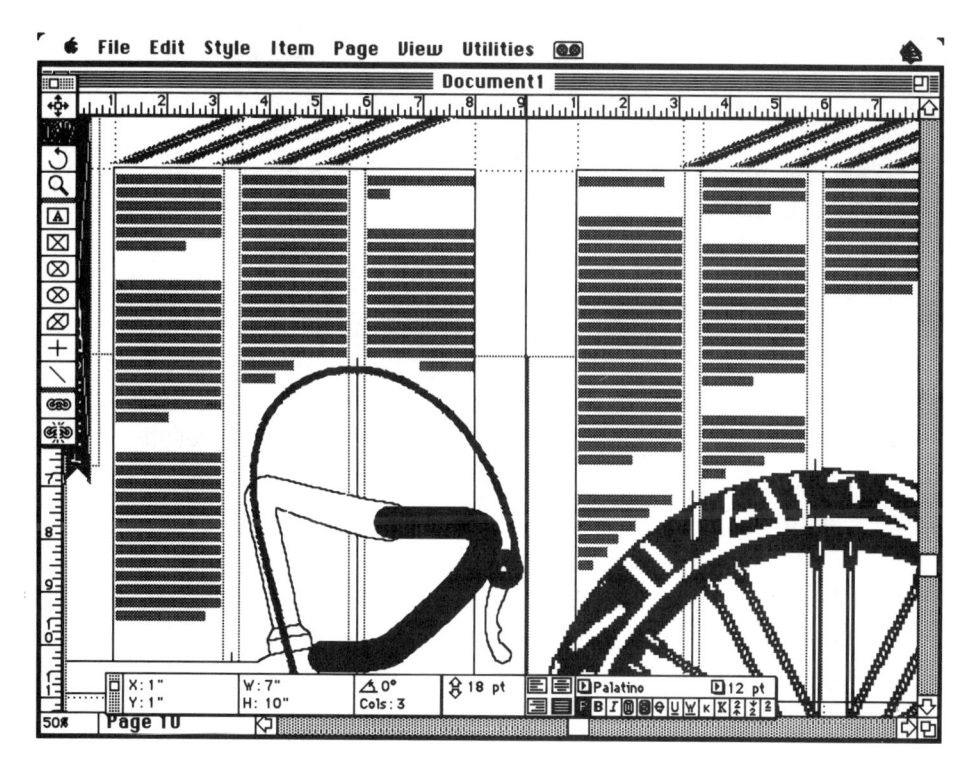

Figure 9-27. Text fitting clean-up of Step 65.

**Keep Lines Together** and **Keep with Next ¶**. This causes the text to reflow and more closely follow the illustration contours. This also gives you the opportunity to do some manual copy fitting to clean up the ends of the paragraphs. Use the keyboard shortcuts to tighten up the character spacing in the paragraphs where lines of type fall alone at the top of a column, as in Figure 9-27.

You can adjust areas by carefully tracking the text in small increments or by changing the hyphenation and justification attributes. Take plenty of time and experiment to find the solution that works best for you. There are advantages to both methods.

66. Finally, the last page of the document. Make a quick response form using **Paragraph Rules**. Give yourself some extra space by pressing Return a couple of times. Then type **Name**, **Address**, **City/State/Zip**, and **Telephone**, with each separated by a line return. Select all four lines and choose **Rules** under the **Style** menu (**Shift+⌘+N**).

Set the rules to appear above the text by clicking on the **Rules Above** check box (see Figure 9-28).

67. Add captions to some of the illustrations throughout the document. Start with the **Handlebars** illustration on page 3. Create a new text box at the bottom right-hand corner under the handlebar. Make it transparent and flow the text file **Text 1** from the tutorial files. Select all of the text and change its style to **Captions.** Use the **Item** tool to select and copy this text box and paste it in a few other places in your document where you need it.

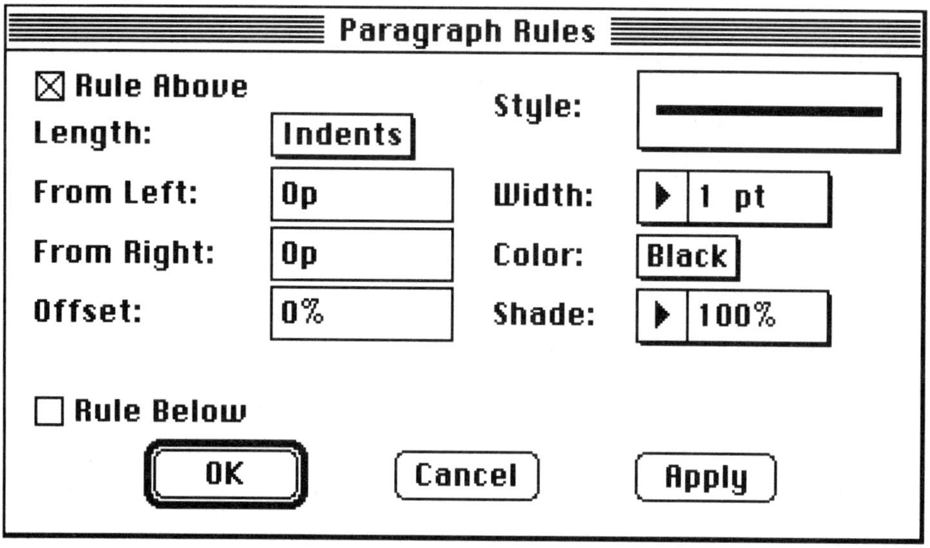

Figure 9-28. Paragraph Rules dialog box (Step 66).

68. Now for the subheads. Choose a few appropriate places to insert your own subheads. Remember, text must be separated by a line return to be considered a separate paragraph, so type in your subheads, followed by return, then place the cursor back in the subhead line and choose the **Subhead** style from the **Style Sheet**s menu. Remember, the paragraph formats you set for your body text call for a space of 1/2 inch after each paragraph, so when you type your subhead and press **Return**, the paragraph jumps down that 1/2 inch. Don't be alarmed — when you move the cursor back into your subhead and change the style, the space closes back up. Your subhead style doesn't have to designate any space. Your layout should now look like the one in Figure 9-29.

315

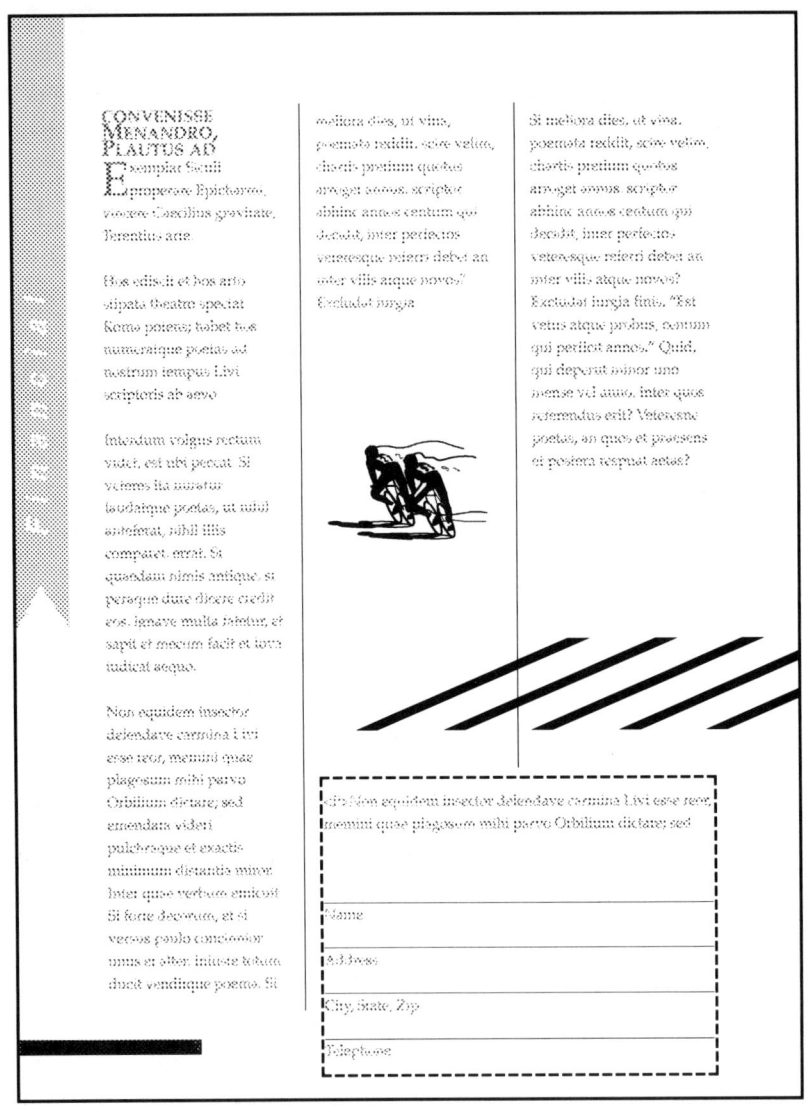

Figure 9-29. The finished project.

Congratulations! Whew! Pat yourself on the back. Finishing this project is a real accomplishment!

# GLOSSARY

**amberlith/rubylith** A vinyl/plastic composite film used to create opaque areas for the mechanical production phase of printing preparation.

**application** A software program designed to perform a specific task. QuarkXPress 3.0 is an application that is designed to facilitate the production of the printed page.

**ascender** The highest part of a type character that extends above the body.

**ASCII** The "lowest common denominator" of text formats. ASCII (American Standard Code for Information Interchange) is the accepted industry standard for information exchange among different software applications.

**auto page numbering** A capability that automatically numbers each page of a document. QuarkXPress 3.0 can also automatically number pages and groups of pages or sections in a document.

**baseline** The invisible line along which the bottoms or bottom serifs of text are aligned.

**baseline grid** An invisible grid that can align columns of text.

**bit map** A graphic image file format that defines an image by "mapping" individual pixels to create the image.

**bleed** An image is said to bleed when any part of it extends beyond the edge of the page.

**body text** Refers to the main blocks of text in a publication.

**cap height** The distance from the baseline of a typeface to the top of the ascender. QuarkXPress 3.0 measures cap height for a typeface by the height of a 0 (zero).

**centered** When each line of text in a column is aligned along an invisible line centered exactly between both column margins.

**choke** When a color is "knocked out" of a background color, QuarkXPress 3.0 automatically adjusts the space where the two colors join by reducing the size of the knocked-out area, causing a small area where the two colors overlap.

**cicero** A unit of measure in typography. Primarily used in Europe (except in Belgium). There are approximately 5.62 ciceros in an inch.

**CMYK** A color model that employs the simulation of different colors by mixing proportions of four basic colors of ink: Cyan, Magenta, Yellow, and Black.

**color breaks** The division between colors in production. QuarkXPress 3.0 automates the color separation to streamline platemaking.

**comprehensive (comp)** A term used to describe a "rough" copy of your design for planning purposes. QuarkXPress 3.0 allows for the production of very accurate comps to show exactly how a printed piece will look when finished.

**constrain** To control the creation of an object. Boxes may be constrained to perfect squares or circles, and lines to perfectly horizontal or vertical, by holding down the **Shift** key while you create them.

**constraining boxes** Boxes that hold items within them and prevent the interior items from being moved outside the boundaries of the box.

**contrast curve** A graphic representation of the relationship between contrast and brightness in an image. QuarkXPress 3.0 allows you to adjust and create your own contrast curve for some kinds of imported graphic images.

**copy** The text of a document.

**crop** To define the part of an image that is to be shown by removing edges and changing the size of the image.

**cursor** The moving symbol on your computer's monitor that indicates the tool being used or the action being performed.

**default** The automatic settings that are enabled when no others are defined.

**descender** The lowest part of any typeface that extends below the baseline.

**desktop publishing (or "electronic" publishing)** The technology that allows designers and artists to sleep later and take longer lunches while at the same time performing more billable work for a client. Intended as such, it exacts a high price in lost sleep and shorter breaks just to learn how to use it.

**document** The end product produced when using an "application." Using QuarkXPress 3.0 produces QuarkXPress 3.0 documents.

**drop cap** An large initial capital letter that begins a paragraph, so large that it "drops" down into the paragraph as deep as several lines of text.

**drop shadow** A duplicate of any object, offset from the original so that it simulates a shadow of the original.

**em-dash** A longer hyphen character that is classically defined as the width of an uppercase "M" in any typeface. QuarkXPress 3.0 defines an em-dash as the width of two adjoining zeros.

**em-space** A horizontal space originally measured as the width of a capital letter "M" in any size typeface. QuarkXPress 3.0 measures an em-space as the space occupied by two adjoining zeros.

**en-dash** Longer than a hyphen, an en-dash is half the width of an em-dash.

**en-space** Horizontal space that is half the width of an em-space.

**EPSF** Initials standing for Encapsulated PostScript File, a high-resolution graphic image file format with great precision and flexibility.

**flush** The alignment of a column of text along either margin. Text aligned along the right margin of a column is called "flush right." Text aligned along the left margin of a column is called "flush left."

319

**grayscale** Shades of gray making up the transition of color from black to white. The larger the number of shades, the smoother the transition.

**greeking** Creating a rough representation of an item on screen to speed up the building of images on your computer screen.

**halftone** The simulation of gray tones in an image by creating tiny dots of variable sizes and proximity to each other. The frequency (or the number of dots that will fit in an inch) dictates the clarity of an image.

**high contrast** A special image effect that reduces the number of steps in the transition of black to white to 2, eliminating gray tones.

**horizontal scaling** Condensed/extended type. The defined width of a character as it is made narrower or wider.

**HSB** Initials standing for Hue, Saturation, and Brightness. HSB is a model by which color is sometimes defined.

**items** The individual components that make up a page layout. In QuarkXPress 3.0 there are three types of items: text boxes, picture boxes and lines.

**justify** To adjust the space between letters and words to align text along both margins of a text box. Text can also be justified vertically.

**kern (letterspace)** To adjust the white space between two consecutive characters of type.

**knockout** When more than one color is used in printing, a "knocked-out" area is the space in a background color that is removed so that a foreground color may be printed over it without being affected by the background color.

**layout** A generic term used to describe the positioning of items on a page.

**leading** The amount of space that occurs between lines of text. QuarkXPress 3.0 measures leading from the baseline of one line of text to the baseline of the next.

# GLOSSARY

**line art** Graphic images that consist of only black and white (no gray).

**master page** A template or format page that contains items that are to be common to all pages that use it as a master.

**mechanical** The physical assembled elements of production, ready to be photographed for negative and plate production in printing.

**moiré** A pattern that is created when two or more halftone screens are misaligned in production.

**offset** When a duplicate element of design is moved from its original location, it is said to be "offset."

**offset lithography** Printing process that uses plates to impress the ink to the paper.

**orphans/widows** Words or lines of text that appear alone at the top or bottom of a column or page.

**output** The final product of the design process; the actual pages of work.

**overprint** To print a color directly on top of another without "knocking out" the background color.

**pasteup** The activity of placing the mechanical page elements together on a production board for reproduction. Before electronic design, this was usually accomplished by placing adhesive wax on the back of typesetting and camera work to affix it to production boards.

**pica** A unit of measure in typography. There are 6 picas per inch and 12 points per pica.

**PICT and PICT2** Not an acronym, PICT is a graphic image file format that can hold more than 72dpi resolution in bit-mapped and object-oriented formats. PICT2 is an advanced version that accommodates color and grayscale information.

**picture boxes** Containers for graphic images in QuarkXPress 3.0. Picture boxes can be rectangles, rectangles with rounded corners, ellipses, and irregular polygons.

**plate** The actual physical device that impresses a single color onto the printed page in the press. Plate also refers to the separation of a single color in the production process.

**PMS** An acronym for the Pantone Matching System, a proprietary worldwide system for matching ink colors.

**point** A unit of measure in typography. There are 72 points per inch.

**posterization** A special-effect treatment of grayscale images that reduces the number of gray tones in the image.

**PostScript** The "language" that most Macintosh desktop publishing software products use to describe an image to a high-resolution printing device.

**process color** Color created using the four component "process" colors; Cyan, Magenta, Yellow, and Black.

**process separations** When color images are composed of process colors, they are separated into individual plates, one for each of the four process colors. These are then called "process" separations.

**registration** The process of aligning each color plate so that colors position properly on the page. Misregistration can cause gaps in adjoining colors and moiré patterns in screens.

**registration marks** Symbols used to align plates on camera-ready art.

**RGB** An acronym for Red, Green, Blue. Computer monitors and televisions use the RGB model to simulate colors by combining different levels of red, green, and blue light.

**RIFF** An acronym for Raster Image File Format, a compressed proprietary image file format developed by the Letraset Corporation.

**scanner** An image recording device that saves images in a variety of machine-readable formats for placement or manipulation with other software products.

# GLOSSARY

**screen angle** The angle at which halftone dots are aligned. Different screen angles can have an effect on tone gradation and appearance of halftone images.

**serifs** The little "feet" that appear at the ends of vertical strokes on a typeface.

**smart page numbering** Automatic updates to page numbers that reference where a text chain is continued on or from, when linked across several pages of a document.

**spot colors** Colors that are assigned their own plate in the separation process.

**stat camera** Another casualty of the electronic age, made obsolete by scanners.

**stripping** The act of placing and separating images and color areas in negatives in preparation for platemaking.

**stylesheets** Automatic assignments of styles and attributes to blocks of text. QuarkXPress 3.0 allows for up to 127 different stylesheets per document.

**text boxes** Containers for holding textual information in QuarkXPress.

**thumbnail** A small, rough image of a document intended to give a general idea of its layout.

**TIFF** An acronym for Tag Image File Format. TIFF images are the most versatile for controlling contrast and screen attributes of grayscale and color images.

**track (letterspacing)** The manipulation of the spaces that occur between characters as applied to a range of text (more than two characters).

**trap** The overlap space that one color extends over another to prevent gaps caused by slight misregistration of color plates on a printing press.

**trim lines** Guides that indicate the boundaries of a page.

**x-height** The vertical height of any lower-case "x" character as measured from its baseline.

*Appendix A*

# Keyboard Shortcuts

**Most Important**

Invoking the Muse (Help) ..................................................... ⌘-**?** (or the **Help** key)

**Getting Things Done With Type**
**Selecting Text**

Previous character ........................................................................ ⇧-← (left arrow)
Next character ............................................................................. ⇧-→ (right arrow)
Previous line ................................................................................ ⇧-↑ (up arrow)
Next line ...................................................................................... ⇧-↓ (down arrow)
Previous word .............................................................................. ⌘-⇧-← (left arrow)
Next word .................................................................................... ⌘-⇧-→ (right arrow)
Previous paragraph ...................................................................... ⌘-⇧-↑ (up arrow)
Next paragraph ............................................................................ ⌘-⇧-↓ (down arrow)
Start of line .................................................................................. ⌘-*option*-⇧-← (left arrow)
End of line ................................................................................... ⌘-*option*-⇧-→ (right arrow)
Start of story ................................................................................ ⌘-*option*-⇧-↑ (up arrow)
End of story ................................................................................. ⌘-*option*-⇧-↓ (down arrow)

325

## Changing Styles

| | |
|---|---|
| Other size | ⌘-⇧-\ |
| Plain text | ⌘-⇧-P |
| Bold text | ⌘-⇧-B |
| Italic text | ⌘-⇧-I |
| Underline text | ⌘-⇧-U |
| Word underline | ⌘-⇧-W |
| Strike through | ⌘-⇧-/ |
| Outline | ⌘-⇧-O |
| Shadow | ⌘-⇧-S |
| All caps | ⌘-⇧-K |
| Small caps | ⌘-⇧-H |
| Superscript | ⌘-⇧-+ |
| Subscript | ⌘-⇧-hyphen |
| Character | ⌘-⇧-D |
| Align left | ⌘-⇧-L |
| Align centered | ⌘-⇧-C |
| Align right | ⌘-⇧-R |
| Align justified | ⌘-⇧-J |
| Define leading | ⌘-⇧-E |
| Define formats | ⌘-⇧-F |
| Define tabs | ⌘-⇧-T |

## Fonts

| | |
|---|---|
| Increase font size | ⌘-⇧-> |
| Increase in 1 pt increments | ⌘-*option* ⇧-> |
| Decrease font size | ⌘-⇧-< |
| Decrease in 1 pt increments | ⌘-*option* ⇧-< |

## Leading

| | |
|---|---|
| Increase leading 1 pt | ⌘-⇧-' |
| Increase in .1 pt increments | ⌘-*option* ⇧-' |
| Decrease leading 1pt | ⌘-⇧-; |
| Decrease in .1 pt increments | ⌘-*option*-⇧-; |

## Baseline Shift

| | |
|---|---|
| Increase by 1 pt | ⌘-*option*-⇧-+ |
| Decrease by 1 pt | ⌘-*option*-⇧-— |

(works only when an absolute or incremental leading value is assigned to selected text)

## Kerning/Tracking

| | |
|---|---|
| Increase by .05 em-space | ⌘-⇧-} |
| Increase by .005 em-space | ⌘-*option*-⇧-} |
| Decrease by .05 em-space | ⌘-⇧-{ |
| Decrease by .005 em-space | ⌘-*option*-⇧-{ |

## Horizontal Scaling

| | |
|---|---|
| Increase by 5% | ⌘-] |
| Decrease by 5% | ⌘-[ |

## Special Characters
Symbol font ........................................................................................ ⌘-⇧-Q
Zapf dingbats font ............................................................................ ⌘-⇧-Z

## Deleting Text
Delete previous character ................................................................ *delete*
Delete next character ....................................................................... ⇧-*delete*
Delete previous word ....................................................................... ⌘-*delete*
Delete next word .............................................................................. ⌘-⇧-*delete*
Delete selected text ......................................................................... *delete*
Delete selected boxes & lines ......................................................... ⌘-K

## Special Characters
New paragraph ................................................................................ *return*
New line ........................................................................................... ⇧-*return*
New column ..................................................................................... *enter*
New box .......................................................................................... ⇧-*enter*

## Spaces
Breaking standard space ................................................................. space
Breaking en-space .......................................................................... *option*-space
Breaking standard hyphen .............................................................. hyphen
Nonbreaking standard space .......................................................... ⌘-space
Nonbreaking en-space .................................................................... ⌘-*option*-space

## Hyphens & Dashes

| | |
|---|---|
| Nonbreaking standard hyphen | ⌘-= |
| Nonbreaking en-dash | *option*-hyphen |
| Nonbreaking em-dash | *option*-⇧-hyphen |
| Discretionary (soft) hyphen | ⌘-hyphen |

## Getting Things Done With Pictures

| | |
|---|---|
| Negative | ⌘-⇧-hyphen |
| Normal-contrast picture | ⌘-⇧-N |
| High-contrast picture | ⌘-⇧-H |
| Posterize picture | ⌘-⇧-P |
| Other contrast | ⌘-⇧-C |
| Other halftone screen | ⌘-⇧-S |
| Increase size by 5% | ⌘-*option*-⇧-> |
| Decrease size by 5% | ⌘-*option*-⇧-< |
| Center picture in box | ⌘-⇧-M |
| Fit exactly to box | ⌘-⇧-F |
| Fit proportionally to box | ⌘-*option*-⇧-F |

## Lines

| | |
|---|---|
| Increase line width | ⌘-⇧-> |
| Increase in 1 pt increments | ⌘-*option*-⇧-> |
| Decrease line width | ⌘-⇧-< |
| Decrease in 1 pt increments | ⌘-*option*-⇧-< |
| Other width | ⌘-⇧-\ |

## USING QUARKXPRESS

## Making Things Happen
### File Menu
| | |
|---|---|
| New | ⌘-N |
| Open | ⌘-O |
| Save | ⌘-S |
| Save as | ⌘-*option*-S |
| Get text/picture | ⌘-E |
| Page setup | ⌘-*option*-P |
| Print | ⌘-P |
| Transfer | ⌘-T |
| Quit | ⌘-Q |

### Edit Menu
| | |
|---|---|
| Undo | ⌘-Z |
| Cut | ⌘-X |
| Copy | ⌘-C |
| Paste | ⌘-V |
| Select all | ⌘-A |
| Find/change | ⌘-F |
| Preferences | ⌘-Y |

## Item Menu

| | |
|---|---|
| Modify | ⌘-M |
| Frame | ⌘-B |
| Duplicate | ⌘-D |
| Step and repeat | ⌘-*option*-D |
| Delete | ⌘-K |
| Lock | ⌘-L |

## ViewMenu

| | |
|---|---|
| Show/hide rulers | ⌘-R |
| Show/hide invisibles | ⌘-I |

## Utilities Menu

| | |
|---|---|
| Check word spelling | ⌘-W |
| Check story spelling | ⌘-*option*-W |
| Suggested hyphenation | ⌘-H |

## Getting Around
### Using the Extended Keyboard

| | |
|---|---|
| Help | **Help** key |
| Beginning of document | home |
| End of document | end |
| Previous screen | page up |
| Next screen | page down |
| First page | ⇧-home |
| Last page | ⇧-end |
| Previous page | ⇧-page up |
| Next page | ⇧-page down |
| Delete next character | ⌦ |

### Using Any Keyboard

| | |
|---|---|
| Beginning of document | *control*-A |
| End of document | *control*-D |
| Previous screen | *control*-K |
| Next screen | *control*-L |
| First page | *control*-⇧-A |
| Last page | *control*-⇧-D |
| Previous page | *control*-⇧-K |
| Next page | *control*-⇧-L |
| Go to page | ⌘-J |

## Moving Insertion Point

| | |
|---|---|
| Previous character | ← (left arrow) |
| Next character | → (right arrow) |
| Previous line | ↑ (up arrow) |
| Next line | ↓ (down arrow) |
| Previous word | ⌘-← (left arrow) |
| Next word | ⌘-→ (right arrow) |
| Previous paragraph | ⌘-(up arrow) |
| Next paragraph | ⌘-↓ (down arrow) |
| Start of line | ⌘-*option*-← (left arrow) |
| End of line | ⌘-*option*-→ (right arrow) |
| Start of story | ⌘-*option*-↑ (up arrow) |
| End of story | ⌘-*option*-↓ (down arrow) |

## Special Tricks
### Automatic Page Numbering

| | |
|---|---|
| Of previous text box | ⌘-2 |
| Of current text box | ⌘-3 |
| Of next text box | ⌘-4 |

### Talking to Dialog Boxes

| | |
|---|---|
| OK (or highlighted button) | *return* or *enter* |
| Cancel | ⌘-. (period) |
| Apply | ⌘-A |
| Yes | ⌘-Y |
| No | ⌘-N |

# Index

## A

Actual size, 40, 41, 241, 242, 272, 286, 295, 297, 303
Alignment, 39, 240, 262, 272, 274, 296, 307, 310
All caps, 287
Anchored graphics, 176, 189, 191
Anchored rules, 145, 163, 165, 252, 253, 281
Append, 90
    Color palette, 188, 213, 217, 224
    Guides, 137
    H&J, 138
Arrow keys, 197, 275, 290
Ascender, 107, 125, 135, 149, 165
Ascent, 39, 129, 134, 149, 165, 273
ASCII, 73, 103, 116, 245, 303, 310, 313
Auto page insertion, 35, 49, 265
Auto page numbering, 50, 51, 52, 53, 233, 238, 239, 281, 294, 295, 296
Auto picture import, 36, 180-182
Automatic text box, 39,
Automatic text inset, 24, 39
Auxiliary dictionary, 75, 98, 100, 101, 102, 103

## B

Background color, 39, 40, 58, 59, 105, 145, 154, 157, 188, 205, 207, 223, 224-226, 228, 231, 243, 275, 288, 290, 295, 297, 299, 301, 302

Baseline, 37, 38, 39, 107, 127, 129, 131, 134-136, 165, 245, 252
    First baseline, 252, 273
Baseline grid, 38, 282
Baseline shift, 131-133, 304
Bit map, 182, 195, 205
Bleed, 147, 171, 265, 291, 292, 293
Box angle, 146-147, 188, 191, 243, 258, 289
Box rotation, 145
Bring to front, 56, 288

## C

Cap height, 135, 273
Centered, 124, 215, 224, 241, 274
Character attributes, 19, 81, 82, 91, 207, 238, 250, 253, 272, 295, 304, 306
Choke, 224-226
Clear, 22, 55, 79
CMYK, 186, 208, 212, 218-219, 221-223, 284
Color, 10-11, 15, 21, 23, 32, 34, 39-40, 57-60, 66, 68-69, 81, 83, 105, 126, 157, 182, 185-188, 192, 194, 195, 196-231
    Adding, 218
    Frame, 172, 203-205
    Images, 205
    Import types, 182-183
    Lines, 160, 162-163, 202
    Models, 219-223

Palette, 206, 209, 217, 224
Reverse, 144, 145, 154, 165
Trapping, 226
Columns, 32, 38, 39, 83, 124, 125, 133, 137, 143, 153, 164
Constrained lines, 23, 24, 157, 229, 235, 259
Constrained shapes, 167
Constraining objects, 37, 56, 65, 142, 167, 179
Content tool, 21, 22, 52, 55, 58, 115, 145, 150, 172, 183-184, 185, 188-189, 201, 238, 240, 244, 245, 249, 252, 259, 263, 288, 295, 297, 299, 303, 310
Contrast, 183, 185-188, 194, 199, 205, 208, 209, 210, 231
Copy, 14, 19, 21, 22, 55, 61, 79, 80, 93, 105, 151-152, 219, 229, 257, 260, 269, 270, 271, 276, 295, 314
Custom borders, 62, 65
Customizing, 24, 307
    Drop shadows, 150-152
    Kerning, 118
    Lines, 160
    Outset, 175-177
    Screen, 186
    Tracking, 121
    Trapping, 226-227
Cut, 19, 21, 22, 55, 79, 80, 105, 189, 193, 297

# D

Default (automatic) text box, 49, 151, 265, 285, 291, 296
Delete, 22, 41, 48, 55, 79, 90, 102, 85, 115, 123, 138, 141, 191, 196, 206, 217, 274, 303
Descender, 107, 125, 136, 165
Dictionary, 75, 98, 100, 102, 103
Document layout palette, 40, 44, 45, 46, 47, 48, 50
Drop caps, 144, 147-151
Duplicate, 55, 65, 90, 91, 93, 126, 138, 155, 157, 197, 208, 217, 219, 230, 235, 285, 290, 296, 301, 306, 307

# E

Element, 230, 234, 235, 263, 269, 286, 290, 291, 296, 299, 301

# F

Facing pages, 32, 45, 235
Find/change, 94, 95, 96, 97, 111
Fit in window, 41, 43, 52, 234, 235, 239, 243, 247, 248, 255, 261, 265, 286, 291, 307
Flush, 124, 240, 296
Font, 37, 38, 81, 97, 105, 107-111, 113-115, 119, 121-123, 139, 144, 245, 272, 278
Font rendering, 36
Font selection, 245
Font substitution, 278
Font usage, 110-111
Format, 43, 44, 45, 47, 48, 50, 51, 53, 60, 137, 139, 142-143, 148, 150, 151, 182, 185, 191, 195, 200, 209, 226, 234, 235, 239, 240, 243, 252, 259, 262, 281, 285, 296, 301, 303, 312

Format lines, 43, 265
Format text, 73, 74, 81, 87, 103
Frame/frame editor, 24, 34, 39, 40, 57, 62, 63, 64, 65, 72, 105, 119, 167, 172-173, 180, 199, 203, 205, 206, 207, 216, 251, 255, 257

## G

Get Picture, 59, 179-180, 267
Get Text, 52, 74, 75
Go To..., 252
Greek below, 36
Greek pictures, 37
Group, 22, 55, 58, 59, 60, 154-155, 157, 192, 196, 203, 229-231, 244, 260, 277, 288, 289, 291, 292, 296
Group specifications, 58
Group/ungroup, 55

## H

H&J, 124, 125, 137-141
Halftone (screen), 182-188, 194-195, 208, 221, 225, 228, 233, 262
Hide, 19, 25, 40, 261, 265, 279
Horizontal scale, 92, 105, 144, 287, 304
HSB, 186, 211, 218-220
Hyphenation, 21, 84, 99, 119, 137-141, 314

## I

Import
    Curved line, 158
    EPS, 191
    Graphics, 36, 54, 157, 166, 208, 209, 218, 255, 259, 268, 276, 297, 303, 307
    Images, 179-183
    Kerning tables, 116
    Picture usage, 193-194, 195
    Text, 9, 35, 71-74, 81, 304, 310, 313
Invert, 126, 178, 275

## J

Justification, 21, 105, 124, 136-140, 262, 272, 277, 314

## K

Keep lines together, 142, 311, 314
Kern, 38, 105, 108, 111-121, 137, 144, 150
Kerning table, 113, 119, 121, 165
Keyboard equivalent, 22, 88, 91, 193, 194, 242, 246, 261, 262, 267, 277, 287, 288, 290
Keyboard shortcut, 14, 19, 51, 52, 77, 78, 79, 81, 82, 86, 98, 99, 174, 231, 235, 241, 244, 245, 247, 252, 253, 265, 272, 278, 307, 314, 324
Knockout, 218

## L

Label, 47, 61, 193, 194, 262, 296, 302
Leading, 37, 38, 84, 105, 108, 125-130, 135-137, 142, 144, 242, 245, 272, 273, 274, 277, 306
    Absolute leading, 128, 272, 273
    Incremental leading, 128-130
    Proportional leading, 129

Library, 57, 60, 61, 62, 192-196, 221, 230, 259, 260, 265, 277, 297, 308
Link, linking/unlinking, 24, 46, 49, 52, 77, 99, 101, 233, 247, 248
Lock/unlock, 56, 157, 244

# M

Master page, 9, 32, 36, 40, 43, 44, 45, 46, 47, 48, 50, 54, 234, 235, 238, 240, 252, 265, 281, 285, 286, 296, 299, 301, 302, 303
Measurement palette, 19, 22, 23, 25, 26, 35, 40, 57, 58, 72, 81, 83, 145-147, 160-162, 168, 170-171, 184, 189, 229, 240, 243, 258, 276, 277
Modify, 21, 22, 23, 24, 39, 40, 57, 58, 59, 60, 62, 71, 126, 132, 134, 145-147, 159-162, 168, 170, 184, 188, 191, 203, 206, 231, 242, 243, 245, 252, 262, 267, 271, 276, 288, 290, 296, 297, 272
Moire, 221

# O

Offset, 37, 40, 55, 152, 164, 165-166, 184, 188, 235-236, 273, 290, 295
Overflow, 35, 52, 231, 246, 248, 271
Overprint, 152, 225-226, 228

# P

Pantone, 209, 213, 217-218, 222-223, 267, 282, 283
Paragraph format, 73, 83, 84, 89, 137, 139, 142, 143, 148, 150, 254, 272, 273, 304, 305, 306, 311, 313, 315

Paragraph rules, 88, 90, 163-165, 253, 314-315
Paste, 4, 20, 22, 54, 58, 60, 62, 78, 80, 105, 151, 189, 193, 255, 274, 297, 314
Pasteboard, 18, 32, 160-171, 229, 274, 278
Pasteup, 4
Picture box, 20, 22, 24, 34, 40, 54, 58, 157-158, 166-180, 172, 174, 176, 178, 180, 183-184, 188-191, 195-196, 207, 248, 249, 252, 255-256, 259, 260, 262, 263, 266, 276, 277, 287, 288, 290, 291, 297, 299, 301, 302, 303, 307, 309
Picture box shape, 126, 166-169, 290
Picture rotation, 188
Picture skew, 24, 40, 188, 277
Picture usage, 193-194
Pixel, 62, 64, 108, 182, 195, 209, 220
PMS, 217, 219, 221, 222-223, 228, 266, 267, 274, 275, 280, 282, 284, 301, 302, 304
Polygon picture box, 126, 166-170, 176-178, 196, 287, 288, 290, 297
Posterized, 186, 187
Preferences, 8, 24, 28, 34, 36, 38, 40, 44, 48, 54, 127-129, 180, 181, 231, 265, 266, 282
Preview, 32, 180, 186, 279

# R

Registration marks, 68, 208, 225, 227, 263, 280
Render, 36
Reshape picture box, 168, 169, 196,

# INDEX

288, 290, 293
Resolution, 109, 110, 144, 180, 181, 182, 193-194
   High-resolution output, 7, 67, 280
RGB, 186, 211-212, 218-220
Rotation, 18, 22, 24, 58, 243, 259, 308
   Box rotation, 145, 155, 157, 188
   Rotation tool, 146-147, 155, 157, 244
Rule above/rule below, 164, 165
Rulers, 35, 36, 40, 41, 42, 72, 85, 150, 179, 269
Runaround, 24, 25, 39, 40, 57, 60, 126, 145, 151, 152, 154, 157, 173-179, 203, 235, 243, 251, 252, 262, 265, 266, 267, 269, 274, 276, 287, 288, 303, 307-309

# S

Save text, 66, 103
Select all, 145, 231, 242, 245, 297
Send to back, 56, 152, 229, 274
Separations, 69, 183, 199, 209, 218, 222, 225, 227-228
Shade, 23, 39, 40, 58, 59, 69, 81, 126, 145, 152, 160, 165, 172, 182, 185-188, 199, 201, 205, 217, 229, 230
Small caps, 81, 242, 274
Smart page numbering, 51, 238, 247
Space/align, 56, 258
Spelling (check), 75, 98, 99, 100, 102, 105
Spread (layout), 34, 35, 197, 229, 235, 239, 240, 281, 290, 296, 299, 301-303, 307
Spread (traps, chokes), 224, 225, 226
Step and repeat, 55, 56, 196, 229, 235, 237, 239, 290, 294
Style menu, 21, 23, 34, 55, 81, 82, 84, 85, 86, 87, 93, 94, 235, 238, 243, 251, 253, 259, 260, 262, 263, 272, 275, 288, 310, 314
   Style menu (text), 113, 120, 124, 126, 128, 131, 139, 142, 143, 144-145, 148, 149, 151, 152, 160, 161, 163, 165, 201, 202
   Style menu (graphics), 185, 194, 203, 205
Stylesheet, 21, 74, 86, 87, 88, 89, 90, 92, 93, 94, 131, 137, 252, 262, 281, 303-307, 312, 315
Suggested hyphenation, 99, 140-141
Suppress printout, 126, 189

# T

Tabs, 73, 83, 84, 85, 88, 256, 259, 260
Template, 29, 30, 31, 32, 33, 34, 43, 44, 60, 64, 66, 67, 192, 206, 261, 262
Text box, 23, 24, 32, 35, 39, 42, 49, 50, 51, 53, 54, 55, 58, 60, 66, 71, 72, 74, 75, 76, 80, 84, 85, 94, 98, 105, 112, 119, 120, 124, 132, 133, 134, 147, 216, 240, 241, 243, 245, 246, 256, 257, 270, 286, 287, 307
Text box specifications, 132, 134, 135, 136, 145, 147, 273, 311
Text inset, 24, 39, 132-133, 135-136, 231

339

Thumbnail, 3, 32, 41, 43, 180, 234, 281, 302, 303, 307
Tile, 69, 263, 264
Tool palette, 18, 19, 21, 22, 23, 25, 39, 40, 52, 71, 126, 158, 167
Track, 38, 105, 108, 111-112, 114, 116-124, 137, 144, 154, 246-247, 277-278, 287, 314
Tracking table, 38, 119, 121
Trap, 214, 217, 223, 224-227
Trim lines, 227, 263
Typesetting, 4, 5, 6, 38, 67, 105, 129, 280
Typography, 105-106, 109, 137

# U

Utilities (Utility menu), 20, 21, 57, 60, 98, 99, 102, 110, 113, 121, 140-141, 193, 260

# V

Vertical alignment, 39, 133-136, 307
View menu, 20, 21, 22, 40, 41, 42, 52, 81, 170, 233, 234, 235, 238, 239, 241, 261, 265, 279, 284, 286, 297, 303, 307

# W

Word processing, 105, 129

# X

X-height, 107
XPress data file, 62, 65, 119, 121

# Z

Zoom tool, 23, 24, 41, 42, 238, 247, 248, 275, 276, 287, 297

# M&T BOOKS

## Running WordPerfect on Netware
### by Greg McMurdie and Joni Taylor

Written by NetWare and WordPerfect experts, the book contains practical information for both system administrators and network WordPerfect users. Administrators will learn how to install, maintain, and troubleshoot WordPerfect on the network. Users will find answers to everyday questions such as how to print over the network, how to handle error messages, and how to use WordPerfect's tutorial on NetWare.

| | | |
|---|---|---|
| Book only | Item #145-8 | $29.95 |

## Graphics Programming in C
### by Roger T. Stevens

All the information you need to program graphics in C, including source code, is presented. You'll find complete discussions of ROM BIOS, VGA, EGA, and CGA inherent capabilities; methods of displaying points on a screen; improved, faster algorithms for drawing and filling lines, rectangles, rounded polygons, ovals, circles, and arcs; graphic cursors; and much more! Both Turbo C and Microsoft C are supported.

| | | |
|---|---|---|
| Book/Disk (MS-DOS) | Item #019-4 | $36.95 |
| Book only | Item #018-4 | $26.95 |

## Object-Oriented Programming for Presentation Manager
### by William G. Wong

Written for programmers and developers interested in OS/2 Presentation Manager (PM), as well as DOS programmers who are just beginning to explore Object-Oriented Programming and PM. Topics include a thorough overview of Presentation Manager and Object-Oriented Programming, Object-Oriented Programming languages and techniques, developing Presentation Manager applications using C and OOP techniques, and more.

| | | |
|---|---|---|
| Book/Disk (MS-DOS) | Item #079-6 | $39.95 |
| Book only | Item #074-5 | $29.95 |

**1-800-533-4372 (in CA 1-800-356-2002)**

# M&T BOOKS

### Fractal Programming in C
### by Roger T. Stevens

If you are a programmer wanting to learn more about fractals, this book is for you. Learn how to create pictures that have both beauty and an underlying mathematical meaning. Included are over 50 black and white pictures and 32 full color fractals. All source code to reproduce these pictures is provided on disk in MS-DOS format and requires an IBM PC or clone with an EGA or VGA card, a color monitor, and a Turbo C, Quick C, or Microsoft C compiler.

| | | |
|---|---|---|
| Book/Disk (MS-DOS) | Item #038-9 | $36.95 |
| Book only | Item #037-0 | $26.95 |

### Fractal Programming in Turbo Pascal
### by Roger T. Stevens

This book equips Turbo pascal programmers with the tools needed to program dynamic fractal curves. It is a reference that gives full attention to developing the reader's understanding of various fractal curves. More than 100 black and white and 32 full color fractals are illustrated throughout the book. All source code to reproduce the fractals is available on disk in MS/PC-DOS format. Requires a PC or clone with EGA or VGA, color monitor, and Turbo Pascal 4.0 or better.

| | | |
|---|---|---|
| Book/Disk (MS-DOS) | Item #107-5 | $39.95 |
| Book | Item #106-7 | $29.95 |

### Programming the 8514/A
### by Jake Richter and Bud Smith

Written for programmers who want to develop software for the 8514/A, this complete reference includes information on both the 8514/A register and adapter Interface. Topics include an introduction to the 8514/A and its architecture, a discussion on programming to the applications interface specification, a complete section on programming the hardware, and more. A sample source code and programs are available on the optional disk in MS-DOS format.

| | | |
|---|---|---|
| Book/Disk (MS-DOS) | Item #103-2 | $39.95 |
| Book only | Item #086-9 | $29.95 |

**1-800-533-4372 (in CA 1-800-356-2002)**

# M&T BOOKS

### The Verbum Book of Digital Typography
**by Michael Gosney, Linnea Dayton, and Jason Levine**

The Verbum Book of Digital Typography combines information on good design principles with effective typography techniques, showing designers, illustrators, and desk-top publishers how to create attractive printed materials that communicate effectively. Each chapter highlights the talents of professional type designers as they step readers through interesting real-like projects. Readers will learn how to develop letterforms and typefaces, modify type outlines, and create special effects.

Book only      Item #092-3      $29.95

### The Verbum Book of Electronic Design
**by Michael Gosney and Linnea Dayton**

This particular volume introduces designers, illustrators, and desktop publishers to the electronic page layout medium and various application programs, such as PageMaker, QuarkXPress, Design Studio, and Ventura Publishing. Each chapter highlights the talents of a top designer who guides readers through the thinking as well as the "mousing" that leads to the creation of various projects. These projects range in complexity from a trifold black and white brochure to a catalog produced with QuarkXPress. More than 100 illustrations, with 32 pages in full-color, are included.

Book only      Item #088-5      $29.95

### The Verbum Book of Digital Painting
**by Michael Gosney, Linnea Dayton, and Paul Goethel**

Contained herein are a series of entertaining projects that teach readers how to create compelling designs using the myriad of graphics tools available in commercial painting programs. Presented by professional designers, these projects range from a simple greeting card to a complex street scene. This book also includes portfolios of paintings created by the featured artists, plus an extensive gallery of works from other accomplished artists and 64 pages of full-color paintings.

Book only      Item #090-7      $29.95

**1-800-533-4372 (in CA 1-800-356-2002)**

# M&T BOOKS

## ORDER FORM

**To Order:** Return this form with your payment to M&T books, 501 Galveston Drive, Redwood City, CA 94063 or **call toll-free 1-800-533-4372 (in California, call 1-800-356-2002).**

| ITEM # | DESCRIPTION | DISK | PRICE |
|---|---|---|---|
|  |  |  |  |
|  |  |  |  |
|  |  |  |  |
|  |  |  |  |
|  |  |  |  |
|  |  |  |  |
|  |  |  |  |
|  |  |  |  |
|  |  |  |  |

Subtotal

CA residents add sales tax ___%

Add $3.50 per item for shipping and handling

TOTAL

**Charge my:**
- ❏ **Visa**
- ❏ **MasterCard**
- ❏ **AmExpress**

- ❏ **Check enclosed, payable to M&T Books.**

CARD NO. _____

SIGNATURE _____ EXP. DATE _____

NAME _____

ADDRESS _____

CITY _____

STATE _____ ZIP _____

**M&T GUARANTEE:** If your are not satisfied with your order for any reason, return it to us within 25 days of receipt for a full refund. Note: Refunds on disks apply only when returned with book within guarantee period. Disks damaged in transit or defective will be promptly replaced, but cannot be exchanged for a disk from a different title.

8018